Surviving Child Sexual Abuse

Dedication

For all the survivors we have known
and for our children, Nicholas, Alison, Diarmuid and Eamon.

Surviving Child Sexual Abuse

A Handbook for Helping Women Challenge their Past

Liz Hall
Siobhan Lloyd

 The Falmer Press

(A member of the Taylor & Francis Group)
London • Washington D.C.

UK   The Falmer Press, 1 Gunpowder Square, London EC4A 3DE
USA   The Falmer Press, Taylor & Francis Inc., 1990 Frost Road, Suite 101, Bristol, PA 19007

First published in 1989. Second Edition 1993
Reprinted 1994 and 1997

British Library Cataloguing in Publication Data available on request

Library of Congress Cataloging-in-Publication Data available on request

ISBN 075070 152 8 cased
ISBN 075070 153 6 paper

Jacket design by Caroline Archer

Typeset in 10.5/13pt Times
by Graphicraft Typesetters Ltd, Hong Kong
Printed and bound in Great Britain by
Biddles Ltd, Guildford and King's Lynn

Contents

Contents

List of Tables

List of Figures

Acknowledgments

The idea for the first edition of this book came to us, with some help, one sunny afternoon in mid-1987. At that time there was a developing literature on the theoretical aspects of sexual abuse, but none, to our knowledge, that described the process of giving help to survivors of child sexual abuse. We decided to try to fill that gap.

It took eighteen months to put our thoughts on paper for the first edition, which was published in July 1989. During that time we were encouraged and helped by a network of supportive friends, family and colleagues. Writing had to compete with many other demands on our time, and we often had to fit it in late at night and at weekends. Since the first edition was published there has been a significant increase in the number of books and articles which survivors and their helpers can use. We have tried to incorporate this new material and our own recent learning in this second edition, which we are very pleased to have been asked to write.

There are many people whom we would like to acknowledge for the support, constructive criticism and ideas which they provided for both editions of the book. All the survivors we have known over the past ten years have made a major contribution to this book. Without their individual and collective voices we would never have begun to understand the reality of childhood sexual abuse and its consequences. To all these women and men we would like to express our thanks and admiration for their courage in challenging their past and for allowing us to be part of that process. Some of these survivors have also allowed us to include their writing in both editions; we offer our specific thanks to them.

Our learning and the roots of our work lie in the rape crisis movement. We were both members of a women's collective which established a Rape Crisis Centre in Aberdeen in the early 1980s. Survivors of child sexual abuse were in contact with the Centre from the first day the telephone lines opened. We all started learning at that point, and we continued to learn with every woman who made contact with the Centre. Our thanks go to all the members of the collective, in particular to women who were involved in the early days.

As the book began to take shape, we were encouraged by colleagues who shared ideas and read or commented on the numerous drafts of our work. Brenda Flaherty, Sue Hunt, Sandra Malley, Elizabeth Shiach and Patricia Smith were enthusiastic in their support and constructive in their criticism. Colleagues in the Departments of Social Work and Sociology in the University of Aberdeen and the Community Psychology Department and Area Psychology Service of Grampian Health Board have also given advice at different stages. Malcolm Clarkson, our editor at Falmer Press deserves thanks too, for his support of our original ideas, encouragement to produce a second edition and willingness to extend deadlines.

One colleague has been a constant source of encouragement, stimulation and new ideas. Alison Peaker has meticulously read early drafts of our work, developed and facilitated training courses with us and has provided much valued support in innumerable ways. Her skills as a therapist, trainer and facilitator, coupled with her warmth, clarity of thought and downright good sense have ensured a realistic response to some of our more impractical ideas. Thanks, Alison!

Another group of colleagues deserve mention in this second edition. Since early 1990 we have worked alongside our colleague Alison Peaker to facilitate multidisciplinary training for working with survivors of child sexual abuse. The courses are six days in length and they take place in Aberdeen twice a year. They bring together paid workers and volunteer helpers from a wide range of agencies, providing a rich diversity of knowledge and experience. The courses have also encouraged the development of local networks and support groups for helpers who work with survivors. The women and men who have attended these and other training courses we have run throughout Britain have been challenging and energizing in equal measure. We have incorporated many of their ideas into this second edition and we extend to them our thanks for extending our knowledge.

We should also like to thank friends and family who kept us going when our energy was flagging and our spirits low. We owe special thanks to partners when we were writing the first edition and to Greg for suggesting that it was time we stopped talking and started writing. Our children have cheerfully lived with the extra disruption and preoccupation with writing. One arrived just as we were starting to commit our thoughts to paper, another made his appearance into the world just after the book was first published and the two older children will be delighted to know that their mother has finally completed the book — again.

We acknowledge Charlotte F. Hoffmann, Sheila L. Sisk and Pandora Press for giving us permission to reprint some poems from their book *Inside Scars: Incest Recovery as told by a Survivor and her Therapist.*

Finally, but by no means least, our thanks to Margaret Donald, Heather Wilson, Esther Gray, Ann Gordon and Karen Stewart for their professional competence in deciphering our messy manuscript and for their eternal goodwill and patience on their word processors.

Preface to the Second Edition

In the three years since the first edition of this book was published, the issue of childhood sexual abuse had rarely been out of the headlines. The way in which child abuse investigations are carried out by police and social workers and the setting up of specialist units to carry out these investigations has put the issue of inter-agency collaboration on child abuse at the forefront of public debate. Research from Britain, the United States and Europe is providing policy makers and practitioners with valuable information about the child's experience of sexual abuse; we hope this will lead to a more child-centered response to children who disclose. We are also beginning to get more information on abusers and non-abusing caregivers. Data on survivors' experiences seeking and receiving help is becoming available; its use will assist support services in the future.

Female survivors continue to seek help in ever increasing numbers; male survivors, too, are beginning to speak out about their experiences of being sexually abused by trusted adults. Partners of survivors, non-abusing caregivers, foster parents and other carers are coming together for information and support as they try to understand the implications of childhood sexual abuse on people who are close to them. Some survivors are seeking legal redress and are using the resources of the police, lawyers and Criminal Injuries Compensation Board to affirm the damage of their childhood experiences. These last acts of courage have been particularly helpful to some women, who may never get as far as a court hearing, but for whom discussing the abuse with representatives of the legal system can be a further indication that they are finally being heard and taken seriously.

Re-reading the first edition of the book, we can identify many areas where our understanding has increased and deepened. Once again we owe an enormous debt to survivors, whose courage, strengths and accomplishments have led the way. Not only have they been responsible for much of our learning, but they have encouraged other survivors and their helpers to commit their ideas and experiences to paper. In many ways this developing body of literature is radical. It is written from a perspective of partnership which truly empowers survivors and has much to teach all of the helping professions and anyone involved in giving support to survivors.

We can also recognize our earlier need for magic answers to all sorts of difficult questions. Our uncertainty may have led us to be too prescriptive; it certainly led us to undervalue the resources which survivors and helpers bring to the helping process. These resources include themselves, their partners, children and friends, all of whom have an important role to play in a survivor's healing journey. We hope we have redressed this imbalance in the second edition.

In recent years child sexual abuse has attracted increasing attention from the legal profession, politicians, policy makers and the media, and from workers who are involved in helping children and their families or who are in mental health work. Attention has largely focused on children who are in abusive situations or who have been abused in the recent past. As a consequence of changes in attitudes and professional practice, there is now some hope that future generations of children may be able to ask for and receive help if they are being sexually abused.

For many adults such help was not available to them as children and, as a result, they have carried the long-term effects of sexual abuse into their adult lives. Some of them have been referred to mental health or social work agencies with a variety of problems, the roots of which lie in their experience of having been sexually abused. In the past they may have found it difficult to talk about their childhood experiences, fearing that they would not be believed or that they would encounter negative attitudes from professionals whom they approached for help. There are also adults who have been unable to seek help. They may continue to remain silent unless they can feel confident that they will be heard and sympathetically understood. There are, sadly, some adults for whom the consequences of childhood sexual abuse are so severe that long-term hospitalization or even suicide results. It is hoped, however, that a growing awareness and understanding about sexual abuse and its effects among professional helpers will enable appropriate support to be offered to all adults who have experienced this form of abuse and who choose to seek help.

One of the most significant recent developments has been the growing voice of survivors themselves, speaking out about their childhood experiences. This has had a number of effects. Firstly, it has encouraged other survivors to disclose details of their experiences, and in so doing to acknowledge problems which are common to all survivors. This has also contributed to our knowledge of the effects of child sexual abuse. Secondly, it has led to an increase in the number of adults who seek help once they discover that it is possible to come to terms with their childhood ordeal. It has also forced helpers with whom they are in contact to evaluate the assumptions on which their work is based and the therapeutic methods which they use. For us, this has been a difficult, but rewarding process which has enabled us to feel more confident in our work with survivors.

In 1983 we started working with a small number of women who had experienced sexual abuse as children. Since then the number of women coming forward to seek help has increased dramatically. We now work with them in individual and group settings. From the outset we were acutely aware of the lack of published material relating to the long-term effects of childhood sexual abuse and appropriate therapeutic methods to use in working with survivors. Material about how to ask critical questions in therapy, or how to respond to disclosure was not widely available. We had to learn largely through personal experience of working with survivors. Since then the literature has increased, and there is now a wide range of material, both theoretical and practical, which helpers can use. We continue to learn from survivors and from colleagues who have shared their work on training courses and in supervision.

We hope that the book will be of interest to an audience of survivors, their partners and others who are close to them, mental health workers and social workers in statutory and voluntary settings, primary care workers, rape crisis groups, voluntary counselling schemes, survivors' groups and any other resources which offer support to women. We hope that it will be accessible across traditional professional, training and agency boundaries.

For a number of reasons the book concentrates on women who have been sexually abused. We are writing from our own experience, which has been of working predominantly with female survivors. We do acknowledge that many of the issues addressed will be relevant to male survivors. These male survivors may face additional issues which are only recently being acknowledged and understood. We are also concentrating on female survivors because our current understanding of child sexual abuse indicates the predominance of male family member abusing female children. We do accept that children are abused by other trusted adults outside the family, including family friends, babysitters, teachers, youth leaders, ministers, social workers and doctors. We also acknowledge that some women have been abused by a trusted female or by other children. A recent Scottish report (National Children's Home, 1992), for example, suggests that one in three abused children has been abused by other children.

The book will focus on sexual abuse within the immediate or extended family. We do acknowledge that many of the issues will apply equally to situations where the abuser is a trusted adult outside the immediate family and, to a lesser extent, to incidents of abuse by a stranger. As more women decide to seek help, it is likely that helpers will meet women who have been subjected to ritualistic and sadistic abuse by family members and other adults. This area of work is beyond the scope of this book, but it is important to acknowledge that these forms of abuse do exist.

We have tried to write the book as free from jargon as possible in the hope that it will be accessible to a wide audience. We acknowledge that readers will be selective in their use of its contents; and we hope that it can be used as a sourcebook, to be referred to on specific issues, or as a way of gaining a wide understanding on a range of topics. Some colleagues have told us that they have used the book as a supervision tool, checking on the work they have done with a survivor and anticipating what might arise in future sessions. Others have said that they use the book itself as a therapeutic tool with survivors. One example of this is giving the 'continuum of abuse' to survivors who may be having difficulty saying what exactly has happened to them. (See Chapter 1) The survivor can use the continuum as a sort of checklist, which can be used by helper and survivor together in future sessions.

The book starts with a definition of terms used in the text and an examination of the ways in which helpers have previously responded to disclosures of sexual abuse. Some of the personal and professional issues which arise for helpers who support survivors are then addressed, paying particular attention to the importance of examining personal attitudes and values and acknowledging any life experiences which may inhibit or add to the effectiveness of the work. A summary of the long-term effects of sexual abuse follows, together with an analysis of the factors which may lead a woman to seek help. The strengths of survivors are stressed, together with the supportive alliances they have forged with helpers, including their own partners and friends.

The theme of disclosure is analyzed in depth, together with a woman's right to remain silent. This is followed by a description of the main themes in therapeutic work with survivors, paying attention to methods which can be used in the work. Attention is given to the issue of confidentiality and a summary of the particular issues which arise in working with individuals, groups and family settings. They are given along with details of methods which can be used in therapeutic work. The book concludes with a look at some of the issues for training. We hope that this book will offer material of value to survivors and helpers alike, that it will act as a sourcebook for useful therapeutic methods, and that it will encourage other helpers to develop confidence in offering help to women who have been sexually abused.

The main changes to the book will be obvious to readers of the first edition. We have added to the 'continuum of abuse' in Chapter 1, drawing on information shared with us by survivors. We have included a description of the practice perspective of 'the child within' (Parks, 1990) which has done much to aid our understanding of the way in which adults can be empowered during the helping process. We have also added to Chapter 2, noting the resources which helpers themselves use to sustain them in their work with survivors. The material on problems faced by survivors in adulthood has been extended and restructured, and we have added a new chapter which acknowledges the strengths and resources of survivors themselves. A short discussion of multiple personality disorder is included in Chapter 3. A fuller analysis of this topic falls outside the remit of this book.

We have substantially expanded the work on disclosure, paying attention to the range of ways in which disclosure of sexual abuse can be made, even if there are no visual memories. New material on sexuality has been included in a separate chapter, and we have taken a more general approach to discussion of training. Finally, we have added to the bibliography and appendices by including new books and writing by survivors. We have also deleted the list of United Kingdom resources for working with survivors, since it is out of date as soon as it is printed.

We again recognize the crucial role which survivors themselves play in helping others to acknowledge painful experiences from their past. For some helpers this will lead to an acknowledgment that they too have experienced child sexual abuse. For these helpers the book may provoke painful memories or bring the pain of parts of their own childhood to the surface. We hope that these helpers will not be deterred from seeking support for themselves or from giving help to others. We also hope that helpers who have not been abused will use the book to increase their understanding and gain confidence for their work with adults who were sexually abused as children. Our experience has taught us to evaluate and appraise our own work. It has also taught us that there is no substitute for listening to and learning from survivors themselves.

The final word rests with Susan Sgroi:

What about the requirement for magic? The magic approach will doubtless be inexpensive, easily learned and effortlessly applied. The reality is that there is no-one just over the horizon to come and rescue the clients or the professionals who are committed to helping them. (Sgroi, 1989)

We hope that this book will help to reduce the isolated feelings of both survivors and their helpers.

Liz Hall and Siobhan Lloyd
Aberdeen
June 1992

Behind the Human Wall

I can hear a noise behind the wall
Like a child crying.
The wall is very high and thick
And still I hear the sound of crying.
Who's in there?

It's me, help me!
I'm trapped, I feel I'm in prison.

Who built this wall and trapped you behind it?

My parents, with their hate and aggression, they didn't love me. They pushed me behind this wall and built the wall brick by brick, day by day, month by month, year by year and they have left me here as a child and I can't break through. The wall is thick, yet I'm afraid of what's on your side. The world frightens me, yet it's lonely behind the wall. I don't know who cares any more for me, yet I'm cold behind the wall. I want this wall to fall down, yet I'm frightened of what will get in with me if I let the wall down. I will get invaded by insects, horrible black creatures crawling all over me. Just that feeling makes me want to stay here.

Then you are a prisoner behind the wall
and the only way out is to break through.

Please, help me, I'm confused, I've been here for so long!
The wall can only be broken the way your parents built it,
Brick by brick, day by day, month by month, year by year.

Why do you scream?

I'm in pain; and there's nothing to stop me from feeling this hurt
that makes me scream

By Lynda E.D. Adams
A survivor

Chapter 1

Introduction

One consequence of the public interest in the issue of sexual abuse has been a dramatic rise in the number of women seeking help because of their childhood experiences. Statutory services and voluntary organizations have had to respond to this increased demand on their resources. People working with survivors have also been forced to examine their own attitudes and working practices, so that women can be offered the help most appropriate to their needs. Wider issues have also been debated; the legal framework for crimes of sexual violence has been examined and prevailing theories about the nature and extent of child sexual abuse have been challenged. Most importantly our understanding of child sexual abuse has been heightened by the testimony of survivors themselves. This chapter covers three main areas:

— a definition of some of the key terms used in the book;
— a summary of the main theoretical perspectives that have been used to understand and explain child sexual abuse;
— a description of sexual abuse.

Definition of Terms

Child Sexual Abuse

Attempts at defining child sexual abuse abound in the literature. Definitions vary according to the abuse activities included, the relationship of the child to the abuser and the age difference between the child and the abuser. Some of the difficulties in the search for an acceptable definition can best be illustrated by examining different but overlapping approaches. One of the most widely used definitions is as follows:

> The involvement of developmentally immature children and adolescents in sexual actions which they cannot fully comprehend, to which they cannot give informed consent, and which violate the taboos of social roles. (Kempe and Kempe, 1984)

This definition has been criticized on two counts by MacLeod and Saraga (1988):

— It takes no account of the possibility or threat of force being used by the abuser.
— It suggests that some acts are abusive only because they are not socially acceptable.

The definition does not acknowledge that young adults can also be sexually abused, even though they may be over the age of informed consent. It also ignores the fact that most children are abused by adults known to them. Survivors themselves have agreed a definition which has also been adopted by campaigning groups. Their definition is:

> The sexual molestation of a child by an older person perceived as a figure of trust or authority — parents, relatives (whether natural or adoptive), family friends, youth leaders and teachers, etc. (Incest Survivors Campaign, quoted in Nelson, 1987)

It is vital that survivors of child sexual abuse have a right to define sexual abuse as they choose. However, by including abuse by babysitters or family friends, it becomes easy for critics who still doubt the prevalence of sexual abuse to discount new statistics. The allegation can be made that the figures are misleading because they include these wider extra-familial relationships (Nelson, 1987). Nelson also argues that 'nothing should be allowed to obscure the fact that the majority of (incest) survivors suffered at the hands of a father-figure or brother.'

A third, more restricted definition is used by Forward and Buck (1981):

> Any overtly sexual contact between people who are closely related or perceive themselves to be ... if that special trust which exists between a child and parent figure or sibling is violated by a sexual act, that act becomes incestuous.

This definition is restricted to family relationships, even though it is recognized that the abuse of trust within the family has particularly devastating effects lasting into adulthood. Nelson (1987) concludes that

Traditionally, professionals have ignored or played down such abuse because it takes place within the family . . . there is no good place for sexual abuse . . . the family is the most destructive place of all.

Sgroi (1982) uses a definition which has fewer problems:

Child sexual abuse is a sexual act imposed on a child who lacks emotional, maturational and cognitive development. The ability to lure a child into a sexual relationship is based on the all-powerful and dominant position of the adult or older perpetrator which is in sharp contrast to the child's age, dependence or subordinate position. Authority and power enable the perpetrator, implicitly or directly, to coerce the child into sexual compliance.

However, its emphasis on the 'sexual act' does not cover the range of sexual activities which children find threatening or unpleasant, for example, being watched in a 'sexual' way whilst undressing or bathing. It also fails to mention the range of other types of abuse which all too frequently accompany sexual abuse.

The search for the perfect definition of child sexual abuse will doubtless continue. Whatever the outcome it should include the following elements:

— the betrayal of trust and responsibility;
— the abuse of power;
— an indication of the wide range of sexual activity involved in the abuse;
— the use of force and/or threats by the abuser;
— the child's perception of a threat even if the abuse is non-coercive, non-threatening or non-violent.

In this way, it will acknowledge that child sexual abuse not only crosses the physical boundaries between adult and child, but it also constitutes a fundamental abuse and betrayal of the power that an adult has in relation to a child. In this book we examine issues relating to child sexual abuse which is perpetrated by an adult who is known to and trusted by the child. We emphasize abuse which is perpetrated by family members.

Characteristics of Sexual Abuse

Child sexual abuse has a number of features which make it particularly difficult for the child and which cause problems for the adult survivor:

Duration of the abuse   A child may be abused by a trusted adult on one occasion only, but more frequently the sexual abuse goes on for months or years (Lukianowitz, 1972; Maisch, 1973).

Frequency of the abuse   The abuse may occur once only or several times a week over a number of years. Often, however, a child experiences sexual abuse on a daily or more frequent basis.

The identity of the abuser   Most sexual abuse is perpetrated by fathers or father-figures. Forward and Buck (1981) suggest that 75 per cent of reported abuse cases involve fathers and daughters, and that 10 per cent involve grandfathers. Brothers, uncles and cousins, or adult men who are in a position of trust with the child, for example, youth leaders, baby-sitters, teachers and doctors have also been identified as perpetrators (Patton, 1991). It is also estimated that approximately 5 per cent of the abusers of girls are female (Russell, 1986; Finkelhor, 1986).

The age of the child   For most abused children the abuse starts well before puberty. Kempe and Kempe (1984) found the median age was between nine and ten years old. Herman and Hirschman's (1977) study found that between six and nine was a common age for the abuse to start. There have been many individual cases reported where the child was under the age of six and even as young as a few months old.

Age of the abuser   Evidence on the age of abusers comes from figures on convicted offenders and the accounts of survivors themselves. In most cases, the abuser is at least ten years older than the child. In relation to abuse by brothers and cousins, the age difference may be less, but the abuser is usually at or past puberty when the abuse starts. (O'Brien, 1991).

Multiple abusers   Some children are abused by several adults, including a number of family members and other adults known to the family.

Sexual Abuse and Incest

Incest is defined by the *New Collins Concise English Dictionary* as 'sexual intercourse between two people who are too closely related to marry'. This definition reflects the legal parameters of the crime of incest, and it confirms that children who have suffered long-term sexual abuse without full sexual intercourse have no recourse in law. We have deliberately avoided the use of the word 'incest' in the book to describe sexual abuse. We consider 'incest' to be a difficult, emotive and confusing word for the following reasons:

— it does not take into account the range of sexual activity which constitutes sexual abuse;
— it omits the fact that one of the 'persons' is a child and is in no position legally, emotionally or socially to consent;
— it is a word which survivors themselves believe implies consent;
— it is too narrow and legalistic a definition.

For all these reasons, we prefer to use the term 'sexual abuse'.

Survivor

Throughout the book we have used the term 'survivor' to describe a woman who has experienced sexual abuse. The term was identified by women themselves in the 1980s as an alternative to the word 'victim' which had been in common use until that time. To describe a woman as a survivor suggests that:

— it confirms that she has survived traumatic experiences;
— she is no longer powerless in relation to the abuse;
— she has identified the cause of her problems and is, hopefully, going to seek help;
— she can identify with other survivors, sharing elements of a common past, a common language and a common wish for change;
— it emphasizes the inner personal resources and strengths which she has used to survive the abuse.

Helper

Throughout the book we use the term 'helper' to describe the person who works with a survivor to help her to deal with the effects of her childhood experiences. The term is not wholly satisfactory, as the helping role may take a variety of forms and can occur in different settings. For example, the helper might be:

— a member of the survivor's family, a partner or friend;
— a volunteer working in an organization such as Women's Aid or Rape Crisis;
— a trained counsellor working in a voluntary or professional capacity;
— a member of a profession dealing with mental health problems in adults and/or children, for example, clinical psychologist, psychiatrist, social worker, psychiatric nurse;

— an education or community worker with a women's group;
— a trained psychotherapist or family therapist;
— a marriage guidance counsellor;
— a sex therapist;
— a minister;
— a GP or other medical specialist;
— a worker in residential hostel;
— a worker in a community project with families;
— another survivor in any of the above situations.

Other words which might be used to describe the helper include 'counsellor', 'therapist' or simply 'worker'. In a group setting, the word 'facilitator' is often used and we have done so in Chapter 10.

Not all helpers have formal training in counselling or a particular therapeutic perspective. Many survivors are supported by partners and friends who have a keen insight into the nature of sexual abuse and its effects. They may be the mainstay of support for a survivor who begins to remember her past, and they might be the only person to whom a survivor can disclose. Partners and friends can also provide invaluable ongoing support if a survivor has sought professional help.

Theoretical Perspectives

Two theoretical perspectives have had a major influence on the way survivors have been helped. These are the psychoanalytic and feminist views of child sexual abuse. This section examines the features of each perspective and considers their impact on the ways in which survivors receive help.

The Psychoanalytic Perspective

Psychoanalytic theory has had a dominant influence on our understanding of male and female sexuality. Its theoretical importance lies in the way in which a set of ideas, originating in the late nineteenth century in one section of Viennese society has dominated society's beliefs and professional practice. Freud formed his seduction theory about the origins of hysteria and the neuroses on the basis that large numbers of his female patients revealed that they had suffered sexual abuse. He linked the symptoms of these women with sexual trauma in their childhood.

Following the publication of his ideas, Freud was heavily criticized and he modified his original ideas. He suggested that a woman who described sexual abuse was really having incestuous fantasies and wishes toward her father. It is now generally accepted that the reasons for Freud's change of mind originated in his wish to protect his standing as a respectable member of a scientific community which had rejected his ideas. After delivering a paper on his findings to a hostile and rejecting audience he wrote, 'I felt as though I was despised and universally shunned' (Masson, 1985). In addition the nature of family life in nineteenth century Europe meant that parents had to be respected, at any cost, and this provided a further pressure for Freud not to believe his patients. Within a few years, Freud had begun to assert that for 'girls who produce such an event (sexual abuse) in the story of their childhood . . . there can be no doubt of the imaginary nature of the accusation or of the motive that has led to it' (Masson, 1985). Giving little evidence, Freud went on to claim 'these separated scenes of seduction had never taken place, and they were only fantasies which my patients made up'.

When Freud abandoned his original theory, he did a disservice not only to his profession but to many generations of men and women whose childhood experiences have since been denied. Freud's followers continued to work on the assumption of childhood sexual fantasies, making this their basis for inquiry when a woman disclosed sexual abuse in analysis as an adult. One serious consequence was that an abuser's desire and capacity for initiating the abuse was ignored. Furthermore, responsibility for allowing or imagining the abuse to have taken place was seen to rest with the child. Nelson concludes:

> We can only guess how momentous might have been the conse-
> quences for several generations of incest survivors if Freud had
> stuck to his original theory and his followers had searched actively
> for an incest history in disturbed patients, from the belief that it
> was a major cause of mental disorder. (Nelson, 1987)

Although psychoanalytic ideas have assisted in perpetuating a denial that sexual abuse has occurred, they cannot be accused of minimizing the trauma of sexual abuse itself. The theory stresses the importance of traumatic childhood events in the emotional, social and sexual development of the individual. In particular, it has made an important contribution to our understanding of the idea of ambivalence, where a woman who has been sexually abused feels both love and hate for an abuser. He has sexually abused her, but he may be the only person in her life who has ever paid her any attention or given her affection. A survivor might feel that,

> Because anger towards the loved person cannot be expressed for fear of losing that person, and cannot therefore be lived out, ambivalence and linking of love and hate remains an important characteristic of later . . . relationships. Many people cannot even imagine that love is possible at all without suffering and sacrifice, without fear of being abused, without being hurt and humiliated. (Miller, 1984)

Freud's emphasis on the unconscious has implications for work with survivors of childhood sexual abuse. He believed that behaviour and personality development is influenced by forces, motivation and childhood patterns of which the individual is totally unaware. It is estimated that up to 50 per cent of survivors of child sexual abuse are not aware of these abusive experiences, and yet there are many signs and symptoms that may lead to a suspicion that a woman has been abused.

Freud's discussion of the mechanisms that the individual uses to defend him or herself against emotional and physical pain are also important. Freud stressed the importance of recovering the repressed or suppressed memories in order to help the individual make sense of his/her problems. This is the cornerstone of therapeutic work with survivors. In the final analysis, however, psychoanalytic theory operates within a patriarchal ideology. It fails to make any links between powerlessness, violence and sexuality. By denying the reality of sexual abuse it has sentenced thousands of women to 'confused guilty silence, whilst exonerating the abusers' (Scott, 1988).

The Feminist Perspective

In the mid-1970s women began to question seriously the assumptions made by Freud in relation to child sexual abuse. At the same time, the issue was being brought to public attention not by professional workers or politicians, but by women in Women's Aid, Rape Crisis and by survivors themselves. Feminist practice in relation to sexual abuse has come from the initiatives of the women's movement in relation to rape and domestic violence. It has raised awareness both nationally and internationally about the numbers of children being abused, about the emotional and social effects of the experience and it has questioned why men sexually abuse children.

Theoretical work from feminist writers began to be published in the early 1980s (Rush, 1980; Herman, 1981; Nelson, 1982, 1987; Ash, 1984; Driver and Droisen, 1989). Moving personal accounts from survivors began to appear (Allen, 1980; Ward, 1984; Danica, 1988; Sisk and Hoffman,

1987; Matthews, 1990) and biographies and novels have also been important (Morris, 1982; Walker, 1982; Angelou, 1984).

A feminist analysis examines the kind of society we live in and sees child sexual abuse as part of the spectrum of male dominance over women and girls. The learning of social roles and gender identity take place initially in the family and are transmitted through male and female gender-roles. As Ash (1984) indicates:

> The feminine role confers passivity, dependence and subordination and casts the female as the emotional caretaker of other family members. The masculine role confers mastery, control and dominance, and casts the man as protector and material provider for the family unit. Father-daughter sexual abuse, like rape and violence against women, occurs in a society which has historically viewed women and children as the property of their male protectors, and which has supported the use of male aggression to maintain dominance.

The contradictions of our society are therefore acknowledged. Men are assumed, through their role as partners and fathers, to protect their women and children, particularly from other men, and yet are sanctioned in their use of aggression to maintain their dominant status, both within the family and in society generally. Our society encourages the exploitation of women and girls through advertising, pornography and the beliefs about rape, a fear with which all women live, serving to keep them watchful and in need of protection from men.

Feminism argues that deep-rooted social attitudes about male dominance and power encourage crimes such as wife-beating and rape and until these attitudes have changed, no amount of work with convicted offenders will seriously reduce the number of these crimes. It calls for the re-evaluation of a system which causes male violence. The belief is that a society without male violence will only happen when society itself changes.

A feminist analysis also sees 'the problem of masculinity' at the centre of any explanation of child sexual abuse. It asserts that we live in a patriarchal society which is reinforced by the social structure of the family, with father as the power holder, mother as nurturer and children as dependent. Male power is also held responsible for the silence surrounding sexual abuse, as mothers and children have no power to break that silence. A need to maintain the family identity prevents a revelation of the truth, since to tell would risk isolation. The analysis also goes some way towards explaining the incidence of sexual abuse of girls. Current estimates suggest that between one in five and one in eight girls are sexually abused by a male adult before the age of sixteen, Russell (1986). Clearly, this level of incidence can only be explained by broad factors, and not the psychopathology of individual men.

Feminist theory has also challenged Freudian ideas and developed new ways of thinking about mothers, abusers and children in families where child sexual abuse has occurred.

Mothers The image produced by society is of a carer and nurturer whose role is to reproduce and develop a happy family. Her function is to provide emotional and physical care and to be sexually available to her partner. A mother is, therefore, held to blame when one of *her* children is sexually abused by *her* partner, because she works, leaves home, fails to protect *her* children, does not see the abuse, does not hear *her* children, fails to sexually satisfy *her* partner, because she is not a well-adjusted woman or chooses a man who abuses her child.

A feminist analysis of mothers in families where child abuse has occurred sees her as isolated, conforming to a feminine role-model where she is the arbiter and carer of everyone else in the family and the keeper of secrets, thus rendering her powerless.

Children Feminist theory has voiced the view that, if children really did share the sexual desires and feelings of adults, they would respond to the 'courtship gestures' which adults use with one another (Nelson, 1987). Instead it points to the means of coercion and holding out of favours which abusers use to maintain a child's silence. Feminism is unequivocal in asserting that responsibility for sexual abuse of children and adults lies with the perpetrator of the abuse.

Abusers Feminism challenged the way in which characteristics that are cited in child abusers have allowed responsibility for the abuse to be deflected from them. By labelling the abuser as a psychopath, alcohol-dependent or a paedophile, his behaviour is to some extent excused as needing treatment. Instead, feminism asserts that abusers should accept responsibility for their actions, thus allowing children to rid themselves of the burden of guilt which they universally feel.

The aims of feminist practice with survivors has four main tenets:

— to reverse the victim-blaming and mother-blaming practices of the past;
— to emphasize the importance of talking, support, self-help and education for survivors of child sexual abuse;
— to influence policy-making in relation to sexual abuse. This might include campaigning for more women-centred resources such as women's therapy centres and refuges for survivors;

— to influence practice within statutory and voluntary settings through discussion and training.

The main shortcoming of a feminist analysis is that it is ideological, and places the major responsibility for sexual abuse on the structure of society. This does not allow for individual differences between families. It has little to say about male children who are sexually abused, or about female abusers. The argument about male children may be unfounded, however, if one accepts that male children, like women and girls, share the same status of powerlessness and dependency within families.

The emphasis on male power, whilst consistent with the testimony of survivors, does not adequately address the issue that sexual abuse is especially problematic because it is sexual. Many of the long-term effects (sexual problems, fear of being touched, body image difficulties) result from the sexual nature of the abuse. (For a more detailed analysis of the far-reaching sexual effects, *The Sexual Healing Journey* by Wendy Maltz (1991) is recommended).

The feminist perspective does not consider the very real issue of some survivors living in a family that was chaotic or dysfunctional prior to the abuse. In this situation, there is a failure on the part of the adults in the family to take responsibility for normal adult tasks and to maintain appropriate boundaries between adults and the children. This is sometimes exacerbated by problems of the abuser, the mother or some other adult in the household, major mental illness, alcohol abuse or violent behaviour. Scapegoating and blaming the child are common, and the effects of being brought up in such a family may add problems over and above those caused by the abuse.

It is our view, however, that a feminist analysis offers a dynamic approach to the issue of child sexual abuse. It is the perspective which is the starting point for our thinking and practice and it underpins the content of this book. Identifying power rather than sexuality as the basis for an abuser's motivation, and emphasizing the importance of talking, support, self-help and education for survivors and those who work with them, are all crucial. It also offers hope for change. The growth in women's self-help groups and in the number of professional workers who practice from a feminist perspective confirms this hope.

Finally, the feminist perspective stresses the importance of giving power back to those who have been silenced and marginalized over the years, and, by listening to and understanding their problems in the light of their experiences, we can continue to make changes in the ways that help is offered. Empowering adults and children, who have experienced sexual abuse, to talk, be believed, and to be given the right to be safe continues to be the mainstay of our work.

Additional Issues Relating to Mothers

Many survivors feel betrayed by their mother because their mother may have known about the abuse and done nothing. We recognize the major difficulties faced by both mothers and daughters in breaking the secret of sexual abuse, but we are also aware that some mothers may initiate, participate in, or condone the abuse. This can leave the child in an impossible position, feeling that a person from whom she expects care allows her to be abused. It can also leave her doubly isolated and unable to tell anyone.

Women are still the primary care-givers in the home and this can give women power as mothers. For some women this is their only source of power. It has to be accepted that women as well as men do sometimes misuse this power, especially in relation to their children. Some women are abusive to their children, not necessarily sexually, but emotionally and/or physically. The ultimate taboo is about women, especially mothers, sexually abusing their children. Sexual abuse by women breaks all society's expectations about women, who are expected to be gentle and protective, putting the needs of others particularly those of children, above their own needs. We do not yet have the evidence to know the extent of sexual abuse by women, whether alone or with a male partner, and it is an area for further research.

The silence about sexual abuse by women has to be broken so that children and adults abused in this way can be given a voice. Sexual abuse by a mother can be more traumatic than that by a father because the child may have a stronger biological and psychological bond with the mother. The young child may be totally dependent on her mother for meeting her basic needs, especially at a very young age. If her mother begins to abuse her, her needs for nurturing, protection and care can be shattered. This can be so overwhelming that the child's isolation and vulnerability can lead her into situations where she is at risk of exploitation from others. This has significant consequences for the adult survivor.

The 'Child Within'

We believe that the concept of the 'child within' or the 'inner child' can be seen as a therapeutic development from the feminist perspective. This approach begins by stating that within all of us, there is a child. If we have been reasonably treated as a child, that 'child within' will allow us to play, have fun, be spontaneous, curious and creative. If, however, our childhood experiences have been fearful, painful, upsetting and/or abusive, our 'inner child' will continue to react to the environment by being frightened, withdrawn, lonely, depressed, sad or showing signs of emotional or behavioural disturbance reflecting the childhood. For many adult survivors, being in touch with the feelings of the 'inner child' is frightening and may lead to the suppression of any associations with themselves as children. This can result in the survivor experiencing a conflict, with the adult part surviving in the world but with a frightened child who comes to the surface from time to time.

By using this approach with a survivor, we are able to:

— listen to the child within her, believe her disclosures of abuse, validate her feelings, survival skills and strengths, and begin to help her recover emotionally;
— empower the child through this process, and through her the adult survivor;
— encourage the adult survivor not to blame the child, and to begin to place the responsibility for the abuse on the perpetrator(s) and for the lack of protection and care both on the perpetrator and other adults in her childhood;
— recognize the powerlessness of children;
— understand some of the origins of the adult's reactions and problems.

The process has been described very succinctly by Tracy Hansen in her book *Seven for a Secret* (1991):

... it was as if I was two people: the adult I am today, and the child I was. I had to learn to listen to the child within me, take her seriously, accept her feelings and encourage her to tell me what she thought, even though it might sound silly to me.

We will refer to this approach to working with survivors throughout the book. It underpins many of our ways of working with survivors in enabling them to face the reality of their childhood experience, and by doing so to regain control and power over their lives through understanding their reactions, beliefs, attitudes and behaviour in the light of those experiences. With this comes the possibility of change and the chance to lead happier and more satisfying lives.

The Meaning of Sexual Abuse

In this section we outline the range of sexually abusive behaviour and other abusive activities that are perpetrated on children. It does not make easy reading, but we feel that it is important to understand what might be involved when a women says she has been sexually abused. A knowledge of what abuse entails also enables helpers to anticipate disclosures and to become more accepting of information which is extremely difficult to describe and equally difficult to share.

There is clearly a continuum of abuse (Sgroi *et al*, 1982), which ranges from an adult exposing his genitals to a child at one end of the spectrum, to rape, accompanied by violent and sadistic abuse at the other. The examples of sexual abuse given in subsequent pages are not isolated incidents; many of them have been disclosed by numerous women. Sexual abuse can take place:

— in everyday situations such as bathtime or bedtime;
— always in the same location (for example, a child's bed, on a chair in the living room);
— at the same time of the day or week (for example, Thursday evenings when the child is left alone with the abuser);
— with or without being clothed;
— as part of a wider range of physical or sadistic abuse;
— in a 'special' place away from the child's home (for example, in a car, shed, or building used for community activities);
— in a fleeting way as the child and adult come physically close to each other (for example, the abuser fondles the child's genital area as he passes her on the stairs or in a swimming pool);
— in her parents' bed;
— whilst she is sleeping;
— whilst she is in the bath/shower;
— in the dark;
— in the presence of other children;
— in a context where the child is rewarded by money or presents for the sexual abuse;
— within the context of a dysfunctional or chaotic family;
— in a context where the abuser has been preparing or grooming her for the later sexual abuse.

Most survivors have been exposed to a variety of sexual activities. It may be difficult for them to pinpoint the start of the abuse, but it often quickly escalates in both frequency and range. The following represents a picture of the continuum of the sexual and other abuse of children. It is important to bear in mind that the abuser is usually a trusted adult, and that the child is therefore likely to have a relationship with him or her that pre-dated the abuse.

Sexual Abuse: A Continuum of Abuse

The abuser watches the child in an intrusive or sexual way as she has a bath, goes to the toilet or gets dressed and undressed;

The abuser exposes his penis to the child;

The abuser walks around naked or half-naked with his penis erect;

The abuser persuades or demands the child to undress and expose her genitals to him;

The abuser has the child sitting/lying on his lap in such a way that her body movements, pressure and position cause him to have an erection;

The abuser masturbates himself in front of the child, perhaps until he ejaculates;

The child is told to masturbate herself;

The child is told to masturbate the abuser, perhaps until he ejaculates;

The abuser strokes the child gently:
her face
her hair
her back
her legs and thighs
her arms
her chest, breasts and nipples
her bottom and anal opening
her vaginal opening
her clitoris

The abuser massages the child:
her back, shoulders and arms
her chest/breasts
her lower abdomen
her legs and thighs
her bottom and anal opening
her vaginal opening
her clitoris

The abuser touches the child in a painful and rough way;

The child is told to touch certain parts of the abuser's body;

The child is forced to kiss the abuser on the mouth, often in an overtly sexual way, with his tongue in her mouth, and/or her tongue in his mouth;

The abuser rubs his penis against the child's body:
  against her thighs
  against her buttocks
  in her genital area
  against other parts of her body

The abuser places his penis in the child's mouth;

The abuser ejaculates in the child's mouth;

The abuser uses his mouth and tongue to stimulate and suck the child in the genital area, or internally in her vagina;

The abuser ejaculates over the child's body and face;

The abuser ejaculates on the child or himself and forces the child to lick up his semen;

The abuser penetrates the child's body by inserting his fingers into:
  her vagina
  her anal opening
  her urethra

The abuser penetrates the child's body with his penis in:
  her vagina
  her anal opening
  her urethra

The abuser uses everyday objects (pen, banana, cucumber, sticks, other long thin objects) to penetrate the child in:
  her vagina
  her anal opening
  her urethra

The abuser uses sexual or gynaecological objects (vibrator or vaginal dilator) to penetrate the child in:
  her vagina
  her anal opening
  her urethra

The abuser uses weapons (gun, sword) or dangerous objects (glass bottle, broken glass or knife) to penetrate the child in:
  her vagina
  her anal opening
  her urethra

The abuser turns ordinary children's games/play into opportunities for sexual activity (tickling, rough-and-tumble, nursery rhymes that mention touch, or bouncing on a knee);

The abuser involves the child in sexual games (strip poker);

The abuser deliberately/accidentally induces sexual arousal and orgasm in the child;

The child is made pregnant by the abuser.

Involvement of Others in the Abuse

The child is forced to watch the abuser having sexual contact with another adult;

The child is forced to watch the abuser sexually abusing another child;

The child is forced to be involved in sexual activities with another child, (for example, sibling);

The child is offered for sexual purposes by the abuser to friends and relatives;

The child is offered for sexual purposes to friends and relatives, but the friends and relatives then sexually abuse the child;

The child is offered to, or is sexually abused by the abuser's friends and relatives for money, gifts or other inducements;

An important adult (mother or older sibling) offers the child for sexual purposes to friends and relatives;

The child is forced to become a child prostitute;

The child is forced to be part of a sex ring;

A group of adults, men and/or women sexually abuse the child one after another;

One adult sexually abuses the child whilst another prevents her from moving, struggling or screaming;

More than one adult sexually abuses the child at the same time;

The child is forced to be involved in pornographic activities, for example, photographed in overtly sexual poses, forced to dress in adult clothes, tied and bound as part of the sexual abuse;

The child is forced to watch the abuser being involved in sexual activity with an animal;

The child is forced to be involved in sexual activity with animals.

Related Sexually Abusive Activities

The abuser places the child in such a position that the child can see the abuse reflected in a mirror;

The abuser approaches the child from behind;

The child is forced to agree to the sexual activity;

The child is forced to ask the abuser to involve her in a particular sexual activity;

The child is told to repeat after the abuser the sexual activities he intends to involve her in;

The child is told to write a letter to the abuser asking him to involve her in certain types of sexual activity;

The child is forced/expected to say that she enjoyed the sexual activity;

The child is expected to wear certain clothes during to sexual activity;

The child is expected to interpret an abuser's verbal and non-verbal signals that he wishes sexual activity with her to occur (a look at the clock, certain gestures or verbal instructions which always precede the abuse);

The child is verbally abused ('your body is like that of a slut');

The child is lured into the sexual abuse by being promised presents, treats or money;

The child is lured into the sexual abuse by being promised treats which turn out to be sexual ('come and suck my lollipop', or 'come and meet my friend' when he is talking of his penis);

The child is forced into the sexual abuse by the abuser who threatens to abuse other children or harm other important adults or the child's pets.

Physical Abuse

A child who is being subjected to sexual abuse may also experience physical abuse. The sexual abuse may form part of a range of physical abuse which is perpetrated on all the children in the family. Alternatively, the physical abuse may be limited to its use as a means of keeping one child silent about the sexual abuse. The following are common forms of physical abuse:

The abuser hits the child with his hands or fists
on her body
on her head
in the genital area

The abuser hits the child with an object
on her body
on her head
in the genital area

The abuser shakes the child;

The abuser throws objects (iron, sticks, bottles at the child);

The abuser throws the child against a wall or furniture;

The abuser bangs the child's head on a wall or furniture;

The abuser dislocates or fractures the child's limbs;

The abuser burns the child with:
cigarettes/matches
an iron
fire
boiling water/fat

The abuser pulls the child's hair;

The abuser pulls the child around by the hair;

The abuser kicks the child;

The abuser cuts the child with a sharp object (razor blade, broken glass, knife, sharp implement);
on the face and neck
in the genital area
on other parts of the body

The abuser traps the child's fingers in a door or drawers;

The abuser puts his hands around the child's throat;

The abuser chokes the child;

The abuser attempts to strangle the child with a belt, rope, his hands;

The abuser keeps the child's face under water;

The child is whipped with a belt, rope, etc.;

The abuser cuts/shaves the child's hair (including pubic hair).

Verbal Abuse

The abuser repeatedly shouts at the child, even when the child has done nothing wrong;

The abuser repeatedly swears at the child;

The abuser sets grossly unrealistic rules/standards for the child;

The abuser repeatedly blames the child for acts, events and behaviour that are not her fault;

The abuser repeatedly belittles the child in front of friends, siblings and other adults;

The abuser repeatedly finds fault with the child;

The child is verbally humiliated in front of others by the abuser;

The abuser repeatedly belittles other people in front of the child.

Other Forms of Abuse

There are other forms of abuse that often accompany sexual abuse. They are sadistic or cruel in nature or they may be a result of neglect. They may include some or all of the following:

The child is deprived of food and drink;

The child is kept away from other family members;

The child is locked up, kept dirty and not fed;

The child is deprived of items necessary for reasonable physical health, (inhaler for asthma, hearing aid, spectacles);

The child's food and drink are contaminated:
with unpleasant tasting substances
with mould
with semen
with urine or faeces
with paraffin/petrol

The child is prevented from sleeping by:
being constantly woken up (shining a torch in the child's eyes, making loud bangs, blowing whistles)
being made to stand up all night

The child is left alone for long periods with no food or drink;

The child is forced to stand for hours;

The child is tied up;

The child is blindfolded;

The child is gagged;

The child is locked up in a small confined area (cupboard, small attic or cellar room, coal bunker);

The child is thrown out of the house, especially in cold weather.

The child is kept naked;

The child is forced to smoke large numbers of cigarettes;

The child is forced to drink a quantity of alcohol;

The child is forced to drink methylated spirits/paraffin;

The child is forced to take tablets or other medication to excess;

The abuser urinates/defecates over the child;

The abuser urinates in front of the child:
  on the floor
  into the fire
  into a bucket
  into a bottle

The child is forced to lick up/drink urine;

The child is smeared with faeces;

The child is forced to eat faeces;

The abuser uses a range of objects to frighten the child (weapons, sharp implements, masks);

The abuser uses insects to:
  hurt the child (for example, wasps, bees)
  frighten the child
  threaten the child during sexual and physical abuse

Unnecessary medical procedures (for example, enema, injections) are carried out on the child by the abuser;

Wounds are deliberately re-opened;

The child's or family's pets are injured or killed in front of the child;

The child is forced to make 'impossible' choices:
  the child is banned from a room/house and permitted to return only if she agrees to sexual activity;
  the child is locked in a cupboard/cellar/other room and released only if she agrees to sexual activity;
  the child is forced to choose between various forms of abuse that will be carried out (sexual abuse versus a violent beating; being burnt versus being locked in a dark room);
  the child is forced to choose between being physically and/or sexually abused or a pet being hurt or killed;
  the child is forced to choose between being put out of the house or being subjected to sexual abuse;

Cold water is thrown over the child and warmth is then denied;

The abuser damages possessions valued by the child (toys, musical instruments, books, records);

The abuser uses treasured possessions of the child in the abuse;

The abuser criticizes or misuses activities valued by the child (religious activities, musical activities, sport);

Presents are given which are then withdrawn or destroyed;

Presents are given which contain frightening or disgusting objects;

The child is forced to be involved in ritual abuse (Black Magic, witchcraft, or systematic torture).

The continuum of child abuse describes individual acts of abuse, but within any one incident of abuse, several of these acts occur together. The following represent some examples:

Example 1 The child is half asleep in her bed, and her brother comes in and masturbates himself in front of her before forcing his penis in her mouth and ejaculating. He puts his fingers into her vagina and kisses her. He then leaves without saying a word.

Example 2 A very young child is locked in her room for several hours, is cold, and hungry. Her father takes her out and allows her to sit with him in the sitting room — not normally permitted — and seen by the child as a special treat. He asks her if she wishes to meet his nice friend and produces his penis. She is told to kiss and suck it. He ejaculates and she has to lick up the semen.

Example 3 The child is grabbed by her step-father and forced to the floor. He then rips her clothes off, and forces his penis into her vagina. He then punches her in the face, turns her over and forces his penis into her anus. He screams at her, insulting her and daring her to make a sound. He frequently beats her and is verbally very aggressive.

Example 4 Every day the child returns home from school at lunchtime to make her father and older brother their lunch. Her mother is out. She is then told to go upstairs and wait for one of them. Her father comes up and silently undresses. He masturbates himself before throwing her on to the bed. He forces his erect penis into her vagina, ejaculates, gets up and leaves just as silently. She gets up and returns to school knowing it will be her brother's turn the next day.

Faced with the reality of child abuse for the first time, helpers may feel a range of emotions including disgust, anger, guilt and helplessness. These are all normal reactions and are developed when we consider the full implications of child sexual abuse for helpers in Chapter 2.

Chapter 2

Issues for the Helper

Working with survivors of child sexual abuse raises a number of important issues for the helper. These should be considered before starting the work and continuously reviewed while it is in progress. Helpers need to consider their personal history, attitudes, beliefs and prejudices about sexual abuse. They also need to have some confidence about discussing matters relating to sex and sexuality in an open and specific way. Sex and sexual abuse are still enveloped in embarrassment, shame, fear, ignorance and secrecy. This serves to confuse and cloud the reality experienced by the survivor and compounds the hidden nature of the subject.

This chapter explores issues which should be addressed by anyone working with survivors. The issues include:

— challenging the myths about sexual abuse and examining the helper's own attitudes;
— issues of touch within the helping process;
— avoiding further abuse;
— the gender of the helper;
— self-disclosure;
— effects on the helper's family relationships;
— emotional reactions to working with survivors;
— coping strategies of the helper;
— training and supervision.

Challenging the Myths about Sexual Abuse

Many commonly held beliefs about the incidence and meaning of sexual abuse have been challenged in recent years. These beliefs have enabled professionals and society at large to fail to acknowledge the prevalence of sexual abuse, its resulting pain and the damage it carries for children and adult survivors. The myths and their consequences for survivors have been well documented elsewhere (Nelson, 1987; MacLeod and Saraga, 1988). Table 2.1 provides a summary of these myths, together with established facts about child sexual abuse. It is worth noting here that in addition to large-scale research studies, the testimony of survivors themselves, through personal accounts and survivors' groups, has done a great deal to challenge the myths. In work with survivors there are two central issues which relate to the myths about sexual abuse which have professional and personal consequences for the helper. These are the questions of believing and responsibility.

Believing

The myths which relate to the issues of believing are:

— sexual abuse never happens;
— sexual abuse is acceptable in some cultures;
— children, and by implication adult survivors, tell lies about sexual abuse;
— women do not sexually abuse children;
— children fantasize about sexual relationships with adults.

Myth: Sexual abuse never happens The first step is for a helper to acknowledge that sexual abuse can and does occur. This may appear to be stating the obvious, but continued disbelief and an inability, or unwillingness, to accept the extent to which such abuse occurs are still widespread.

We do not know how common sexual abuse by a trusted adult is. There are difficulties in interpreting the available data because:

— there is no consistency between studies in their definition of sexual abuse;
— there is no agreement on the age limits of childhood;
— early studies, carried out before 1975, were based on small clinical samples, which made it difficult to draw firm conclusions.

Finkelhor (1986) has examined the prevalence rates of sexual abuse in the United States in thirteen studies carried out between 1975 and 1985. They ranged from 6 per cent to 62 per cent for females, and 3 per cent to 31 per cent for males. He concludes that the incidence of child sexual

Table 2.1: **Sexual abuse: Myths, consequences and facts**

Myth	Consequence	Fact
Sexual abuse never happens.	Survivors' and children's accounts are dismissed as fantasy. The abused are disbelieved by helpers. Consequences of abuse are ignored.	Sexual abuse is widespread. At least one in eight girls experiences abuse before the age of 16. The abuse often lasts for years.
Sexual abuse occurs only in certain communities/ cultures/classes.	Helpers do nothing. Myth prevents adults accepting responsibility for their actions. Myth perpetuates silence about child sexual abuse.	Sexual abuse happens in all sorts of families, communities and social classes. Men who abuse come from all walks of life.
The mother is to blame because she colludes with the abuser, because she is ill/disabled/pregnant or because she does not meet the sexual needs of the abuser, or because she has chosen a partner who sexually abuses her child, or because she was sexually abused herself.	Myth removes responsibility from the abuser. Myth blames the mother for situations that are beyond her control. Belief compounds the guilt a mother feels. Belief makes the survivor fearful of being a mother.	The abuser is responsible for the abuse, no matter what the circumstances. The abuser should protect the child from harm. Where the mother knows of the abuse and does nothing, she is failing to protect her child. The mother may be unable to protect her child due to illness, disability, or her absence from the house. The abuser may abuse the mother, too, leaving her frightened, injured or victimized. The mother may be under threat not to disclose the abuse.
Mothers never know about the abuse.	Survivor is unable to face the reality of her mother's knowledge of the abuse.	Some mothers do know about the abuse and do nothing. Some mothers do not know about the abuse. Some mothers actively condone or participate in the abuse.

Table 2.1: Continued

Myth	Consequence	Fact
Women do not sexually abuse. Women and especially mothers cannot be violent.	Helper might not believe if survivor discloses abuse by a woman. Myth contravenes the stereotype of a woman being nurturing and protective.	Research suggests that approximately 12 per cent of adult survivors have been abused by a woman. Some women do abuse their power over children. Women can be violent and aggressive.
Men who abuse are deviant, sick or alcoholic.	This removes responsibility for the abuse from the abuser. Myth allows excuses to be made for the abuser.	Biased research sampling has created the myth by studying only convicted offenders. It is not normal to sexually abuse a child, but many abusers appear to be normal in all other respects. Some abusers do have alcohol/psychiatric or other problems.
Men have a right to get their sexual needs met however they choose. They are victims of their uncontrollable sex drives.	The child is perceived to have no rights. This makes excuses for the abuser. Women and children are at risk of abuse from men. Many men do not abuse women and/or children.	Sexual needs should not be met through the abuse of women and children. Men can control their sexual urges.
Abusers have been abused in their own childhoods.	Myth justifies cycle of abuse theory. Belief assumes that people cannot change because of their past. Survivors may be seen as potential abusers by helpers and themselves. This assumes that only people who have been abused are capable of child abuse.	Most female survivors do not abuse their children. Many male survivors do not abuse their children. The experience of being abused can affect parenting skills.

Table 2.1:   Continued

Myth	Consequence	Fact
Sexual abuse is condoned in the Bible.	Belief provides an excuse for the abuser.	The Bible demands the protection of children, and the banning of immoral sexual acts.
Children are abused by strangers.	Belief denies the reality of child sexual abuse.	Research shows that in approximately 85 per cent of cases, the abuser is known to and trusted by the child.
Sexual abuse is the product of a dysfunctional family.	Myth pays less attention to power structures within families and society. This ignores the causes of sexual abuse and its effects on a family.	Power within most families is unequal. Families do not sexually assault children but many men do. Dysfunction is a consequence of abuse, not necessarily the cause of it.
Children are sexually provocative.	Children and survivors are blamed for the abuse. The child or adult survivor feels guilty and confused. Myth ignores the threats and bribes used by the abuser to make the child participate in the abuse.	Adults are responsible for interpreting a child's behaviour as provocative. Children do not behave in an overtly sexual way unless they have previously been abused.
Sexual abuse does not do the child any/much harm.	Accounts of sexual abuse are dismissed by helper. Survivors are told they were too young for it to matter. Survivors are told to forget about events in their past. Survivors are told not to worry about something that happened only a few times.	Short and long-term consequences of child sexual abuse are now recognized to be considerable.
Children and adult survivors lie about sexual abuse.	Professionals take no notice of the child and adult survivors.	Children do not have the awareness or sexual knowledge to lie about sexual abuse. A child or adult survivor has little to gain by lying about sexual abuse.

Table 2.1: Continued

Myth	Consequence	Fact
Children fantasize about sexual relationships with adults.	Helpers attempt to 'correct' fantasies and do not deal with the reality of the abuse. The child/adult survivor is not believed.	Unless they have been abused, a child does not have the sexual knowledge to have sexual fantasies.
Helpers lead women on to make up stories of sexual abuse.	Survivors of sexual abuse continue to be discounted and disbelieved. Helpers involved in work with survivors are isolated, discounted and/ or discredited.	Helpers do not need to make up stories of abuse; the survivors are telling helpers without any prompting.

abuse is not trivial, even if one accepts the lowest prevalence rate of 6 per cent of females and 3 per cent for males. The figure of 6 per cent would give a prevalence in the United States in 1984 of 62.7 million children under the age of seventeen having experienced sexual abuse (Fields, 1988).

In Britain there have been three recent studies of the problem (Baker and Duncan, 1985; West, 1985, Research Team, 1990). The MORI survey conducted by Channel 4 and analyzed by Baker and Duncan had a sample of 2019 people. Ten per cent said they had been sexually abused by the age of sixteen. Thirteen per cent refused to answer and 77 per cent said they had suffered no such abuse. The survey reported that one in eight girls and one in twelve boys in the total sample had suffered sexual abuse. When the figures for abuse by a family member were abstracted, there were five girls for every one boy.

The incidence study conducted in Northern Ireland (Research Team, 1990) reported an incidence rate for sexual abuse of children under 17 years of 0.9 per 1000. The rates for males and females were 0.33 and 1.49 respectively — a ratio of 4:5 females to every male.

Overall, there is some indication that the figures may be an under-estimation. The MORI survey, for example, had a thirteen per cent refusal rate. The researchers noted that some respondents refused to answer questions because they did not want to recall painful memories. This was confirmed by a large random survey (Russell, 1986) where definitions of sexual abuse were carefully chosen and interviewers were selected and trained before matching with possible respondents in terms of age, race and class. The study concluded that almost one in five women of all ages had been sexually abused by a family member before the age of sixteen.

Work with adult survivors has indicated that many totally repress all memories of the abuse. As a result, research studies are likely to produce prevalence figures that are an underestimation of the true prevalence of child sexual abuse.

Myth: Sexual abuse occurs only in certain communities/cultures/classes. Early studies (Flugel, 1926; Guttmacher, 1951) concluded that sexual abuse was more likely to occur in isolated communities, in families where there was a strong influence of alcohol, in working-class families, in poor families, in cultures where men and women did not conform to traditional sex roles, in families where men themselves were abused or where women who were abused in childhood married abusers and became colluding mothers. The sampling methods of these studies and their conclusions have been challenged by Cavallin (1966), MacLeod and Saraga (1988) and Nelson (1987). Susan Forward examined data relating to the abusers of almost three hundred women treated in her practice. She concluded that:

> They come from every cultural, economic, racial, educational, religious and geographical background. They are doctors, policemen, prostitutes, secretaries, artists and merchants. They are heterosexual, bisexual and homosexual. They are happily married and four times divorced ... they are emotionally stable and they have multiple personalities. (Forward and Buck, 1981)

Myth: Children, and by implication adult survivors, tell lies about sexual abuse. Children do not have the explicit knowledge to enable them to talk about this sort of sexual activity unless they have experienced it. Dismissal and disbelief of adult survivors' accounts can be destructive, driving them away from sources of help or causing them more distress with the professional denial of what they know to be a reality.

Myth: Women do not sexually abuse children. We still do not know the extent of abuse by women, but to assume that women always conform to the stereotype of being caring, nurturing and protective is to deny the reality of childhood for many people. Children abused by women, especially if the woman was in the primary caretaking role, are left in a particularly vulnerable position. Children still usually spend more time with their mothers especially in their early years. Some survivors have been abused by both men and women, mothers and fathers, and are therefore likely to have greater problems as an adult.

Myth: Children fantasize about sexual relationships with adults. This myth originated with Freud's work at the end of the nineteenth century, and has had the result of silencing survivors throughout the twentieth century. Children do not have the explicit sexual knowledge to be able to fantasize in the detail that disclosures of sexual abuse can indicate. If the helper attributes disclosures to fantasy, he/she is denying the reality of and suffering caused by sexual abuse, and will not be able to help the survivor come to terms with her past.

Personal and professional implications

Once a helper has acknowledged the prevalence of sexual abuse, the personal and professional implications need to be considered.

Personal implications include:

— wondering when the helper will meet someone socially who tells her/him of experiences of being sexually abused;
— fear of discussing any aspects of the work with friends or family members in case a close friend/relative discloses sexual abuse in her/his past;
— wondering if male friends or acquaintances abuse their children in this way;
— fear for the safety of her/his own children with male friends, relatives and baby-sitters;
— wondering if behaviour with her/his own children could be construed as abusive;
— beginning to feel that every conversation leads to the subject of sexual abuse;
— wondering if she/he is one of the many adults who have forgotten or repressed the experience of childhood sexual abuse.

It is understandable and normal for heightened awareness of child sexual abuse to lead to these feelings. In order to maintain a sense of perspective, it is useful to discuss them with colleagues, a support person or supervisor.

Professional implications include:

— wondering how many survivors have been 'missed' in past work;
— fear of being 'overloaded' with survivors;
— concern about asking routine questions about childhood sexual abuse for fear of being unable to cope with the number of women who might disclose;
— fear of being over-zealous in looking for signs of sexual abuse;
— being accused of being over-zealous in looking for signs of sexual abuse.

Again, these feelings are normal. They should be discussed in supervision if they become problematic.

Believing Individual Women

Whilst we are now beginning to accept the frequency and reality of sexual abuse in general, helpers may still have a tendency towards scepticism about the disclosures of individual women. They should remind themselves that:

— a woman has little to gain by lying about sexual abuse;
— if a helper can believe everything else that a woman has told about herself, there is no reason to doubt the sexual abuse;
— survivors have learnt to minimize the effects of sexual abuse and this can make it easier for a helper to minimize or deny the harm caused by the abuse;
— a survivor may minimize the frequency or nature of the abuse;
— a survivor may not feel justified in having any help because the abuse is in the past.

A helper has a responsibility not to diminish or deny the effects of a woman's childhood experiences but to acknowledge the important role the experience of being sexually abused has had on her development.

Responsibility

The myths which relate to the issue of responsibility for the sexual abuse are:

— children are sexually provocative;
— children do nothing to stop the abuse so they must enjoy and encourage it;
— mothers are to blame because they collude with male abusers;
— sexual abuse is the product of a dysfunctional family;
— the abuser is sexually deviant, mentally ill or abuses alcohol.

Myth: Children are sexually provocative. Young children have strong needs for physical and emotional affection and reassurance from their parents. They are also capable of sensual feeling and enjoyment. This does not mean, however, that they understand their behaviour in the way that adults do, nor that they see any sexual meaning in the verbal and non-verbal messages they give to adults. An acknowledgment that children are sexual beings does not imply that they are physically or emotionally ready to engage in a sexual relationship. It is sometimes easy for a helper to forget that a child's sexuality is open to interpretation and exploitation by adults. The point is well made by Jackson (1978) who suggests that to interpret a wide range of child behaviour as sexual has mistakenly imposed the language of adult sexual experience on the behaviour of children. It should never be forgotten that it is adults who are responsible for interpreting a child's behaviour as sexual.

Myth: Children do nothing to stop the abuse so they must enjoy and encourage it.   A helper may feel that a child could have told another adult or done something to stop the abuse as she got older. These suggestions take little account of the threats and bribes which have been used to maintain a child's silence. For some children, the relationship with the abuser is the only semblance of affection they have ever received. This can make them reluctant to condemn the abuser, and only adds to their sense of blame and complicity. Finally, many children do not recognize that the abuse is wrong until they are older, and because it is done by someone they trust and care about, assume that it is 'normal' behaviour.

Myth: Mothers are to blame because they collude with the abuser.   Mothers are often referred to as 'the silent partner' in families where sexual abuse has occurred. They are held to be responsible for the abuse on three counts:

— inadequate or flawed personalities;
— abandonment of wifely and motherly duties and therefore forcing daughters into a maternal or adult role;
— failure to take action on the abuse even when they know that it is going on.

Nelson (1987) carefully dismantles all three assertions by looking at the difficult choices facing mothers in families where sexual abuse occurs and at the feelings of powerlessness experienced by them. She suggests that it is easy to absorb the ideology of motherhood which asserts that mothers should be with their children twenty-four hours a day, and that they should accept responsibility if things go wrong. If children are being abused, the argument goes, then their mothers should somehow know about it. Often the anger expressed by survivors at their mothers is taken as evidence that they knew what was going on. If an abused child or adult survivor manages to tell her mother that she has been sexually abused by a family member or other trusted adult, the mother's reaction is often one of loss. She has lost her view of herself as a partner and as a protective mother, and her relationship with her family will never be the same again.

It is also important for a survivor to examine her mother's reaction if she told her about the abuse. Some mothers immediately accept their daughter's account whilst others deny that such a thing could happen within their family. If this is the case the child may be rejected because her mother cannot accept what she is being told. Dempster (1989) suggests that discovery of her daughter's abuse is not a discreet event. Rather, it is a process which can be complex and prolonged. It can be prompted by other events, for example, moving house, a recurring childhood illness or can be disclosed when the child reaches adulthood. Dempster also argues that confirmation for a mother that sexual abuse has occurred can replicate aspects of the abuse for her. She too can experience of trauma factors which include stigmatization, feeling powerless and a strong sense of betrayal by the abuser.

Whatever a mother's reaction to discovering that her daughter has been sexually abused, it has important implications for a survivor's recovery. Denial or disbelief from her mother, for example, can have serious consequences for a survivor's ability to form good relationships with women in adulthood. A survivor can also carry strong and sometimes justifiable feelings that her mother failed to protect her from the abuse.

Myth: Sexual abuse is a sign of a disorganized, dysfunctional family. This myth ensures that the focus of concern is the family, rather than individuals within a family who perpetrate or have been subjected to sexual abuse. Sexual abuse is interpreted as a symptom of what is wrong in a family rather than the cause of it. The problem is perceived to be the underlying dysfunction of the family. This theory offers no explanation for the fact that the overwhelming majority of abusers are men, nor does it place responsibility for sexual abuse firmly with the abuser. An alternative perspective is to identify sexual abuse as a problem, and the disorganized family as a consequence of the abuse. Either way, the issues are never clear-cut.

Myth: Men who sexually abuse are deviant. Abusers have been variously described as deviants, as the product of their own abused childhood, obsessive in their compulsion to abuse, mentally ill or disturbed in other ways; they have also been described by survivors as normal men and responsible fathers in other respects. If an abuser is seen as normal by his family, friends, neighbours and colleagues, it becomes harder to accept that he is totally responsible for sexually abusing a child. The only logical explanation is that some of the blame must lie with the child, her mother or anyone else who can be implicated. In reality, abusers come from every walk of life, from every social class, geographical location and racial background.

Personal and Professional Implications

Personal implications include:

— helpers need to acknowledge the reality of male power in relation to women and children within families;
— helpers may feel the need to reassess their relationships with their own partners and children.

Professional implications include the following outstanding issues:

— helpers should make the distinction between responsibility for the abuse and responsibility for failing to protect the child;
— they should acknowledge that a mother had failed her child if she knew about the abuse and did nothing. She is, however, left with a considerable dilemma if her partner is the abuser;
— financial and social considerations may weigh heavily with a mother who knows about the abuse and does nothing;
— professional pursuit for evidence of mother-collusion can threaten the entire therapeutic process, erecting a permanent barrier between mother and daughter;
— helpers should not automatically label a mother 'collusive' if she did not know the abuse was happening, or if she did nothing. They should recognize the complexities of mothers' situations and feelings and explore these with the survivor. It can be helpful to note that:

> For many survivors, part of their anger with their father is that he denied them the possibility of a good relationship with their mother. Therapy ought not to collude with this. (MacLeod and Saraga, 1988)

— helpers also need to acknowledge that some mothers do participate in, initiate sexual abuse or set their children up for being sexually abused and may even involve the child in child prostitution or pornography;

— survivors often forget that they were children at the time of the abuse. It is easy for helpers to do the same.

Issues of Touch Within the Helping Process

Working with survivors inevitably raises questions about touch and personal space. These boundaries have been violated for the survivor by the abuser, and she may have considerable difficulties in allowing anyone to come close to her. The helper, too, has her/his own boundaries concerning touch and personal space.

For a survivor, touch may be seen in a number of ways that largely reflect her experience of being abused. She may not have worked out what would be considered to be safe and non-intrusive touch. She may believe some of the following:

— touch is an unhealthy form of communication;
— touch is mechanical, unemotional and often painful;
— all touch is violating, intrusive or frightening;
— touch indicates that the person touching her has sexual designs on her;
— intrusive/violation or sexually harassing touch is acceptable if it is done to her;
— touch between adults is always sexual;
— there is no such thing as safe touch.

The whole issue of touch is therefore difficult, and the helper should consider some of the following questions:

— if the survivor gets upset, am I prepared to comfort her?
— if she asks me to sit beside her, hold her hand(s) during disclosure, what will I do?
— if she begins to harm herself during the session, what can I do to stop her?
— what boundaries of touch do I feel comfortable with, that are appropriate for working with a survivor?
— what effect does my gender have on the question of touch?

There are a number of types of safe touch that are acceptable in work with a survivor, though issues of gender must be considered:

— shaking hands with a survivor on meeting her for the first time;
— holding her hand(s) during disclosure or times of distress;

— putting an arm round her shoulder during disclosure or times of distress;

— preventing her from hurting herself by holding her hands;

— giving her a hug at the end of her work with the helper.

These forms of safe touch can be more readily acceptable from female helpers but some, such as an introductory handshake and holding the survivor's hand during disclosure may be also acceptable to the survivor working with a male helper. Of crucial importance, however, is that the survivor should be asked what would be acceptable to her and that the helper should be entirely clear what her/his professional limits are in this area.

Avoiding Further Abuse

One of the most alarming issues to have emerged from survivors is evidence that many have been sexually abused by helpers within the context of a therapeutic relationship (Armsworth, 1989, 1990). There is no justification or excuse for such behaviour and it adds considerably to the survivor's problems.

Helpers can also unwittingly behave in ways that remind the survivor of past abusive experiences. The helper might use words, gestures or behaviour that are similar to that of the abuser. In addition, the survivor may think that the helper is going to hurt her if she/he moves suddenly or quickly towards her. This may trigger a strong emotional reaction or flashback in the survivor. The helper should be aware of the fact that she/he is in a position of authority in relation to the survivor and that this power should not be misused. This can be achieved by:

— being clear about issues of confidentiality;

— not intruding on the personal space of the survivor by sitting too close to her, or touching her without her permission;

— setting clear boundaries on inappropriate touch;

— giving the survivor the choice about where she sits and where the helper should sit;

— the helper being aware of her/his emotional reactions, and seeking support and/or supervision to discuss these in detail;

— handing the control and choices back to the survivor, whilst maintaining a sense of direction throughout her work.

By being aware of the power and gender issues in work with a survivor, the helper is more likely to achieve a therapeutic relationship with the survivor that gives her the power and control over the work and is therefore enabling her to take real control over the issues that affect her. This means that at times the helper may have to review her/his usual ways of providing help.

The Gender of the Helper

In this section we examine issues in relation to the gender of the helper as they affect work with survivors.

The Female Helper

The female helper starts off with a number of advantages. The majority of survivors have not been abused by women, and this can allow them to feel much safer with a female helper. It may be easier for them to disclose details of the sexual abuse because there is a shared gender experience in relation to certain aspects of female sexuality. The helper herself may have a more empathic understanding of a survivor's experiences, especially if she has ever felt vulnerable, victimized or exploited in adult sexual situations or in other contexts. Physical comfort, which can be very useful in facilitating the healing process, may also be more acceptable and less threatening if it is offered by or requested from a female helper.

An area of potential difficulty for a female helper and a female survivor relates to the survivor's relationship with and feelings towards her mother and other significant females who failed to protect her from the abuse. The survivor may transfer her expectations and feelings about women onto the helper. This can raise concerns for her about caring and competence, and result in a desire to protect the helper. It can also allow the helper to become the focus for the survivor's suppressed feelings of anger, disappointment and neediness.

Further difficulties are described in Table 2.2.

The Male Helper

The legacy of bad feelings about men in general that the survivor has carried from her childhood can inhibit or prevent the start of any therapeutic work with a male helper. If she can tolerate these feelings and come through the initial stages, there are a number of important benefits for her. First, she can discover that not every man will abuse her, be only

Table 2.2: **Issues for the female helper**

Potential difficulties	Consequences	Action by helper
Disbelieves or denies sexual abuse. Overidentifies with survivor, becomes overwhelmed with fears of helplessness and despair.	It may be worse for survivor if another woman disbelieves her. Helper distances herself from survivor. Gets angry. Difficulties in listening to the survivor.	Review beliefs and evidence about sexual abuse. Discuss with colleagues to maintain objectivity.
Remembers sexual abuse from her own past.	Angry with survivor for triggering memories. Too distressed to continue work. Relief.	Seek help for herself and stop working with survivors in the the meantime.
Takes on role of rescuer.	Unable to set a limit on referrals. May engage women in help who are not yet ready. Burn-out.	Discuss with supervisor, support person or other colleague. Set limits on the work.
Over-involvement with a woman's problems.	Risks reducing survivor's control over her life. Helper angry or distances herself from survivor. Unable to set boundaries or limits on the work. Burn-out.	Discuss in supervision or support group. Set limits.
Anger towards abuser.	Ignores any positive feelings, comments, survivor makes about abuser.	Support to offload anger. Supervision to understand feelings.
Frustration or anger at slow pace of recovery. Feels that the survivor should not continue to behave as a victim.	Lack of understanding of survivor's situation and continuing feelings of helplessness. Personal beliefs impede work.	Discuss justification for anger.
Becomes anti-male.	Leads to providing an unbalanced and unhelpful view of the world to the survivor.	Discuss with supportive colleagues/friends/ supervisor.

Table 2.2:   Continued

Potential difficulties	Consequences	Action by helper
Becomes sexually aroused at details of survivor's abuse.	Survivor may be unaware of this as it may not be obvious.	Acknowledge this and discuss with support person.
	Helper feels guilty/ embarrassed/angry.	May need to terminate this work if unresolved.
Excessive need to be a 'good mother' to compensate for survivor's early experiences.	Leads to over-involvement or inappropriate re-parenting.	Explore if this is a general feature of work or relates to one survivor.
Difficulty with terminating contact.	Survivor feels she is not really coping after all.	Discuss helper's needs in supervision/support.
	Intrusion of helper's needs — can't let go.	
Unable to accept that mothers could not know/ do not protect their children from the abuser.	Misunderstanding of the abuser and his behaviour.	Discuss in supervision. Review facts about sexual abuse.
Does not fully understand survivor's reactions to the abuse, especially if it was limited to fondling or masturbation.	Minimizes her reactions. Survivor feels misunderstood and withdraws.	Review understanding of long-term effects of child sexual abuse.
Difficulties in validating woman's experiences because of own view of women's role in society.	Believes some of the myths about sexual abuse. Indicates that problems are less to do with the abuse and more to do with a woman's personality.	Read survivors' accounts of their past and some feminist literature on sexual abuse.

interested in her sexually or exploit her. Secondly, she can learn that it is possible to trust a man, perhaps for the first time in her life. Finally, her attitude towards men can improve significantly by experiencing the male helper's concern and understanding for her without fearing that he will abuse her trust.

On the other hand, issues that repeat her childhood experiences are likely to be a constant source of difficulty with a male helper. She is likely to expect betrayal, intrusion and that he will overwhelm her with his apparent power over her. She may even expect him to sexually exploit or abuse her.

Physical comfort from a male helper during a period of distress is another issue which may echo her childhood experiences. Survivors have problems with touch in any case, but comfort from a male helper whom she perceives to have power over her is likely to bring many of her childhood feelings to the surface. Unfortunately, her distress is likely to be at its highest initially and during periods of disclosure, neither of which are easy times to learn to trust a man in this way.

Beyond these specific issues, there are other problems which women can have in relation to male helpers. They may be particularly noticeable in a group setting. Firstly, women often have greater difficulty discussing sexual matters with a man. Secondly, women are likely to be more passive and less assertive with a man and to defer to him. In work with survivors, where encouraging her to take control of her life and of her past is one of the key aims, she may be more likely to acquiesce to a male helper's ideas and decisions and find it difficult to challenge him sufficiently to become a woman in her own right. Finally, women find it harder to express their anger to a man, and may try to protect him from it, fearing his reaction.

So far, we have examined a survivor's potential problems with a male helper. There are, however, a number of unhelpful reactions from the male helper himself. These are summarized in Table 2.3.

Choice of Gender of Helper

In a one-to-one therapeutic setting, we believe that most survivors find it easier to work with a female helper, particularly in the early stages. Some women will always find it impossible to entertain the possibility of working with a man. It is vital therefore that survivors should, where possible, be given a choice of the gender of the helper from the outset.

In group settings there is a debate about whether the group leaders should both be female or whether one should be male and one female. Having a male and a female group leader can facilitate the working-through of the conflicts from the survivor's family situation. It may be, however, that the male-female combination could be too close to the original family situation for the survivor to find it helpful. Survivors, who join a group in the latter stages of their therapeutic work, may be able to tolerate these difficult feelings. Women nearer the beginning may need careful preparation for the group with particular reference to the gender of the helpers. Having two female workers as group leaders overcomes some of these difficulties, and avoids feelings of passivity, powerlessness and unassertiveness that women can feel in the presence of a man.

Table 2.3: **Issues for the male helper**

Potential difficulties	Consequences	Action by helper
Possible over-identification with abuser.	Survivor feels betrayed.	Discuss with colleagues.
	Helper excited by sexual aspects of the abuse.	Review the work.
Over-emphasizes the sexual aspects of the abuse rather than issue of power.	Survivor feels that he is only interested in the sexual content.	Review understanding of sexual abuse and its effects.
	Survivor disgusted and withdraws.	
Sexually aroused by details of the abuse.	Survivor may be very aware of male sexual arousal.	Discuss in supervision to examine effects of the woman's history on him.
	Survivor feels betrayed and angry.	If unresolved, stop working with survivors.
	Withdraws from helping situation.	
	Helper feels guilty, becomes over-compensating or distant.	
	In rare cases could lead to therapeutic relationship becoming sexual and thus repeating the abuse.	
Feels guilty about being male/about thoughts and actions in relation to his and others' children.	Overcompensates to show that he is 'safe' man.	Examine own experiences with colleagues.
	Overprotects survivor and own family.	
Feels anger towards abuser.	Ignores any positive feelings/comments that the survivor makes about the abuser.	Support to offload anger.
		Supervision to understand feelings.
Does not fully understand survivor's reactions to the abuse, especially if it was limited to fondling or masturbation.	Minimizes her reaction.	Review understanding of long-term effects of child sexual abuse.
	Survivor feels misunderstood and withdraws.	
May be seen as genderless by survivor.	Helper feels devalued.	Discuss with colleagues.
		Understand her reaction in the context of the abuse.

Table 2.3: Continued

Potential difficulties	Consequences	Action by helper
Physical appearance may remind survivor of abuser.	Can cause flashbacks, strong emotional reactions for the survivor.	Help survivor work through the memories. Help her to see the differences rather than the similarities.
Difficulties in validating woman's experience because of own view of woman's role in society.	Believes some of the myths about sexual abuse. Indicates that problems are less to do with the abuse and more to do with a woman's personality.	Read survivors' accounts of their past and some feminist literature on sexual abuse.

Self-Disclosure

Work with survivors can be sometimes facilitated by self-disclosure on the part of the helper. The helper can find that she/he may be more open about personal experiences as they relate to issues raised by the survivor. Self-disclosure should never be used to discuss any personal difficulties which the helper might be experiencing. Problems can also be caused, for example, if a helper inappropriately discloses a history of sexual abuse. This can result in a survivor's problems being overshadowed or minimized. It can also severely test the therapeutic relationship.

Self-disclosure can be helpful, however, to enable a survivor to have a benchmark for more normal experiences and to work out which aspects of her difficulties are related specifically to the sexual abuse. Examples of appropriate self-disclosure include:

— sharing experiences of being a parent;
— drawing on the female helper's life experiences as a women;
— comparing a helper's and survivor's responses to difficult or threatening situations;
— discussing the normality of emotional reactions.

Effects on Helper's Family Relationships

Working with survivors can raise issues in relation to a helper's partner and children. It is important to be aware of these at the outset. They vary according to the gender of the helper.

The Female Helper

Anger When a female helper works with a survivor for the first time, she may feel anger towards all men for the consequences of the actions of one of them. These feelings are common but can become harmful if they begin to affect her relationships with a male partner, colleagues or friends. They can be compounded if the helper is unable to explain the reasons for her anger. Although it is not appropriate to discuss details of her work, the helper should at least try to say to a male partner:

— that she is working with women who have been sexually abused;
— how the work makes her feel;
— what she would find helpful from her partner (a quiet space for a short while, a hug, something to take her mind off her work or several cups of tea) if she comes home angry or upset about a disclosure from a survivor.

Discussing issues relating to sexual abuse with her partner The issue of male power is usually present when men and women discuss sexual abuse together. It is now generally acknowledged that child sexual abuse is a reflection of wider power relationships between men and women in society. This in itself can make the issue difficult to discuss, even with a supportive partner or colleague. Female helpers should try to voice their fears and feelings with their partners, before deciding whether it will be helpful to discuss it further.

Trusting male partners When a helper learns from survivors about the context in which sexual abuse occurs, what it entails and the threats and bribes which are used to maintain silence, she can seriously question whether she can trust a male partner with her own children. She might find herself saying:

'I know that he wouldn't ever abuse any of our children but I've found myself watching how he plays with them. . . .'

She might find herself becoming over-vigilant at home, watching the way her partner relates to their children, how and when he cuddles, baths or dresses them. She might find herself making excuses for being present when she would normally be doing something else, or curtailing her own activities so that she is at home as often as possible. Again, this is a normal reaction, if experienced in moderation, and it will pass. It is hard to share with a partner, however, since it implies a lack of trust. It could also seriously damage the trust which exists between partners if it persists. A sensitive partner may notice the signs and raise it himself. Otherwise. the helper should share her feelings in supervision or with other helpers in order to get them into perspective before she raises it with her partner.

Effects on her sexual relationship   A helper's own sexual relationship can be affected by work with a survivor, especially during periods of disclosure and she may find herself rejecting her partner. More disturbing, however, is the experience of a flashback if a sexual experience with a partner reminds her of something which a survivor has disclosed. This can be very upsetting both for the helper and her partner. It can be helpful to discuss it with her partner to resolve the specific problem or with a supportive colleague or friend.

The Male Helper

Guilt   There are two issues for a male helper in relation to guilt feelings. Firstly, if the survivor was abused by a man, the helper can feel guilty on behalf of all men. Secondly, if he is a parent, he can become more aware of and feel guilty about his behaviour towards his own children, particularly daughters. It would be important to raise these issues, if they become problematic, with his partner or in supervision.

Fear   A male helper can sometimes have fears about how he treats his own children. After hearing about the way an abuser started to abuse his child, he may no longer have any certainty about what is acceptable behaviour between father and child, in relation to nudity, bathing, privacy, cuddling. Discussing these fears with his partner and in support and supervision should help him to gain some perspective on his own behaviour.

Effects on his sexual relationship   Having listened to a survivor describing distressing sexual experiences, a male helper may begin to question his own sexual relationship. He may need to reassess what is acceptable or pleasurable to his partner by discussing aspects of their sexual relationship together. Difficulties can also arise if he has a flashback to a distressing experience for a survivor when he is involved in similar sexual activity with his partner. Again, he should consider raising the issue with his partner.

For All Helpers

Fears for safety of helper's children   The over-protectiveness which some survivors experience towards their own children can also be felt by helpers. They can find themselves becoming reluctant to engage a babysitter, to allow their children to play outside, to spend the night in a friend's house or to go on a school outing for fear of encountering a potential abuser. These signs of anxiety are often picked up by a partner or friends if they know that the helper is working with survivors. Again, by discussing them, the helper can be reassured that these feelings are normal and that they will pass.

Sexuality of the helper   Crucial to the process of giving help to survivors is the helper's understanding of her/his own sexuality and sexual development. Account should also be taken of personal views and values in this area, openness about sexual matters and ease of discussion of sexuality. Helpers should also be aware of the ways in which their values, experiences and boundaries affect their perception of a survivor's experience. The most important factor is that helpers should be relatively comfortable with their own sexuality and that the ways in which they express it are acceptable generally.

Common Emotional Reactions to Working with Survivors

Work with survivors often produces emotions and reactions in the helper which can affect both the therapeutic relationship and style of work. It is essential that helpers are aware of their reactions and examine them carefully, perhaps with the help of a supervisor, colleague, or other support person.

Some reactions are the result of an empathic response to the survivor. For example, the helper can become very distressed after a detailed disclosure of sexual abuse, because the woman herself is very upset. However, it ceases to be empathic if the helper is unable to contain her/his feelings and reacts inappropriately.

Example: Joanne was very distressed disclosing that her father violently raped her when she was ten. The helper reacted initially by feeling upset too, but could not hold her distress and burst into tears. Joanne was then concerned about the helper's reaction to such an extent that she minimized her own feelings and also the importance of the incident she had been discussing.

This section now examines the common reactions of helpers to disclosure and the consequences for therapeutic contact and work. It is necessary to discuss these during support and supervision so that they do not impede the work. This is especially relevant if a helper finds that she/he is reacting in a way that keeps producing the same problems in the work.

Guilt

This is expressed in a number of ways:

— I feel bad about having had a good childhood;
— I was spared what she experienced;
— I feel guilty because I'm angry about what happened to her. She's suffered enough;
— I feel guilty for thoughts about and behaviour towards my children;
— I made the woman feel suicidal because I asked her for details about the sexual abuse;
— I feel guilty that I felt aroused by her disclosure.

These feelings can lead to the helper being unable to say or ask about things that might hurt the survivor, or not wanting to hear any more about the sexual abuse. In addition, the helper may have difficulty in setting realistic limits on work with a particular woman in order to compensate for her/his feelings of guilt.

Fear

This can be expressed in the following ways:

— she might kill/hurt herself if she tells me what happened;
— she'll feel worse if she tells me, and I'm frightened for her;
— I am frightened to listen to her in case it reminds me of something bad from my own childhood;
— I'm scared of how I'll cope with my own feelings.

These feelings result in the helper not asking a woman about the abuse, thus giving an impression that a woman's history of sexual abuse is too difficult to discuss.

Anger and Rage

These are expressed in the following ways;

— how could anyone do that to a child?
— how dare he/they (abusers in general) do these things?
— why on earth didn't she do something to stop it?
— where was her mother while all this was going on?
— she made me remember what happened to me;
— I feel angry with her because she won't forgive the abuser;
— I feel angry because she won't move on in the work;
— I feel angry because my view of the world has been shattered.

These reactions are common but can lead a helper to disbelieve or minimize the abuser's responsibility for the abuse. A helper can easily mistake her/his anger for the survivor's anger, resulting in a blind spot about the woman's true feelings. As we have already noted, the helper's anger with a particular woman's abuser can spread to anger with men in general. This can result in problems with male colleagues, friends and family members.

Shock/Horror

These feelings are often experienced when a helper starts to work with survivors, when she/he listens to women who have experienced both physical and sexual abuse, and when the abuse has had particularly sadistic features. These feelings can be expressed in the following ways;

— surely nobody could do anything so dreadful to a child;
— I feel sick and horrified by the appalling things which this woman has had to suffer;
— I can't bear to listen. It's too horrible;
— could a child really survive all of this?

High levels of shock or horror about the nature and extent of the abuse will lead to the helper distancing him or herself from the woman as a self-protective mechanism. The helper may avoid asking the woman for details of the abuse or may find it impossible to believe her. This is likely to result in the therapeutic contact being shortened if allowed to go unchecked.

When a survivor is disclosing particularly violent and sadistic abuse the helper can experience nightmares. It may be helpful to share these with a supervisor or support person.

Dread

This is related to reactions of shock and horror and occurs particularly during periods of detailed disclosure about the incidents of abuse. It is expressed by the helper saying:

— what else is she going to tell me?
— I don't want to ask in case she tells me something even worse;
— where is it all going to end?

Again this is liable to lead to the helper distancing him or herself from the woman, and not allowing her to disclose the details of the abuse.

Grief, Sadness and Distress

These are very common reactions and occur both during disclosure of memories when the woman herself gets upset, and during periods when the woman is grieving over the losses which are a result of the abuse.
They can be expressed in the following ways:

— I can get so upset by what she's telling me that I don't want to hear it;
— I wish I could make it all go away for her (and for me).

This leads once again to the helper becoming distanced from the woman for fear of getting upset. A survivor herself may suspect that her helper is overwhelmed by her distress, and she, in turn, may try to protect the helper. This is not generally helpful for the survivor.

Disgust

Feelings of disgust occur most often during periods of detailed disclosure about the sexual abuse. They are also common if the helper has just started working with survivors. After some time, most helpers can cope with these feelings because they can anticipate what a woman has to tell. These feelings can be expressed in the following ways:

— this makes me feel sick. I don't want to listen any more;

— how could he do anything so sick/base/obscene to a child?

The survivor is likely to pick up these feelings in her helper, and she may protect the helper by not disclosing any more details of the abuse.

Feeling Overwhelmed and Burnt-out

This often occurs when the helper is going through a particularly unpleasant period of disclosure with a woman or if the helper is trying to work with too many survivors at any one time. It is expressed in the following says:

— I can't bear to hear anyone else say they have been sexually abused;

— I can't remember which woman I'm talking to — they've all merged into one;

— I don't want to hear any more;

— I'm too tired to hear any more disclosures.

If these feelings emerge with an individual woman, it can lead to the helper becoming distressed and exhausted, and results in a general distancing from her. As a consequence, the helper may try to get the woman to minimize the effects of the abuse rather than helping her to face very distressing events from her past.

If a helper is working with several survivors at any one time, it is essential to have supervision and support. Attempts should be made to set clear limits both on the number and amount of time spent with survivors. It may also be time for the helper to take a break!

No Emotional Reaction

Whilst overwhelming emotional reactions in the helper are troublesome, being totally unaffected can also produce difficulties. Helpers sometimes express this in the following ways:

— I don't/can't feel anything;

— I shut myself off so that I won't feel anything;

— this survivor might affect/contaminate me with her feelings.

These feelings are likely to make a survivor think that the helper is not interested in her. A lack of response may also indicate that the helper has learnt that the expression of feelings is dangerous. A complete absence of emotional expression is not uncommon in people who have themselves been abused (see Chapter 3).

Idealization of the Survivor

This is expressed in the following ways:

— it is a great privilege to work with her;
— I admire her for surviving and for her courage;
— my problems are nothing compared to hers;
— she has done so well.

It can lead the helper to minimize a survivor's pain or her problems, and can make it difficult for her to express her distress. It is important for the helper to maintain a balance, reaffirming a survivor's strengths whilst acknowledging her pain.

Delight/Praise

Expression of a helper's more positive emotions is necessary but can be problematic. Statements such as:

— I am pleased that she finally got round to telling me;
— she is doing so well

can encourage a survivor to continue doing the work, but can encourage her to carry on just to gain the helper's approval, rather than because it meets with her own needs and wishes. A woman who has been abused can also find it extremely difficult to hear and believe praise. As a consequence, she may not be able to tell the helper about any of her positive achievements or may not be able to assess whether there have been any.

Voyeurism/Sexual Arousal

An extremely problematic reaction in the helper is when she/he actually gets some satisfaction, or becomes sexually aroused by the sexual details of the abuse. The latter reaction is reported to be more common among male helpers (Herman, 1981). It may be expressed in the following ways:

— I enjoy hearing all the details of what happened to her;

— I want to know everything that happened. It's so interesting hearing what an adult can do to a child;

— it turns me on to hear the sexual details;

— I feel guilty because I have these feelings.

A survivor may pick up these indications of sexual arousal, and she may distance herself, miss appointments or remove herself altogether from the situation, because she feels misunderstood or at-risk of abuse once again. Helpers should be aware that there may be some instances where they may feel aroused by some things which a survivor tells them. This is normal. It is never acceptable, however, to act on any of these feelings in the therapeutic relationship. If they persist, helpers have a professional and ethical obligation to remove themselves from the work in a way which does not endanger the survivors further.

Rescuing/Over-protective Reaction

A common reaction is the desire to help any survivor who comes to the helper's attention without regard to setting reasonable limits on numbers. The helper feels a need to protect survivors from feelings of vulnerability, pain and distress. It can be expressed in a number of ways:

— I must protect her from getting upset. She's had enough pain already;

— she's too fragile/vulnerable for me to ask any detailed questions about the abuse;

— I'll try to make everything all right by keeping her safe.

This clearly ignores the survivor's inner strengths and resources which have enabled her to reach adulthood. It can also contribute to a slower pace of recovery and increase the survivor's dependency on her helper.

Other Issues for the Helper

Confidentiality

Survivors have the right to know from the outset what the boundaries of confidentiality are going to be. Sharing this information and discussing issues about which the survivor might be unhappy can be a way of building trust. It is also an important step in enabling the survivor to feel more in control of her destiny and returning power to her. It will be important to discuss:

— what sort of notes, if any, will be kept on each session;
— where these notes will be kept;
— who else will see them;
— will the survivor be able to read them;
— what will happen to any material (notes, writing, artwork) kept by the helper when contact has ceased.

In addition the survivor may wish to know:

— whether any information about her will be shared with other professionals (family doctor, hospital);
— if there will be any unforeseen consequences of recording her history of sexual abuse, — will it be used in assessments for childminding, fostering, adoption, job references;
— how and if information shared with the helper might be used if she decides to take the abuser to court.

These are also a number of issues for the helper in relation to confidentiality. These include:

— the ground-rules regarding confidentiality may vary between agencies. The helper needs to discuss confidentiality issues with workers in any other agency which might be involved;
— getting the survivor's permission to share information is vital;
— being careful about information that is shared over the telephone;
— being careful that files are not left lying around the office;
— letting the survivor know what sort of discussion might be undertaken in supervision, and the boundaries of confidentiality;
— being aware that there might be particular issues regarding confidentiality in a small or rural community;
— who types notes or letters about her.

Membership of a survivors' group can raise additional issues of confidentiality. They include:

— fear about other group members speaking about the group or individuals within it, outside the group;
— information shared between facilitators and a survivor's individual therapist. Here the ground-rules need to be clearly established at the outset and adhered to during the group;

— group members knowing each other, or knowing the families of origin of each other.

The survivor may require reassurance about confidentiality so that she feels more in control in this respect. This may include:

— being clear from the outset about confidentiality;
— letting her know of any circumstances under which the helper might have to break confidentiality (for example, where a child is in danger or at risk of being abused);
— letting her know early on if the helper is going to share anything about her with anyone else;
— letting her see the sort of records which are being kept by the agency;
— showing her where records are kept;
— considering the possibility of the survivor keeping a log or diary of the sessions, which would be lodged in a safe place. This could be an alternative to the helper keeping a record. The material could then be handed back to the survivor at the end of the contact.

In the final analysis, helpers should be aware that the sharing of information about a survivor should only be for the benefit of the survivor. Any breaches in confidentiality or inappropriate sharing of information will feel like a further abuse of trust for the survivor.

Rejection

Most survivors are extremely sensitive to being rejected. Their experience has taught them to expect to be rejected and they can easily interpret aspects of the helper's behaviour as rejecting. For example, not returning a phone-call, appearing to be tired during a session, not reading a piece of writing immediately, being late for a meeting with the survivor, getting her name wrong, can all be interpreted as signs of rejection or lack of interest on the part of the helper.

Why Me?

Helpers often ask themselves why the survivor chose them to disclose to. They may feel flattered, honoured or burdened by the disclosure. In reality, it is likely to be a result of two main factors. Firstly, the survivor herself may have reached a point of having to tell someone. Secondly, the helper may have already provided her with a safe and accepting environment and atmosphere so that she feels it will be safe enough to reveal the secrets of her childhood.

Testing Out

Some survivors test out the helper to see how much they can be relied on. This testing out may take the form of lying, threatening suicide or making huge demands of the helper in terms of time and emotional commitment. It is important for the helper to have a consistent attitude, setting limits with a woman where necessary. A helper may have to endure a long period of testing before a woman can begin to accept that the helper is prepared to work on her problems with her.

Regression

During disclosure work, some survivors regress to being a small child. This is explored in detail in Chapter 7. In this situation, the helper can be a trigger for the regression to occur. Regression demands high levels of support and involvement from the helper, a safe place in which to allow the regression to occur and time to allow the woman to return to her normal adult state afterwards.

Working with Several Members of the Same Family

Considerable problems can be caused if the helper is seeing several members of the same family separately because of their individual needs. The helper is likely to hear conflicting perceptions of events and there will be reasonable concerns about confidentiality regarding information from other family members.

The helper may also find that therapeutic work proceeds at very different rates for different family members. Sometimes, a helper will be asked to help a woman's sibling with expectations that the brother/sister will gain as much as the woman herself from getting help. This does not always happen as the sibling may feel pressured into seeking help, or may not be able to use the helper in the same way as his/her sister.

Isolation

It can be particularly stressful if the helper is working in a setting where sexual abuse is not generally acknowledged or where she/he is the only person involved in working with survivors. It can result in a lack of immediate support which exacerbates the sense of isolation. In these circumstances the helper should seek support from others working in this field, while bearing in mind the issues of confidentiality.

Survivors as Helpers

Table 2.4 summarizes the ways in which a helper's personal experience of childhood sexual abuse might enhance or hinder work with other survivors. Many survivors have forgotten all or some of their childhood experiences, and this can create difficulties in helping other survivors. Forgotten memories, flashbacks and nightmares can be triggered by hearing another survivor's history. It is essential for any helper who finds him or herself in this situation to seek support and help before she/he continues working with women who have been sexually abused. This may necessitate transferring the survivor to another helper in order to allow time for the helper to deal with her/his own past.

Table 2.4: **Survivors as helpers: Some advantages and areas of difficulty**

Potential advantages	*Potential areas of difficulty*
Can immediately identify with survivors	Greater possibility of becoming over-involved
No difficulty about believing	Own past may intrude inappropriately (My experience was worse than/not as bad as yours)
Can help her understand her feelings more easily	
Easier to help disclosure	May bring previously forgotten memories to the surface
Can accurately guess what survivor is trying to say	Some issues may be more difficult to deal with (sexuality, physical abuse)
Helps survivor to break the silence ('me too')	May get angry with other survivors because they are not 'trying' hard enough to come to terms with their past
Reduces isolation	
Helper may be able to personally recommend useful books.	Helper's self disclosure could intrude into the survivor's work

Coping Strategies for the Helper

Working with survivors can be very rewarding for the helper, but as we have seen, can bring strong and uncomfortable emotional reactions. It is therefore important that the helper takes time to look after her/himself. In this section, we suggest some common coping strategies that helpers can use to sustain themselves during work with survivors. The following are ways often used:

— *Immediate support at work* There are many times when immediate support from a trusted colleague can be enough to off-load some of the feelings resulting from working with a survivor. It may be necessary to share the secret of the abuse that has just been disclosed, without breaking the confidentiality of the survivor;

— *Sharing the positives with a supervisor or colleague* The ways the survivor used her resources to survive the abuse, her progress and writing (with permission of the survivor), along with the more difficult feelings, enables the helper to keep a balance and be reminded of the progress the survivor is making;

— *Writing/dictating notes after a session with survivor* This can be a useful way of allowing the helper to set a particular survivor's story, problems and emotions to one side until the next session;

— *Ensuring that there is some balance in the helper's workload* This can be achieved by not seeing too many survivors at one time, or by having survivors at different stages of their work, with not too many in painful disclosure work. This is sometimes difficult to achieve where the helper is one of the few resources in an area known to work with survivors;

— *Use of other activities at work and at home* This can balance the intensity of work with survivors. At work this can include working with people who do not have sexual abuse in their history, or the myriad of other tasks that are required of the helper in the workplace. At home, many helpers find physical activity — sports, gardening, walking — beneficial in enabling them to get away from the emotional reactions from their work. Any activity that enables the helper to wind down and relax is useful in this context;

— *Support at home* This can be important so that the helper's partner, family or close friends are aware of the kind of work that the helper is doing. Working with survivors can impinge on personal relationships, and it can be worth discussing the issues with family members and close friends where appropriate so that potential difficulties can be anticipated. This can have the effect of mitigating any problems that do occur;

— *Rest and scheduled breaks from the more intensive work* It is far better to schedule a few days' holiday that can be planned and anticipated by the survivor than to have to have a few days off because of exhaustion or being overwhelmed by the work;

— *The expression of emotional feelings* This is a task the helper is likely to encourage in the survivor in a safe way. The helper needs to do the same with trusted colleagues, supervisor, partner, family members or friends;

— *Physical comfort for the helper* This can be important and useful in allowing the expression of the more distressed feelings;

— *Establishing a support network in the area of other helpers who are working with survivors* This can be very beneficial. In this way, the helper is likely to have a range of support resources available at any one time;

— *Receiving training for work with survivors* This is important and can enable helpers to make contact with others engaged in similar work. We are very conscious of the fact that there are many individuals working with survivors in isolation, often without support within their agency. Taking part in local training allows some of these helpers to get together and give mutual support;

— *Supervision* This is an important part of any therapeutic work, but in practice is often difficult to obtain from other helpers who are experienced in working with survivors. However, good supervision should be sought. This issue will be examined in more detail in a later section;

— *The use of humour* This can be a way of balancing some of the more painful emotional reactions. For example, the helper and survivor may find themselves being able to laugh at some of the ways the abuser behaved. Sometimes, the less serious side of the mixed messages that the survivor was given can strike her as an adult in a way that could not be seen as a child.

Example: Sharon was talking about the way she was constantly blamed for everything that happened when she was a child. She recalled an incident when her father blamed her for the breaking of a plate that occurred whilst she was out at the shops. His logic was that if Sharon had been at home looking after her little sister, he would not have had to get up and see to her and would not have tripped over the plate that he had left on the floor. Also, if Sharon had been there, the plate would not have been on the floor. As Sharon was describing this, she suddenly looked at the helper who was looking puzzled, and started to laugh at her father's reasoning. This led her to question the authority and power of her father for the first time.

Whilst the above suggestions are only some ways that helpers might use to deal with some of the effects of working with survivors, it is essential for the helper to take the responsibility for looking after her/himself using whatever methods are helpful. The dangers of emotional overload and burn-out are present in many types of care-work; working with survivors is no different. Often, the fact that a survivor is clearly changing and feeling better makes the hard work for the helper feel worthwhile and will encourage the helper. Overcoming the effects of childhood trauma is hard emotional work. It can also be very positive and satisfying for both the survivor and her helper because changes in survivors can be dramatic and lead to significant positive developments in their lives.

Support and Supervision for Working with Survivors

There is a need for good support and supervision to be available for anyone who is working, or planning to work with survivors. We would define a support person as someone to whom the helper would choose to turn for informal discussion about the work and for personal reassurance. It could be a colleague, friend or partner. A supervisor, on the other hand, is a colleague, or group of colleagues, formally involved in detailed discussions with a helper about the work.

The main criteria to be met for good supervision are:

— the supervisor should be someone who is currently involved in helping survivors come to terms with their experiences. Helpers may wish to arrange supervision with someone outside their agency/ setting, for example, facilitators in a small self-help group may arrange supervision from a health or social worker. However, helpers employed by large bureaucratic organizations may experience some difficulty from their managers if they request supervision from outside that setting. This problem might be solved by ensuring confidentiality and stressing inter-professional co-operation.

— supervision should take place in a safe and supportive climate. Working with survivors can raise difficult personal issues and provoke feelings of anger, distress, uncertainty and anxiety in the helper. Creating a climate in which the helper feels safe enough to express these feelings is an important step towards resolving them. It also helps to ensure that concerns and doubts raised by the helper are balanced with recognition by a supervisor of the positive work being done.

In order for it to be of maximum benefit, supervision should be held on a regular basis (weekly or fortnightly).

Helpers may find they need support immediately after seeing a survivor. In this case, seeking support from a colleague may be necessary. Different types of support from friends, partners and colleagues may be useful.

Content of Supervision

Supervision should cover the following areas:

Content and process of work with survivor   Detailed feedback on the work should be given by both helper and supervisor. In this way the helper can be encouraged to reflect on what was said or done and to note the successful and problematic aspects of the work. The way in which the work is progressing can also be reviewed at regular intervals. Any parts of a survivor's personal history that are causing difficulties for the helper, in emotional terms or in relation to the helper's personal life, could be discussed in supervision.

Help with planning ahead   Supervision should be used to anticipate the likely consequences of different courses of actions taken by the helper. Role-playing difficult situations can enable the helper to see things from the perspective of the survivor and to consider different courses of action.

Discussion of personal issues   If issues raised by a survivor evoke painful memories for the helper, these should be addressed in supervision. If a helper remembers being abused as a child, she/he may initially have to consider giving up the work with survivors until her/his own problems have been resolved. This should not be undertaken in supervision, but in another therapeutic environment. Supervision might cover *how* to hand over the work to another helper, without the survivor feeling that this is a personal rejection.

Sharing the secret   When a survivor discloses new information about her past, the burden of the secret passes to the helper. This is a stressful experience, especially if the disclosure is particularly horrifying. The helper can feel that she/he alone now holds the secrets of the abuse. Supervision then becomes an important place for sharing these secrets whilst maintaining their confidentiality and enabling the helper to maintain objectivity. Sometimes, a helper will find it difficult to wait until the next supervision session to share the disclosures made by a survivor. Good support is vital during this period. To share, in confidence, a survivor's disclosures is not a further betrayal of trust; it is one means of breaking the silence surrounding childhood sexual abuse.

Difficulties with believing   These should always be raised in supervision as a survivor will be hypersensitive to any suggestion that she might not be believed. Clarifying any reasons for doubt on the part of the helper is crucial. These reasons might include:

— a disclosure of abuse which is more horrifying than any previous disclosure;
— any doubt that a survivor has about the occurrence of an incident. This in turn can influence a helper's ability to believe;
— knowledge that a survivor has lied in the past;
— lack of emotional reaction in a survivor, suggesting that nothing really happened.

We know that survivors often react unemotionally during disclosures of sexual abuse and previous discrepancies do not mean that sexual abuse did not occur. It is essential that the helper believes a woman who says she has been sexually abused; any doubts should be reserved for discussion in supervision.

Preparing for disclosure   During supervision it is sometimes possible to anticipate the likely content of a woman's future disclosures; she may have had nightmares, or express unspecific fears about people, situations or events. The helper may be able to help her to connect these feelings with her early experiences and can be enabled to examine any anticipated disclosures in the safety of a supervision session. Any distressing or strong emotional reactions can then be dealt with before having to hear the disclosure from the survivor herself.

The 'style' of the helper   This may involve taking a close look at how the helper organizes the meetings with a survivor, and the style and method used in the work. We suggest that work with survivors has to be both active and creative. Sitting back with minimal intervention from the helper often allows the woman's passivity to dominate the session and so reduce the pace of the work. Being active means that the helper may sometimes exaggerate her/his facial expression and tone of voice so that a survivor can learn different forms of communication with others.

Creativity in work with survivors is important. Methods and ideas for achieving a particular goal with a survivor should never be disregarded, just because they are different from a helper's normal way of working. Sometimes, the most unexpected idea causes a breakthrough. Sharing these ideas in supervision is useful, as it can often lead to development of new techniques, or of different methods to use with a particular woman.

Sharing literature and new methods   Supervision provides a good forum for helpers to share and discuss new literature on sexual abuse; it is also useful for discovering new ways of dealing with the issues which women raise.

Questions for supervisors   Supervisors might find it helpful to ask these questions of the helper in supervision:

— What were your reactions to the situation?
— What made this situation easy/difficult for you?
— What issues does it raise in relation to your own life?
— How might your feelings affect the process of helping this survivor?

Models for Supervision

Helpers should consider the type of supervision which will be most useful to them and to try to arrange this if it is available. There are three possible alternatives outlined in Table 2.5, together with their advantages and limitations. The ideal situation may be a combination of one-to-one and group supervision, with the latter occurring less frequently and taking place with a pre-planned agenda.

Support for Working with Survivors

Support can be gained in a variety of ways. It can include:

— letting off steam when you get home after a difficult session with survivor/s;

— letting friends/partner/colleagues know why you are feeling angry, upset or elated after a session;

— asking for a hug, cup of tea, some advice or a ready ear after a session.

Table 2.5: **Models for supervision: Advantages and limitations**

Model	Advantages	Limitations
One-to-one.	Trust established with supervisor.	Supervisor may feel wider pressure.
	Personal material more easily disclosed.	Can't check out how common feelings are.
	Confidentiality more easily ensured.	
Group (peer group).	Common issues identified.	Not enough time for in-depth discussion.
	More scope for new ideas and approaches.	Less likelihood of helper disclosing personal issues.
Group (with a leader).	Approaches from other settings shared.	Common ground may be limited.
	Supervision may be more structured.	Supervision may feel more like training session.
		Less time available for individual women's problems.

Making Links with Other Resources

It is easy for helpers who are working with survivors to feel isolated and unsupported, unless they are working in a setting where the main focus of work is sexual abuse. In order to give the best resources to survivors, it is essential to pool skills, knowledge and resources. Finding just one other person with an interest in this type of work can be the trigger for support, joint training sessions, seminars, or case discussions to share ideas on ways of working. Making links could start by finding out about all the resources available locally for survivors. A letter could be sent to clinical psychologists, psychiatrists, social workers, health visitors and others working in the field of mental health and support for women (for example,

Rape Crisis, Women's Aid, hostels for women). The letter might ask about any work undertaken with survivors, the support and training available for this work and any interest in joint seminars or training.

This chapter has outlined the main issues for helpers. It is our view that no one should undertake such work without adequate minimum training. A system of support and supervision should also be established otherwise helpers may find themselves feeling confused, doubtful and burned-out.

Training Issues

Chapter 12 examines aspects of training in more depth, but here we note that the minimum training needs for anyone offering support to survivors should include:

— acknowledging the helper's own life experiences and how these could help or hinder work with survivors;
— recognizing the nature and consequences of childhood sexual abuse;
— reading life stories of survivors;
— becoming open about using language specific to sexual abuse;
— ensuring that adequate supervision and support is available when undertaking work with survivors.

It is often the case that helpers will not have had the opportunity to plan for working with survivors of child sexual abuse. By whatever means they come to the work, it may be helpful for them to ask themselves some of the following questions when they start:

— how prepared do I feel to do this work?
— how ready do I feel to do it?
— do I need to talk over the implications of doing this work with a partner or friends?
— do I know where to go for reading/preliminary training to enable me to work with survivors?
— do I have adequate support to enable me to do the work?
— do I have adequate supervision?
— What personal resources do I have to sustain me in the work?

Chapter 3

Problems in Adulthood

Factors in Childhood Relating to the Development of Problems

In the last decade, there has been a gradual accumulation of empirical evidence indicating that a history of child sexual abuse is associated with considerable mental health and adjustment problems in adulthood, long after the abuse itself has stopped (Bagley and Ramsay, 1986; Finkelhor, 1984; Fromuth, 1986). There are a number of factors in childhood which are relevant to the development and severity of these problems (Browne and Finkelhor, 1986; Lister, 1982; Russell, 1986). These include:

Traumatic sexualization (Brown and Finkelhor, 1986) This occurs when a child is subjected to sexual activity. Consequently she develops misconceptions about sexual behaviour and norms, learns to associate sexual activity with negative feelings and may confuse sex with love and affection.

Betrayal The child's trust and vulnerability are betrayed by adults who are in a position of trust with the child and should therefore be protecting and caring for her.

Powerlessness The child is powerless in that her wishes and needs are constantly undermined and disregarded. She is forced into experiences that leave her fearful and from which she is unable to protect herself.

Stigma The child's sense of being stigmatized results from the many negative messages associated with sexual abuse. They may come directly from the abuser who blames or condemns her, or from other adults who imply blame and shame to the child about the sexual abuse. Additionally, her perception of cultural and religious taboos may convince her that she should feel guilty, bad or ashamed.

Enforced silence   The child is expected, told or forced by use of threats, to keep the secret of sexual abuse. Lister (1982) emphasizes that this enforced silence is important in the development of adult mental health problems. It encourages the woman to continue to live in fear and isolation with considerable feelings of guilt and shame. He states that 'in silence, the pain and subliminal memories of pain festered'. Once this silence has been broken, the adult survivor can be terrified that the abuser's threats will come to fruition, and yet relieved that the burden of secrecy is removed. She may feel a sense of disloyalty towards her family for breaking the secret, and this may cause difficulties during any therapeutic work (Gelinas, 1983).

Factors Relating to the Nature of the Abuse

Duration and frequency of abuse   There is strong evidence linking the duration and frequency of the abuse with the severity of its long-term consequences (Bagley and Ramsay, 1986; Browne and Finkelhor, 1986; Tsai and Wagner, 1978; Briere and Zaidi, 1989). However, it is also clear that a single incident of sexual abuse can produce very significant problems for a woman in her adult life.

Type of sexual abuse   There is some suggestion that the type of sexual abuse is related to its damaging effects (Russell, 1986), but the empirical evidence is as yet inconclusive.

Relationship with the abuser   Greater damaging effects are reported following sexual abuse by a father or father figure (Russell, 1986). The effects of being abused by other family members may depend on the degree of trust in the relationship. It is also possible that abuse by trusted neighbours or babysitters can be more damaging than abuse by distant relatives. Abuse by women is now being reported more frequently, and the damage, especially if the abuse is perpetrated by the child's mother, seems to be particularly devastating.

Use of physical force   An association between the abuser's use of force or violence and the degree of later long-term effects has been confirmed in a number of studies (Finkelhor, 1979; Russell, 1986).

The number of abusers   The empirical research does indicate greater traumatic effects where the child has been subjected to abuse by several individuals (Briere and Zaidi, 1989). In our experience, for women who were sexually abused by both parents, or were abused by one parent with the knowledge or encouragement of the other, the negative consequences are more severe.

The age of the child   There is some suggestion that the younger the child at the start of the abuse, the greater the consequences in her adult life (Gil, 1988).

These explanations for the occurrence and severity of the long-term consequences of child sexual abuse should be used only as a guide, since significant problems can and do result from a single incident of sexual abuse by a more distant relative. What is clear, however, is that being sexually abused as a child by a trusted adult does have a number of long-term consequences for mental health and relationships in adult life. The evidence from research studies has enabled us to construct a picture of the common problems of adult survivors that is remarkably consistent regardless of the family background and severity of the abuse. These difficulties should therefore be construed as the *normal* consequences of child sexual abuse though their pattern varies from one individual to another.

The Long-term Consequences of Sexual Abuse

Table 3.1 summarizes the long-term consequences of sexual abuse. Clearly not all the problems are present in every survivor and their severity varies from one woman to the next and from one period of her life to another. They do provide a sobering account, however, of the real and severe difficulties faced by many women as a result of their childhood experiences.

The effects of sexual abuse into adulthood can be largely understood and predicted from the effects on and the reactions of the child, in conjunction with a knowledge of the factors relating to the abuse (see previous section). The childhood effects, reactions, beliefs and behaviour often continue unmodified or generalized into adulthood.

Low Self-esteem

Low levels of self-esteem are fundamental to many survivors' difficulties. Kempe (1980) reported that sexually abused children revealed a view of

Table 3.1: **Summary of long-term consequences of child sexual abuse**

Low Self-esteem.	Further Assault/Revictimization.
Confusion.	General Fear of Men.
Emotional Reactions — guilt — anger and rage — sadness and grief — complete absence of emotional reaction.	Interpersonal Difficulties. — in relationships with men — in relationships with women.
Depression	Sexual Problems — impaired sexual arousal — difficulties with orgasm — lack of sexual motivation — lack of sexual satisfaction — guilt during sexual contact — vaginismus — pain during intercourse.
Anxiety Problems — generalized anxiety — panic attacks — specific fears and phobias — pronounced startle response.	
Isolation and Alienation	Problems with Touch.
Bad Reactions to Medical Procedures — hospital admissions — gynaecological procedures — dental procedures.	Parenting Problems.
	Abuse of Self — self mutilation and injury — suicidal attempts.
Physical Complaints.	Substance Abuse — alcohol — drugs — tranquillizers.
Sleep Disturbance.	
Eating Disorders — compulsive eating and obesity — bulimia — anorexia nervosa.	Compulsive and Obsessional Problems.
	Under-achievement in Education and Occupation.
Multiple Personality Disorder.	Difficulty in Sustaining Positive Experiences.
Dissociative Problems — perceptual disturbances — flashbacks — nightmares/bad dreams — out-of-body experiences.	Other Effects.
Problems with Trust.	
Victim Behaviour.	

themselves as defenceless, worthless, guilty, at-risk and threatened from all sides, especially from their parents. This picture continues into adulthood with a woman often displaying overwhelming helplessness, hopelessness and an extremely negative view of herself. The self-esteem problems are compounded by the extreme sense of guilt and shame that most survivors carry about the sexual abuse and their inability to stop it. Self-blame often generalizes to other experiences in adulthood, leading to further situations where a woman is taken advantage of and exploited.

Survivors often have a very negative self-image. They feel bad about many aspects of their life. They express guilt about their failings, particularly in meeting the demands of others, and they blame themselves constantly for things that go wrong. This leads to difficulties in liking and accepting themselves, in accepting that anyone else might like them, want to be with them, or care about them. This can result in further isolation and alienation. This poor self-image and self-esteem is at the root of victim behaviour, and underlies much of the depression, alcohol and drug abuse and relationship difficulties experienced by survivors. A lack of assertiveness, feelings of powerlessness and helplessness are also consequences of low self-esteem which leads to a failure to protect themselves from further abuse and to a denial of emotional needs.

Survivors often fail to see the many emotional strengths and resources which have enabled them to survive and cope with the negative consequences of their childhood experiences (see Chapter 4). Thus, a negative, helpless picture of themselves persists, although they may show great courage, fortitude and determination in dealing with problems in their lives. Part of their difficulty in seeing these positive aspects of themselves is that they have experienced little positive feedback about their good qualities, especially when they were children.

Confusion

Survivors often experience intense confusion about the nature of their difficulties, the causes of their problems and the reactions of others to them. Gelinas (1983) suggests that this confusion, in the absence of severe psychiatric problems, is one of the most common indicators that a woman has been sexually abused as a child. It is likely that this confusion originated in childhood, partly as the result of a lack of understanding about the sexual nature of the abuse, and partly because the child was abused and hurt by an adult whom she could have reasonably expected to protect and care for her. Her difficulty in understanding or making sense of the childhood experiences continues into adulthood.

Emotional Reactions

Guilt   Guilt is the predominant emotional response for many survivors. It relates to their feelings of responsibility for the sexual abuse and generalizes to many situations and relationships. The high levels of guilt about childhood experiences can be attributed to several factors (Tsai and Wagner, 1978):

— silence about the abuse, suggesting that the abuse was an experience to be ashamed of and not to be revealed to others;
— feelings of responsibility for the sexual abuse, often compounded by the reactions of the abuser and other significant adults blaming the child;
— believing that she had behaved badly and that her punishment was to be abused;
— failing to stop the abuse, giving the survivor the idea that she 'allowed' it to continue;
— any feelings of physical arousal felt during the abuse.

As a child, therefore, she learns to feel guilty about the experiences. Without the reassurance that she was not responsible for the abuse, these feelings continue into adulthood, and lead her to feel guilty about all aspects of her life and any problems encountered by people she is close to. This in turn results in a lowering of her self-esteem, the establishment of depression and a sense of hopelessness.

Anger and rage Some survivors show considerable anger and hostility towards the world in general, and family and friends in particular. This manifests itself in angry outbursts, aggression and an ability to produce conflict in many situations. It is extremely disruptive for relationships and can lead to isolation from other people. As with the guilty feelings, the anger is unfocused and is displaced from the childhood experiences into adulthood.

It is a set of complex responses to the abuse and abuser and to other potentially protective adults, especially the mother. It relates to the widespread occurrence of sexual abuse and to the fact that so much was lost through the experience of being abused. For example, it is not uncommon to find survivors becoming extremely angry because they perceive other people to have normal, caring sexual relationships, and good relationships with their parents and children. Anger and hostility are also used as a protective shield preventing others from getting close (Hays, 1985). Many survivors have never learned appropriate ways of dealing with their anger, and frequently turn it in on themselves. This leads to self-mutilation, alcohol and drug abuse and suicidal attempts.

Sadness and grief Many survivors experience periods of extreme sadness which they are unable to understand. They rarely appreciate the extent of the losses in their lives which are due to being sexually abused (for example, loss of normal relationships with parents, of normal childhood and adult opportunities, of normal emotional development). This sadness can have all the signs of an unresolved grief reaction (see Chapter 11), and may result in considerable depression. The survivor is usually confused by the intensity of these emotional reactions and her lack of explanation for them (Hays, 1985).

Complete absence of emotional reaction As we will see in Chapter 7, when a child is being sexually abused she will often learn to dissociate herself from the abuse and its accompanying feelings. Such dissociation usually continues into adulthood, with the result that the survivor remains unaware of emotional reactions and can be devoid of any emotional expression. She may therefore describe the abusive experiences without any feeling, and may misinterpret, ignore or deny the existence of any signs of emotion.

Depression

Periods of depression and low mood are common in survivors (Bagley and Ramsay, 1986; Browne and Finkelhor, 1986). During these times, it is usual to find intensification of feelings of guilt, very low self-esteem, withdrawal from social contact, and sometimes an inner deadness or lack of emotional reaction (Herman *et al.*, 1986). Suicide attempts, disturbed sleep and eating patterns and marked changes in weight are common occurrences.

Survivors often come into contact with psychiatric services when they are depressed. In-patient treatment may be necessary for those who experience severe depression, and anti-depressant medication and electro-convulsive therapy (ECT) may be used. For a woman who has not felt able to discuss her childhood experiences at all, these contacts with the statutory services can help to maintain her capacity to cope with normal life. Because her secret remains unbroken, however, the medical responses listed above do not enable her to deal with the root cause of her difficulties.

Anxiety Problems

Most survivors experience considerable anxiety, as well as multiple fears, often of phobic intensity. Anxiety shows itself in three main ways:

— It is experienced physically (headaches, dizziness, dry mouth, palpitations, pains/tightness in the chest and other parts of the body, sweating, shaking and nausea). It is accompanied by physical exhaustion, sensitivity to noise, and sleeping problems;

— Anxiety affects an individual's behaviour, in that it leads to avoidance of feared situations, difficulties in making decisions, restlessness, constant checking of tasks already done and irritability;

— Anxiety affects an individual's way of thinking. Following the work of Beck and his associates (Beck, 1976) it is possible to identify the types of negative thinking that occur during periods of anxiety and depression (see Chapter 11). These negative thoughts contribute significantly to the maintenance of high levels of anxiety, and form part of a vicious circle of physical anxiety leading to avoidance and negative thinking. This, in turn, leads to further physical anxiety.

Panic attacks　A panic attack is defined as a distinct episode that is characterized by the following features:

— a high level of anxiety;

— strong physical reactions (dizziness, heart palpitations, sweating, shaking, trembling, nausea, feelings of unreality, going hot and cold, chest pains, breathlessness/choking sensation);

— loss of the ability to plan, think or reason;

— a strong fear of doing something uncontrolled (of going 'crazy', or of dying).

A panic attack is usually experienced during periods of high anxiety, but it may come out of the blue. It is common for panic attacks to become more frequent during recall of the details of sexual abuse.

Specific fears/phobias　Survivors often have a number of specific fears which can be extremely disabling, and can lead to a woman avoiding certain situations. They can be categorized as follows:

— Places that have similar qualities to the place where the abuse occurred, for example, visiting a house that has many of the same characteristics (room layout, stairs, colour of decor, etc.) as the house she lived in during the time of the sexual abuse. Similarly, claustrophobia (intense fear of being in a confined space) is quite common for women who were abused in a small room.

> **Example:**　Moira was abused by her father in a small dark attic room. As an adult she experienced intense anxiety and panic attacks in a number of confined spaces — lifts, attic rooms, sitting as a passenger in a car or being on a crowded bus. These symptoms led her to avoid all these places.

— Specific phobias, for example, for animals, insects. This may relate directly to the abusive situation where her abuser may have used her fears of animals/insects to frighten and threaten her further. Even without this direct link to the abuse, survivors often experience insect phobias. Insects are seen as dangerous, out of control, able to creep in unseen and behave in incomprehensible ways. The women themselves often come to see their insect phobias as a way of describing the abuse situation;

— Phobic reactions to violence are particularly common in women who have experienced physical as well as sexual abuse, and result in avoidance of all violent or potentially violent situations in everyday life and of all violent scenes on television, video or films;

— Phobic reactions to sexual activity or nudity in the media are frequently experienced by survivors. This results in avoidance of television, video or film material which portrays sexual activity or nudity. A woman may also avoid situations such as sporting activities or a visit to the beach where people may not be fully clothed;

— Situations in which high levels of anxiety or panic attacks have been experienced previously. The woman is likely to anticipate further anxiety/panic symptoms and become frightened of the symptoms themselves. Over-sensitivity to any physical signs of anxiety is common, and leads to predictions that she will have further unpleasant symptoms or panic attacks, so she will try to avoid being in similar situations. This can rapidly generalize to other situations, and can lead to agoraphobia (complete avoidance of all places outside her home);

— Situations that generate fear that the women herself describes as irrational or unfounded. These can then become the focus of all her anxiety symptoms and can lead to considerable disruption of her everyday life.

Example: Penny described being frightened of plugging in any electrical equipment for fear that the electrical socket would harm her in some way. She knew these fears were unfounded but continued to avoid electrical equipment, with obvious consequences for her everyday life.

Pronounced startle response   Survivors often exhibit a significant startle response to any sudden noises, such as the ringing of the telephone or door bell. It is as if they are on edge all the time listening for noises. Most describe this response beginning when they were children. It is also a response which is seen as part of a post-traumatic reaction.

Isolation and Alienation

A sense of isolation and loneliness is often experienced by a survivor. She often prefers to lead an isolated life even within the context of her family. In this way, the secret of the sexual abuse can remain unbroken. She frequently fears that others will find out or guess about her childhood experiences, and will blame her, so it becomes safer to remain withdrawn from people. From childhood, she is likely to have felt alienated and different from her peer group because she has had experiences that cannot be discussed openly. The sense of being different results from the many negative associations and feelings (feeling bad, dirty, ashamed and guilty) that she has with the abuse. These feelings may have come directly from the abuser who may have blamed her or at least communicated a sense of shame. They may have come from other adults whom she tried to tell, or from the child's own knowledge about the fact that the sexual activity was wrong (Finkelhor and Browne, 1986). This sense of being different from others usually inhibits the formation of close relationships, and without the reassurance that she is not to blame for the abuse, will continue into adulthood. Many survivors do, however, see their isolation as a way of keeping themselves safe.

Negative Reactions to Medical Procedures

Hospital admissions   Routine admission to hospital can produce difficulties. For a survivor, being in hospital can present a lack of control, a lack of privacy, having unexplained procedures done to her, often by male doctors, and a feeling of being trapped. Hospital admission can therefore result in distress, panic or extreme hostility within the woman. Admissions to psychiatric hospitals produce a number of different reactions including:

— a sense of safety;
— fears of being trapped;
— fears of being in hospital forever;
— fears that she is going 'mad';
— extreme anger and hostility.

Gynaecological procedures Internal vaginal examinations, cervical smear tests, and pregnancy and fertility investigations often produce acute panic, flashbacks and even regression for a survivor. Procedures under general anaesthetic are not usually so difficult, although a woman may express fears that a male doctor might abuse her whilst she is under the anaesthetic.

Dental procedures Visits to the dentist revive memories of being trapped in a potentially painful or frightening situation. If her dentist is male, a woman may avoid attending the dentist until it is absolutely necessary, and then may only manage to undergo treatment with the help of tranquillizers.

Physical Complaints

A number of physical problems are often noted in survivors. Most commonly headaches, stomach problems, chronic backache, psychosomatic pains and illness, cystitis, asthma and eczema are found (Faria and Belohlavek, 1984).

It has also been documented that epileptiform seizures, sometimes called pseudo-epilepsy or hysterical epilepsy, are to be found in survivors (Gross, 1980). Goodwin *et al.* (1979) suggest that at least ten per cent of 'hysterical seizures' are associated with childhood sexual abuse. For survivors who have a confirmed diagnosis of epilepsy, the frequency of epileptic fits can greatly increase during flashbacks and recall of memories of sexual abuse.

Example: Julie had been diagnosed as epileptic as an adolescent. Her epilepsy was well controlled with minimal anti-convulsant medication. Suddenly, during her twenties when she got married, the frequency of fits increased dramatically. Increased medication made little difference, and it was only when she disclosed that her marriage had revived memories of being sexually abused by her uncle during childhood, that her epilepsy reverted to its previously well-controlled level.

For women who have experienced very severe sexual abuse, gynaecological problems, pelvic infections and the effects of damage to genital and rectal organs may continue to cause problems well into adulthood.

Sleep Disturbance

Disrupted sleep patterns are very common in survivors, especially at times of extreme distress or when they are reliving the memories of their abusive past. Recurring nightmares and bad dreams often occur and may lead to a fear of going to bed.

Eating Disorders

There is growing evidence that between one-third and two-thirds of women with eating disorders have experienced childhood sexual abuse (Oppenheimer *et al.*, 1985).

Compulsive eating and obesity   Compulsive over-eating and its associated weight gain and loss of self-esteem is often part of a survivor's difficulties with control. Meiselman (1978) noted that a third of her sample of abused women were significantly overweight.

Bulimia   This involves secret bingeing and self-induced vomiting and is accompanied by extreme feelings of guilt and shame. Oppenheimer *et al.* (1985) found that as many as two-thirds of women with bulimia had been sexually abused before the age of fifteen.

Anorexia nervosa   Anorexia is characterized by self-starvation, purging through laxatives, self-induced vomiting, distorted body-image, cessation of menstruation and very significant weight loss. Sloan and Leichner (1986) presented evidence linking anorexia with a history of childhood sexual abuse.

Multiple Personality Disorder

When a very young child is subjected to prolonged and severe abuse, she may dissociate during the abuse so that she has no knowledge or awareness of it having occurred. This can lead to the development of a separate part or personality of the child, with separate memories, experiences and identity. This process may continue until the child has several alternative personalities, who may or may not be aware of each other.

Multiple personality disorder is not usually identified until adulthood by which time the survivor may have developed other personalities with particular roles and functions which have helped her to survive into adulthood. There is little published work in the United Kingdom about multiple personality disorder largely because it is not included in the British psychiatric diagnosis system, but survivors with multiple personalities are presenting themselves to helpers, often in the context of coming to terms with their experiences of sexual abuse.

From the American work with multiple personality survivors, it is widely recognized that the abuse these survivors experienced has a number of features:

— it began before the survivor was four or five years old;
— it was very severe sexual abuse;
— the sexual abuse was accompanied by high levels of physical and emotional abuse;
— it was perpetrated by a number of adults.

Detailed discussion of multiple personality disorder is beyond the scope of this book, but helpers are directed to books by Gil (1983, 1988), Ross (1989) and by the Troops for Truddi Chase (1987). With an understanding of the origins of the development of the multiple personalities, which can be seen as a creative response to intolerable and overwhelming abuse, these survivors can be helped considerably.

Dissociative Problems

Many children who have been sexually abused learn to deal with the abuse by denying its reality, by dissociating themselves from it or by repressing it partially or completely. These methods of dissociation and their implications for disclosure will be discussed in more detail in Chapter 7. However, it is clear that these dissociative processes are rarely totally successful and evidence that a woman has been sexually abused as a child often breaks through in quite frightening ways.

Perceptual disturbances   A number of perceptual disturbances are experienced by most survivors (Ellenson, 1985, 1986). They can be visual, auditory, olfactory and related to taste and touch, or more usually some combination of these.

Visual disturbances
These include:

— Shadowy figures: these are nearly always described as dark, featureless shapes, usually male, and evil or dangerous. Seeing such figures at night-time at the foot of the bed is very common. During the day-time, these figures are often seen to move quickly and furtively;

— Partial figures: the face, eyes or hands of the abuser, or of an unknown male, are often seen, especially during sexual activity;

— Elaborated images: sometimes the perceptions of male figures are more elaborate in detail. Clear pictures of the abuser are often seen and may be superimposed on a partner in sexual situations;

— Movement in peripheral vision: seeing a rapidly moving object or person out of the corner of the eye is common;

— Images of objects used during the abuse: where the woman's abuser has used objects (for example, knife, rope, bottle), or insects, such as spiders, to frighten or abuse her, images of these often occur and add to her fear and terror.

Auditory disturbances
These include:

— Intruder sounds: these occur mostly at night and include footsteps, heavy breathing, bumps, scrapes, doorknobs turning, doors and windows being opened and closed or tampered with, and creaking floorboards;

— Vocal sounds: these usually take the form of a child crying, screaming or calling out, hearing the child's name called out by an adult known to the survivor. Sometimes, a survivor will hear words spoken by the abuser or by herself as a child during the abuse;

— Booming sounds: these are less common but usually sound like a heavy door banging shut or an explosion;

— Persecutory/hostile/threatening voices: these are heard particularly by women who have been subjected to prolonged violent or sadistic abuse. The voices often condemn her and may encourage her to do something violent to herself or others. Sometimes, these voices are interpreted by the woman as the voice of the devil;

— Sounds associated with the abuse: women sometimes hear sounds that were present before and during the abuse (for example, music, creaking floorboards, radio sounds, running water).

Tactile sensation

A sensation of being touched by a human hand or face is common among survivors especially when they are in bed. Ellenson (1986) suggested that this occurs less frequently than visual and auditory disturbances. For women who have experienced physical abuse along with the sexual abuse, tactile sensations often relate to the physical abuse.

Sensations of pain

During recall of abusive incidents or during flashbacks, it is quite normal for a survivor to experience sensations of physical pain. These sensations frequently amount to re-experiencing the abuse. Internal and external genital pain, pain in the chest and ribs (due to the experience of a heavy body weight on top of her) or in other parts of the body are common.

Perception of smells

Smells that have particular associations with the abuse or the abuser are often experienced by survivors. Common examples are bodily and sexual smells, and the smell of cigarettes and alcohol.

Perception of taste

This often occurs in conjunction with the perception of smells and usually involved being able to taste body and sexual secretions.

Recurring illusions   These are common and occur with visual or auditory sensations. They can include:

— a sensation that there is a threatening evil male entity in the room, sometimes described as a monster or demon;
— a sense of a poorly defined evil presence.

Flashbacks   Memories of childhood incidents return in the form of flashbacks which occur frequently and are beyond the control of the woman herself. A flashback has several distinguishing features:

— It occurs when she is suddenly and unpredictably taken back to an abusive incident in her childhood;
— The flashback produces a vivid recollection or picture of this incident and include the intense emotional reactions and physical pain experienced at the time, and visual, auditory and tactile memories of the abuse itself. At times, the survivor may experience such intense flashbacks that she feels as if she is re-experiencing the abuse. Bleeding from the genital area can be triggered by a flashback;

— It can be triggered by an experience in the present that instantly reminds her of the sexual abuse. Common examples of such triggers are:

- the tone of someone's voice;
- sexual situations including sexual positions, arousal, being touched in certain parts of the body;
- touching certain fabrics, such as blankets or nylon shirts;
- hearing certain sounds, such as music or heavy breathing;
- hearing certain words spoken;
- seeing a man who resembles the abuser in some way (for example, clothes, facial appearance, build);
- certain smells e.g., alcohol, cigarette, sexual or bodily smells.

Example: Mandy experienced flashbacks every time she heard military bands playing march tunes. Her father was a member of an army band and regularly sexually abused her on the way to ceremonial occasions at which he was playing.

— It can be triggered by an experience in the present that is apparently unrelated to the abuse itself. These triggers may involve general reminders of her childhood, discussions with friends about sex, families, discipline methods or children, and conflict with family members.

Flashbacks are very alarming experiences and often lead to fears of ensuing 'madness', increased self-mutilation and suicidal attempts, alcohol and drug misuse. For some women who have experienced very violent abuse over a number of years, the flashbacks often occur in large numbers, and as one is dealt with, it is replaced by others. Flashbacks are also particularly common during therapeutic work. When a survivor is experiencing a flashback, it is usual to see changes in body position, breathing rhythm and ability to maintain eye-contact. A woman will often avert her gaze or appear to be gazing into the middle-distance. Her body movements may clearly indicate that she is re-experiencing the abuse, with avoidance actions and obvious discomfort in the genital area being common.

Nightmares and bad dreams The sleep patterns of a survivor are often disturbed by nightmares. They can be very realistic and appear to be exact replications of various incidents of abuse. The content of nightmares can therefore be used as a basis for disclosure. Nightmares are accompanied by extreme emotional reactions of distress, terror or pain. The consequences for the woman range from a fear of going to sleep to suicidal attempts, and may involve increased self-mutilation, running away, and drug and alcohol misuse. The bad dreams of a survivor are often characterized by fear, being chased or trapped, or they include a child being hurt in some way.

Out-of-body experiences   A survivor may describe feelings of being 'out of her body' and floating (Briere and Runtz, 1986). She may feel that situations and experiences are unreal, and that she is watching herself go through life as though she were another person. She can often trace this dissociative process back to the abusive situation, where she learned to survive by believing that the abuse was not really happening to her but to someone else. It enabled her, therefore, to escape from any unpleasant or painful feelings associated with the abuse.

Lack of sensation of pain   Many survivors report having dissociated themselves from the pain of the abuse with the result that they have reduced perception of pain. This may result in the lack of sensation of painful stimuli in certain areas of the body. This sensation may gradually return as disclosure of the painful memories progresses.

Problems with Trust

Sexual abuse of a child by a trusted adult is not only a physical violation of the child, but also represents a betrayal of the trust that the child has for the adult. The child rapidly learns, therefore, that it is not safe to trust others. This is compounded by the secrecy, blame and shame attached to the abuse which results in her being unable to tell anyone, and these problems with trust continue into adulthood and create difficulties in establishing and maintaining relationships. Many survivors have particular problems in trusting people who love them or to whom they feel close. This can be a strong echo of the abuse, and trust may be less of a problem in other situations. Survivors often see trust as an all-or-nothing matter, they believe they should trust totally or not at all. In addition, they do not pick up normal cues about the levels of trustworthiness in others.

Victim Behaviour

Survivors often behave as victims, believing they have no rights or choices. They therefore feel helpless, submissive and compliant in relation to others. They often have no recognition of their own emotional needs or personal space, and allow others to violate both on a regular basis.

Revictimization/further assault   Survivors are particularly vulnerable to being sexually assaulted or raped as adults (Fromuth, 1986; Russell, 1986). Russell also indicated that survivors are more likely than non-abused women to have physically violent husbands and to be sexually assaulted within marriage. It suggests, therefore, that the experience of childhood sexual abuse may prevent a woman from learning how to protect or assert herself as an adult.

General Fear of Men

Some survivors have a general fear of men which results in avoidance of any situations where they might have to speak to or pass too near a man (for example, shops, medical facilities, walking down a busy street). It can be difficult for them to call in tradespeople to do essential repairs and even the usual regular calls of the milkman of window-cleaner for payment of bills can cause alarm and fear.

Interpersonal Difficulties

The problems faced by a survivor in her relationships with others are often coloured by mistrust and insecurity. Forming and sustaining relationships can be difficult. Baker and Duncan (1985) suggest that this results not only from the experience of being sexually abused as a child, but also from the abuser's misuse of his power and responsibility, from the betrayal of her trust, and from the distortion and disruption of family relationships. Normal emotional development of a child in this situation is likely to be disrupted, especially if the sexual abuse remains hidden, ignored or condoned by other significant adults. Even more problems result if both parents are involved in abusing the child, thus giving her no respite from the abuse. Further difficulties arise because abused children are often prevented from having normal childhood friendships, leading to additional isolation.

Many relationship problems take the form of repeating patterns the survivor learnt as a child in order to cope with her childhood experiences. These patterns may be subtle and involve relating to a partner, friends, work colleagues and children in ways that she learned as a child. For example, she may have learned that she could get some of her needs for closeness met through the abuse, and as a result, sex gets confused with closeness leading to problems and confusion in her adult relationships. Common patterns of relating learned as a child might involve:

— excessive care-taking where the abused child was forced or attempted to look after the adults and other children in her family in order to pacify or please the abuser and others;

— trying to be invisible so that no-one would notice her and her distress, or that the abuser might not notice her and leave her alone;

— being rebellious, argumentative and difficult;

— being the scapegoat of the family, taking the blame or being blamed for anything that goes wrong;

— behaving in a sexual way with adults other than the abuser in order to get her needs for affection, closeness and love met;

— behaving as the family/class 'clown' so that others are diverted from the real reasons for her behaviour. This can lead to superficial patterns of relating to others;

— behaving as the always 'good' child, perhaps to please the abuser and others, or in the hope that by being very well-behaved, the abuse will stop;

— withdrawing from others, fearing rejection, dislike or mistrust.

It is important to acknowledge that, within any relationship, both partners may be survivors of sexual abuse, and that this is likely to cause a range of problems that relate to the different long-term effects, patterns of relating and recovery process experienced by each. However, to have a partner who is a survivor can be a source of support and help, as it is possible to develop a deeper understanding with someone who knows about the experience of being abused in the past.

Relationships with men   Survivors report difficulties in relating to men. Courtois (1979) found that over three-quarters of her sample of survivors had such problems and their relationships were characterized by disappointment, fear, hostility, mistrust and the likelihood of betrayal. Herman (1981) also reported that many survivors tend to over-value and idealize men. These problems have several consequences:

— *Avoidance of relationships with men* Complete life-time avoidance is relatively rare, although many survivors go through long periods of avoidance of relationships with men;

— *Avoidance of long-term intimate relationships with men* Some abused women avoid close relationships with men and end up being involved in brief unsatisfactory relationships instead;

— *Difficulties in long-term intimate relationships with men* Many survivors do manage a significant close relationship with a man, but this can be fraught with problems because of its parallels with the abusive childhood relationship;

— *Oversexualized relationships* Many survivors have difficulties in distinguishing between affection and sex. Sex may therefore be used to gain attention and affection (Herman, 1981), or conversely a man's affection is seen to be genuine and worthwhile only if the relationship is sexual (Jehu and Gazan, 1983). Brief unsatisfactory sexual relationships with men are thus more likely to occur, and the survivor may be seen by others as promiscuous;

— *Prostitution* It is now well-established that many prostitutes were sexually abused as children (James and Meyerding, 1977; Sheldon, 1987). As children, they may have been given rewards for the sexual activity or for maintaining the silence which, when combined with their poor self-esteem and self-image, made them more vulnerable to prostitution. Female adolescents who run away from home to get away from sexual abuse are more likely to be exploited and abused and may get involved in prostitution (McCormack, *et al.*, 1986). It is, however, relatively unusual for adult women to seek help during a period of prostitution;

— *Abusive relationships* Survivors often become involved with men who mistreat them (Meiselman, 1978; Tsai and Wagner, 1978). This probably results from the woman's poor self-esteem, leading her to believe that she deserves to be abused or mistreated. She is likely to have never learned to assert or protect herself in relationships;

— *Marriage* Many survivors marry early to get away from home and the abuse. These early marriages often fail because the legacy of the sexual abuse intrudes and causes problems with trust, sexuality and intimacy. The divorce and separation rate is known to be higher in women who were abused as children (Russell, 1986);

— *Jealousy* Some survivors feel so insecure in a relationship with a man, that jealousy of him, his thoughts and actions can lead to considerable problems. This can erupt in accusations that any time her partner looks at another woman on television, films, at work or in the street, he is obviously wanting to have sex with that woman. It reflects the survivor's low self-esteem, confusion about sexuality and deep insecurities about relationships with men.

Relationships with women Difficulties in relationships are not confined to those with men. A survivor often has problems with trusting other women, partly as a reflection of her feelings about her mother. Her relationship with her mother may be affected by feeling betrayed, let down, rejected or ignored, and these feelings can intrude into relationships with other women. This can prevent the development of normal supportive relationships with women. Severe mistrust of women results if the survivor has actually been abused by her mother or other female relatives.

Sexual relationships with women There is no evidence that a lesbian sexual orientation is caused by the experience of sexual abuse. Although research has indicated that about 38 per cent of lesbian women have experienced child sexual abuse (Loulan, 1987), these figures are matched in the total female population. When a lesbian woman is also a survivor, she is likely to have to confront two major issues that are surrounded by secrecy. Some lesbian women do believe that their sexual orientation is a result of their experience of being sexually abused. Others believe that they are safe from the intrusive effects of sexual abuse, although this is not always the case, as flashbacks and nightmares can occur in any situation. Finally, it may be more likely for two women in a lesbian relationship to both be survivors. This may increase the problems that they experience in their relationship.

Sexual Problems

These are almost universal among survivors and take a number of forms. It is very often the occurrence of sexual problems which encourages a woman to seek help and to disclose the childhood sexual abuse.

One of the major difficulties for a survivor in a sexual relationship is that sexual activity in itself can produce flashbacks to the childhood sexual abuse. It can take the form of a brief image (for example, seeing the face of the abuser) or a vivid memory which is very disturbing to her. They may occur when her current sexual partner touches her in ways that remind her of the abuse, makes demands or forces her into unwanted sexual activity, and when there are certain bodily and sexual smells. When these flashbacks occur, the woman is likely to experience feelings of intense anxiety, panic and distress, and immediately 'freeze' physically. This will obviously disrupt any on-going sexual activity, and is likely to restrict the range of and motivation for sexual experiences.

Once flashbacks have occurred in this way the woman is likely to anticipate further problems so that even very limited sexual contact begins to produce anxiety. As a result, sexual activity may be avoided completely, with difficulties for the woman's partner and associated guilt for the woman herself. Beyond these very general problems, survivors often have a number of specific sexual difficulties (Gelinas, 1983; Sheldon, 1987):

Impaired sexual arousal   For some women, sexual arousal appears to be disrupted (Becker *et al.*, 1982). This may result from the intense anxiety produced by flashbacks as described above, as it is well known that high levels of anxiety can impair arousal level. Resulting restrictions on sexual activity may then limit sexual stimulation. For some women, sexual arousal is completely lacking (Jehu *et al.*, 1985), either because she dissociates herself totally from potential sexual sensations or because she does not allow herself to be aware of any stimulation she is receiving from her partner.

Difficulties with orgasm   It is well documented that survivors often have orgasmic difficulties (Meiselman, 1978; Becker *et al.*, 1982). Orgasm may be possible in certain circumstances, such as with a new partner, with a patient and undemanding partner or during certain types of sexual activity (McGuire and Wagner, 1978). Where orgasm does occur, it is often not associated with pleasure. If it is pleasurable, this can be extremely threatening and can lead to intense feelings of guilt, especially for women who have experienced sexual arousal during the sexual abuse. If a woman experienced sexual arousal in association with violence, she may only become aroused as an adult if her partner is violent with her. This can be deeply upsetting and confusing for her.

Lack of sexual satisfaction and motivation   Lack of interest in and motivation for sex is quite common, and may be partly a result of depression, problems with the sexual partner or generalized negative feelings about physical contact. Lack of sexual satisfaction has also been found in survivors (Tsai and Wagner, 1979).

Guilt during sexual contact   For the survivor who is able to participate in a sexual relationship, she is frequently overwhelmed with feelings of guilt either for enjoying the sexual activity, becoming aroused or for initiating any part of the sexual contact. This usually relates to feelings experienced during the sexual abuse.

Vaginismus   This is a condition that occurs quite frequently in survivors. It involves an involuntary reflex response of the outer vaginal muscles and of the perineum to any threat of vaginal penetration.

Pain during intercourse Survivors often report pelvic pain especially during intercourse (Gross *et al.*, 1980). This may be due to internal injuries resulting from the sexual abuse, to chronic vaginal infections, or to anxiety leading to extreme muscle tension and pain.

Problems with Touch

Fundamental to all close relationships is the issue of touch. Many survivors find it extremely difficult to tolerate being touched physically. This results in:

- fear and avoidance of crowded and social situations in case someone brushes against her;
- inability to shake hands when being introduced to someone;
- any physical contact on greeting or leaving friends or family members;
- refusal to allow anyone to physically comfort her when she is distressed;
- extreme problems in intimate or sexual relationships;
- fears that she will contaminate/infect someone through her touch;
- difficulties in touching her children;
- problems with medical and dental examinations;
- dislike of hairdressing.

This problem with touch can affect many aspects of a survivor's life, and lead to increased anxiety.

Parenting Problems

For survivors with children, there are a number of common difficulties:

Difficulties in meeting her child's emotional needs Some survivors have problems with their parenting skills partly because they did not experience adequate parenting when they were children. They may be unaware of a child's emotional needs, or may over-compensate for their own difficult childhood by being unable to set appropriate boundaries and limits for the child.

Overprotection of children Fears for the safety of a child, especially if the child is left in someone else's care, are usually very pronounced. This may extend to fears that the child's father will abuse the child. If the woman's abuser is still alive and in contact with her family, she will be justifiably vigilant, and fearful when her children are in his presence. These fears can lead to general over-protection of the children and can sometimes prevent the children from becoming independent. She may also underestimate the risk of abuse to her children, believing that there was something about herself as a child that singled her out for abuse.

Fears that she will abuse her child   A survivor often fears that she will abuse her child because she believes that sexual abuse runs in families or that an abused child becomes an abuser as an adult. These beliefs are confirmed for her if she is in any way angry or frustrated with her children. She is unable to distinguish normal methods of discipline from the abuse she experienced, with the result that her children may not get appropriate disciplining.

Difficulties in showing physical affection towards children   Survivors are often frightened to comfort or show physical affection towards their children for fear they will be seen as an abuser. This shows the confusion they have about the boundaries between physical affection and sexual closeness. Therefore many survivors are very frightened to touch their children in any way. This means that physical care of their children becomes problematic, and normal parenting tasks such as bathing, dressing, nappy-changing, toilet-training are difficult.

Difficulty in protecting her child   If a survivor has not remembered her experience of being sexually abused, or has not recognized its effects, she may be unaware of signs that her children are in danger or may not be able to react appropriately to them. For example, if one of her children is being abused, she may be paralyzed by fear, deny that her child could be abused or ignore any warning signs. She may be unable to deal appropriately with other potentially difficult situations such as allowing a child to play at a friend's house without adequate supervision, asking a young child to run errands for her, or allowing children to cross roads before they are old enough to do so safely.

Actual abuse of her child   For some survivors, the obvious lack of adequate parenting in their own childhood, and the lack of an appropriate model of parenting, leaves them poorly equipped to deal with the demands of caring for their own children. A lack of warmth and an inability to be protective leaves her children vulnerable. Without help this can sometimes result in abuse and neglect, thus perpetuating a cycle of abuse and deprivation. As yet, we do not know the percentage of female survivors who do go on to abuse or neglect their own children, although our impression is that it is extremely small.

Abuse of Self

This is very common in survivors (de Young, 1982), particularly when they are depressed, angry or remembering the details of the sexual abuse. It includes:

Self mutilation   This usually takes the form of making small cuts with a sharp object on the arms, legs and other parts of the body. These are often superficial wounds, and should be distinguished from suicidal attempts. A woman's explanation for this type of self-injury is usually one of the following:

— the pain of these cuts diverts me from the pain of the memories;
— I know I should feel something about these memories but I don't so I cut myself to prove to myself that I can still feel pain;
— I feel so bad about myself that it doesn't matter what I do to myself;
— I don't even notice what I am doing to myself;
— I want to hurt myself because I don't deserve any better.

Other self-injury   Some survivors go through periods of head-banging and hitting themselves. This occurs at times of particular crisis or desperation, and serves the same kind of function as the self-mutilation.

Suicidal attempts   Repeated suicidal attempts (often overdoses or wrist-cutting) are common (Briere and Runtz, 1986). They occur when the pain of the past is too much, when control over her current life experiences disappears or during periods of severe depression (Gelinas, 1983). Paradoxically, survivors sometimes appear suicidal because they keep the means of terminating their lives always to hand in the form of pills, glass, etc. Their explanation is that they need to have the safety of an 'escape route' if they feel that things are getting 'too bad'.

Substance Abuse

Alcohol abuse   The use of alcohol as a way of blocking out the memories and their associated pain has been confirmed in a number of studies summarized by Finkelhor and Browne (1986).

Drug misuse   Misuse of drugs such as amphetamines, cocaine, LSD and heroin is less common than alcohol misuse in adult survivors, but sometimes begins in late adolescence and continues into adulthood (Peters, 1984).

Tranquillizer dependency   Tranquillizers (e.g., Valium, Librium, Diazepam, Ativan) may have initially been prescribed to help a woman with her anxiety symptoms or sleep difficulties, but they also help to blank out memories of childhood experiences.

Compulsive and Obsessional Problems

Obsessional concerns with cleanliness and fears of harming others, especially children, are not uncommon in survivors. This obsessional behaviour usually develops in an attempt to gain control over her anxieties and fears, or to preoccupy her sufficiently to allow her to block out the past.

Example: Alison described difficulties in dealing with household tasks. She had to do things in a set order, and could not rest until her house was cleaned in this rigid way every day. If she was interrupted, she had to start again at the beginning. She had developed this rigid routine as a way of distracting herself from her memories, fears and guilt about being sexually abused by her father.

Compulsive behaviour such as shoplifting (Winestine, 1985), and compulsive lying and stealing have been noted in women who were abused as children. The function of lying is often to prevent others from getting close or learning the true nature of her childhood experiences.

Under-achievement in Education and Occupation

Educational under-achievement is widespread among survivors, yet their poetry and writing skills indicate that many have the potential to achieve at a much higher level than they managed during their formal education. The disruption of education caused by sexual abuse during childhood and enforced silence about the abuse is known to have a significant effect on a child's ability to concentrate on and cope with formal education (Nakashima and Zakus, 1977).

Under-achievement in employment is also widespread. It partially reflects the educational difficulties, but Russell (1986) also found that unemployment was much more likely in a sample of survivors, regardless of educational levels.

Difficulties in Sustaining Positive Experiences

Survivors often describe problems in allowing themselves to enjoy anything or in sustaining positive experiences. If they do enjoy any aspect of their lives, guilt manifests itself and manages to spoil the experience.

These difficulties usually originate in childhood where they learned to believe:

— I don't deserve anything nice happening to me;
— if I enjoy something, I am bound to be punished;
— I am not worthy of anyone wanting to do good things for me;
— if an experience is nice, there is bound to be something nasty about to happen;
— no-one does good things to or for me without expecting something in return.

These negative appraisals of herself prevent the survivor from deriving pleasure, enjoyment or any anticipation of positive experiences, and they contribute to her low self-esteem and episodes of depression.

Other Effects

So far we have considered the major consequences of child sexual abuse and its associated family disruption. However, there are many smaller consequences that can disrupt or distort survivor's life. These are usually habits learned during childhood. The following examples were given by survivors:

— wearing pyjamas (increases feelings of safety);
— shutting all internal doors of the house before answering the doorbell (so that no-one can see what might be happening in the house);
— sleeping with the light on;
— sleeping with the bedroom door open/closed;
— sleeping along the very edge of the bed;
— always checking and double-checking that any children in the house are safe when they are in bed;

— not able to have a bath/shower with someone in the house;
— making sure that bedclothes/sheets are tucked in very tight;
— never wearing clothes of a particular colour/fabric/style;
— playing loud music to block out memories.

The long-term effects of being sexually abused as outlined here can be devastating. It is important to recognize that these effects do not occur in isolation from each other, and they often weave together in more subtle ways. For example, the cluster of effects relating to feelings of guilt are considerable, and affect many aspects of a survivor's life. In addition, some of these common long-term effects have their own consequences, for example, substance abuse which may result in problems of withdrawal and other difficulties. Many of the effects do, however, recede once the memories of the abuse and the origins of these problems are understood. Sometimes dealing with long-term effects of sexual abuse occurs dramatically without specific intervention beyond the disclosure work.

Example: Gemma had a significant problem with obsessionally checking her house. She felt that she could hear a tap running all the time. She knew she had been abused, but could not recall the details. During disclosure work, she recalled that her father would come upstairs, run a bath for her, and whilst it was filling, would abuse her. She would then be placed in the bath. Once she recalled this, her obsessional behaviour concerning the checking of the taps disappeared. She understood the origins of her behaviour, and this was enough to enable her to stop the checking.

It may seem a daunting task to begin to help the survivor with the long-term effects that she is experiencing. As we have seen, through understanding their causes, some of these effects do disappear. It is also important to recognize that survivors have strengths and resources that have enabled them to cope with the sexual abuse, and these can be used in the helping process.

Chapter 4

Strengths of Survivors

For a child or an adult, surviving childhood sexual abuse involves developing all sorts of personal resources and enhancing the inherent strengths which a survivor already has. Much work with survivors involves difficult and painful memories and feelings, however, and it is often difficult to confirm strengths. This chapter honours those strengths by examining:

— how she developed and used them as a child;
— how she has sustained them as an adult;
— how the strengths of survivors are reflected in their writing;
— how their strength has been used to teach helpers the best way to support them;
— how their strength has ensured that the issue of childhood sexual abuse has been put onto the public agenda.

There is a continuum of coping behaviours used by survivors. At one end of the continuum are strategies like alcohol and drug abuse, suicide attempts and other self-injury; at the other there are survivors who channel all their energies into being high achievers — in education or employment. Some survivors see their coping mechanisms as something to be ashamed of and they may not wish to admit to some of the things they did to survive. Coping is, however, a means of survival and an indication of resourcefulness and strength.

Some coping mechanisms develop into clear strengths, such as becoming self-sufficient, being steady in a crisis, whilst others develop into self-destructive patterns of behaviour like stealing or compulsive overeating. There are also behaviours which have both healthy and destructive aspects — high achievement in academic matters may secure a college place and a good job, but may lead the survivor to become even more isolated from other people as she channels all her energies into the pursuit of success.

The task for the helper is to identify and examine, with the survivor, her survival mechanisms and to determine which of these skills, if any, may still be useful to her. This will involve looking at the origins of them and assessing their worth to the woman's adult life and her potential for change. When this work is carried out in partnership with her helper it can be very empowering for the survivor.

Childhood Survival Strengths

Many of the ways which women use to survive the experience of childhood sexual abuse have their roots in their childhood survival strategies. These include:

— *minimizing*   Pretending that what is happening is not really that bad, painful or frightening;
— *rationalizing*   Inventing reasons for the abuser behaving in the way that he did;
— *denying*   Pretending that what happened did not happen;
— *forgetting*   Repressing memories of the abuse even as it is happening;
— *dissociating*   Shutting off from aspects of the abuse such as the pain, the associated emotions or particular behaviour of the abuser, so that she can tolerate the situation. It may feel as though she is watching the abuse from a distance, or that the abuse is happening to someone else;
— *sexualizing the experience*   Focusing on the sexual activity itself as a means of not having to bear what was happening to her;
— *hiding*   Being a 'good'/hardworking girl so that no-one knows.

All of these coping mechanisms can be seen as strengths. They did not allow the child to be overwhelmed by the abusive experiences, they enabled her to find ways of keeping herself separate from the abuse, and they laid the foundations for adult survival strategies. A survivor can also be enabled to see herself as the 'healthy' family member of her family of origin, since she showed normal reactions to an abnormal and traumatic situation.

Adult Survival Strengths

There are also a number of coping mechanisms which are carried into adulthood in a positive way. These include:

- *Surviving*   The adult has the courage to heal and to get on with life.
- *Writing*   This may have been used as a way of expressing pain and grief in childhood and adulthood. It can be rediscovered as a way of gaining a perspective on her life, disclosing aspects of the abuse when she cannot convey this verbally, and expressing emotions which are too difficult to express verbally.
- *Work/career achievement*   Survivors can feel a great need to achieve in their work environment, to make up for internal feelings of low self-esteem. Success in this area is highly valued in our society, so a survivor can feel accepted and strongly motivated to succeed.
- *Parenting*   Because of her knowledge about the effects of child sexual abuse on a child, most survivors are clear about the way they want to relate to and raise their own children. Spending time looking at the positive aspects of this area of their lives can be very affirming for a survivor.
- *Developing a sense of humour*   Often survivors have learned to use humour, cynicism or wit to get them through difficult times. Humour also serves a function as a protector and distancer for someone who is hurt. In adulthood it can be a social asset and can enable a survivor to be accepted by other people.
- *Being alert*   Children in abusive situations become very aware of their surroundings. Although this hyper-vigilance can be intrusive to an adult, it can also be an asset. It can be put to good use in professional contexts, for example in the helping professions, police, medical contexts (Bass and Davis, 1988).

Survivors' Writing

Recent years have witnessed an important development in the writing on sexual abuse. The voices of survivors themselves in prose, poetry, song, letters and novels have provided courageous testimony and a conceptual framework for a greater understanding of the reality of childhood sexual abuse (see Appendices 1 and 2). The existence of survivors' writing, published and unpublished, has had a number of consequences:

— it has broken the silence surrounding sexual abuse in a very direct and accessible way;
— it has provided a vehicle to encourage other survivors to disclose details of their experiences. In so doing it has acknowledged issues which are common to all survivors, and it has begun to address the strengths which they have. This has led to a greater professional and societal understanding of sexual abuse and its long term effects;
— it has forced helpers to re-evaluate the assumptions on which their work is based and the therapeutic methods which they use. This has, in turn, empowered survivors and given them validity as experts in their own lives;
— it has been a self-help process for survivors as they struggle to come to terms with their past and look towards a more optimistic future.

Survivors' writing includes the following:

— personal accounts of sexual abuse by a trusted adult. There are a number of short and longer autobiographical accounts. Some focus on the way in which the child coped with the abuse when it was happening (Brady, 1979; Allen, 1980); others detail the impact of sexual abuse on adult life (Armstrong, 1978; McNaron and Morgan, 1982; Bass and Thornton, 1983). All of these accounts are invaluable for survivors to identify a common past with others. Other personal accounts go further. They detail the effect of sexual abuse on the growing child and adolescent (Angelou, 1984, Danica, 1988). A third group provides a graphic insight into the ways in which childhood memories have been suppressed, only to emerge in later life (Matthews, 1986; Fraser, 1987).
— accounts which describe the process of recovery from sexual abuse, some with professional help and others with the support of volunteers and other survivors (Evert and Bijkert, 1987; Spring, 1987). Some of these accounts have been co-authored by survivors and their helpers or therapists (Sisk and Hoffman, 1987; Utain and Oliver, 1989). These give a valuable insight into the process of a shared work which is empowering, in the sense that responsibility for the therapeutic work and the writing is shared between the survivor and her helper.

— novels dealing with the subject of child sexual abuse (Hart, 1979; Morris, 1982; Murphy, 1987; Gaitskill, 1991).
— letters and poetry which give an account of the abuse and its effects (Walker, 1982). We have included poems written by survivors in Appendix 1. They are very helpful in reaching an audience which might not otherwise have addressed the issue of childhood sexual abuse.
— self-help handbooks and workbooks aimed at individual survivors and groups (Bass and Davis, 1988; Davis, 1990; Parks, 1990; Kunzman, 1990; Parrish, 1990). A key feature of these books is the way they work towards empowering survivors by stressing their strengths and the possibility of recovery. They include a rich blend of personal accounts, identification of the long-term effects of sexual abuse, themes in the recovery process and exercises to help this recovery process. At their best they are written in a clear, straightforward style which directly addresses the survivor and her helper. In so doing they also demystify the helping process itself. Most of these handbooks have been written for a general audience of survivors. There are, however, books which have been written for particular groups, or on specific topics. Younger survivors (Bain and Saunders, 1990), survivors who are Christian (Wilson, 1986; Hancock and Mains, 1987; Woititz, 1989), partners of survivors (Davis, 1991; Graber, 1991) and mothers of children who have been abused (Byerly, 1985) are all given a voice for their particular needs. Specific topics such as sexuality (Maltz and Holman, 1987; Maltz, 1991) are also addressed.

Survivor Resources for Teaching Helpers

The types of books referred to above have had a considerable impact on the way in which therapeutic work is undertaken with survivors. The underlying theme for this collective voice of survivors is that they will be silent no longer and they have a vital role to play in extending knowledge for helpers. Survivors can also teach helpers in a number of other ways:

— they can take responsibility for what happens in the helping process itself, guiding the helper and entering into a partnership;
— they can alert them to effects of abuse which they have not previously considered;
— they can, as the result of their own creativity, encourage helpers to be more innovative and creative in the methods they use.

Survival Strengths and the Public Agenda

Sometimes survivors use their collective strengths to contribute to the public debate on sexual abuse of children. Some of the ways in which this can happen include:

— contributing to television and radio programmes, newspaper and magazine articles;

— organizing or participating in conferences on issues relating to sexual abuse;

— attending conferences where a survivor's voice needs to be heard;

— contributing to research projects by telling of their experiences;

— contributing to prevention strategies by saying what sorts of resources they would have found helpful as children;

— lobbying members of parliament and other public figures on specific issues;

— becoming involved in public education programmes about sexual abuse in schools, colleges and the community;

— organizing one-off 'celebration' events where survivors can have a platform for their writing, artwork and other creative talents;

— involving themselves in helping other survivors.

Acknowledging and building on the strengths of survivors is the cornerstone of good practice. Although they may feel and show that the toll of the abuse has weighed heavily on their lives, they have the capacity to recover and to have good relationships as adults with their children and other adults.

They can be encouraged to use and draw on the strengths of partners and friends and to acknowledge that they are raising the issue of sexual abuse in a society which is slow to change. The prevalence figures for child sexual abuse are high and, just as there are survivors who have great difficulties as adults, so too are there survivors who are surviving — and thriving.

Chapter 5

Seeking Help

When a survivor decides to seek help, she is taking an important first step in coming to terms with the experience of childhood sexual abuse. She may have spent months or years getting to this point, and much will depend on her finding a setting in which she feels safe enough to disclose the painful details of her past. Finding out what resources are available locally can be difficult. There are, however, a range of organizations and professional helpers who can offer support, undertake therapeutic work or refer a woman to a more appropriate source of help.

This chapter outlines the main sources of help available to survivors, together with information on how to make contact with them. It also examines some of the contexts in which help can be given and the issues which arise in these contexts.

Choosing a Source of Help

Until she has access to reliable information, a woman will be unable to make an informed choice about the source of help most appropriate to her needs. There are a number of questions she might ask before deciding which route to pursue. These are listed in Table 5.1. Not all of these questions will have clear or immediate answers, and they will vary according to the context in which help is given.

Where and How to Get Help

Table 5.2 lists the main sources of help available for survivors, not all of which will be available in any one locality.

Table 5.1: **Questions to ask about sources of help**

Can I refer myself?
If not, do I need to have a letter from my doctor?
Will notes be kept on my visits?
Who will see these notes?
Will information about me be sent back to my doctor?
Can I see what is written about me?
Will I be able to get time off work to attend for help?
Will I have to pay?
Are child-care facilities available?
How regular will the session be?
How long will each session last?
Who will be present?
Where will we meet? (hospital, own home, helper's office).
Who else will my helper speak to about me?
Can I stop attending if it gets too difficult?
How will I know when it is time to end my contact?

Table 5.2: **Source of help for survivors**

A woman may refer herself to	*Her GP can arrange referral to*
Family doctor.	Community or hospital clinical psychology services.
Other members of primary care team (for example, health visitors).	Psychiatric services.
Walk-in counselling services.	Sex therapy clinic.
Counselling services at place of work or study.	Psychotherapy services within National Health Service.
Voluntary agencies — Survivors group* — Rape crisis group* — Other voluntary group relating to specific problems (for example, Women's Aid, Marriage Guidance (Relate), Anorexic Aid, Phobia group, Alcohol Advice Centre) — Women's groups in the community.	A professional worker with particular interest and expertise in working with survivors (regardless of agency).
Social work department.	
Some psychotherapy services (often private).	
Private counsellor/therapist.	

* Indicates services specifically for women who acknowledge that they were sexually abused.

Family doctor   A woman's family doctor, or GP, can be an important source of help initially. Her GP may be the first person a woman tells about her childhood experiences; her/his reaction to the woman's disclosure can determine whether further help is sought or made available. A family doctor can refer a woman to other services within the National Health Service (NHS) for specialized help. Referrals can be made to a psychologist, psychiatrist or psychotherapist. A woman may be able to ask her doctor for a referral to a particular individual within the NHS if she knows about someone with particular expertise or knowledge in the area of sexual abuse.

Clinical psychologists   These practitioners usually work within the NHS and in both hospital and community settings. They study psychology before undertaking the clinical psychology training. Their aim is to help people deal with their psychological difficulties by gaining an understanding of the effects of a person's history, life experiences and conditions on his/her behaviour. They work with individuals and groups using counselling skills together with a number of techniques to deal with specific problems. Although some psychologists may have the title 'Dr', this is a research qualification, and they are not allowed to prescribe drugs.

Psychiatrists   They are medical doctors who have chosen to specialize in the field of mental illness. They usually work in psychiatric hospitals or special units in general hospitals. Some provide services in doctors' surgeries. They can prescribe medication and may have had training in psychotherapy and counselling.

Psychotherapists   They work within a number of settings (NHS, private practice, social services departments and voluntary organizations). A registered psychotherapist should have undergone recognized training and aims to help people resolve their personal difficulties with the use of verbal techniques. A psychotherapist does not necessarily have a medical training.

Social workers   They work for local government and voluntary organizations, and some are attached to hospitals or doctors' surgeries. They deal with a wide range of social and emotional problems and have statutory responsibilities, including taking children into care and arranging a compulsory admission to a psychiatric hospital under the Mental Health Act. They usually have a large and varied caseload so their opportunity for doing intensive work is limited. Some local authorities have a community-based mental health team specializing in mental health problems. Social workers can be contacted through the social services department (social work departments in Scotland, health boards in Ireland), and they are listed in telephone directories.

Rape Crisis Centres They are now established in many towns and cities in Britain and Ireland. Each centre is run as an autonomous group. They provide a support service by women for women who have experienced sexual abuse in their childhood or as adults. Rape Crisis Centres usually offer telephone counselling or one-to-one support from volunteers. They may also have survivors group. Rape Crisis members also ensure that the women who contact them have control over the contact they wish to have; help is given in a supportive, non-judgmental atmosphere where the women are encouraged to make decisions that are right for themselves.

Survivors' Groups They have been set up by Rape Crisis Centres, Women's Aid, in local community centres and in psychiatric hospitals. Telephone contact lines for survivors have been established in at least eleven towns in Britain and Ireland. There is a wide variety in the way groups operate (see Chapter 9). Contact with a survivors' group can usually be made through a Rape Crisis Centre or Mental Health Advice Centre. Even if the Centre does not have a group, it may be able to suggest other local sources of help.

Advice Centres Many towns now have a range of advice agencies and support groups which deal with specific issues such as, Alcohol Advice Centre, Women's Aid, Relate. There are also advice centres operating under the auspices of local associations for mental health. They offer a range of counselling resources, on a one-to-one basis and in groups.

Choice of Context

In addition to knowing what resources are available locally, a woman should also consider whether she will feel more comfortable in a one-to-one setting or in a group with other survivors. At a later stage she might also wish to do some work with her siblings, mother, in a family context or with her partner.

The main distinction between the services listed in Table 5.2 is between statutory (e.g., social work department, health services) and voluntary organizations (e.g., Rape Crisis Centre). Table 5.3 summarizes the relevant distinguishing features.

It is preferable for a survivor, if she is able to make use of facilities located in the community or those provided by hospital out-patient

Table 5.3: **Statutory and voluntary organizations as sources of help**

Statutory organizations	Voluntary organizations
May have to be referred by GP.	Greater ease of self-referral.
May have to wait some time if there is a waiting list.	More likely to be seen soon after making contact.
Setting may be formal, (office, hospital).	Flexibility in meeting place and time of meeting.
They have trained and professionally qualified staff.	May be staffed by volunteers or trained workers.
Records may be centralized and passed to other professionals.	Each organization has own records.

departments. Sometimes, however, it is necessary for a survivor to be admitted as an in-patient to a psychiatric hospital or unit, because of symptoms of severe depression, suicidal behaviour or other problems. Admission to hospital at a time of great stress can provide a number of benefits to a survivor.

— it allows her a period of rest in a safe place away from the pressures of her normal life;
— she can receive medication or other treatment for her symptoms;
— it allows the woman to be in a supportive and safe environment whilst she does some difficult disclosure work.

Helpers in these settings should also be aware of the potential difficulties for a survivor. The most obvious problem relates to confidentiality and trust:

— a woman may be expected to talk to several members of staff about her experiences. Consequently no one member has all the information to help her to deal with them appropriately;
— she may feel upset or angry if she feels that staff members are sharing her 'secrets' without her permission;
— some staff members may feel excluded if they are not told details of her experiences.

It is important that these issues are resolved by the staff team, and the woman should be assigned to an individual therapist who is able to involve her in the necessary therapeutic work. The staff team's policy regarding confidentiality should be clarified and discussed with the survivor allowing her some freedom about what she chooses to talk about.

Table 5.4: **Individual help: Issues for helpers and survivors**

For the woman	Consequences for a helper
Can establish a long-term trusting relationship with someone who believes her.	Concern about over-involvement or dependency. May ask, 'Will she lean on me so hard that I'll collapse?'
Details of her abuse are confidential to one person.	Feels the need to share burden of the 'secret' of the abuse with colleagues for support.
Work can be done at her own pace, in her own time.	Pace of work may be too slow for the helper and this can be frustrating.
Feels helper is someone she can rely on.	May be difficulties at holiday periods or if helper is ill/absent.
Intensity of the work can be frightening. Asks herself, 'Will I go mad if this carries on?'	Helper asks 'Can I get her through this?', 'Can I cope with her pain?'
Feels that she is going mad.	Needs to reassure the woman that she is not going mad. Asks, 'Can I get her through this?'
Does not want to burden her helper with details of the abuse.	Should emphasize the continued importance of disclosure.
May not fully resolve issues of secrecy, isolation and stigma.	Suggest that woman joins survivors' group at appropriate time.
Can become over-dependent on helper.	Can feel overburdened by woman's dependency.

Group and Individual Settings

A woman needs to decide whether she will feel more comfortable in a one-to-one context with an individual helper, or in a group with other survivors.

Individual Setting

Many women choose a one-to-one therapeutic situation, preferring the confidentiality and sense of security which it offers. Individual help can be arranged by referral to a clinical psychologist, psychotherapist, psychiatrist, social worker or counsellor in a specialist advice agency. Table 5.4 lists some of the issues which can arise for the survivor and her helper in one-to-one work.

Group Work

A woman may decide to move on from individual therapy to a self-help or other group. Alteratively a survivors' group could be her main source of support from the outset. Chapter 10 examines issues relating to groups

Table 5.5: **Group settings: Advantages and limitations**

Advantages	Limitations
Women share burden of the abuse with other who have been through similar experiences.	Group setting may be too threatening for some women.
Emotional and social isolation reduced when women realize they are not the only ones to have been abused.	Confidentiality may be more difficult to maintain.
It can help women to face the reality of what has happened.	Individuals may feel excluded or need more individual attention.
It can validate as normal a woman's feelings of guilt, anger, grief, loneliness and other long-term effects.	Women may need more regular support than group can offer.
More established members can acknowledge progress they have made and can give hope to newer members.	Hearing about the experiences of others may be too painful.
Group can be a place of safety to express true feelings and emotions.	There may be reluctance to participate in group if woman fells she has not suffered as much as others in the group.
Women can work together to build trust and alleviate guilt.	

for survivors in some detail. Table 5.5 lists the main advantages and limitations of groups.

Work with Families of Origin

Therapeutic work with a whole family usually involves children in families where abuse is suspected or confirmed. In adulthood, it may be beneficial for the woman to work with siblings or her mother in either a family or group setting.

Work with Siblings

When a child has been sexually abused by a trusted adult, she is likely to ask herself if her brothers or sisters have had similar experiences. Sometimes siblings have attended for help at the same agency. If this is the case, it may be possible to bring them together to talk about their past. Table 5.6 gives an indication of issues which might arise in this context.

Mothers and Daughters

In individual therapy and in group work, the question of a mother's knowledge about the abuse is a recurring theme. A woman may want to

Table 5.6: **Issues in working with siblings**

Issues for siblings	Implications for the helper
This may be first time the abuse is openly acknowledged to each other.	Helper needs to check out knowledge with each sibling about the abuse, and may need to perform mediating role.
Siblings may have been abused in different ways.	Helper must ensure that both experiences are acknowledged and validated without minimizing either.
Siblings may be at different stages of recovery from the abuse.	Helper must acknowledge this and take it into account in the work.
Abuse may have had different consequences for each sibling.	Helper must acknowledge and encourage dialogue on the issue.
One sibling feels responsible for allowing abuse of others to happen.	Helper must examine threats and bribes used to maintain silence and secrecy, and issues of responsibility for the abuse.
Siblings may have different views of the same event.	Helper must check out reasons for discrepancies, and emphasize common elements.

confront her mother with issues relating to the extent of this knowledge, her failure to protect her and her responsibility for past events. A survivor may wish to enlist the support of her helper in confronting her mother. Clearly, this can only take place if her mother is also willing to do the work. It might be possible for a mother to undertake individual work before coming together with her daughter. Some of the issues which arise in joint work with mothers and daughters are given in Table 5.7.

Table 5.7: **Issues for mothers and daughters**

Mothers	Daughters
Mothers must acknowledge that the abuse has occurred.	Did she know about it? How could she *not* have known?
Mother may have feelings of guilt and failure to protect her child, and of not being a good-enough parent.	Why did she not see that something was wrong? What did she do/could she have done to stop it?
Mother will feel vulnerable when confronted with the facts about the abuse.	Daughters may want to protect mother from details of the abuse.
Mother will find it difficult to cope with daughter's feelings.	Daughters may want to protect mother so they disguise their true feelings.
Is she able to let daughter know what it was like for her, especially in her relationship with the abuser?	Daughters may not want to hear and find it difficult to acknowledge her mother's own difficulties.
Mother may have been abused by the same man.	Why didn't she protect me from him? She knew what he was like.

Working with Partners

As more survivors seek help in dealing with issues from their past, their partners are looking for support for themselves, in which they try to understand the difficulties which survivors face. A partner is often the only person whom a survivor trusts enough to disclose details of her past. This can result in a range of problems for both partners and their relationship.

There are three areas where work with partners of survivors can be helpful. These are:

— enabling them to understand the effects of sexual abuse on their partners. This can be done through discussion, reading or talking to other partners of survivors;

— supporting them whilst their partners are receiving help in coming to terms with their childhood experiences. Partners may be confused about the way a survivor is behaving as she remembers details of the abuse or gets in touch with painful feelings;

— helping them to renegotiate their relationship as the survivor changes.

Laura Davis' book *Allies in Healing* (1991) provides a full account of many of the issues faced by partners of survivors.

Chapter 6

Stages of Recovery

This chapter examines the stages of work that a survivor is likely to have to pass through before finally coming to terms with being sexually abused as a child. The details and emphasis of the work will vary from individual to individual, and may also reflect the setting in which the work is carried out. For example, some women may only attend a group that is time-limited and has a restricted set of aims. Others may attend for individual counselling, or be involved in both group and individual work simultaneously. Progress through the stages is not an orderly process, since it is affected by a number of factors within the woman and in her circumstances.

The six stages are:

— acknowledging that help is needed;
— initial disclosure of childhood sexual abuse;
— finding an appropriate source of help;
— beginning of therapeutic contact;
— the middle phase of therapeutic work;
— ending the therapeutic contact.

Stage 1: Acknowledging That Help is Needed

An acknowledgment that the woman needs some help for her present or past difficulties may come from herself, through the concern of her family, friends or work colleagues, or through agencies dealing with other members of her family (e.g., education and child health agencies). At this stage, she may not be aware that she was sexually abused or that being abused as a child could have links with her present difficulties.

Stage 2: Initial Disclosure of Child Sexual Abuse

The first disclosure from a survivor that she was sexually abused as a child may take place with family members or friends, or may not occur until she is established in a therapeutic relationship and has already begun to work on some of her difficulties. The reactions of those whom she first tells will determine whether she feels encouraged to seek further help. If this disclosure is made in a context where help is not available, such as in a community-based women's group, it is essential that potential sources of help are discussed with the woman immediately, so that she can seek them out for herself. Contact with the health service can be made through her family doctor, or she may prefer to avail herself of help from voluntary groups, social services or community agencies.

Once she has decided to seek help, there should be as little delay as possible between a woman's request for help and her first contact with her chosen helping agency. Significant delay could result in:

— a woman feeling that her history of sexual abuse is too shocking/ disgusting for her to have help;
— a woman feeling rejected after she has plucked up courage to ask for help;
— a woman retracting/minimizing/denying that she has been abused;
— a woman feeling that her story of abuse is not serious enough to warrant attention;
— a woman requiring emergency or urgent psychiatric help because, once she has broken the secret about her past, she cannot contain the feelings associated with it any longer;
— an increase in her suicidal, or self-injurious behaviour, perhaps requiring emergency treatment.

Detailed discussion of the management of and issues arising from initial disclosure is given in Chapter 7.

Stage 3: Finding an Appropriate Source of Help

Sources of help can be found both in the statutory (medical, mental health and social services) agencies and within voluntary agencies. A woman may come to them by a number of different routes. Her selection of an appropriate source of help depends on whether or not she can remember or disclose that she was sexually abused. Chapter 5 discussed the various helping agencies available; where possible she should be encouraged to choose an agency that best meets her needs and circumstances.

Stage 4: Beginning of the Therapeutic Contact

Therapeutic work to overcome the effects of being sexually abused as a child begins with a woman's initial acknowledgment that she was abused. For some survivors, however, this acknowledgment is not possible for several reasons:

— she does not remember that she was abused;
— she does not feel ready to disclose this information;
— she does not feel safe enough to do so with the particular helper;
— she does not believe that her early experiences are having any effect on her life.

In these cases, the woman may need to be involved in a therapeutic situation which allows her to prepare herself for a confirmation that she was sexually abused as a child.

Establishment of a Therapeutic Relationship

A survivor may come for help with many problems relating to her childhood experiences. Some of these problems may make it difficult for her to be involved in a therapeutic relationship. Her feelings of guilt, shame and helplessness, combined with her fears of being betrayed and exploited in close relationships, may lead her to want to run from the helper; she may fear disbelief, blame and rejection.

From the very beginning of contact, therefore, the helper should aim to establish a relationship with the woman that will allow her to feel that she is believed and taken seriously. This will involve:

— actively listening and attempting to understand her problems from her point of view (i.e., with empathy);
— suspending judgments and preconceived ideas about the woman and general issues about child sexual abuse;
— responding warmly, with support and interest;
— allowing her to discuss her problems, her past and other issues at her own pace;
— respecting her right to remain silent about any issue.

The experience of sexual abuse as a child is surrounded by secrecy. It involves a misuse of power, betrayal of the child's trust and compounds the child's helplessness and lack of control over her situation. These issues are likely to be very much in evidence at this stage of therapy. An assurance of confidentiality, not forcing her to talk in detail about the abuse and giving her choices in the therapeutic situation are vitally necessary to avoid betraying her trust and leaving her feeling helpless a second time.

Establishing a relationship with a survivor that is safe enough to allow her to reveal her childhood memories and their associated pain can take a long time — perhaps many months. She may be very tentative, ambivalent or suspicious with the helper and she must be given time to feel secure before the work progresses.

Engagement Difficulties

It may take a long time for a survivor to trust her helper and to engage with her. Non-attendance at initial appointments is normally seen as a sign of poor motivation in professional helping services. The helper will follow up non-attendance and use other means to encourage a woman to engage with her. The helper could do the following:

— visit the woman in her own home initially;
— see the woman initially with someone she already trusts and with whom she has already shared some of her experiences;
— meet on neutral territory. An office or hospital, for example, may have unpleasant memories or be seen as too authoritarian. Alternatively, some women feel safer out of doors;
— place the survivor in a comfortable place in the room. Some women need to feel that they can escape quickly if necessary, so sitting near and in view of the door is important. A woman may be unable to relax if the helper is seated between her and the door;
— make telephone contact with the survivor in order build up the relationship before having a face-to-face meeting. This is more likely to enable the woman to feel in control. She is also able to terminate the call herself if necessary.

Framework and Specific Aims

Therapeutic work with a survivor can be a lengthy and intensive process and it is not likely to begin unless the therapeutic environment allows the woman to feel in control and offers her some assurance of confidentiality. There are five important principles which should be explained to a woman at this stage:

— she will be gradually helped to gain control of her past so that it stops intruding into and affecting the present;

— she will be encouraged to take more control of and exercise choice in the therapeutic situation and in her current life circumstances;

— during her therapeutic work, she will be given control and choice of when and how much she discloses about painful and distressing memories and experiences of her past;

— the work will proceed at a pace that she can tolerate;

— extra support will be given or sought from other agencies where necessary with prior discussion with the woman.

The specific aims of the work will vary from woman to woman, and will also depend on the setting in which she receives help. There are a number of aims which apply to any setting. These are outlined in Table 6.1.

Table 6.1: **Aims of Work with Survivors**

1 Helping her to gradually talk in detail about her childhood so that she gains some understanding of the effects of being abused as a child;
2 Gaining an understanding of the long-term effects of being abused;
3 Facilitating an understanding and safe release of emotional reactions;
4 Gaining an understanding of her family and its interactions;
5 Exploring the losses resulting from her childhood experiences, and helping her to reverse some of them;
6 Breaking the secret of her past with others;
7 Working specifically on the long-term effects of the abuse (for example assertiveness work, sex therapy, anxiety problems, depression);
8 Gaining an acceptance of the past so that it allows her to look forward to the future.

Establishing the Arrangements for the Therapeutic Work

It is essential at the beginning of any work with a survivor that the helper clarifies what the offer of help entails. The issues which should be discussed with her are:

— when, where and how often the therapeutic sessions are to take place;

— the length of these sessions;

— whether the sessions will be discussed with anyone else (as support or supervision for the helper(s));

— whether the helper will be communicating with a referring agency (this is usually only necessary in the statutory services) or with anyone else;

— whether there are any details of her experiences which the woman does not wish to be communicated to the referring agency;
— what level of or alternative arrangements for support the helper might organize for the survivor, her partner and the helper during difficult periods of the therapeutic work, holidays, etc.

Explanation of the Therapeutic Process

It is helpful at this stage to acknowledge that coming to terms with childhood sexual abuse is a painful process that can take considerable time. A useful analogy is to explain the healing process by likening it to the healing of a wound. The helper might say:

> I want you to think of this process like the healing of a deep wound. First, imagine you have a deep wound on your arm. Think what would happen if you kept it covered up with plaster or a bandage for a long time. It would not heal properly and might even go septic. If you then take the plasters off, the wound will hurt a great deal, but once it has been cleaned, it will begin to heal properly. Now if we imagine that what your . . . (father, uncle, brother, cousin, grandfather, etc.) did to you caused a deep wound inside you, but for a number of reasons it has been bandaged up ever since. What we will be doing is gradually peeling back those bandages until the wound is exposed. This is going to hurt, but then it can be cleaned and will begin to heal properly leaving just a scar. Eventually, it will stop hurting, except when the scar is knocked sharply.

This analogy can be both hopeful and realistic, and offers some explanation for any setbacks.

The following information about what may happen during the process of receiving help should also be discussed:

— the process may take a long time, extending to several months or years;
— the woman is likely to feel worse before she begins to feel better;
— there will be times when she wishes she had not embarked on this process;
— it may have some effects on her relationships with her partner, her children and her own family;
— she may need time off work during or after particularly upsetting periods of the work.

Table 6.2: **Relevant factors for the start of therapeutic work**

Issue	Implications	Questions to be considered
Motivation to work on the past	If low, she may not be able to involve herself with the work and may fail to attend meetings or appointments.	Who referred her? Was she willing to be referred? Did she seek the help herself? Did she seek help for the problems of another family member (child, spouse, sibling)?
Life circumstances	If complicated, disrupted, busy or unsupported, it may be difficult to embark on the work.	Is this the right time for her? Does she have very young children and little support? Is she going through another major life crisis? Does she have any support for herself?
Her willingness to get involved with a particular helper	Issues of trust, gender of the helper are critical here.	Can she trust the helper? Can she talk more easily to a male or female helper? Has she any expectations or prior knowledge that the helper has worked with other survivors?
Previous attempts at getting help	Issues concerned with being believed are important, as are the reactions of helpers.	Has she received help before and when? What were the reactions of the helper(s)? What gender were they? Was she believed and taken seriously?
Concerns about confidentiality	She will be concerned about trust and may be overwhelmed by the power of the secret.	Who else will find out that she has been abused? Who will be told details of the abuse? What will be written down about her in notes, letters?

At this stage the woman's courage in seeking help should be acknowledged. She should also be assured of ongoing support during the work she is about to undertake.

Difficulties at this Stage

The helper must examine any factors at this stage which may inhibit the start of the therapeutic process. These are summarized in Table 6.2 above.

Finally, some survivors are extremely unsure about the benefits of receiving help or may be ambivalent about embarking on the process. If this is the case it is useful to consider the following options:

— initially she might be offered a limited number of therapeutic sessions to allow her to examine the importance and relevance of her history of being abused as a child;

— she may need more time to make her decision, and another meeting with the helper might be arranged for several weeks later in order to give her that time;

— she may need to have time to see how she will react to making her initial disclosure before committing herself to working on the problems.

Ultimately, it is the woman's choice whether or not she accepts the offer of help.

Confidentiality

The issue of confidentiality should be discussed at the start of the work. The issues to be explored with the survivor are:

— any statutory requirements that the helper has to communicate with the referring agency (for example, within the NHS, helpers are expected to communicate some information to the woman's family doctor);

— any information that she does not wish the referring agency to know (for example, if she lives in a closely-knit community, she may find it difficult to cope with the possibility of anyone in the community knowing that she was sexually abused);

— whether the helper discusses her/his work with a supervisor or support person;

— what other staff in the helping agency need to know. This is particularly relevant in situations where there is a team of helpers (for example, in psychiatric hospital settings, Women's Aid or a hostel where the woman is living).

Stage 5: The Middle Phase of Therapeutic Work

Once a woman has accepted the offer of help, the most intensive part of the work can begin. Some women find their decision to accept help too frightening and withdraw from the helping situation fairly quickly. In our experience, most survivors who manage to cope with the initial stages do continue long enough to gain some benefit from the contact.

The content and process of the middle phase of therapeutic work depends largely on the needs and problems of an individual woman.

Levels of Support

During a period of disclosure, when there is often an increased need for support, survivors frequently worry about becoming over-dependent on their helpers. This can also become an issue for helpers. If this is the case, it can be useful to conceptualize the process in terms of recovery from a physical injury. The helper might say:

> I want you to imagine this process is like recovering from a broken leg. When you break a leg, first you have to have bed rest, then you get on to two crutches with lots of help from the nurses. After that you learn to walk on two crutches, then one until you can manage just with a stick. For a while you will hobble about. That's what is happening here. Just now you are needing crutches but eventually you'll be able to throw them away, though you may need them back again occasionally if there are any setbacks.

This will enable a woman to see that it is quite reasonable to need and use the support that is available to her, and that there may be times when a high level of support is needed. Kenward (1987) noted that in individual work at least, the need for high levels of support occurs mainly during the early stages, but may increase again about a year later, before reducing to more manageable levels prior to ending contact with a helper.

The level of support required by a survivor varies from one woman to another and depends on the stage which she has reached in the recovery process. Weekly sessions at the outset, moving to fortnightly or monthly contact later is a common pattern. Sometimes a woman needs much more intensive support; this can amount to daily contact, perhaps by phone. If she needs more contact than this, it is likely that a short admission to a psychiatric unit or an alternative place of safety (such as a women's hostel or Women's Aid refuge) may have to be arranged. Use of community and voluntary organizations, church facilities (if appropriate) and community psychiatric nurse teams should be considered as additional sources of support for any woman who can continue to manage in the community.

Stage 6: Ending of Therapeutic Contact

The process of ending therapeutic contact with a survivor will begin once it becomes clear that her past is no longer intruding into the present, and that she has moved from being a victim to becoming a survivor. The management and timing of the termination of contact is important and should be done in consultation with the woman herself, as the ending of contact can be painful for the survivor and her helper, especially when the contact has lasted a long period of time. Some women prefer not to consider this issue openly, and may terminate the contact suddenly by not keeping their last appointment. Where possible, however, the ending should be planned. It may be useful to consider some of the following strategies:

- reduction in the frequency and/or length of sessions;
- determining how many more sessions are required, setting a fixed date for the last one and spacing out the remainder to fit in before that date;
- not setting the date for a further session, but allowing the woman herself to request a further meeting. If no contact is made within say, three months, agree that the helper will make contact to discuss future sessions.

In some situations, such as a time-limited group, the number of sessions and the date of the last session may be fixed at the beginning. In this case follow-up meetings or sessions with an individual helper may be arranged by agreement.

At the end of any work with a survivor, the helper should discuss the of following issues:

- the usefulness of the contact to her;
- any arrangements for follow-up and the helper's availability to see her again in the future;
- any writing that she has done during the course of the work for the helper. Is this to be kept, destroyed or returned?
- any contact that the helper intends to have with the agency that referred her.

These issues may be problematic if the woman terminates her contact early.

Finally, helpers should remember that survivors, having worked through many issues and terminated their contact with a helper, are quite likely to find that future life events can trigger off further memories. It is important therefore for a helper to operate an 'open door' policy if possible; the ability to do this will obviously reflect the demands on the helper. If an open door policy is not possible, then women should be made aware of other sources of support.

Special Considerations for Women who have Experienced Physical and Sexual Abuse

For a woman who has experienced severe levels of physical and sexual abuse, usually within her family, there are a number of features that relate to the stages of therapy (Rocklin and Lavett, 1987):

- — she may have great difficulty in asking for help, assuming rejection, disbelief and hostility;
- — similar fears are likely to emerge at the start of any therapeutic contact. As a result, the helper may have to be more active in engaging the woman in the work, perhaps requiring more frequent contact than would be usual. There may be a trial period with the helper, the main goal being to indicate to the woman that her helper is trustworthy, concerned and not rejecting;
- — issues of trust and being believed are predominant especially at the beginning, and reassurance about these concerns is essential.
- — periods of disclosure are more likely to provoke a regression to childhood with its associated terror, despair and child-like behaviour (see Chapter 7). Higher levels of support may be needed at this time. Fears about any threats made by the abuser may also be activated at this time;
- — the helper may be actively involved in 're-parenting' the woman, assuring her of safety, protection and care. This again represents the need for a greater level of involvement from the helper;
- — the ending of the therapeutic contact should be planned, and involve a gradual reduction in contact over a period of time;
- — concerns about confidentiality are likely to be more pronounced particularly if the woman is still in contact with the abuser. She is likely to re-experience fear of the threats which he used to maintain her silence as a child.

Outlining the stages of recovery can be a useful exercise. It can help a woman to acknowledge the progress she has made, and it allows her to look ahead with some degree of optimism, even when she may be feeling that her pain is increasing rather than diminishing in intensity.

Chapter 7

Disclosure

The long-term consequences of child sexual abuse are considerable, but many women are unable to disclose their experiences until many years after the abuse has stopped. In this chapter, we will examine the management, difficulties and consequences of a survivor's initial and subsequent disclosures of being sexually abused as a child.

Disclosure: General Comments

Survivors, their partners, families and helpers frequently ask how much the survivor will have to remember and disclose about her childhood experiences in order to come to terms with her past. There is no simple answer, but the survivor has a right to know what happened to her. By gaining this knowledge, she can begin to make sense of reactions, feelings, behaviour and attitudes that perhaps were previously inexplicable or confusing. She can also decide how much she herself needs to tell someone else about her memories.

The disclosure process may come in three stages:

— acknowledging to herself what has happened to her;
— sharing this knowledge with someone else;
— understanding the implications of what she is remembering in terms of her reactions, survival strategies, and the effects on her childhood and adult life.

These stages do not necessarily come in this order, particularly since the disclosure to someone else may be the first time she has recalled aspects of the abuse. It is, however, important that she is encouraged to complete the stages. This will help her to release the emotional energy that is bound in keeping the secret and no longer to react in ways that may be unhelpful to her.

Few survivors ever remember all of the incidents of abuse even if they have been abused on very few occasions. The amount of disclosure will vary enormously from one survivor to another. However, it is our experience that survivors tell what they need to tell in order to understand the effects of and come to terms with the abuse. By remembering and disclosing, the survivor has her experiences and feelings confirmed and validated. She reclaims her knowledge of the abuse, but also the many resources and strengths she used to survive it. For many survivors, this process also allows her to reclaim other memories of her childhood which have been lost to her along with the memories of abuse.

Sharing the secrets of the abuse with someone the survivor trusts is, in itself, important as it lessens the burden and the power of the secrets and their associated shame. It allows the survivor to begin to work actively on dealing with the abuse and its aftermath. Telling someone who believes her and who then accepts her, knowing about the abuse, is often a significant turning point for an improvement in the survivor's self-esteem.

Disclosure of a history of sexual abuse or of specific details of abuse should *never* be sought just for the sake of disclosure. Survivors find it particularly difficult if they give the information and the helper does nothing with it except record it as part of her history.

A woman can be encouraged to consider the possibility of sexual abuse if:

— there are clues in her background or the nature of her difficulties (see Table 7.1);
— a sibling reports having been sexually abused;
— one of her children reports being sexually abused, particularly by a member of the survivor's family of origin;
— she is suffering from nightmares or perceptual disturbances;
— her work situation is beginning to trigger memories, for example, if the survivor is working with people who have experienced sexual abuse.

She should be encouraged to disclose specific memories if:

— she is having frequent nightmares, body memories, perceptual disturbances or flashbacks to the abuse;
— she is trying to make links between her past and her current difficulties (for example, understanding difficulties in sexual situations);

— she is trying to deal effectively with feelings of guilt and self-blame;

— sharing the secrets of the abuse with someone who believes her enables her to challenge the abuser's claims or her own beliefs that no-one would believe her;

— she has started to injure herself as a diversion from the memories;

— she has started to use alcohol or drugs to block the memories;

— the memories are flooding back once she stops using alcohol or drugs to block them.

Table 7.1: **Clues to child sexual abuse**

Combination of some of following factors:

Combination of long-term effects (especially sexual problems, nightmares, perceptual disturbances, fear of men or avoidance of relationships with men, self-mutilation);

Previous psychiatric history and several different diagnoses without significant improvement;

No memories of childhood/over-positive descriptions of childhood;

Significant memory gaps about childhood;

Reasons for seeking help now (see Table 7.2);

Certain features during childhood including:

        Significant behaviour disturbances
        Running away from home
        Persistent urinary tract infections
        Sexually transmitted disease
        Frequent unexplained school absences (especially if evidence of physical violence in family)
        Withdrawal or isolation from peer group
        Nightmares/sleep disturbances/night terrors;

Certain features during adolescence including:

        Running away from home
        Pregnancy, especially during early adolescence
        Sexually transmitted diseases
        Pronounced fear of men
        Self-mutilation or self-injury
        Prostitution or significant promiscuity
        Fire-raising
        Truancy
        Criminal Behaviour;

Family history:

        Another child (especially sibling) sexually abused
        Evidence of violence and/or alcoholism in parents;

History of prostitution.

Many survivors attend helping agencies unaware of the links between their current difficulties and their early experiences of sexual abuse. For others, their history of sexual abuse remains hidden or repressed, even to the survivors themselves, until an event in their adult life brings the past to the surface. Gelinas (1983) has likened this process to having a time-bomb inside that ticks away until a trigger or triggers in the present detonate the bomb and brings a sudden and intolerable increase in psychological difficulties and distress. Common triggers are described in Table 7.2.

For some survivors, memories surface only because it has become safe enough to do so. This may be because:

— the survivor lives a long way from the abuser and therefore does not feel she has to maintain contact;
— the abuser is old and infirm and she feels he cannot bother her;
— the abuser and/or her mother has died;
— she is in a safe, supportive relationship with a partner. In this case the relationship provides a feeling of safety and security perhaps for the first time. Survivors and their partners are often confused about and resentful of this as their security can be shattered by the memories of her childhood;
— she has just left an abusive adult relationship, and by doing so she feels safer.

Factors Influencing a Disclosure of Abuse

The factors which influence or facilitate a disclosure of sexual abuse, especially when it has remained hidden for many years, are critical. Some of these lie within the survivor herself (Courtois and Watts, 1982; Josephson and Fong-Beyette, 1987) and include the following:

— whether or not she has told anyone before;
— the reactions of others to previous attempts to disclose as a child and as an adult;
— her predictions about the reactions of the person she is about to tell;
— the extent of her recall of the abuse;
— her emotional reactions to the memories of the abuse;
— whether she had close relationships with non-abusive adults during childhood.

Other factors influencing the timing of a disclosure of abuse are related to the abuse itself and the reactions of the survivor as a child to the abuse (Herman and Schatzow, 1987; Kendall-Tackett, 1991):

Table 7.2: **Triggers linking current difficulties with childhood abuse**

Context	Trigger
Adult relationships	— After a long-term intimate relationship with a man has been established. — Having a sexual relationship. — Being in an abusive relationship. — Partner disclosing sexual abuse.
The abuser	— His terminal illness or death. — Making further demands on survivor. — His denial of abuse when confronted. — His denial of any problems with her childhood. — Fear of abuser in presence of her own children.
Her mother	— Terminal illness or death. — Confrontation and denial of abuse. — Separation/divorce from father (where partner was abuser). — Revealing that she was abused by same abuser (e.g., her father, and survivor's grandfather).
Siblings	— Disclosing their sexual abuse. — Sibling's children (especially daughters) reaching age woman was when abuse started. — Siblings in presence of abuser. — Discovery that siblings' child is being sexually abused by woman's abuser or by another family member.
Her children	— Birth of a daughter. — Daughter reaching age that woman was when abuse started. — Her children in presence of abuser. — Discovery that her child is being sexually abused by woman's abuser or by another family member.
Abusive situation as an adult	— Rape. — Physical assault. — Marital abuse. — Abuse in adult relationships.
Experience of loss	— Death of important family member. — Loss of job. — Miscarriage/stillbirth/abortion. — End of relationship.
Gynaecological examination/procedure	— Cervical smear test. — Fertility problems requiring treatment. — Pregnancy investigations.
Media	— Television or radio programmes about child sexual abuse. — Films depicting sexual abuse. — Magazines and newspaper articles about sexual abuse.
Employment in a helping profession or membership of a voluntary group/other work situation	— Client/other women disclosing that they were sexually abused as children. — Training/workshops/discussion on child abuse, sexuality or violence in the home, childhood. — Colleague disclosing sexual abuse.

— the severity of the abuse;

— whether there was violence associated with the sexual abuse;

— the age of the child when the abuse started (if the abuse started at a very young age, she is more likely to seek help many years after the abuse has stopped);

— whether she dissociated during or immediately after the abuse;

— whether she repressed the memories of the abuse;

— her emotional reactions to the abuse at the time, particularly the extent to which she blamed herself;

— her fear of the abuser(s) and other family members if she discloses.

Finally, there are a number of factors that can facilitate or block disclosure from an adult survivor that lie within the helper or the therapeutic situation:

— if the helper is known to be knowledgeable about sexual abuse and its effects;

— if the survivor feels safe with the helper;

— if the helper shows understanding for and empathy with the survivor;

— the attitudes and values of the helper;

— the gender of the helper;

— where the helper works, such as, in a community setting, in a psychiatric setting, or in a voluntary agency where she can self-refer;

— the location of the woman's sessions. For many survivors, any institutional setting can inhibit disclosure.

The reactions of any past helper to a woman's attempts at disclosure are also relevant, in that many survivors have learned that some therapists or helpers cannot 'hear' information about sexual abuse and may treat it as an irrelevancy from the past (O'Hare and Taylor, 1983). Many survivors have had their disclosures positively discounted or disbelieved in the past. This can lead to increased wariness on the part of a survivor about making further attempts at disclosure.

Dissociation

A key factor in disclosure is the extent to which a woman learned to dissociate herself from the abuse and its accompanying emotional reactions when she was a child. The trauma of sexual abuse is likely to make a child feel overwhelmed, extremely frightened and anxious. That the abuser is usually a trusted adult adds to her confusion, so much so that she may doubt the reality of the abuse. By denying the reality, she learns to dissociate herself from the accompanying psychological and physical pain.

It seems likely that if the abuse started at a very young age, involved severe sexual abuse and violence, even if it was of short duration, the child is more likely to spontaneously dissociate from it and repress the memories completely (Herman and Schatzow, 1987). This is partly a reflection of the developmental stage of the child in that she has fewer alternative survival strategies available to her, but is also a normal response to overwhelming trauma. For the child, it may have allowed her to continue with some semblance of normality in her ordinary life and enable her to face the abuser in ordinary everyday situations.

There are a number of ways that an abused child uses to cope with and dissociate herself from the abuse. Ultimately, these methods help her to survive the experience. Common examples are:

— pretending that the abuse was not happening to her;
— believing that the abuse was being done to another little girl;
— forgetting each incident so that each time seemed to be the first time;
— thinking of other things, such as a dream world, chores, homework, a favourite book during the abuse;
— focusing all her attention of some feature of the room, such as a spot on the ceiling, the curtains, the pattern of the wallpaper during the abuse;
— thinking about how bad she was or how much she deserved what was happening and so not paying any attention to the abuse and/or its pain;
— over-breathing/breath-holding during the abuse;
— pretending to be asleep;
— 'coming out of her body', so that she has the experience of looking down on herself during the abuse but not feeling the pain, fear or hurt until later;
— shutting off so completely mentally that she has no conscious awareness of the abuse.

As an adult, a survivor may experience feelings and problems without understanding their origins, because she has no conscious knowledge that she was sexually abused a child. The process of linking her feelings and current difficulties with her early life can be terrifying and very distressing. The dissociative process continues into adulthood with some of the following consequences:

— *the abuse is not recalled at all*   Such total amnesia is often found in adult survivors, though there may be clues that something unpleasant has occurred in the survivor's childhood. An excellent example of complete repression of a traumatic and painful childhood is to be found in *Breaking Through* (which incorporates *No Longer a Victim*) by Cathy-Ann Matthews (1990), who believed she had a happy childhood until she was in her late forties. The memories of herself as a child who was physically and sexually abused emerged during her training as a marriage guidance counsellor.

Example: Elizabeth had completely repressed her memories of being raped by her grandfather at the age of six. She knew, however, that from the age of six that she had become a difficult child with eating problems, sleeping difficulties and a great fear of people. Her parents had told her that she had measles at the age of six and had never been same since. During therapy, some thirty years later, she started to question this explanation and suddenly recalled the sexual abuse with all its terror, pain, and great distress.

— *the woman remembers the sexual abuse but transfers the memories to a less upsetting place (e.g., outside the home), or less threatening abuse stranger rather than father)*

Example: Sarah had been severely abused by her father, but had a vague memory of being fondled genitally by a friend of the family when she was four. During counselling, she recalled this incident properly, and remembered that the family friend had not touched her but had been concerned about her. This provoked an angry reaction from her father, who, when the family friend left the house, showed her 'what men do to people they care about', tore her pants off and started to touch her roughly and painfully inserted his fingers into her vagina.

— *the abuse is recalled amidst feeling of guilt and shame*   Here the overwhelming nature of stronger and more frightening emotions of terror, panic, pain, isolation, despair and rage is denied.

— *the abuse is recalled but with none of the accompanying feelings*   In this case the survivor may recall the abuse as if she was remembering a shopping list. All the accompanying emotional reactions are forgotten or minimized;

— *only certain incidents/parts of the abuse are recalled* whereas other more traumatic incidents are forgotten:

> **Example:** Susannah initially remembered that her stepfather had touched her from the age of seven. During therapy, she recalled that the sexual abuse had started when she was four, and far from involving genital touching alone, had involved forced intercourse and oral sex.

— *the memories of the abuse are vague and without much detail* This often occurs with incidents that have particularly unpleasant implications, for example, if the incident demonstrated that other important adults knew about the abuse.

> **Example:** Jan remembered an incident of abuse when she thought that her father had tried to touch her. In fact, when she finally recalled this incident, her father had demanded to have intercourse with her, had then become very violent and beaten her up. But of crucial significance for Jan, she remembered that her mother had walked in and found her father having intercourse with her. Both parents then abused her physically as a punishment for being a 'dirty girl'. In this way, Jan learned of her mother's knowledge of and attitude toward the sexual abuse, and the fact that she was blamed and punished by both parents.

The Nature of Memories

When the memories of sexual abuse return to the survivor, they may return in a number of different forms.

— *Sensory memories*:

Visual
The survivor may get visual images of the abuse and the context in which it occurred.

Auditory
The survivor may hear the voice of the abuser, herself as a child or other sounds associated with the abuse or the context of the abuse, (for example, sounds of music or TV in the background, or other children playing outside);

Tactile

The survivor may remember the sensation of being touched during the abuse, the touch of clothes, bedding, or other materials associated with the context of the abuse, the feel of the abuser's skin, hair, or his body weight, or the sensation of body fluids on her body (for example, semen, urine, vaginal discharge, blood);

Taste

The survivor may experience memories of the abuse as sensations of taste (semen, bodily secretions and vomit); tastes transferred from the abuser's mouth (for example, garlic, cigarettes, alcohol);

Olfactory

The survivor may remember smells associated with the abuse (sexual and bodily smells, perfumes used by the abuser); the smell of other substances used by the abuser (for example, cigarettes, alcohol); smells associated with the context of the abuse (for example, the place, room, fabrics).

— *Body memories*

The survivor may experience pain or the emergence of marks on her body that are consistent with the current disclosure of abuse. It is as if her body has stored the memories of abuse even if she was unable to do so mentally. The pain and any marks usually disappear after disclosure. She may also re-experience the physical after-effects of the abuse (for example, bleeding, fits, unconsciousness or bruising).

— *Body position memories*

The survivor may remember the abuse through her body being in a similar position (for example, lying in a certain position). She may also feel as though her body has been in a certain position, or that she been thrown into the air.

— *Emotional memories*

The survivor may remember the emotional reactions she had at the time of the abuse, or as a child generally. She may experience these emotions even in the absence of sensory or body memories.

— *The 'child's view of the world' memories*

The survivor may have memories of her thought processes, her understanding of the world at a given age, and her beliefs about many aspects of her life. For example, she may recall how she thought about some aspect of her family life, or how she reasoned out an understanding of what was happening to her. A survivor might say that she remembers thinking that it was because she was bad that her mother was not interested in her.

A survivor may recall the abuse in any of the above ways or may experience some combination of sensory, body and emotional memories. For those survivors who have experienced severe abuse, it is common for them to experience a more intense combination of memories, with body memories being particularly frequent.

Sometimes the survivor remembers her childhood experiences from the perspective of a child. She may report that everything in her memory seems large and/or distorted. This can be very frightening. The concept of the 'child within' (Parks, 1990) is useful here — it is as if she has a child inside herself who is remembering/reliving the past on her behalf.

A survivor may never have visual memories. She may find this disturbing, resulting in her beginning to doubt whether she was abused, or that the helper will start to have similar doubts. It is important to recognize that she may never have clear visual memories because:

— she could not see during the abuse as she was blindfolded or face down on a bed or the floor whilst she was being abused;
— she may have been abused in the dark;
— she had shut out all visual input by staring at a particular point in the room;
— she had been hurt on the head causing unconsciousness or concussion;
— she was very young (under five) and was so overwhelmed with emotions and shock at a time when her understanding of her world was at a relatively undeveloped stage;
— she was in a severe state of shock and therefore any processing of visual information was incomplete or absent;
— she was at a preverbal or precognitive state of development and could not identify or distinguish what was being done to her;
— she had eyesight problems.

Types of Memories

There are a number of different types of memory that are common in survivors of child abuse.

Composite memories
Memories relating to abuse of a similar nature, or of a number of incidents occurring in the same location are rolled into one memory.

Example: Angela had been sexually abused by her foster father on a daily basis between the ages of eight and twelve. During the recall of this abuse when she was in her early twenties, she had one memory of oral sex, one of being forced to touch his penis, and another of being raped. She knew, however, that the abuse had occurred every day, but it was always in the same place, at the same time of day and involved a rigid sequence of sexual activities.

Snapshot memories
The memory in this case is as if a photograph was taken of one moment of the abuse, and the survivor cannot recall what happened before or after this moment.

Cine film memories
The survivor recalls incidents of abuse in a sequence, although they may not have actually followed one another in this sequence when she was a child.

Flashbacks
A memory of the abuse comes back to the survivor suddenly and without warning, and is often an intense combination of sensory, body and emotional memories (see Chapter 3).

Nightmares
These can be similar to flashbacks but occurring during sleep. The survivor may re-live the abuse during sleep.

Aftermath memories
The survivor may only recall her feelings, thoughts, reactions and body sensations after the abuse. For example, she may remember lying in bed feeling sick, dizzy and distressed.

Tip-of-the-iceberg memories
The memory is a small fragment of the whole story or a frequently experienced memory blocks the view of a more serious one.

Example: Caroline thought that she had remembered all the abuse that her teacher had perpetrated on her, in that she had always remembered him forcing her to masturbate him. Once this was disclosed, she then remembered that on at least three occasions he had raped her.

Blocking memories
The survivor has a memory that repeatedly returns but which, when disclosed, unleashes a flood of other memories that had remained hidden.

Intrusive memories
For some survivors, the memories do not return in a controlled way, and intrude into every aspect of her life.

A survivor may appear to get stuck on a particular memory of abuse. This may be because:

— she has not been able to tell the whole incident;

— she has managed to disclose some of the dimensions of the abuse but not all of the relevant ones, for example she may have visual recall of the incident accompanied by the emotional reactions but has not been able to disclose the auditory dimension;

— she has not been able to recall a critical part of the incident;

— it is safer to stick with an incident of abuse because she has an inkling of worse to come;

— she needs to go over and over the incident of abuse until she can talk about it without it causing any pain.

Initial Disclosure

A woman's first contact with a helping agency is likely to involve discussions about her difficulties and the context in which they have occurred. Questions about her family, marital and work background may be routinely asked. Helpers should consider whether to ask similar routine questions about any experiences of being sexually abused. The advantages and disadvantages of routine questions are outlined in Table 7.3.

Table 7.3: **Routine questions about sexual abuse**

Advantages	Disadvantages
They help to remove the stigma of being a survivor.	The helper who asks the questions may not be in a position to offer the woman help. She then feels exposed and unsupported.
They enable the helper to become comfortable asking difficult questions about sexual abuse.	Unless help is available to her immediately on disclosure of abuse, the woman is likely to find it increasingly difficult to cope with the burden of the secret.
They raise the subject of sexual abuse in a non-threatening way.	
Questions provide relief that sexual abuse can be discussed openly.	The helper may not want to hear confirmation that a woman has been sexually abused.
	The woman may not be ready to disclose.
	The woman may feel that the helper is intruding.
	Routine questioning may suggest to the woman that the helper views sexual abuse as no worse than other stressful life experiences.
	A woman may feel trapped into acknowledging that she was sexually abused.

An initial disclosure of a history of child abuse can come in a number of ways:

— the woman herself has requested help to enable her to come to terms with the abuse. Here, she is taking the initiative for disclosure and can be assumed to be ready to tell the secrets of her childhood;
— the woman has established herself in a therapeutic situation, and feels she can trust the helper. She is taking the initiative to disclose once she has established that it is safe to do so;
— she responds to routine questions from the helper about her family and sexual history;
— she responds to *specific* questions from the helper who has been alerted to the possibility that the woman had been sexually abused because of the nature of her difficulties and aspects of her history. Table 7.1 examines the potential clues that might lead to such questions;
— the woman makes a desperate response when she can no longer contain the information. In this case, she is more likely to blurt out the information and possibly say more than she wanted to.

In this situation, the helper should take responsibility for asking about sexual abuse as the woman may be unaware of the links between her current difficulties and her past. In this way, the helper is indicating to her that the subject of child abuse can be raised and is assisting her with the very difficult task of breaking the secret. As with routine questions, however, she may not be ready to disclose, but may feel pushed into doing so. As a result, she may fail to keep further appointments, retract her disclosure, deny its importance or refuse to discuss it further.

Therapeutic work to overcome the effects of sexual abuse begins at the moment of the initial disclosure. It may also have started before, if the survivor is or has been in an established relationship with the helper. Unfortunately, it can also end there, if the disclosure is managed in an insensitive or intrusive way. Both the style and nature of the questioning about sexual abuse and the helper's subsequent reactions are critical. Therefore, enquiry about a history of sexual abuse must be handled in a sensitive and non-judgmental way. Questions should be tentative, allowing the woman the choice to remain silent or deny her history of sexual abuse. She should not be forced or persuaded in any way to admit she was abused. Examples of useful questions are set out in Table 7.4.

Table 7.4: **Examples of questions to elicit a disclosure of sexual abuse**

'This may be a difficult question to hear, but I am wondering whether you were ever sexually abused as a child?'

'You have been describing a number of difficulties that are often found in women who report that they were sexually abused as children. I wonder if this has ever happened to you?'

'The problems you are describing suggest to me that something very unpleasant may have happened to you as a child. Were you ever abused, physically?' (wait for answer) 'Sexually?'

'I'm wondering if anyone touched you when you were a child in a way that made you feel uncomfortable and/or frightened?'

Where there is evidence that she was physically abused as a child:

'Did he ever do more than physically abuse you? For example, did he ever also sexually abuse you?'

Helpers' Reactions to Disclosure

It has been shown that if the woman perceives a negative reaction in the helper when she makes her initial disclosure, she may refuse to discuss the sexual abuse or to return for further sessions (Josephson and Fong-Beyette, 1987). Examples of such reactions are:

— the helper ignores or minimizes the effects of being sexually abused;
— the helper shows an excessive interest in the sexual details;
— the helper appears very angry, shocked or disgusted by the disclosure.

Therefore, if a woman confirms that she was abused, the helper should respond positively. Examples of helpful ways of responding are as follows:

— congratulate the woman on taking the step of disclosing, and acknowledge the difficulty of doing so;
— remain calm, and do not show any feelings of shock, disgust or distress. These reactions will prompt the woman to retract her disclosure, stop the contact with the helper, or remain silent;
— identify child sexual abuse as a primary cause of some of her difficulties;
— do not minimize the sexual abuse even if it occurred infrequently or on one occasion.

— offer her immediate support in the days following disclosure;

— encourage her to explore her feelings about her disclosure;

— ask her if she wishes to talk about the abuse. Her answer will determine the helper's course of action.

> — if the answer is Yes, encourage her to do so, but in her own time and at her own pace;
>
> — if the answer is No, respect her right to remain silent, but leave her with an invitation to talk about it should she change her mind.

— if she is to be referred on to another helper, she should not be encouraged to talk too much about the details of the abuse as she may not be able to cope with the accompanying emotional reactions. This is best done within the safety of an established therapeutic relationship;

— indicate to the woman that she is believed.

These responses acknowledge a woman's difficulty in disclosing, indicate that she is believed and is being taken seriously, and begin to help her understand that child sexual abuse has significant consequences into adulthood. It is essential that the helper avoids certain unhelpful responses (see Table 7.5) as these are likely to make the woman leave the therapeutic situation.

Table 7.5: **Unhelpful responses to disclosure**

'It's in the past. Do try to forget about it.'

'Did you enjoy it?'

'It only happened a few times, so maybe there isn't really anything to worry about.'

'You were much too little for it to have any effect.'

'That is not as bad as some sexual abuse that I have heard about.'

'Do you really expect me to believe that your father/cousin/brother/uncle, who is obviously such a successful man would do such a thing.'

'What a disgusting thing to have happened to you. It makes me very angry when I hear women describe these sorts of experiences.'

'Please don't go on just now. I find this sort of thing very distressing to hear.'

'But why did you let him carry on when you got older.'

'Why didn't you tell someone?'

'I'm a safe person. You can tell me.'

Once a woman has confirmed that she was sexually abused as a child, she may react in a number of ways:

— she may feel relieved that she can begin to make sense of her difficulties;
— she may be shocked, leading to feelings of numbness and distress;
— she may feel bewildered, frightened and/or confused;
— she may have very mixed feelings about remembering and disclosing her childhood experiences;
— She may be angry or resentful towards the helper for encouraging or enabling her to remember;
— she may be totally calm, misleading the helper into thinking that her childhood experiences held no negative feelings for her;
— she may be pleased/relieved that she managed to tell;
— in the days following disclosure, she may attempt suicide, abuse alcohol or drugs heavily or injure/mutilate herself in some way.

These are obviously strong emotional reactions. If the woman has been helped to recall the sexual abuse for the first time for many years, the helper must be alert to her needs for support, safety and reassurance, and once the confirmation of a history of sexual abuse has been made, it is useful to gather certain general information about the abuse:

— the age she was when the abuse started and stopped;
— the identity of the abuser(s);
— who else now knows that she was abused;
— who she told/tried to tell as a child;
— what were the reactions of those she told;
— whether she knows if any brothers, sisters or other family members were also abused.

Beyond these general facts, a woman should not be pressed at this stage for any specific details unless she indicates that she wants to talk further. At this point it is useful to check on the available support she has when she leaves the helper. It may be important to discuss telling someone else so that she has some support when she leaves. For instance, her partner, a friend or relative or a worker from another agency may be able to provide support before she attends for another session.

Some women may have experienced sexual abuse but still deny the fact. This may be for one or more of the following reasons:

— she has no recollection of being abused;
— she was abused but does not wish or is not ready talk about it;
— she was abused but does not wish to talk to the particular helper about it;

— she was abused but she is too frightened to break the secret because of threats from the abuser, or fears about confidentiality;
— she fears she will not be believed if she discloses;
— she feel she will 'go mad', 'crack up', 'go to pieces' if she breaks
the secret;
— she thinks the helper will feel disgust or revulsion towards her.

In this situation, the helper has no choice but to respect her silence.
However, she may be able to disclose at a later date when she feels ready.
In our experience, women who have been abused, but who cannot yet
acknowledge it, often feel relieved that the possibility of child sexual
abuse has been recognized and put to them by a helper.

Subsequent Disclosures

An initial confirmation of sexual abuse is only the beginning of the work
needed to come to terms with these childhood experiences. Subsequent
disclosures of particular incidents and details of the abuse are also very
important. A survivor should be encouraged to talk about the details of
being abused. The helper's task here is to facilitate disclosure in a non-
threatening and safe way, and to carefully monitor the woman's reactions
during disclosure.

A disclosure can be made in a number of different ways — through
writing and artwork, verbally, in face-to-face contact with the helper or
with childhood objects. Table 7.6 examines these methods, and tables 7.7,
7.8, 7.9 and 7.10 examine the advantages, disadvantages and implications
for the helper of each of these contexts and methods. It is useful to
discuss each of them with a survivor so that she can choose those with
which she feels most comfortable at different points. In addition to making
decisions about the method of disclosure, survivors can be helped by:

— the use of the concept of the 'child within' (Bass and Davis, 1988,
Parks, 1990). A woman should be reassured that her 'child' was
abused and might need to tell a safe and trusted adult. The feelings which emerge during this process are those that belong to the
child, and the little girl needs to be reassured that she is now safe
and was not to blame for what happened;
— being given the choice and control over how, when and how much
to disclose. The helper's task is to monitor whether a woman wishes
to continue and to respect her right to stop when she feels that she
has told enough. If she does not wish to share a particular memory,

Table 7.6: **Methods of disclosure**

Method	Materials/other requirements	Variations
Talking face-to-face	Person(s) the survivor trusts.	Talking on the telephone.
	Safe environment.	Talking in a group.
	Confidentiality.	Talking into a cassette recorder.
Writing	Enough time.	Using a word processor.
	Paper and pens.	Writing poems.
	Undisturbed time to write.	Writing short stories.
	Safe place to keep writing.	Writing life story.
		Sentence completion exercise.
		Courage to Heal writing exercises (Davis, 1990).
		Writing letters.
		Diaries/Journals.
Drawing/artwork	Paper, pens, crayons, paint brushes, felt tip pens.	Use of artwork in design.
	Undisturbed time.	Drawing pictures for children's books.
	Safe place to keep artwork.	Working in other media, such as clay, embroidery.
		Recreating pictures drawn as a child.
		Art therapy.
Use of childhood objects	Toys, teddies, dolls.	Play therapy.
	Other play material.	Regression.
	Survivor's own childhood.	Childhood photographs.
	Memorabilia.	Use of reports of survivor as a child (medical, school, social work).
	Suitable environment for play if necessary.	
	Trusted person(s) to help if necessary.	

her right to silence must be respected, though the reasons for not disclosing should be explored with her. Examples of such reasons and subsequent appropriate action to be taken by the helper are given in Table 7.11.

She should be encouraged, rather than pressured, to disclose and reminded that only by breaking the silence about her memories will they

Table 7.7: **Methods of disclosure: Talking face-to-face**

Advantages	Disadvantages	Implications for helper
Disclosure lessens the power of the secret of the abuse.	It has to be done at a certain time within a time-limit.	The helper can tune in more easily to the survivor.
Survivor may be able to get comfort if she wants it.	She may be too frightened to say much.	The helper can provide the woman with a safe environment in which to complete the disclosure.
She may need to hold onto the helper whilst disclosing.	She may be scared of the helper's reactions.	Comfort, maintenance of physical safety, and grounding may need to be provided.
She can be grounded before, during and after disclosing.	Disclosure can provoke strong unexpected or uncontrolled reactions.	Helper can monitor the survivor's emotional reactions.
Disclosure enables her to use previously avoided words.	It may be difficult to find the right words.	Helper has to maintain careful control over own reactions.
She can disclose with support.		
The information can be clarified.		

lose some of their pain and power. Where she has already disclosed memories, it is useful to remind her of any benefits of that process. She may need to be constantly reassured that it is safe to tell, and that she will be believed.

However, her feelings about making the disclosure may have to be considered first; this allows exploration of any concerns she may have about the helper. Two examples of such pre-disclosure work now follow. In the first, the helper deals with a woman who is disclosing detailed memories for the first time. In the second example, the woman has already experienced the benefits of disclosing details of her abuse.

Example 1
Pre-disclosure work:

> *Jane* I have been having horrible thoughts about what happened to me with my stepfather. I am scared to tell.
>
> *Helper* What are you scared of?
>
> *Jane* It'll get worse, and then I'll never be able to cope again.
>
> *Helper* Usually telling someone about what happened during the abuse is the beginning of being able to get over it.
>
> *Jane* But doesn't it get worse?
>
> *Helper* Yes, women often feel more upset for a while, and may

Table 7.8: **Methods of disclosure: Writing**

Advantages	Disadvantages	Implications for helper
Details of the abuse can be described without having to say the words.	She may still need to say what happened.	The helper may not be able to tune into the survivor in the same way.
It can be done in own time and at own pace.	She may be inhibited by literacy problems.	There may be a lot to read and too much to be done in the session, so feedback is delayed.
It can be kept as a record, compared over time, and reflected on at a later date.	She may fear that her writing will fall into the wrong hands.	Helper can read and react to the writing without the survivor being present.
She can write what she cannot say.	She may not remember what she has written. She may not want to discuss the writing.	Helper may have to read it under the scrutiny of the survivor.
Other people can read it, for example, her partner.	There may be a shock of seeing the abuse described on paper.	Writing can inhibit the building up of the relationship with the helper.
She has control over who reads it.	She can keep it too controlled, ambiguous, or intellectual.	The writing can only be shared with others with the permission of the survivor.
The writing can be destroyed even before anyone reads it.	Writing is usually done without support.	
Writing can be used to help other survivors.	It can be expensive.	Helper may be asked to keep writings in a safe place.
It can be the first signs of creative work and can lead to an improvement in self-esteem.		Helper may have to supply materials.
It can be published.		

need a lot of extra support while they are telling the memories. That could happen for you.

Jane   But why does it get worse?

Helper   I like to think of it like the healing of a wound. Think about having a cut on your hand, and covering it up for weeks and weeks with a bandage. The cut won't heal properly and might go septic. If you take the bandage off, it will hurt a lot, but once it's cleaned it can begin to heal.

Now, imagine that what your stepfather did to you was like a deep wound inside you, and it's been hidden and covered for years. It has been going bad and causing problems. What we'll be doing is gradually peeling the bandages off until the wound is exposed. It will hurt a lot more but then it will have a chance to heal. Does that make sense?

Jane   Yes.

Table 7.9: **Methods of disclosure: Drawing/artwork**

Advantages	Disadvantages	Implications for helper
Memories are those of a child, who may find it easier to draw than to use words.	There may be problems of misinterpretation.	The helper may not be able to interpret the drawings.
It has an immediate direct impact.	Survivor may feel silly, or threatened by the drawings, especially if she does not feel she can draw.	The helper may have to do the drawings, including sexually explicit drawings.
Artwork can be helpful if survivor does not find it easy to explain.	The details of the abuse may be hard to draw.	The helper may have to draw out the interpretation of and emotions associated with the drawings.
It is useful if survivor has hearing or speech problems.	The simplicity of the drawings may limit their usefulness.	
Helper can guide drawing.	Words are still needed to clarify the drawings.	The helper may have to provide appropriate materials.
Drawing may be the only way that the survivor can communicate about the abuse, especially if it occurred when she was very young.		The helper may have to keep drawings in a safe place.
Certain visual images may stand out, giving clues about the abuse to the survivor and helper.		
She can do it at home in her own time.		
Helper can do the drawing.		
It can be a stepping stone to verbal disclosure.		
It can be framed, exhibited, and published.		

Helper   Part of exposing that wound will be telling someone you feel you can trust with the details of the memories and flashbacks — then they will start to lose some of the pain, and the panic you feel will gradually get less until you can cope with the memories. Do you feel you want to tell me about these memories today?

Jane   No, not now, I'm not ready. I might try and write it down for you.

Helper   That is fine. You can let me know when you feel ready. Sometimes it is easier to write it down. If you want me to

Table 7.10: **Methods of disclosure: Use of childhood objects**

Advantages	Disadvantages	Implications for helper
Disclosure can prompt the survivor to remember how it actually was for her as a child.	Disclosure can remind her of her despair as a child.	Helper may not feel comfortable using toys.
It enables her to get in touch with her 'inner child'.	She may feel silly or childish.	It may remind the helper of her own childhood.
Objects can enable her to feel safe.	She may have never learned to use toys.	Helper may have to deal with regression.
She can disclose through play, or with the help of soft toys.	She may not be able to play.	Helper may not feel skilled in disclosure using toys or play.
The objects can help her remember ways she survived as a child.	She may regress.	
	She may have nothing from her own childhood.	
	It may provoke emotional reactions.	

see what you've written, I'll be happy to read it, but if you decide you don't want me to read it, that's all right too. It's up to you.

In this example, the woman is given choices about disclosing, and the helper respects her right not to disclose on this occasion. Explanations about the benefits of disclosing and the suggestion about writing the memories down whilst leaving her with choices are also given. The helper is realistic about Jane's fears that she may feel worse before she feels better, but through the use of the wound analogy helps her to understand the process of coming to terms with being abused.

Example 2
Pre-disclosure work:

Anne   I have been thinking about something that happened with my father.

Helper   Do you want to talk about it?

Anne   If I tell you, you won't believe me, because it's so horrible.

Helper   I know that these memories are horrible for you, but that doesn't mean they didn't happen.

Anne   But I feel so horrible about what happened.

Helper   I get the feeling that you would like to tell, but are worried about whether I will believe you and how you'll feel afterwards.

Anne	I know in the past it has helped to tell you, but this incident is much worse.
Helper	How has it helped?
Anne	Well, remember last time, I stopped being bothered by those memories, and although I was upset I got much better. It was a relief to find out that someone believed me.
Helper	Do you think the same will happen this time?
Anne	Probably. Maybe I should tell you; perhaps I won't have to think about it any more.
Helper	Do you want to tell me today?
Anne	Yes, I think so.
Helper	How would you like to tell me? Sometimes you like to write it, and sometimes you just tell me.
Anne	I think I could manage to tell you, but I might get upset.
Helper	It is all right to get upset. The memories are quite upsetting, and it is quite understandable to get upset.

In this example, the helper gradually prepares the ground for a new disclosure. Anne is given choices about whether she wants to tell and how, and is reminded of the benefits of disclosing previous memories before being reassured that being upset is normal and acceptable.

There are several situations in which disclosure about a particular incident of abuse becomes essential:

— if the woman is having flashbacks or nightmares about a particular incident which are causing considerable distress;
— when she has become so anxious about making the disclosure that she is unable to cope with her normal life;
— when certain memories continually intrude into her current relationships.

The helper should encourage her to disclose in these situations. Flashbacks, nightmares and related perceptual disturbances will decrease in frequency and intensity once all the important details of the incident have been revealed and discussed. Avoidance of disclosure intensifies the emotional reactions and is therefore usually much worse than revealing the details of the incident. The helper should reassure the woman that the worst happened at the time of the incident, nothing worse can happen now and that it is safe for her to tell.

Once a woman had decided to tell the helper, it is useful to remind her again of the analogy that everyone has a 'child within' and it is her 'child' who needs to be encouraged to tell her about her bad experiences,

Table 7.11: **Difficulties with disclosure and action of the helper**

Reasons for not disclosing a particular memory	Helper action
The memory is too horrific or upsetting.	The helper can give reassurance that nothing can happen to her now by telling. The worst happened at the time of the abuse.
She is not sure the helper will believe her.	The helper can give reassurance that she does believe her.
She does not want to believe it herself, and telling will make it real.	The helper can remind her that the memory is already real to her. Not wanting to believe it does not mean it did not happen.
She is not sure it really happened.	The helper can comment that the main issue is that this memory/ thought is bothering her and that she needs to discuss it in order to decide whether it did happen.
She is scared of her own reactions later such as a suicide attempt, self-mutilation, rage.	The helper can offer more support perhaps, if appropriate, arranging and admitting survivor to a psychiatric unit, or other place of safety.
She is scared that the abuser's threats will come to pass (even if he is dead), if she tells.	The helper can assure her of confidentiality. The survivor is only telling the helper. If the abuser is dead, remind her that he can do nothing further to harm her.
Her current life is so full of problems that she does not wish to add to her difficulties.	This may be realistic, but the memories are likely to cause more problems as long as they remain undisclosed.
She has some important event in her life that she does not wish to upset such as exams, marriage, or the start of a new job.	This is realistic, and she should not be pressurized to disclose. It can be useful to set a time after the 'event' to do the disclosing.
She has no support at home, and feels unable to cope with being by herself after she has disclosed.	The helper can offer more support. An admission to hospital or the support of other community agencies can be arranged.
She wants to protect her helper from her memories.	The helper can remind her that these memories need to be disclosed if she is to get over them, and that the helper's reactions to her disclosures are the helper's responsibility.
She feels pressurized to tell.	The helper can remind her she has choice and will not be forced to tell.
She fears that if she tells about a particular memory, she will remember more unpleasant incidents.	The helper can encourage her to disclose and can reassure her that any other memories will be dealt with as they appear.
She feels ashamed or guilty about the memory and fears the helper will pass judgment on her.	The helper can reassure her that these are normal feelings and that the abuser was responsible for creating the situation in which these feelings arose.
She knows what the next disclosure will be, but the implications of the memory are too frightening to consider.	The helper can give reassurance that she/he will continue to work through the issues associated with the abuse with her.

knowing that she will be believed. Helping the adult part of her stay in touch with her current life situation and in control of it can be achieved in a number of ways:

— she can be asked to hold firmly onto the arms of her chair, or to some other piece of furniture near her chair;
— the helper might hold the woman's hand whilst she makes her disclosure;
— in a group situation, two group members (perhaps one of the facilitators and one other survivor) might hold on to her, one at each side;
— at the end of the disclosure, she could be asked where she is now, how old she is and encouraged to look around the room to establish that she is still the adult.

As we have already seen, disclosure can be made in a number of different ways (see Table 7.6). If the woman has decided to disclose verbally, the helper should also be aware of her non-verbal communication. It is often possible to facilitate the telling through the use of her body language.

Pushing for Memories

Disclosure of sexual abuse rarely comes easily to a survivor, and she will usually require some help not only to begin the process, but also to complete the telling of a particular memory. It may not be necessary for her to disclose every part of the memory, but the significant features should be drawn out where possible. It is important to recognize that the abuse is only part of the memory. It takes place in a context, consisting of a place and the overall circumstances of the child's life at the time. The incident does not stop with the last moment of the abuse; the survivor's feelings afterwards are an integral part of the incident.

The helper can therefore facilitate the disclosure by:

— asking specific questions about the context in which the abuse took place;
— initiating discussion about the circumstances of the survivor's life at the time;
— enabling the survivor to gain a picture of herself as a child through the study of photographs or mementos of her childhood;
— asking specific questions about the abuse;

— asking the survivor to focus on her emotional and physical reactions to her recent thoughts about the memory, the imminent
disclosure she feels is about to come and her concerns about it.

For many disclosures, using the context of the abuse is a more bearable
lead-in to the more difficult work around the abuse and the implications
of the disclosure. It is also important to recognize that the abuse is only
part of the overall situation that the survivor was in as a child, and that
the implications of a disclosure have to be considered within that context.

Reliving

During disclosure, survivors sometimes re-experience the incident of abuse
during the telling process. This can be alarming for both survivor and
helper when it happens for the first time. This should be distinguished
from regression, where the survivor behaves as if she is the age she was
at the time of the abusive incident (see later section). Re-living is common amongst survivors of trauma generally and can occur during sleep.

Obviously reliving is not the same as experiencing the abuse for the
first time. The survivor is now an adult, disclosing to someone she trusts,
who will take her through the disclosure. She is in a safe place and the
abuser is not present. Also the length of time taken to disclose is usually
less than the original incident and its aftermath. For the survivor, however, it may feel as though she is back in the past.

Example: Irene was trying to disclose about an incident when her uncle
attempted to rape her. It was obvious to the helper that she
was experiencing discomfort in the genital area and was
writhing about on the chair as if she was being hurt in that
part of her body. The helper was able to feed this back to
Irene, thus enabling her to begin disclosing.

This example shows how the survivor's re-experiencing of the abuse
can be used to facilitate the start of her disclosure. The fact that the
helper indicates her/his awareness of the woman's non-verbal behaviour
can enable the survivor to begin to describe what happened.

During some disclosures, however, this would not be enough to facilitate disclosure. In these cases, the re-living begins after the survivor
has begun to disclose, and she gets so involved in the reliving that she
momentarily loses a sense of where she is. Survivors report that it is useful here if the helper can keep them grounded by talking to them in a
reassuring way about:

— where they are now (for example, the helper's office, the survivor's home);
— who the helper is;
— that she is remembering something that happened a long time ago;
— that she is safe now;
— that she will feel better once she has let the helper know what she is re-experiencing.

The survivor is likely to need some help in actually telling the helper what happened to her. If the survivor is unable to speak, either because of what she is re-experiencing or because of her strong emotional reactions, such as distress and/or fear, the helper will need to establish a means of communicating with her. Useful ways are:

— asking closed questions and asking her to nod or shake her head;
— where acceptable, holding the survivor's hand and asking her to grip more tightly if the answer to a question is 'Yes';
— get the survivor to slightly raise her hand or finger if the answer to a question is 'Yes'.

Beyond this, it is likely that the helper will have to ask fairly explicit questions about the nature of the incident she is trying to disclose. This may mean asking very closed questions so that the survivor can respond 'Yes' or 'No'. Helpers sometimes fear they are leading the survivor, but our experience has shown that the survivor in these circumstances will answer 'No' if the helper asks about some form of abuse that did not take place. Such a method would not be appropriate if the disclosure was being used to gather evidence for legal proceedings, but this is rarely the case with adults.

For the survivor who can talk, the following gives an example of such a disclosure, with the helper making the link between her present physical experiences and the abuse:

Example:

Anne   I keep feeling shooting pains in my legs. I haven't fallen or anything. They just hurt, especially round my thighs.

Helper   Does this pain remind you of any particular time when you were a child?

Anne   (Look of surprise) Well, yes I used to get these pains in my legs especially after my father had finished with me.

Helper   What caused the pains?

> *Anne*   He was a big man and I was quite a small child. He used to
> sprawl across my legs. It was heavy, like a dead weight, and
> I think my legs got numb.

This disclosure continued with Anne re-experiencing a previously forgotten incident of abuse. It involved oral sex and forced intercourse, and ended with her father, who was drunk, falling asleep across the lower part of her body. She was too small to move him and her legs become numb and then very sore. During the disclosure, she began to cough and splutter but was able to tell that helper that 'he' (meaning the father) had shoved something horrible into her mouth. She was clearly reliving the oral sex. She confirmed this afterwards. Following disclosure she was very distressed and frightened but the pains in her legs subsequently stopped.

Whenever a survivor relives an incident of abuse, it is important to check that she is in contact with the here-and-now before she leaves. The helper can achieve this by using any of the following methods:

— ask the survivor to say where she is now (the place, town etc);
— ask her to say her name, age and address now (this is particularly useful if she no longer has her childhood surname);
— ask her to say with whom she lives now;
— ask her to name the month and year now;
— ask her to look around the room and look closely at the things she sees there (this is especially useful if she is in her own home);
— ask her to say the helper's name;
— ask her to describe what she did before coming to see the helper;
— ask her to explain what has happened during the session, that she has been remembering something from her childhood and that she is an adult;
— ask her what she is planning to do when she leaves the session.

Thus, it should be possible to reorientate the survivor and check that she is no longer reliving any aspect of her childhood.

After the first 'reliving' disclosure, the helper and survivor should together plan for the possibility that this may occur again. It is useful to work out ways of maintaining contact during future disclosures, and anything else that the survivor feels may be helpful. One of the key issues may be the planning of sessions that are long enough to allow the reliving to occur together with reorientation and discussion of the implications of the disclosure. We have found that survivors who do relive the memories of the abuse become increasingly efficient at using this method.

Disclosure Through Flashbacks

We have discussed 'reliving' disclosures and that these may be triggered by flashbacks of the abuse. If the survivor feels ready to disclose, her flashbacks can be used to facilitate the remembering process. Flashbacks usually lose their power and intensity once the content has been disclosed. In this situation, the survivor should be encouraged to describe the content of her flashback giving as many details as she feels able to. Even if she begins this description calmly, she may begin to re-experience the feelings. Where this occurs, all the methods described in the reliving section should be used.

Sometimes, however, the emotional reactions contained in the flashback are so intense that the survivor may be unable to speak. In this case, the helper should keep talking to the survivor, calmly grounding her in the reality of her adult life until the emotions subside. At this point, encouraging her to talk about the content of the flashback is important, although this may take some time to complete.

When the same flashback keeps recurring, it is likely that some aspect of the particular incident of abuse has not been disclosed. The undisclosed material may represent a dimension of the memory, the sensory, emotional, or body memory dimensions, or additional information about the circumstances or nature of the abuse. In this case, the helper should assist the survivor to look more closely at the recall of this incident of abuse to assess the possible missing aspects.

Disclosure Through the 'Child Within'

The concept of the 'child within' is a useful aid to disclosure for some survivors. The idea is that within each of us is a 'child', who represents the child that we were in terms of spontaneous reactions, feelings, memories and behaviour. This 'child' remembers events from that time, with all their accompanying feelings.

Some survivors like this concept and can work with it in order to facilitate disclosure. It is possible to learn to tune into the inner child and listen to what she has to say. By becoming aware of the child within herself, the survivor can listen to and report back on what the 'child' is beginning to tell her. She is likely to talk about the 'child' in the third person for example, 'she is telling me that . . .', 'she is doing . . .', 'she is frightened because. . . .'.

In this situation, the survivor remains in touch with the reality of her adult world, and may act as a parent or protector of the young girl she once was. The helper's task is to encourage the adult part of the woman to act as a spokesperson for the 'child'. The woman therefore listens to the 'child' and reports the disclosures to the helper.

Once the disclosure is complete, the survivor may need some help in making sense of the information and to understand the implications of the disclosure. She may also be quite shocked or distressed. It is useful to help the survivor make her 'inner child' feel safe. She should be asked what might make the 'child' feel safe. This may involve:

— taking her to a safe place (a real place where the survivor feels safe or one that she uses her imagination to create);
— checking that the 'child' has all she needs to feel safe and warm (a safe place that the abuser cannot come to, a warm and welcoming place/room/house with all the necessary equipment to make a child feel comfortable);
— giving the 'child' a hug;
— getting another adult to hug the 'child'.

After the disclosure and the discussion of its implications, the helper should once again check that the survivor feels safe to leave, and check that she is re-orientated to the here-and-now using the methods described in the section on reliving.

Example: Sue was sexually abused by her stepfather, and had a clear image of herself as a child of eight. She was asked to watch the little girl, and ask her a number of questions about the events in the little girl's life. She told her helper that the little girl was frightened because her stepfather had just come home. The little girl then told Sue what had taken place the previous day. This incident of sexual abuse was one that she had not previously recalled. Once the disclosure was over, she was encouraged to make the little girl feel safe, and in her imagination, Sue took the little girl to a room which no-one could enter and played with her. The helper then had to help Sue to deal with her feelings about this incident of abuse, before checking that she felt safe to leave.

Regression

During disclosure, some survivors regress to the age they were when the particular incident of abuse took place. In this case, the woman's behaviour, language, feelings, thinking, comprehension and gestures will change to that of a child. It is as if the 'child within' the woman is doing the disclosing. The woman will therefore talk as if she is a child, often in the present tense, suggesting that she is not aware that the abuse happened long ago. It is important for the helper to be aware of these changes and to modify her/his behaviour accordingly.

The reasons for the occurrence of regression are by no means clear although they may be related to:

— the extent of the memory gaps and dissociation about the abuse;
— the terror engendered by the abuse;
— the age at which the abuse started;
— prolonged, violent or sadistic abuse (Gil, 1988).

A good description of regression is contained in *When You're Ready* (Evert and Bijkerk, 1987). The survivor behaves as if she has become a child again, and may show behaviour that is typical of a sexually abused child, for example:

— she may withdraw and be uncommunicative;
— she may expect the helper to hurt or abuse her;
— she may try to run away (to places where she hid as a child);
— she may roam the streets, unaware of potential dangers such as roads and traffic;
— she may have temper tantrums, with breath-holding, head-banging and other self-injury;
— she may start cutting herself;
— she may become verbally or physically aggressive;
— she may not have words to describe the abuse, and may be able to disclose only through play or drawings.

It is essential that regression should occur in a safe place, preferably with comfortable furniture and a supply of cushions. The helper should try to prevent self-injury, if necessary by holding the woman. Occasionally, the 'child' may be more actively involved in hurting herself, and come prepared with tablets or a sharp object (for example, broken glass, razor blade or knife) for this purpose. The helper may have to remove these from the survivor.

The start of the regression can be detected in a number of ways:

— the woman's tone and pitch of voice changes;
— her breathing quickens and she shows signs of extreme fear;

— she begins to use simple sentences and vocabulary consistent with that of a child;

— she appears to become distant and seems to be unable to maintain her usual eye contact with the helper;

— her behaviour suddenly changes to that of a frightened/distressed/ hurt child.

The helper's presence may be a trigger for the woman to regress, or it may result from direct questions about any memories/flashbacks, from the woman's sudden awareness of pain in her body (Evert and Bijkerk, 1987) or from heightened emotional reactions. During disclosure, the helper should facilitate the disclosure using methods and language appropriate to work with an abused child. These might include drawings, use of books, play or anatomically correct dolls. The language of the helper will also have to be modified to suit the age of the child that the woman has regressed to.

Example: The initial part of this disclosure is as the adult, then the woman regresses before returning to being an adult.

Suzanne	I can remember my father's face — leering — the look in his face.
Helper	What did this look say to you?
Suzanne	Lust. I don't know why this is so bad. He was only touching my breasts — no, I didn't have any then.
Helper	Do you want to talk about it?
Suzanne	I can see it so clearly, even the shade over the light. It was pink. The strange thing is that I keep thinking that Mummy is in the next room.
Helper	How is that strange?
Suzanne	I never called her Mummy, at least I don't remember ever doing so.
Helper	What did you call her?
Suzanne	Mum, mother, but never Mummy.
Helper	I wonder if you called her Mummy when you were very little.
Suzanne	I don't know. I can't remember that far back.
Helper	Sometimes very small children call their mothers Mummy, but when they start school, they start to call her Mum.
Suzanne	(Head down, holding and wringing hands. Fighting tears) *Regression* (voice rises in pitch)

Mummy's in the next room. She's feeding the new baby. She wouldn't do anything anyway. She had just bought the baby at the hospital. We wanted a boy, but she said boys were too expensive. We didn't want another girl. Daddies make little girls sore (Tears).

Helper	So you didn't want a baby sister?
Suzanne	No, Daddies hurt little girls.
Helper	Does Daddy hurt you?
Suzanne	(Nod) (tears)
Helper	Where does he hurt you? (Too confusing a question as she had regressed to being a pre-school child).
Suzanne	(Shake of the head)
Helper	Can you point to where he hurts you?
Suzanne	(Gesture towards the top of her legs and genital area)
Helper	So Daddy hurts you in places that he shouldn't touch little girls?
Suzanne	(Nod) (Sobbing) But where was Mummy . . . she didn't come . . . I cried . . . she was too busy with the baby.
Helper	What was the baby's name?
Suzanne	Margaret (more sobbing) Poor little girl . . .

She changed her position in the chair and obviously reverted to being an adult. Suzanne then realized that the sexual abuse had already started when she was four and a half — the age she was when her youngest sister, Margaret, was born. Previously she had thought that it had started at the age of seven.

It is noticeable that in this example, the woman's language becomes simpler, child-like and in the present tense during the regression phase. The helper's language has to match the survivor's or lack of understanding results.

Before leaving the helper, it is vital that the survivor is re-orientated to her adult life in the ways we have described above in the section dealing with re-living. The survivor is likely to feel exhausted, and possibly sore, if she has re-lived the disclosure, or if she is experiencing body memories. Encouraging her to take care of herself is therefore worthwhile, and in so doing, she can begin to look after her 'child within'. There are many ways of doing this. The following examples come from survivors themselves:

— have a bath and go to bed for a while;
— curl up in bed/on a settee with a teddy-bear;
— do adult activities in order to stay grounded;
— discuss the session with her partner as soon as possible;
— go to sleep;
— treat the pain in her body with analgesics, or using support bandages for pain in her arms or legs;
— have a warm drink, or something nice to eat.

Example: Ruth was violently sexually abused by her father. She started to experience pain in her ribs, and on questioning from the helper, regressed to being herself when she was six. The pain intensified, and she became very fearful that the helper would hit her. She started to bang her head against the chair and had to be restrained. Gradually, in very simple language, with drawings and her doll, she was able to disclose a particularly brutal incident of abuse involving being beaten around her rib-cage before being raped by her father. Once the disclosure was over, she was noticeably calmer, was physically comforted by the helper and told she was now safe. She and the helper then looked at some children's books, before being asked to focus on furniture, ornaments and pictures in the room. Gradually she returned to her adult state, and discussed the disclosure. She was by then exhausted.

When a woman has experienced severe painful sexual and/or physical abuse that has induced a state of terror, she may regress to such an extent that the methods she used to cope as a child are in evidence during the disclosure. For example, singing songs to herself, reciting poems or nursery rhymes, over-breathing or breath-holding, trying to run out of the room or becoming detached from what is going on around her may have been used to block out the worst of the abuse. These may re-emerge during the disclosure. She is, after all, recalling an incident that consisted not only of the abuse but also the behaviour she used to cope with it.

Post-disclosure Work

A disclosure of abuse does not end with the remembering process. The implications of the significance of the disclosure should be explored.

Sometimes the implications can have a devastating effect on the survivor, especially if the disclosure shatters her beliefs about herself, or about other family members, for example, learning of her mother's knowledge of the abuse.

Example: Lisa thought she knew what had happened to her as a child. She knew she had been abused by her elder brother who made her believe that she was protecting her twin sister by taking the abuse. She had built her picture of herself around the 'fact' that she had saved her sister. But when she remembered an incident in which she found him abusing her sister, her belief in her own self-worth disappeared. She felt very guilty and began to be very suicidal.

A survivor's reactions after a disclosure should be explored, to assess both her psychological state and the methods used to facilitate the disclosure. Common responses are relief, anger/rage, extreme distress and panic, fear, guilt, physical pain, and sometimes a desire to retract the disclosure because the associated emotions are so strong. Some of these reactions are the result of her childhood fears of the abuser, and his threats to maintain her silence. For example, she may suddenly fear retribution from the abuser for breaking the secret, especially if he threatened to hurt her physically if she ever told anyone.

For a survivor who was subjected to severe physical and/or sadistic abuse as well as sexual abuse, any disclosure may induce intense terror and continuing fears that the helper will not be able to believe her. These fears may prevent her from disclosing further until she is again reassured that she is believed. The demands on the helper are therefore high, and frequent contact, reassurance and careful management of the disclosure are essential.

It is essential, therefore, that the helper is very flexible about offering her extra support and time during periods of continuous disclosure. It may be necessary or appropriate to enlist support for her from other community or health agencies, such as rape crisis group, community psychiatric team, health visitors, or voluntary counsellors or if she wishes, the support of friends or members of her family. If any members of her family are involved in supporting her, they may need support themselves. Not all disclosures require this level of support, but it must be recognized that even a small disclosure can produce a very significant reaction in the woman.

The Survivor with No Memories

Some survivors have great difficulty in recalling any incident of abuse. However, they may believe or know that they were sexually abused. It is commonly assumed that if memories return they do so in visual form. This need not be the case. We have already discussed the different forms that memories can take — sensory, physical/body or emotional — and the survivor may be remembering aspects of the abuse, but not visually. The memories may be hidden from the survivor's view partly because she is still searching for visual clues. Williams (1991) discusses this in more detail and stresses the importance of looking for clues in the survivor's adult life that she may have previously ignored as memories. For example, a survivor may have particular sexual difficulties, such as being unable to tolerate certain aspects of touching by her partner in her genital area. This could either be an effect of the abuse or an indication of a memory of the abuse.

A way of describing this process is to imagine throwing a large boulder into the middle of a muddy pond. The boulder disappears without a trace, but sets up ripples on the surface that are an indication of the size and shape of the boulder. The boulder represents the abuse, and the ripples are not the effects of the abuse, but represent the features of the abuse. Common examples are:

— specific problems in sexual situations;
— significant emotional reactions to ordinary, everyday events, such as music being played, the woman's partner leaning over her, being in bed, the bedroom door being opened from the outside by someone, particularly her partner;
— significant emotional reactions to smells, the feel of fabrics, certain colours, the look or taste of certain foods;
— behaving in certain ways that do not seem to relate to the situation that she is in, such as jumping out of bed suddenly when her partner gets into bed with her;
— physical or body memories, body position, emotional or non-visual sensory, memories;
— the content of perceptual disturbances, nightmares and bad dreams.

The key feature when looking for hidden memories is to examine the survivor's emotional reactions that seem out of proportion to the situation and to hypothesize that the strength of the reaction may be an indication of some aspect of the abuse. For the survivor who is desperately searching for some clues to the nature of the abuse that she suffered, it can be a relief to discover that there may be some indicators. Once a survivor begins the search for such clues, some of the memory blocks may be released, giving her more direct access to the memories.

Example: Frances is certain she was abused by her father at a very young age (two or three), but she has no memories of the abuse. She is suffering intense emotional pain and has very frequent and distressing nightmares. In her search for memories, she discovers that she does not like her partner wandering around the house naked, especially if he leans over her when he is naked or partially dressed. She has an intense emotional freezing at the thought of oral sex, and starts screaming if her partner makes sexual advances when she is half-asleep. She feels that her recovery would have been quicker if she had not had to go to bed at all as lying in bed makes her very anxious. She hypothesized that these reactions were an indication of what her father might have done to her, and the nightmares started to diminish in intensity and frequency, and she began to feel generally better. She believed, therefore, that these and other features were memories.

The effects of traumatic experiences such as sexual abuse often continue to reverberate within the survivor's life, even in the absence of clear memories. These echoes, and the survivor's reactions to them, can be a useful source of information about the nature of the abuse and the hidden effects that may have previously gone unnoticed. A further useful source of hidden memories can be any writing done — especially poetry by the survivor. In Appendix 2 a survivor's account of her understanding of hidden memories is published, and is recommended as a demonstration of this process.

Both helper and survivor have to be aware that strong emotional reactions, which may seem out of all proportion to the situation and have no explanation in the present, are not always hidden memories of the abuse, but may represent reactions from other unresolved issues. However, the survivor, who has no visual memories, is often greatly relieved to find that there may be other sources of memory available to her.

This chapter has reviewed the methods for facilitating disclosure together with problems which can arise during periods of disclosure. The helper may need to enlist support for her or himself during periods of disclosure, particularly if the woman is reacting in a highly emotional way to the memories. Ultimately, however, the key to coming to terms with the abuse is in breaking the secrets of childhood. Through disclosure, memories lose their power and pain. A woman can then be enabled to begin to shift the burden of responsibility from herself to the abuser. She has to take the risk of disclosing and begin to understand that the pain of her childhood can be significantly reduced by sharing her secrets with adults whom she trusts.

Chapter 8

Themes in Therapeutic Work

Chapter 5 examined the overall guidelines and aims for therapeutic work with survivors. Beyond these general guidelines, there are a number of specific and recurrent themes which arise in the work. These include:

— the 'child within';
— being believed;
— the nature of the abuse;
— responsibility for the abuse;
— her family of origin;
— flashbacks and memories;
— regression;
— trust;
— loss;
— getting in touch with feelings;
— anger;
— confrontation;
— forgiveness;
— living in the present: from victim to survivor.

The Child Within

We have already discussed the usefulness of the concept of the 'child within' or the 'inner child' in Chapter 1. In this section we will examine the ways in which this idea can be used in therapeutic work with a survivor. The concept has already been described in relation to disclosure work in Chapter 7. Many survivors have a very strong sense of their inner child. However, for others, thinking about the inner child produces a great deal of anxiety. The survivor may:

— have covered up her childhood vulnerability in order to survive;
— fear that getting in touch with herself as a child may increase her vulnerability and therefore cause her to have additional problems;
— hate herself for having been small, powerless and vulnerable;
— dislike herself for needing affection or comfort as a child, which in her mind contributed to the occurrence of the abuse;
— have no memories of herself as a child;
— fear facing the pain, terror and other feelings of herself as a child;
— blame, or feel ashamed of herself as a child for causing, not stopping or getting bribes for the abuse.

Before helping a survivor to get in touch with her inner child, these fears should be addressed, in addition to looking at positive reasons for doing this work. There are a number of reasons for helping a survivor get in touch with her inner child:

— it can enable the survivor to remember not only the abuse but the feelings she had, the patterns of behaviour that existed in her family and her reactions to them;
— it can enable her to explore the ways she coped with her childhood experiences;
— it can help the survivor remember how small she was, and the power which adults had over her;
— when the survivor is behaving in a puzzling or childlike way, it can be useful, where appropriate, to see that behaviour as belonging to the inner child;
— it can give the survivor permission to express feelings she had as a child;
— it can help the survivor relate to her own children;
— it can help her look more rationally at the issues of guilt and responsibility;
— it can lead to an awareness of the losses she experienced as a child and could therefore provoke an understandable but distressing grief reaction;
— it can help the survivor identify when situations in her adult life are triggering the feelings, behaviour, thoughts and beliefs that she showed as a child;
— if she can care for and like her inner child, it can be the beginning of the survivor caring for, valuing and liking herself;
— it can free spontaneity and creativity.

For many survivors, the suggestion that there is a hurt, lonely, frightened child inside that is causing her to behave in ways that she would have done to survive the abuse, comes as a great relief. It is the helper's task to help the survivor find ways of communicating with the inner child before going on to do more detailed work with her.

Ways of Getting in Touch with the Inner Child

There are many ways of contacting the inner child, and once the general concept has been explained to a survivor, it is important that the helper discusses any fears and concerns that the survivor may have about being in touch with the 'child'. It does not follow that getting in touch with the 'child within' will lead to the survivor regressing and behaving like a child again. This should be explained by the helper. For some survivors, however, regression is a possibility, and it is better if the helper can be honest about this. As we have seen in Chapter 7, regression is more likely if the abuse has been severe, violent and sadistic and has started early in childhood.

The following represent some ways of helping the survivor to get in touch with her inner child:

— getting the survivor to think of herself as a child, perhaps with the help of photographs. She should be encouraged to get as clear an image as possible and identify the age of the child in her image;
— identifying any childhood pet names or nicknames that she could use to communicate with the inner child. The 'child' should not be addressed in a derogatory way (for example, the brat), or with a name that was used only by the abuser;
— identifying times and situations when the survivor feels that she is reacting to situations in ways that she learnt as a child. In this way the survivor begins to become aware of the 'child's' reactions and feelings and her intrusion into the adult's life.

Example: Jessie was abused by her father between the ages of 8 and 10. As an adult, she often found herself sobbing quietly to herself after sexual intercourse with her boyfriend. All she could think of was that no-one would hear her, and that she was too scared to move. This was proving to be disruptive to their relationship. Her helper explained that it was as if her inner child was reliving aspects of the abuse, and that she was probably behaving like a small child. Jessie immediately spoke of feeling as though she was 9-years-old. In this way she was able to identify her inner child through feelings she was already experiencing.

— writing a letter to her inner child, introducing herself and explaining that she, the adult, wants to help her, the 'child', with what was happening to her. Sometimes, a survivor may find this difficult as she has never thought that she was worthy of being taken care of as a child, and may have very negative feelings towards the 'child', perhaps blaming her for getting herself abused;

— drawing pictures relating to her childhood home, the abuser her family, and herself as a child;

— choosing a photograph of herself as a child and beginning to talk to the child in the photograph. Initially, any dialogue should begin with introductions and safe topics, rather than immediately discussing issues relating to the abuse;

— using toys, especially soft toys to think of herself as a child;

— disclosing, with the helper asking what the 'child' feels and remembers;

— writing nursery rhymes, poems or stories for the 'child'.

The main aim here is to enable the survivor to be aware of the inner child before going on to begin communication with her. The next step is to examine ways of communicating with her. Survivors use various techniques but are often frightened to allocate time to the task when they are on their own because of an understandable fear of the emergence of very strong and painful feelings. If the survivor has a supportive partner, friend or other family member, it may be possible for her to enlist their support whilst she tries to communicate with her inner child.

The following are ways that two-way communication can be encouraged:

— writing letters to the 'child', and getting the 'child' to write back. In this situation, the survivor might be asked to imagine herself as a child, and write a letter to an adult who wanted to help her. Alternatively, the letter could be addressed to the adult survivor;

— writing a dialogue between herself as an adult, and the inner child, with the adult gently asking questions about the 'child', and trying to help her talk to the adult. This can be modelled by the helper first so that the survivor can initially experience this with support;

— encouraging a dialogue between the helper, the survivor and her inner child during a session with the helper. The helper encourages the survivor to report back on what the 'child' is saying, thinking and feeling. Questions such as 'What is 'she' saying?', 'What does the child (using her name if possible) think or feel about what we are discussing?' may be useful;

— encouraging the 'child' to play, disclose or just 'be' with the survivor whilst the survivor plays with toys and childhood objects;
— talking to the 'child' as if she was a real child, using appropriate language and concepts;
— encouraging the survivor to go to places that she thinks she would have enjoyed going to as a child, and talking to her 'child' whilst she is there. Any dialogue should be quite direct. For example, a survivor might say to the 'child': 'We are going to the park today because I know you weren't allowed to go there as a child, and I know you have always wanted to go.' The dialogue could be developed as though the survivor was talking to a real child.

Looking After the Inner Child

Throughout the process of working with the inner child, the helper should encourage the survivor to look after the 'child'. As we have already discussed in Chapter 7, this is particularly important following disclosure. It is the 'child's' memories that are being disclosed, and the 'child' will need reassurance, caring and practical help, such as feeling safe following the telling of painful memories.

The following general principles are useful in helping the survivor look after her 'child':

— believing the 'child' her feelings, understanding and her memories;
— never blaming her, the 'child', for any aspect of, or behaviour associated with the abuse;
— honouring the ways she, the 'child', survived the childhood experiences;
— taking care of herself, the adult, in ways that she would have liked to have been taken care of as a child, such as getting a cuddle from a partner/friend, having a hot drink before she goes to sleep, having a warm bath, eating food that she likes, going to sleep hugging a teddy-bear;
— involving herself, the adult, in activities that she would have enjoyed as a child, such as play, drawing, clay work, painting, embroidery, writing, reading children's books, playing with children, and physical activities (for example, swimming, sports.)
— telling the 'child' that she is now safe and that she no longer lives with the abuser, but with the adult survivor. This can present problems if the survivor does still live with the abuser, or is in an abusive relationship. The 'child' should also be informed of any-

one else living with the survivor (partner, children, friend) and if and where the survivor works;

— telling the 'child' about the helper so that the therapeutic situation does not produce additional feelings of fear.

The Use of the Inner Child in Therapeutic Work

Once a survivor has discovered her inner child, the therapeutic possibilities are numerous. They will vary from survivor to survivor, but many revolve around understanding how the survivor's childhood experiences, beliefs, emotional reactions and behaviour are still in evidence in her adult life. In addition, it allows the 'child' to begin to recover from the traumatic experiences and regain her spontaneity, appreciation of the world, and learn new skills which she may not have been able to do as a child, such as literacy skills. The main therapeutic uses are:

— enabling the survivor to recall in disclosure work the details of the abuse through the eyes and understanding of a child;

— allowing both the helper and the survivor herself to be able to give the 'child' accurate information about the abuser, his intentions and the criminal nature of his behaviour. This may be the first time the survivor has been in a position to challenge her own ideas about the abuse, and as such it is an important step in resolving some of her feelings about her childhood experiences;

— working around the issues of guilt and responsibility, where the survivor may blame herself, but may have had much more difficulty in blaming the 'child'. It allows the helper to make comparisons between other children and the inner child, encouraging the survivor to see her inner child as the same as other children and therefore not responsible for the abuse;

— understanding how she reacted, felt, thought and behaved during childhood, and looking for evidence of these reactions in the survivor herself. This can lead to learning new ways of responding, particularly in relationships that can allow the adult survivor to feel better and to have more satisfying relationships with other people. For a detailed account of the childhood reactions in sexual situations, we would recommend *The Sexual Healing Journey* by Wendy Maltz (1991);

— encouraging play, having fun, doing activities that she was unable to do as a child or teenager whilst working on reclaiming the losses of her childhood;

— overcoming problems the survivor may have with her own children. Enabling the survivor to be in touch with her inner child will often free the survivor to develop new ways of relating to children, and may also help her to play with and enjoy her own children;

— improving her self-esteem. As the origins of poor levels of self-esteem usually lie with the childhood abuse and its effects, enabling the survivor to take care of, like and value her inner child may be the first time that anyone has done that for the child part of her. In addition, it can help the survivor change some of the negative messages about herself that she received either directly or implicitly when she was a child;

— resolving issues of anger. Allowing the inner child to express her anger can be important. Writing a letter (that is never sent) to the abuser on behalf of the 'child', or imagining herself as a child and writing her angry feelings down can shed important light on her childhood feelings. A child might be angry with the abuser, but it might be about something that is discounted by an adult.

Example: Vicky was sexually abused by her uncle between the ages of six and ten. He used to make her feel in his trouser pockets for sweets, but sometimes there were no sweets there, and he would force her to rub his penis through his trousers. When she was a child she often felt angry because there were sometimes no sweets. The reality of what her uncle was doing escaped her. As an adult, she discovered this through working with her inner child.

The helper's attitude towards the survivor's inner child and to children and childhood generally is very important in modelling useful and encouraging attitudes in the survivor. Other suggestions for working with the inner child are contained within *The Courage to Heal* (Bass and Davis, 1988), *The Courage to Heal Workbook* (Davis, 1990), and *Rescuing the Inner Child* (Parks, 1990).

Being Believed

The issue of being believed is central to all work with survivors. It is particularly important at the beginning, when the establishment of a working relationship between the helper and the survivor is made. Any suggestion, however slight, that the helper does not believe the woman, will make it extremely difficult to engage her in therapeutic work. The problems relating to being believed originate in the woman's childhood. She may have experienced one or more of the following situations:

— she may have tried to tell other adults about the abuse, but was not believed. She may have behaved in a sexualized way with other children, written about it in her school work, resisted being left alone with the abuser or shown concern or anxiety if one of her siblings had to stay with the abuser. Adults frequently deny or ignore these verbal and non-verbal messages. If this is the case the child is led to believe that sexual abuse is not a subject which can be safely raised with adults;

— she may have told someone, her mother, a neighbour, a teacher or relative who did believe her, and who then confronted the abuser. If the abuser denied the accusations the child may have been accused of lying or making it all up. As a result she continued to expect adults not to believe her or tell her that the abuse did not happen;

— sometimes the child is told by the abuser that if she tells someone, she will not be believed. This threat is used to maintain her silence;

— if the abuser is seen by others to be a 'good person', 'a thoughtful neighbour' or 'doing a responsible job', the child may have, or feels she will have, even greater difficulties in making other adults believe her;

— she may have told someone in authority, who then confronted the abuser. As a result, the abuser may have put her under pressure to retract the disclosure.

These experiences can continue to colour the woman's expectations of others when she reaches adulthood. It is important therefore for the helper to understand the significance for a woman of being believed. Any hint of disbelief on the part of the helper can be very distressing for the survivor. She is often so hypersensitive about being believed that questions asking for clarification, changes in voice tone and expressions of surprise on the part of the helper can easily be misconstrued as disbelief.

Frequent testing of the helper's capacity to believe may represent a more fundamental conflict about a survivor's desire to be believed; this was summed up by one woman who said,

'I want you to believe because these terrible things really did happen to me, but if you believe, I will have to face up to them and that might be even worse for me'.

Further questioning of the helper's level of belief can occur in relation to the sexual abuse itself. A woman may describe what she thinks is a less serious incident before moving on to discuss her more painful experiences. The woman may wonder how anyone could believe that such experiences could happen to a child. In these situations the helper should reassure her simply and directly by saying, 'Yes, I believe you. I have no reason to doubt what you are saying.' This should be sufficient to allow the woman to continue, and it is important for the helper to do this regularly and without prompting.

A woman who has experienced physical and sexual abuse of a particularly horrifying or sadistic type, may need constant reassurance about being believed. She may find it difficult to disclose new memories for fear that the helper will not believe her and will then disbelieve everything else that she has disclosed. It may then be necessary for the helper to state clearly the reasons for believing the survivor. These might include:

— an incident of abuse may be horrifying, sadistic or terrible, but that does not mean that it did not happen;
— there is no reason to doubt what the woman is saying;
— the helper knows that children are sometimes abused in a very brutal/violent way;
— if the woman has disclosed previous incidents of abuse, the helper should remind her that she was believed on those occasions, and that she will be believed now.

The helper should check regularly with a survivor as to whether she is concerned about being believed. A survivor may constantly ask 'Do you believe me?' needing repeated reassurance from her helper. It is a mark of progress when she asks the question less frequently, knowing and trusting that the helper believes her.

The Nature of the Abuse

An obvious theme in working with survivors is the nature of the abuse itself. It can be difficult to encourage a woman to talk about the details of these experiences, but it is essential to do so. It is only by sharing them with an accepting adult that they lose some of their power to hurt. It has been recognized (Lister, 1982) that enforced silence about traumatic events is likely to contribute to the development of psychological problems later. Once a woman feels she can trust her helper with the details of the abuse, it is likely that a history of increasingly upsetting experiences will be revealed. The helper must be prepared for this so that she/he can remain calm and not show reactions of shock, disbelief or disgust. These reactions are likely to prevent a survivor from disclosing further information.

Children frequently learn to cope with being sexually abused by dissociating themselves from all or part of the experience (see Chapter 7 for a full discussion of dissociation). This dissociation is likely to continue into adulthood. As a result, a survivor's memories of the abuse are often partial, vague or absent altogether. This has clear implications for her therapeutic work, as it is easy to assume that a woman has disclosed everything about a particular incident. The helper should therefore be aware that:

— the survivor may not remember the first incident of abuse. This may reflect the insidious onset of sexual abuse. It often begins with a look, or a touch that may be only slightly different from normal behaviour. It may then start to happen more often and include a wider range of sexually abusive behaviour. It is not unusual for a woman to remember that the abuse began at a much earlier age that she had previously recalled. This can be understandably alarming and upsetting for her;

— she may have a clear memory of a particular incident, and initially be fairly certain that it took place at a certain age. Later memory work may reveal that she was mistaken about her age at the time of this incident. This does not mean that she was lying, but that she made an error, just as we might all do if we tried to recall a series of childhood events;

— she may have a clear memory of an incident of abuse which may have been condensed from a number of incidents, or moved in time or place. It might also involve a less threatening abuser (e.g., a stranger rather than her father). The helper should be aware that this may happen;

— particular memories of the abuse can act like a dam, preventing the woman from remembering other incidents. In this situation, once the blocking incident is disclosed and dealt with, other memories will be released.

Example: Kathy remembered that her father sexually abused her in a particularly frightening way when she was 9-years-old. She discussed this incident with her helper and no longer felt bad about it. However she began to have flashbacks to previously forgotten incidents from the age of five.

— talking about the details of the abuse is important since it is these details that have caused great distress. Not only was the woman abused by a trusted adult, but the context in which the abuse was carried out can have alarming effects. For example, a woman who was abused in the bath may, in adulthood, find it impossible to feel safe in the bath. A woman who as a child was forced to have oral sex with her father, may never be able to initiate this sort of sexual contact as an adult because of her intense feelings of guilt about her early experiences. Discussing these sorts of details can lead to an increase in fear, pain, distress and despair in the woman. She is therefore likely to need a higher level of support from the helper at this point;

— a woman may not remember all the details of a particular incident of abuse. Chapter 7 outlined some methods for facilitating disclosure. The helper's aim here is to enable the woman to talk about the sexual abuse within a safe, calm and accepting environment.

The nature of the abuse is usually only part of the relevant disclosure. It is important for helpers to remember that abuse occurs in a context, at a particular time in the survivor's life and that these factors are often critical in understanding the effects the abuse had on her. Discussing the ways she survived the abuse as a child is also useful.

For many survivors, remembering the abuse can be a frightening prospect, particularly where the memories return gradually, leaving the survivor feeling that they will never stop. However, as one survivor put it:

'I believe my memories only come at the speed I can cope with them, and that it is like doing a jigsaw. There will be a last piece. Each memory I get of the abuse allows me to understand more of my reactions now'.

Responsibility for the Abuse

The issue of responsibility, often expressed in terms of blame and guilt, should be addressed in the early stages of therapeutic work. It is not uncommon for a woman to come for help with guilt feelings about having allowed the sexual abuse to have happened in the first place and for allowing it to continue. As a child she may have known that what was happening to her was in some way wrong for a number of reasons including:

— she had feelings of pain, discomfort or shame;
— she was told by the abuser not to tell anyone about what he was

Table 8.1: **Survivors' explanations for the abuse**

Childhood explanations

> I was a naughty girl so I deserved to be punished.
> I let him do it.
> I asked him for a cuddle/I sat on his knee.
> I told my Mum and she said it was my fault.
> I did it because I loved him.
> There is something about me that made it happen.
> I asked him to do it so he wouldn't hit me.
> It only happened when I was there. It never happened when I wasn't.
> If only I had made his tea, he would not have done it.

Adult explanations

> I am a slut, so of course he knew it was all right for him to do what he liked.
> I used to run around in my nightie, so what else could I expect?
> I must have been a very seductive little girl.
> I must have led him on.
> I was told I was a very precocious little girl.

doing, otherwise he would go to prison or the family would be split up;
— she realised that the sexual abuse was at odds with her family's attitudes towards physical contact, nudity and basic bodily functions.

Part of her distress has arisen because she was abused by an adult whom she trusted and whom she may have assumed cared about her. Furthermore, the abuse was not usually an isolated incident, but may have continued over months or years. The question asked by many women is, 'How could he do that to me for so long when he was supposed to love me?' The only answer which initially seems to make any sense for her is that the abuser must have been disturbed. He could not have known what he was doing and was not responsible for his actions, therefore the logical conclusion for the woman is that she was in some way to blame. Self-blame is often compounded by the reactions of others whom she tried to tell, and by feelings of guilt and shame. These feelings are expressed by the woman in the explanations she gives for the abuse occurring. These are summarized in Table 8.1. These explanations ignore the fact that she was a child when the abuse occurred, and that the abuser was in a position of trust, power and responsibility in relation to her. Such explanations need to be gently challenged by the helper, so that the woman can be helped to understand that:

— she was a child when the abuse occurred;
— as a child she was expected to respect and obey trusted adults;

— as a young child she did not have sexual knowledge prior to being abused;

— the only obvious factor which made the abuser 'choose' her was that she was too young to complain;

— her inability to break the secret was because of her fear of the reactions of others, of breaking up the family, or of threats made by the abuser, not because she was in any way responsible for the abuse;

— in families where the woman was not the only child who was abused, she was not responsible for failing to protect her siblings. That was the responsibility of the abuser and other adults in the family;

— the adult abused his position of power and responsibility by sexually abusing her. He should have been protecting her from, rather than exposing her to, harm;

— the abuse was done *to* her. This can be difficult for a survivor to understand, if she has been forced to masturbate the abuser or have oral sex with him. Similar difficulties arise if she has been sexually aroused by the abuser's actions;

— it was the adult's responsibility for interpreting any of her behaviour as sexual. Young children who have been sexually abused sometimes learn that by using sexualized behaviour, they can get adult attention which may be absent in their lives. It remains, however, the adult's responsibility for reinforcing that behaviour with sexual attention;

— if the abuse has continued into adulthood, the survivor is still not responsible. The abuser is still misusing his position of trust with her, and she will remain extremely frightened even if she is older. There is no magic day that the survivor becomes an adult in relation to the abuser.

A survivor may find it very difficult to understand that she was not responsible, particularly if her feelings of guilt have generalized to other aspects of her life. It is important that she works through these issues, gradually understanding the position she was in as a child. The helper may have to encourage the survivor to distinguish between issues of responsibility, feelings of guilt and those of regret.

Re-entering the World of Her Childhood

The therapeutic task here is to help the woman to become more objective about the issue of responsibility by re-entering the world of her childhood. This approach acknowledges that she had the physical size, power-lessness, sexual knowledge and understanding of a child when the abuse took place. This needs to be contrasted with the responsibilities of the abuser. Relevant methods for doing this are described in Chapter 11. She may wish to use the 'child within' methods described above.

One important aspect of being a child is the expectation that a child will respect and obey trusted adults, particularly family members. The sexually abused child is in an extremely difficult position, since part of that obedience involves complying with the abuser. Survivors often forget this feature of their childhood, and should be reminded of it. It is helpful if the helper can include it in any summarizing remarks she/he makes about the survivor as a child. For example, 'As a child you were small and expected to obey the adults around you ...' This enables the woman to become aware that compliance cannot be equated with complicity in the abuse. Survivors frequently question whether there was something about them that made the abuser single them out for his sexual attention. This may need to be tackled directly, particularly with the use of photographs of the woman as a child.

Her childhood knowledge of sexual matters should be explored in detail to help her to understand her level of sexual awareness and know-ledge before the start of the sexual abuse. This can also enable her to see that she was not in any position to question the abuser's wishes or desires. In this context the woman will often berate herself for being stupid for allowing the sexual abuse to have occurred, and it is vital for the helper to again remind her: 'You were only a child of ... (age)' Her confusion about her sexuality may have been compounded by physical reactions to the abuse.

Example: Jane described the experience of feeling a 'tingling sensation' when her father touched her 'down below'. She subsequently associated these sensations with feelings of sexual arousal as an adult.

It is essential that a woman understands that a child can and does have sexual feelings which she cannot control when she is touched in certain ways. It is the adult abuser, however, who has sole responsibility for creating the situations which produce these sensations.

Survivors often feel excluded or isolate themselves from peer group discussions about sexuality and sexual relationships because they become conscious of the fact that their early sexual experiences are similar to those described by their peers during adolescence. This contributes to their feelings of shame and guilt.

Finally, survivors often mention the prevailing attitudes which existed in their families about sexuality in its widest sense (such as those about nudity, bodily functions, physical contact). It is not unusual for them to describe extremely repressed and constrained attitudes in the family. Not only does this create difficulties for a woman in comprehending how the abuse could take place in this atmosphere, but it also makes it harder for her to tell anyone about it. By giving the woman permission to think of herself as a child again in a fairly non-threatening way, she can gain new understanding of her life at that time. She can then begin to shift the burden of responsibility for the sexual abuse from herself to the abuser.

The Child's Inability to Stop the Abuse

A survivor's inability to stop the abuse when she was a child remains a source of guilt even when she has gained some insight into the fact that she was not responsible for starting it. It may be necessary to help a woman to acknowledge that she was powerless and small as a child and that the abuser was powerful and big. This can help her to understand that any attempt to withstand the sexual abuse would have been to little or no avail. In addition, frequent threats or bribes may have been used to maintain her powerlessness and silence (see Table 8.2).

Table 8.2: **Threats and bribes used by an abuser to maintain silence**

Physical threats	Threats to split family
Threat to kill or injure child	The child will be put into a home.
Threat to kill or injure mother	The child will be taken away.
Threat to kill or injure siblings	The abuser will be put into prison.
Threat to kill or injure pets	The abuser will be taken away.
Actual injury to child	The child will be sent to prison.
Actual injury to others	
Actual injury to pets	
Verbal threats	*Bribes*
'No one will believe you.'	Special presents
'You will be called a liar.'	Special treats
'You are a slut.'	Special outings
Frequent criticism	'You are my special little girl.'
Ridicule	

With hindsight, a survivor may wonder why she failed to tell anyone about the abuse when it was happening. She usually underestimates the difficulties involved in doing this. The question of who she told and with what result should be explored. There is a general reluctance on the part of an abused child to disclose that she is being abused. There are a number of reasons for this:

— she has a sense of loyalty and/or love for the abuser that makes it impossible for her to speak out against someone who is supposed to be protecting and caring for her;
— she fears the reactions of others, or has had unhelpful responses from people she has already told;
— she is passive because she believes the abuser when he says that the sexual abuse is acceptable;
— threats and bribes are used by the abuser (see Table 8.2) to maintain her silence;
— she feels too much guilt and shame to tell anyone;
— she fears breaking up the family;
— she fears that she will be blamed;
— she does not know what to say.

It is important to help a survivor to understand that her reasons for not breaking the secret were because of her fears of the reaction of others, or because she felt responsible for the abuser or for the potential break-up of her family. It is vital to recognize that these fears do not imply responsibility. Only by encouraging a woman to challenge her childhood beliefs about these areas of responsibility will she be able to make this distinction.

Sometimes women persist in asking 'Why didn't I stop him?' In this case a brainstorming exercise may be useful; she could, for example, be asked to think of as many ways as possible she might have used to try and stop the abuse.

Example: Annette produced a list which included telling her father to stop; fighting him off; telling him she didn't like it or that it hurt; running away from home. She was then able to recognize that none of these alternatives were possible. She had tried telling him to stop and that it hurt but to no avail; he was too strong for her to fight him off. She had run away on one occasion but a neighbor had brought her home. As a result of doing this exercise Annette remembered for the first time that her father used to start abusing her in the middle of the night when she was asleep. In reality there was nothing she could do, but for years she had believed that she should have been able to stop him.

It can also help to explore with a woman whether she can recall any ways in which, as a child, she tried to 'break the secret' of the sexual abuse.

Many survivors recall incidents such as running away from home, taking tablets, doing drawings which indicated the abuse, pretending they were ill, saying that they were sore and so on. By remembering these signals, a woman can be enabled to see that she did not passively accept what was happening to her. It also helps her to realize that she was asking for help but that adults did not recognize the signs or chose to ignore them.

The Child's Responsibility Towards her Siblings

This is of particular concern for survivors who know or suspect that their siblings were also sexually abused. The oldest child in a family is likely to feel responsible for failing to protect her younger siblings from the abuser. The woman needs to acknowledge that, even though she was bigger and older than her siblings, she was still a child and there was little she could do to protect them. Paradoxically, when survivors come from families where several children have been sexually abused, they can usually deal with the issue of responsibility for the abuse more effectively, recognizing that the abuser was guilty of initiating and perpetrating it.

Abusers and the Issue of Responsibility

There is an increasing amount of evidence that abusers spend a great deal of time planning how, when and where to sexually abuse a child in their care (Conte and Smith, 1989; Berliner and Conte, 1990). This process is known as 'grooming'. It may take place over many months with the abuser desensitizing the child to touch before feeling confident enough to sexually abuse her. The process usually occurs in the context of an existing relationship (such as father-daughter), and it is accompanied by types of behaviour designed to engage the child in sexual activity, and to enable it to continue over a long time. There are four overlapping processes which take place:

— *Sexualization of the child* This takes place gradually, beginning with normal physical affection such as hugging, tickling and back rubbing. Reports from adults and children describe the process as moving from non-sexual to sexual touching, and then gradually to increasingly intrusive forms of sexual activity.
— *Justification for the abuse* Two common themes presented by abusers are that the activities were not really sexual, or if they

Table 8.3: **Excuses used by abusers**

'She asked for it.'
'She knew that I found that dress/nightie/pyjamas provocative.'
'I mistook her for her mother.'
'I did it to show her how much I loved her.'
'I wanted to teach her about sex.'
'I didn't want her doing it with the boys in the neighbourhood.'
'She needed to know what to expect from men when she grows up.'
'Isn't that what all fathers do?'
'Her mother didn't mind — she didn't like sex.'
'Her mother was pregnant/disabled/out at work.'
'Her sister didn't seem to mind, so I thought she wouldn't mind.'
'She liked it.'
'I only did it once to her, and I promised I wouldn't do it again.'
'I needed her to do it to make me relax.'
'I was just having a look at how her body was developing.'
'I knew that she couldn't get pregnant.'
'I never actually had sex with her.'
'She never told me to stop.'
'She never said she didn't like it.'
'She told me she wanted me to stop, but I knew she really wanted more.'

Whatever spurious reason an abuser presents, it is clear that, as a participant on a training course succinctly put it:

'Survivors look for reasons; abusers look for excuses.'

were, they were acceptable to the child. Other abusers focus on the child's compliance with the activities. Table 8.3 gives an indication of some of the excuses that abusers use to justify sexually abusing children.

— *Co-operation* Another part of the process relates to the ways in which abusers keep the child involved in the abuse and prevent her from telling. This can be through threats or intimidation. Often, however, it is by finding a particular child's vulnerability and exploiting it. This enables abusers to convince themselves that the child is consenting to the abuse, thereby reducing the abuser's responsibility.

— *Abuse disguised as . . .* Finally, abusers often pretend to the child that the abuse is a legitimate activity, because it is disguised as something else. The common pretences that abusers use are:

— the abuse is seen as a game;
— the abuse is seen as sex education;
— the abuse is seen as love;
— the abuse is a preparation for adulthood;
— the abuse is a punishment for the child's behaviour.

These leave the child more confused, and are likely to prevent the child from understanding that sexual abuse is never an acceptable activity.

When a survivor begins to resolve her feelings of guilt for aspects of the sexual abuse, she will be able to shift responsibility for the abuse from herself to the abuser. This is a positive achievement for her but it can have unforeseen consequences. For example, she may have built up a positive picture of the abuser; she might have been ignored by all the adults in her life apart from him; she may care about and love him. This leaves her with a confusing sense of loyalty towards him. Even when the abuse is disclosed, she may continue to defend and idealize the abuser. She might find herself saying, 'He was a nice man' 'He was a good father' or 'He wouldn't hurt anyone'. This can blind the survivor to the harm which the abuse has caused her.

If a woman can acknowledge the abuser's responsibilities for sexually abusing her, she will have to reassess her view of him, often with painful consequences. She will also have to face emotional reactions, especially anger, which have been submerged under her guilt feelings. A starting point for examining an abuser's responsibilities is to build up a picture of the abuser with the survivor. She could be asked to describe:

— what he looked like;
— how he related to other adults and children in the family;
— what made him angry and how he expressed his anger;
— how he disciplined children in the family;
— what others thought or said about him.

It is useful to ask her to list all the responsibilities an adult, particularly a parent, has towards a child in his or her care. This list could then be compared with the picture of the abuser already drawn up. In this way the woman can discover how the abuser met and abdicated his responsibilities. She may also find that the picture of the abuser which she has held over the years can be challenged and dismantled, allowing her to gain a more realistic and probably ambivalent view of him. In this way, some of her suppressed negative feelings towards him can be allowed to surface.

A reminder of the abuser's responsibilities should be made when a woman lapses into self-blame. A survivor should be enabled to see that the abuser was an adult with particular responsibilities towards her, including protecting her from harm, caring for her and allowing her to mature in a safe environment. If the abuser was her father or in a father's role (stepfather, foster father or her mother's boyfriend), these responsibilities may be even more important.

Another difficult area for a survivor involves the interpretation of her behavior by the abuser. His excuse for abusing her may have been that her behaviour was sexual or provocative. The woman herself may believe this too. There are two tasks here for the helper: the first is to remind the woman that she is interpreting her childhood behaviour from an adult's perspective and giving it a sexual meaning which it did not have for her as a child; secondly, she should be helped to understand that it was the adult's responsibility for interpreting her behaviour in this way.

A problem can arise if the woman has learned, as a child, that sexualized behaviour earned some adult attention. This produces a major conflict for her, expressed as: 'If I behave in a particular way I can get some affection and attention, but I don't like the nature of the attention.' Abusers are often well aware of the emotional needs of a child. They fail as responsible adults by using this awareness to manipulate a child into sexual activity. They may give or withhold treats or love as a way of obtaining a child's involvement in sexual abuse. The resulting confusion between physical affection and sexual attention often continues into adulthood.

Mothers and the Issue of Responsibility

A recurring theme for a survivor involves the extent of a mother's knowledge about the sexual abuse when it was happening. Equally vexing is the question of a mother's response to any suspicions or disclosure about the abuse. The main task for helpers in relation to both issues, is to enable a survivor to distinguish between responsibility for protecting a child and responsibility for or involvement in the abuse itself. This is also one of the most difficult areas for helpers themselves to address. It raises questions about a mother's competence and responsibilities, and can be particularly difficult if the helper is a mother herself. There are five possibilities which relate to a mother's responsibilities towards her daughter. These are when:

Her mother definitely did not know about the abuse A survivor often knows, without question, that her mother had no knowledge of the abuse. She may know from her mother's reaction to disclosure or from the circumstances in which the abuse took place. As a child, she may have told her mother about the abuse and her mother's response was to confront the abuser, to seek help from a welfare agency or to inform the police. If she has been told about the abuse by her daughter in adulthood, her response may be one of shock followed by acceptance or complete denial of what she has been told. A mother may have known nothing about the abuse because:

— she was not in the house when it was taking place;
— she was doing housework or tending to other children or dependents;
— the abuser had ensured silence by saying 'it would kill your mother if she knew about this';
— the abuse occurred in normal family situations, (for example, putting to bed, bathing);
— each incident lasted a very short time and no-one else could possibly have known about it.

If a woman can accept that her mother did not know about the abuse, she will also accept that her mother was in no way responsible for it. She may, however, continue to wonder what prevented her from telling her mother. Fear of not being believed, or of upsetting her mother are two of the most common reasons.

Her mother suspected that sexual abuse was taking place but could not acknowledge it Some mothers pick up signals from their daughters that something is amiss, only to block or disregard the information. Sometimes a mother can doubt her perceptions; she may be convinced that she was crazy to believe that such a thing could happen to her own daughter, or that she was reading too much into the situation. A mother can respond in this way for a number of reasons:

— she finds it impossible to accept that a family member, especially if it is her partner, is capable of sexually abusing her daughter;
— it causes her to question her own judgment in choosing a partner who could sexually abuse a child. If she is forced to accept that possibility, she may blame herself for making this choice. As a result, her guilt prevents her from acknowledging the information;
— she may have been sexually abused herself in childhood and cannot face up to the possibility of this happening to her daughter;
— there may be difficulties in her adult relationship with her partner which she blames herself for.

If a woman has tried to disclose the abuse to her mother only to have the information ignored, she may justifiably conclude that her mother failed to protect her from further abuse. The helper should enable her to examine the reasons for this so that she may be more able to understand her mother's reaction and position whilst acknowledging her mother's failure to protect her. This experience may make her feel ignored or invalidated by her mother. The helper should examine all aspects of her relationship with her mother, to see if these feelings have been repeated in other situations. The survivor may want to re-establish a more positive relationship with her mother, and some of the related feelings should be worked through first. Joint work between mother and daughter can be helpful in this context.

Her mother knew about the sexual abuse but did nothing to stop it A survivor may have told her mother about the abuse on more than one occasion, and she responded with:

— disbelief, saying that her daughter was lying or that she must have dreamed or imagined it;
— anger at her daughter for making such allegations;
— acceptance, saying that there was nothing she could do to stop it.

A woman with this experience is likely to feel intense anger towards her mother. She will again ask why her mother failed to protect her. Her mother's response might be explained by the following:

— she may fear the abuser, especially if he was violent or sexually abusive towards her too;
— the mother is forced to choose between her daughter and her partner. If she chooses her daughter she is likely to lose her partner, particularly if the police and social services department become involved. If she chooses her partner, her daughter will still be with her, but the abuse is likely to continue. The choice is therefore very difficult;
— the mother has mixed feelings towards the abuser. Despite the abuse her mother may still feel that she loves him and this makes her daughter doubly confused about her mother's reactions;
— she may fear the shame and public disgrace of a disclosure that sexual abuse is occurring in her family;
— she may have been financially dependent on the abuser and cannot contemplate breaking up the family.

The task for the helper is to explore the possible reasons for her mother's inaction in order to help the survivor to make sense of it, and to help her to express her feelings about it.

Her mother knew about the abuse and condoned it   This is likely to be very difficult for a survivor to admit at all. Her mother may have 'set up' her daughter to be abused by putting her into situations where she would be alone with the abuser, by arranging for the child to be abused by a family member, or by making her available for child prostitution or pornography. If this is the case the survivor is likely to feel intense rage, anger and disgust towards her mother. She should be reassured that these are all valid and justified emotions. She should be encouraged to express them, so that she can come to terms with the fact that her mother did not protect her, thus increasing her sense of isolation and vulnerability. In addition, she may have great difficulty in understanding her mother's behaviour.

Her mother sexually abused her   Research to date indicates that this only happens to a small number of women (Bass and Davis, 1988), and our own experience confirms this. The feelings experienced by a survivor in this situation will probably be more intense than those felt towards a male abuser. She will feel doubly isolated and there will be an added sense of betrayal that her mother, of all people, misused her authority and trust in this way. It is likely that the survivor will have difficult in understanding how a mother could abdicate her maternal role completely in this way. She may have much clearer expectations of her mother's role in the family than she does about the role of male family members. The helper's task is to help her to understand that not all mothers can fulfil their expected roles and that her mother, in particular, left her in an impossible position.

Disclosing that her mother abused her sexually can be even more difficult for a woman than if the abuser was a male family member. Society's rules and expectations in relation to mothers are so strong that she is at even greater risk of being disbelieved.

Her Family of Origin

A survivor often has conflicting loyalties when it comes to questions of family relationships, in particular her relationships with the abuser, her mother and her siblings.

The Abuser

Where the abuser was her father, or was in the role of father, the survivor probably lived with the man who abused her. She was expected to love,

179

obey and respect him, and could reasonably have expected from him a measure of parental care and protection. His parental role meant that he had the opportunity to carry out the sexual abuse behind the closed doors of the family home. Where the abuser was a grandfather, uncle or trusted male adult, the abuse may have occurred less frequently and in locations other than the family home. If this was the case, the child may have felt safe enough in her own home to tell other adults about the abuse.

Some of the issues which preoccupy survivors in relation to abusers include:

— his level of disturbance or 'madness';
— his treatment of the family as a whole;
— his use of subtle manipulation to gain control over herself and other family members;
— his use of threats and other forms of abuse to maintain her silence;
— his use of physical abuse;
— any pleasure he gained from the abuse;
— his understanding of, or explanations for the abuse.

For some women, gaining an understanding of the balance between the 'good' and 'bad' in the abuser is her aim. This can be very difficult when the evidence points to physical and sexual abuse on a huge scale. It is not uncommon to hear a woman say, 'But I loved him. He was a good person. I just didn't like what he was doing to me and I wanted it to stop.'

A woman may start therapeutic work by blaming herself for the abuse in order to protect the abuser. As her protective excuses diminish, her anger is likely to increase and she may go through a period of intense dislike and hatred for him. Finally, she may be able to come to some understanding of him, although she may never be able to protect or like him again.

If a woman is still in contact with the abuser while she is seeking help she may become more vigilant about him, especially in relation to her own children. She may also express fears of meeting him. On the other hand, a survivor may feel the need to confront the abuser. The helper should encourage her to consider the benefits and costs of this course of action, together with the methods she proposes to use. It is important not to underestimate the level of fear experienced by a survivor if she is determined to face the abuser alone. The helper's task is to help her to look at the situation realistically and to offer support for whatever course of action she decides upon. Even if the abuser has died, the use of letter-writing or other techniques can facilitate the emotional reactions associated with confrontation. This can be particularly important in enabling a survivor to discover the depth of her feelings towards the abuser.

Her Mother

Examination of a survivor's relationship with her mother almost always begins with the extent of her mother's knowledge about the abuse. Exploration of feelings associated with this issue, together with some understanding of her mother's position within the family is also necessary. An important aspect of the work is to examine her mother's ability to protect her at the time of the abuse. A woman may assume that her mother should have been perpetually vigilant and always available, with the implication that if this had been so, the abuse would not have happened.

It can be helpful to ask a survivor to:

— describe the role of her mother within the family;
— describe the situations, time of day and presence of other people when the abuse took place;
— describe a typical day in her mother's life when she (the survivor) was a child.

She may find that her mother did try to protect her or that she was not around when the abuse took place.

For a survivor who was abused by her father, key questions about her mother's loyalty to the abuser are often asked. She may say:

'How could she continue to live with him knowing that he was abusing me?'

or

'How could she love a man who was the type of person who abused his daughter?' (Regardless of whether her mother knew or not.)

or

'How could she sacrifice me to him?'

These questions are often unanswerable. It is important, however, for the survivor to gain a more realistic view of her mother's concern for her and to remember that her mother may genuinely not have known about the abuse.

Throughout all of these discussions, it is vital to acknowledge feelings of rage and disbelief. A survivor should also be helped to see that, following the discovery or disclosure of sexual abuse, her mother may experience a range of emotions:

— anger at her daughter for not telling her sooner;
— guilt that she failed to protect her child. She may also feel that she is responsible for the abuse occurring;
— betrayal by her partner for abusing her daughter;
— anger and hate towards her partner for the consequences of his action, the damage to her daughter, the damage to the relationship between her daughter and herself and the damage to her relationship with her partner;
— revulsion when she thinks about him abusing her daughter;
— confusion about her own feelings in relation to her partner;
— failure as a parent and a partner.

With this may come the need for confrontation if her mother is still alive. Again, this should be considered carefully and adequate preparation time allowed for it. If her mother has died, it can be very beneficial for a survivor to write her thoughts and feelings into a letter.

Her Siblings

Questions about a survivor's siblings usually revolve around whether she was the only child in the family to be abused. Sometimes she already knows or has suspicions that her siblings were also abused, and she may begin to search for clues to confirm or deny her suspicions. She may see similar long-term effects in her siblings, or may remember situations from her childhood which now suggest to her that another child in the family was being abused. Confirmation of these suspicions can only be made by discussing them with her siblings. Many survivors are reluctant to do this for fear of causing extra pain or distress to their brothers and sisters. This is particularly the case when their father is still held in high esteem by other family members. A woman who shatters the myth of 'the perfect father' can easily blame herself or be blamed for the subsequent pain experienced by her siblings.

Where there is confirmation that others were abused, a survivor is likely to feel relief, but also guilt and responsibility for breaking the secret and causing more pain. Where several children in a family have been abused, it is often easier for them to deal with the issue of responsibility. They may have gained support from each other as children, but it is particularly difficult if one or more of them feels they have coped with the experiences better or suffered less abuse than their siblings. If the survivor is the oldest child in the family she is likely to feel an extra burden of responsibility for caring and protecting younger members of her family. For her, the discovery that they too were abused can be devastating, and can contribute to her poor self-esteem and sense of failure. For the woman who discovers that she was the only child of the family to be abused, many questions remain about why she alone was selected by the abuser. A woman will need help to talk about feelings where she was not the only sibling to be abused, but was treated as the 'bad' child by one or both parents, receiving less material comforts and affection and more punishment.

Flashbacks and Memories

Throughout any therapeutic work with a survivor, recall of childhood incidents occurs frequently. Sometimes these memories have been repressed or blocked, or they are shadowy or poorly defined. Other memories of childhood incidents return in the form of flashbacks (see Chapter 3).

A flashback is different from normal memories which return or are facilitated during therapeutic work. It is an alarming experience and often leads to fears of ensuing 'madness' for the woman. It is important, therefore, for her to know that flashbacks are to be expected and that they happen frequently to women who have been sexually abused as children. The helper's task is to explain that the memories and flashbacks will lose their pain and associated emotional intensity once she is able to disclose details of them. If the woman chooses to remain silent, however, the helper should draw her attention to the fact that she will probably remain distressed or continue to have similar flashbacks until she is able to talk about them.

Disclosing individual memories can be as painful for the survivor as her original disclosure of sexual abuse. Her language and behaviour may become that of a young child, her voice may rise in pitch, she may use words appropriate to the particular age that the memory relates to, and her mannerisms and non-verbal behaviour may revert to those of a child.

Example: Pauline was discussing the effects of being raped by her father at the age of seven, and suddenly said, 'But Mummy, it hurts, it stings.' Her voice became that of a little girl and she began to sob. She was writhing in her seat, experiencing what she later described as a physical pain and burning sensation in the genital area.

The helper should be alert to the possibility that the survivor may experience flashbacks during a therapeutic session. Common signs that this is occurring include:

— a sudden silence from the woman, sometimes in the middle of a sentence;
— a sudden increase in distress, anxiety or general tension;
— the woman suddenly begins to look into the middle-distance, often with a glazed expression on her face;
— a sudden increase in body movement, indicating increased discomfort.

She may be unable to speak during the flashback and may need help to regain control when it is over. Discussing details of the flashback is likely to be impossible at this stage because of the incapacitating nature of the woman's fear. The helper should therefore:

— reassure her that she is safe and that the flashback is over;
— remind her that the events in the flashback happened when she was a child;
— help to calm her breathing, which often becomes shallow and quick during a flashback;
— reassure her that flashbacks are normal experiences for any woman who has been sexually abused as a child.

Female helpers should be aware that physical comfort can be very useful to a survivor during a flashback. Male helpers should be extremely cautious and careful about offering physical comfort at this stage as it may be misconstrued as abusive. When a woman has calmed down sufficiently, she should be encouraged to discuss the details of the flashback.

During a flashback and subsequent discussion about it, it is normal for a survivor to feel intense physical pain. Thus usually relates to the incident being recalled.

Example: Katherine recalled a particular incident of abuse when her foster father forced her to have sexual intercourse with him, and then beat her around the head and body for crying. During this recall, she experienced deep vaginal pain, soreness and a heavy feeling around her ribs. This latter pain reminded her of being crushed by the weight of her foster father. She also experienced a severe pain on the side of her head which enabled her to recall the pain associated with the incident.

After experiencing a flashback and discussing it with her helper, a woman should be encouraged to look after herself as if she had had a recent injury. This could involve going to bed, having a warm bath, taking mild pain-killers but most of all giving herself permission to comfort and take care of herself (see Chapter 7). For many survivors, this is a totally new experience and can lead to better self-care.

For some women, recalling memories of the abuse can lead to an increase in the number of perceptual disturbances and nightmares. Where visual images occur, the use of visualization techniques (see Chapter 11) can help the woman gain some control of the disturbing images.

Example: Joanne recalled an incident of physical and sexual abuse that occurred when she was 8. For some weeks after, she kept getting an image of her naked father coming towards her, laughing at her. Through the use of visualization techniques, she discovered that she could gain control of this image, and send him out of the room. Initially she had to imagine two large policemen handcuffing him and taking him away, but she quickly discovered she could send him away herself.

The way which a woman feels about herself when she was a child can also prevent her from disclosing details of her abuse. If this attitude is unduly negative, hostile, or critical, she may not allow herself to remember specific details. A woman can be encouraged to disclose if the helper reminds her, as one might with a child, that part of her/his job is to protect children and make them feel safe enough to talk about the abuse. It can be helpful to remind her, if appropriate, of previous occasions when she has told of particular memories and of the positive consequences for her of telling.

The question of whether the helper can believe details of a woman's sexual abuse is tested to its limits when flashbacks occur. It is easier for a helper to accept general statements about sexual abuse but the actual details can be extremely unpleasant and horrifying to hear, especially where the sexual abuse is combined with physical violence, threats, or pornographic use of the child. However, a helper's inability to picture the sexual abuse should not be equated with a denial by her/him of its occurrence. It is vital for the survivor to know that her memories can be accepted by her helper in a non-judgmental and calm atmosphere.

Regression

We have already discussed the tendency of survivors to use child-like behaviour and language during disclosure of memories of sexual abuse.

Some women cannot properly disclose their memories of sexual abuse without regressing to being a child again. In this situation, the concept of 'the child within' becomes very important, as it is as if that 'child' emerges during the regression. The helper should:

— be prepared to allow enough time for the regression to occur and for the woman to return to her adult state;
— remember that the 'child' is most likely to be quite young, having regressed to an age that the 'adult' cannot remember;
— use the opportunity to help the woman/'child' disclose as many of the incidents of abuse as she feels able to;
— remember that the woman is behaving as a small child, and will therefore have concepts, language and behavior appropriate to the age of the child. This includes methods that the woman used as a child to survive the abuse (counting, reciting poems, over-breathing and blanking out);
— be aware of the 'child's' vulnerability and not inadvertently misuse it;
— be prepared for the woman to be extremely tired after the regression is over;
— spend some time after the regression helping her, the adult woman, to remember the incidents that the 'child' has disclosed. This may involve telling her directly what has been disclosed or helping her to piece together the incidents from half-memories she already has.

Bringing the woman back to her adult state may involve the use of photographs, objects or concepts that only the adult knows. This can only occur once the 'child' has been told that she is now safe, that she has done well to tell, and that the abuser is no longer here.

Example: Following a period of regression during which Anne had disclosed a number of incidents of sexual abuse that occurred when she was four, the helper reassured her that she was safe, that her father (the abuser) was not there and could not do any harm to her. Anne was then shown a photograph of her daughter aged 11 who was in her school uniform. She was asked questions about the photograph, including what was the girl in the photo doing, what she was wearing, what her name was. Gradually Anne began to talk of her daughter going to a new school and was able to give her daughter's name and state she was her daughter's mother. This allowed the helper to check that Anne had now returned to her adult state.

Regression can be alarming for both the woman and the helper when it occurs for the first time, but can also be an extremely useful way of enabling the woman to understand how she coped as a child. Chapter 7 gives further information on how to deal with regression.

Trust

The betrayal of a child's trust is a central feature of child sexual abuse. Problems with trust continue into adulthood. At the beginning of any therapeutic relationship with a survivor, trust is of crucial importance. It may represent a woman's first real attempt to trust someone, particularly with her childhood secrets. The helper should therefore be alert to the fact that a survivor may expect to have her trust betrayed again. For example, she may:

— expect the helper to tell her 'secrets' to other colleagues without her permission;
— not expect the helper to keep appointments with her;
— assume that the helper will tell her doctor all the details of their sessions;
— assume that if the helper met any of her family, the helper would automatically believe them, and not her.

With some survivors, the helper may have to work hard at proving and demonstrating her/his trustworthiness. Reliability, confidentiality, punctuality and respecting her rights not to have certain information about her history transmitted to other helpers are all important issues here.

Survivors tend to believe that trust is an all-or-nothing concept. As a result, if someone betrays a survivor's trust in a small way, she is likely to stop trusting that person completely. In reality, trust is built up gradually through the discovery that a person's behaviour, words and actions can be relied on; trust is therefore earned. For a woman who has difficulty in trusting, it can be useful to encourage her to begin to trust certain people in small ways or in simple situations. These situations should be specified and should not include broad generalizations, for example, 'I don't expect you to ever betray me', 'I want you never to be cross with me!' Examples of situations include:

— asking her partner to do some shopping for her;
— asking a friend to come and spend a short amount of time with her when she is feeling low;
— asking a friend to baby-sit for her.

In this way, she can learn that some people can be trusted. If a situation fails in some way, she should be asked to reflect on what went wrong. For example she might ask herself:

— whom did I pick to trust?
— how long have I known the person?
— has this person let me down in the past?
— what did I trust him/her with?
— did I communicate my wishes clearly?
— was it a good time to ask this person to do this task for me?

Gradually, however, she can discover that she can begin to trust again, and this will lead to the possibility of more positive social relationships.

Loss

A survivor will need to acknowledge and grieve for the childhood and adult losses she has experienced as a result of being sexually abused. These losses relate to her lack of a normal childhood and its opportunities for normal development. For many survivors, the fear and negative feelings associated with the sexual abuse will have coloured normal childhood experiences. Play, peer group relationships, educational achievements and participation in a whole range of childhood activities may have been severely curtailed by the abuser for fear that a child might talk about the abuse. The consequences of these sorts of restrictions are far-reaching. For example, fun and enjoyment may be difficult to attain in adulthood, and many survivors find it difficult to allow their own children to play freely. Poor peer group relationships, educational and employment underachievement are also very common.

For some survivors, the feeling of loss of their childhood resulted from having the responsibility for running the household.

Example: Anne was the eldest of five children. At the age of 9 she was expected to get the younger children up and ready for school. She had to make breakfast, and take all the children to and from school. She was expected to do the washing and cleaning with some help from her younger siblings. She cooked the evening meal, then put the little children to bed, hoping to protect them from their father.

Losses are also described in terms of the lack of normal relationships with parents and siblings. Acknowledging that sexual abuse and its associated secrecy can spread its effects so widely is a painful process. Many survivors have little ongoing contact with their families and, even after the death of their parents, find it hard to have normal relationships with brothers and sisters.

Loss may also be experienced through the death of family members. A survivor often finds it particularly difficult to come to terms with the death of the abuser. She expects to be relieved but discovers to her dismay that his death releases many of the feelings, flashbacks and memories associated with the sexual abuse. She will often feel cheated that 'he got away with it' and that she is denied the opportunity for confrontation and revenge. She may also feel that the manner in which he died was too peaceful, given the suffering and pain which he inflicted on others. Birthdays and the anniversary of his death can be stressful in this respect.

Coming to terms with the death of her mother can also present problems. Questions about her mother's knowledge of the abuse have to remain unanswered if a survivor has never had the opportunity to raise this with her. A woman may also mourn the lack of opportunity for forming a normal adult relationship with her mother.

A bereavement counselling approach can be very helpful in establishing the extent of these losses. It can also focus on the tasks of the mourning process. The features of this approach are described in Chapter 12.

Getting in Touch with Feelings

A recurring theme for survivors is the emergence of well-defined feelings and emotional reactions. These are characterized not only by their range and intensity but also by their unpredictability and newness for the woman. Many survivors have restricted emotional responses, especially in relation to the sexual abuse. They talk about their emotions in general terms such as guilt, fear, depression, or good and bad feelings. As a young girl, a woman may have learned that her emotions were too painful and frightening to show to others, and this may have led to a complete blocking of the feelings. Once she begins to feel a range of emotions she will need to learn different ways of describing her range of emotional states.

Initially, feelings of guilt and shame are predominant. These are usually associated with the issue of responsibility, discussed earlier in this chapter. Challenging guilt can be a complex task as a survivor will often have a range of self-blaming statements that have to be challenged before she is able to relinquish her guilt. Guilty feelings will usually give way to underlying anger and rage.

Work with a survivor often involves extremes of emotional reaction. Complete lack of emotion may be seen at the beginning of the therapeutic work, with descriptions of upsetting experiences being given in a detached and impassive manner. Any attempt by the helper to elicit feelings is met with a lack of understanding on the part of the woman. In this context, it is important to gradually show her that the expression of feelings is acceptable. The helper might say:

'Many women in that situation might have felt a bit . . . (name the emotion — angry, guilty, upset) I wonder if you felt like that?'
or
'There are lots of different ways women might have felt in this situation. For example, they might have felt angry, sad, guilty, frightened, scared (give appropriate examples). I wonder if you are feeling any of these emotions?'

It is likely that a woman will gradually become able to name and differentiate her emotions. The emotional detachment and dissociation should progressively disappear, to be replaced by more intense emotional reactions. These can be alarming for the survivor and are likely to be at their most difficult when she experiences flashbacks or new memories. They can amount to deep sobbing, acute pain reactions and distress of such power that the survivor can become rigid or motionless, agitated or intensely angry. In these situations, the helper must remain calm in spite of feeling very concerned or even frightened by the intensity of emotion being experienced. Feelings of such intensity do pass for the woman once the memories or flashbacks have been discussed.

During work on emotional reactions, the helper needs to facilitate the survivor's awareness of the ways in which they link with her past, particularly with the abuse that she has experienced. Making these connections can be achieved by taking a fairly non-threatening line of enquiry (see Figure 8.1). By following the flow-chart, it can be seen that potential links between past and present experiences and emotions can be clarified by the helper, and the emergence of new emotions can be noted. Where emotional blocking appears to have taken place, it is useful to remind a survivor that it is quite normal for women who have been

Figure 8.1: **Pathway to disclosure: Helper's and survivor's responses**

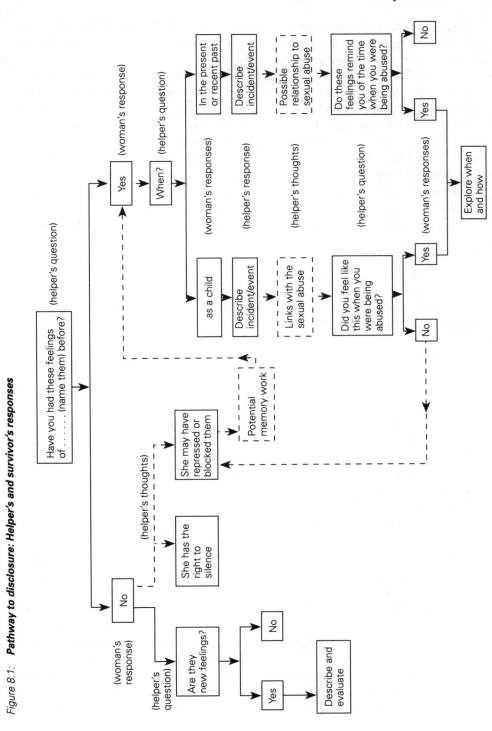

abused to have these feelings in the present and during childhood. This sometimes enables a woman to trust the helper with her feelings, if not at the time, then on a later occasion.

Experiencing these new emotions can also cause problems. For example, intense emotional states can lead to an increase in self-mutilation or suicide attempts, and the emergence of rage can produce murderous thoughts and fear that she might lose control.

It is likely that a survivor will eventually be able to experience a wide range of emotions without linking them all to her experience of being sexually abused. Eventually she will be capable of reacting emotionally, without fear of losing control. She will also be able to allow herself to feel conflicting emotions about people and situations. Table 8.4 summarizes these problems, and indicates possible courses of action open to the helper.

Anger

Many women find anger an extremely difficult emotion to deal with because they have been brought up to believe that:

— anger should never be shown;
— anger is a dangerous emotion;
— as a woman, she must be polite, peacemaking, understanding and forgiving at all times;
— anger is associated with aggression and hate;
— anger is so overwhelming that she cannot bear it.

Anger can be expressed constructively and released in a safe way, and is an important part of recovering from being abused as child. Bass and Davis (1988) have called anger the 'backbone of healing'. It is a natural and normal response to abuse and violation. For many survivors, anger is an emotion that has been hidden behind feelings of guilt and depression. Anger has probably been denied or turned in in a self-destructive way. For others, anger and rage have been expressed indiscriminately and without control, so that people around them have borne the brunt of it.

The aim in dealing with a survivor's anger is not only to become aware of it, but to learn to direct the anger where it belongs in a safe and non-destructive way. Without this, anger can remain suppressed and can eat away at the survivor in bitterness and desire for revenge. We examine ways of dealing with and expressing anger in Chapter 12. It is important to recognize that anger is a useful emotion that can facilitate change. Survivors may have to acknowledge their very justifiable feelings of anger

Table 8.4: **Emotional reactions and consequences**

Feeling	Consequence for woman	Helper's action
Shock	Like any normal severe shock reaction with both physical and emotional reactions.	Reassurance that this is normal.
Numbness	Increased self-mutilation (I know I should feel pain but I don't, so I'm just making sure I can.)	Reassurance that it is a normal experience for survivor.
Guilt	Increased self-blame, depression and helplessness.	Reality-testing of guilt — leading to discovery that she is not help-less, or to blame.
Shame	Feels dirty. Increased self-blame.	Reassurance that this is normal, but that the abuse was not her fault.
Fear/Anxiety/ Panic Attacks	At times paralyzed by fear, extreme shaking, withdrawal from supports, and avoidance of any situation where physical symptoms of anxiety are experienced.	Anxiety management techniques. Giving understanding of anxiety — physical, behavioural, cognitive components.
Terror	Perceptual disturbances and nightmares become more frequent.	Acceptance of these consequences as normal. Discussion of perceptual disturbances and nightmares in detail and establishing any links with the sexual abuse.
Hurt	Intense pain sometimes experienced as physical pain. Leads to suicide attempts and self-mutilation.	Explanations of association of the pain with the abuse. Assessment of suicide risk with aid of appropriate professional agency. Increased support.
Anger/rage	Murderous thoughts, increased guilt, and fears of loss of control. Projection of anger on to others and consequent guilt.	Reassurance that this is normal for a survivor. Detailed discussion of the murderous thoughts. Methods for dealing with and understanding anger, such as writing, drawing, physical activities.
Disgust	Fears of rejection by any helper who hears her secret, but also too frightened to face that person. Over-concern with cleanliness.	Reassurance that the helper is not disgusted by her. What was done to her was dreadful, but she is not disgusting. Over-concern with cleanliness sometimes needs to be dealt with if it has obsessional and compulsive qualities.
Grief	Confused feelings, deep sadness, anger, guilt.	Bereavement counselling methods.
Pleasure	Increased guilt.	Help survivor to accept that pleasure and enjoyment are reasonable and normal emotions.

about their childhood experiences without letting these feelings transfer onto their current relationships. The helper's task is to help the survivor direct these feelings where they belong — namely to the abuser and any other adults who failed to protect her. The loyalty she feels towards family members may make this difficult.

This may be a difficult task for a survivor, particularly if she is still blaming herself. In this situation, dealing with feelings of guilt and shame may be a first priority. It may also be hard if the survivor is turning her anger in on herself by injuring herself in some way. It may be important for the survivor to begin to express her anger outwardly and safely whilst she is also looking for the triggers for her self-injury.

The constructive use of the survivor's anger may lead to a number of changes in her life. For example, she might use it to:

— recognize and confront the situations in which she feels victimized;
— confront family members about her childhood experiences;
— begin to express her true feelings about a range of issues;
— become more assertive;
— discover that she can handle powerful emotions;
— make changes within her current relationships (see Lerner, 1986);
— write about her experiences;
— publicize the plight of adults abused as children;
— raise awareness about sexual abuse and its effects.

Once she has discovered that the expression of anger need not destroy her, she can become more energized and in control of other emotions. However, expression of anger can also release other feelings particularly of distress.

Confrontation

The issue of confronting and challenging members of the survivor's family of origin is one that frequently arises. It can create confusing feelings, and the survivor is often given conflicting advice by family, friends and professional helpers. Sometimes, advice is given that a family meeting where the issue of the abuse is discussed and resolved is all that is needed for her to feel better. This type of advice may be well-meaning but could lead the survivor into a potentially very damaging encounter long before she is ready or before she has prepared herself for the meeting.

The survivor should never be pressurized into a meeting with the abuser or other family members unless she herself is ready for it. If such a meeting is to happen at all, it is not to be recommended until she has resolved some of the issues surrounding the abuse in relation to her family of origin. If such a meeting does take place too soon, the survivor may feel that:

— she is still the vulnerable 'child' of her family;
— there is no hope for change;
— the person(s) who pressured her into the meeting has taken away her control and lacks understanding of the situation;
— she is in danger of further abuse and/or violent or aggressive reactions from the abuser;
— there is no chance of future resolution with the abuser;
— she is guilty of the abuse and breaking its secret;
— the family's reactions are her responsibility;
— in the face of her family's reactions, that the abuse did not take place at all, leading her to retract her disclosures.

These and other reactions can lead the survivor to withdraw from the helping situation. It may take a long time for her to return thus prolonging her suffering.

The survivor therefore should not rush to confront her family. A paramount consideration is her safety, and if a return to the family situation could lead her or other family members to be in physical danger, it should not be an option. There is no good reason for the survivor to have to expose herself to further danger.

The first stage of any potential confrontation is to consider the reasons for seeing the abuser or other family members, and to plan in detail what she wants to say, to whom and for what reason. Examining the potential reactions of the abuser and other family members and her reactions to them is also important. The detailed process is set out in Chapter 11.

At any stage of the preparation role-play is a useful technique, as it allows the survivor to practise and try different scenarios with the helper or other support person who may be helping her to prepare for the task. Role-play can also be useful where the family member has died or is unavailable. Even in this situation, the survivor can be helped to make sense of her reactions and be allowed an opportunity to express her feelings.

Use of letter-writing is also beneficial (see Chapter 11). Here, the survivor can be encouraged to write a letter that will, in the first instance, not be sent. This allows her the freedom to say all that she wants to say.

She may eventually write a letter that does get sent. In both cases, she is spared the initial reactions of the person she wishes to challenge. However, if she does confront by letter, the survivor is less likely to get the person's spontaneous reactions.

Another form of confrontation can take place if a survivor decides to seek legal redress for the abuse and its effects on her life. Special units which have been established in some police forces to deal with crimes of violence against women and children can be a source of help. Often a survivor will discover that there is insufficient evidence for criminal charges to be pursued. It can be helpful, however, to be taken through the potential process by a sympathetic police officer. Where there are several adults and/or children who have all been abused by the same abuser, criminal charges may be possible.

As with any form of confrontation, the consequences of pursuing legal action should be considered very carefully, not only for the survivor but also for other significant people in her life.

Forgiveness

Forgiveness is an area of considerable difficulty for the survivor. Establishing the survivor's understanding of the concept of forgiveness is important, and will be influenced by any religious beliefs she holds. The helper's task is to facilitate some better understanding of forgiveness, making clear that forgiving is not to be equated with excusing. Hancock and Mains (1987) state that:

> A good definition of forgiveness is 'to give up all claim to punish or to exact penalty for the offence' (sic). As long as we are unforgiving, we hold the person responsible for us. We demand an account.

By forgiving, therefore, the survivor learns to give up her desire for revenge and deal with the associated resentment and anger.

The survivor may have been told that forgiveness of the abuser is essential before she can recover. This unfortunately leaves many survivors feeling that they can never come to terms with what happened because they cannot forgive. This can lead to despair and a sense of hopelessness. A suggestion that forgiveness of the abuser is the ultimate goal denies the feelings she has about what has been done to her. It is more helpful to start from the premise that child sexual abuse is unforgivable, even if the survivor may come to some understanding of or compassion for the abuser, and for others who knew about the abuse but did nothing to protect her.

Whatever the circumstances, child sexual abuse is never justifiable or excusable.

Some authors suggest that the survivor should consider forgiving herself for her childhood actions (Bass and Davis, 1988). However, this puts responsibility back onto the survivor for actions she took as a child to survive an intolerable situation created by an adult, and can lead to the survivor feeling guilty once again. The survivor may wish to forgive herself for childhood actions or for actions she has taken as an adult, particularly if they have hurt other people. Ultimately, it is her choice and she should not be pressured into seeing forgiveness as the only path to recovery.

Living in the Present: From Victim to Survivor

So far we have been concerned with themes which relate directly to a woman's sexual abuse and her childhood experiences. In this section, we consider the very real difficulties which a survivor experiences in adulthood. She may have concerns about relationships, sexual difficulties or have considerable anxiety symptoms. Therapeutic work should acknowledge these problems and, where necessary, help a woman to deal with them. This may require referral to an appropriate professional helper such as a sex therapist or marriage guidance counsellor.

Many survivors come for help feeling victimized, helpless and unable to make positive changes in their lives. The therapeutic work will hopefully enable them to take more control of their lives and to stop seeing themselves as victims. The boundary between victim and survivor is by no means clear, and it can be very upsetting for a woman to feel that she has made progress, only to suffer a setback which puts her in the role of victim or abused person once more.

Being a Victim

Being a victim may relate almost entirely to a survivor's childhood experiences and the ways which she learned to survive them. Statements which arise in therapeutic work include:

— 'I cannot say no.' This affects all relationships, and is a particular problem in sexual relationships. A woman may find herself being taken advantage of by friends or colleagues, becoming resentful but unable to assert herself enough to break out of the circle.

— 'I get myself into situations where I am taken advantage of. I know it to be so but I can't do anything about it.' This mirrors the experience of being sexually abused as a child.
— 'I have no rights or choice.' This is often reflected in a survivor's inability to ask for anything for herself. It can create a problem when she feels that she has no right to take up the helper's time or says that she does not know why anyone should spend time helping her.
— 'I have no control over what happens to me.' Again, this mirrors the experience of sexual abuse.
— 'I am not able to speak for myself. No-one will listen to or believe me.' The origins of this lie in her childhood experiences.
— 'I am totally passive — it's easier that way.' Extreme passivity is one way in which a survivor learned to cope with the experience of being sexually abused. It also allows her to believe that by being passive she will not provoke further abuse or exploitation.

All of these issues have considerable implications for relationships in adulthood. Survivors frequently find themselves in abusive relationships and explain this by saying that they do not expect anything better for themselves. It is possible that members of her current family find it difficult to acknowledge that she has needs, opinions and rights, and they may therefore resist her attempts to introduce some choice into her life. It is also probable that she puts everyone else's needs first and is unable to accept that she is a person in her own right.

The therapeutic task is to begin to increase the woman's awareness of her 'victim behaviour' and to gently challenge her assertions that she has no needs, rights or choices in her life. This can be done in small ways, initially by pointing out occasions on which she is able to make choices or state her own needs. Ultimately she may need to learn how to say 'No', to be assertive and to deal with situations in which she is taken advantage of. Further discussion of assertiveness training is to be found in Chapter 11.

Low Self-esteem

A survivor's extremely low self-esteem is at the root of many of her difficulties. During therapeutic work, it is essential to help her gradually see herself in a better light, and to begin to like herself; the helper's task is to help her examine and challenge her misperceptions and negative thinking about herself. For some women, being accepted and heard by the helper is sufficient, but many women require active work, constant feedback and challenge from the helper when they belittle themselves. Many survivors cannot understand why anyone should want to help them or spend time with them. Improvements in self-esteem usually come very gradually, but a lessening of victim behaviour and increased assertiveness both produce significant gains in self-esteem.

Relationship with a Partner

The experience of child sexual abuse can have many repercussions for a survivor's partner. Disclosure of the abuse can help a partner to understand a survivor's behaviour. It can also put a great strain on a relationship, as the survivor begins to remember incidents of abuse. Many of the long-term effects noted in Chapter 3 may become more acute as the survivor starts to change, adding further stress to the relationship. All of this can be particularly difficult for the survivor who may be in a relationship where she feels safe and secure, perhaps for the first time. The safety of such a relationship may enable her to remember details from her past, but she may feel that the work with her helper is jeopardizing her sense of security, at least in the short term, and her relationship in the longer term.

Issues for partners are extensively dealt with in *Allies in Healing* (Davis, 1991). We also note in Chapter 9 the impact of sexual abuse on the survivor's sexuality. Although there may be important differences in experience between heterosexual and lesbian couples, especially in relation to the power dynamics, conditioning and role expectations, these differences are outweighed by the common problems faced by all couples where one or both partners are survivors of sexual abuse.

Here we would briefly draw attention to the following issues:

— *Intimacy*   For many survivors, sex and intimacy have become confused. Sex may be used as a way of expressing intimacy without the accompanying honesty, trust and respect for a partner. As a survivor begins to heal she may be able to distinguish between them and build on her relationship with a partner. Learning how to be intimate can be threatening for a survivor as it challenges many of her survival strategies. If her partner knows that she is frightened of being close to someone, the couple may concentrate on these feelings, rather than dwelling on feelings of rejection.
— *Withdrawal and isolation*   Sometimes a survivor may be so overwhelmed with issues from the past that she withdraws

completely from her partner. She may find it difficult to meet her responsibilities at work or in the home, and a greater share of domestic responsibilities falls on her partner. This can cause resentment and frustration, with a partner feeling personally responsible for what is happening and shut out of the relationship.

— *Issues of control*   For a survivor who felt that she had no control over her life as a child, she may become very controlling as she begins to recover. She may have a need to exert control in her relationship with a partner, perhaps by making all the decisions that affect them both. It will be important for a partner to know that the survivor's need to control is related to her powerlessness as a child. Talking about it can help the survivor to see that by sharing control she is not returning to a position of powerlessness but is acknowledging her ability to feel safe in the relationship. Where a survivor has previously felt powerless in her adult relationships, the changes due to her recovery can put a relationship that had previously felt safe under considerable strain.

— *Expressing feelings*   When a survivor begins to find words for and to experience feelings that are new to her, she can bring this newly found knowledge into her existing/new relationships. This can bring both rewards and difficulties especially in an established relationship.

— *Concern that her partner is not to be trusted near their children*   Her knowledge about her own experiences of being abused as a child may lead her to be more vigilant and untrusting when her partner is near any children. Inevitably, this can cause problems for the couple. Sometimes, however, this knowledge does allow her to see that her children may be at risk in a way that she had previously been unaware of.

— *Changes in her relationship with a partner*   There may be times when the survivor's relationship with her partner will be severely tested, as she begins to challenge learned behaviour and begins to heal. Sometimes a temporary separation may be needed, although in other situations, a permanent separation is the only outcome possible. This can feel like a further failure for the survivor and her partner but, with help from an outside source, may come to be seen as a positive outcome. If the couple decides to stay together, other difficulties may become apparent. For a partner who has provided much of the early and ongoing support, positive changes in the survivor may be

threatening. A partner may feel no longer needed. In this context, support groups for partners can be useful to confirm the normality of these feelings.
— *Becoming allies* It will be important for the survivor to explain to her partner that difficulties they are facing may be a result of her experiences as a child. It will, however, affect their joint lives, and partners may get very angry about the abuse and its consequences. Communicating feelings on this issue is vital if the survivor and her partner are to work as allies on the difficulties.

There are a number of specific exercises for partners who do remain together during and after the process of a survivor's recovery. These include:

— each partner should make a list of the things which they love about each other. The list is put somewhere where they can both see it, especially when things are difficult;
— they should try to spend time together every week, without anyone else present. They might take turns to plan an enjoyable activity during this time;
— they should arrange sessions with the survivor's helper or with another helper to look at specific issues.

Relationships with her Children

Chapter 7 has noted that among the triggers that cause a woman to seek help are those that relate to her own children. The birth of a baby, a child reaching the age she was when the abuse started and fears for the safety of her children can all be important. There are a number of specific issues that may arise as a survivor begins to recover from her childhood experiences. These include:

— *Inability to care for her own children* Sometimes, especially during periods of disclosure and memories, a survivor may be unable to meet the needs of her own children. She may project her own feelings of rage, helplessness and despair on to her children. In this situation, she may need practical help with looking after her children so that she has enough space each day to keep her own work going. The helper may have to facilitate this process, without being judgmental about her behaviour. If a survivor is unable to care for her children at all, arrangements may have to be made for someone to look after her children temporarily. In this situation, partners, supportive family members and friends can be extremely important.

— *Over-protectiveness of her children*   Survivors often report that they are over-vigilant of their children, to the extent that it impedes the social development of a child. It is important for a helper to raise this issue with a survivor so that she can gradually learn to set appropriate and safe boundaries for her children. She may have unrealistic expectations about her ability to totally protect her child, especially after the child reaches school age. However, she can begin to inform her child realistically of some of the dangers that he/she may face. We recommend the use of books listed in Appendix 3 for this.

— *Fear of being abusive to her children*   Some survivors go through a period when they fear that, because of their own experiences, they are in danger of abusing a child in their care. Here the role of the helper is to support the survivor in examining how real these fears are and to what extent they are related to the myths about victims of abuse becoming abusers. She may have problems in deciding whether normal physical care of a child is acceptable, for fear of being seen as a potential abuser. These fears should be explored, enabling her to understand the difference between having thoughts of this nature and acting upon them. She may also need help in being aware of what constitutes safe, acceptable and necessary touch in relation to her children.

— *The physical and sexual development of her children*   Survivors often report feeling confused about this issue. Their main concerns are:

> — establishing safe boundaries for a child with regard to nakedness and personal hygiene;
> — sexual development and sex education;
> — how to teach a child to deal with unwanted physical or sexual advances and making this topic safe for discussion;
> — dealing with teenage children, particularly with regard to sensitive issues such as sex, contraception, sexuality, AIDS and drug misuse.

These issues should be raised and discussed openly with the helper so that the survivor has an opportunity to resolve any problem areas. Clearly, where the survivor has a partner, some of these concerns can be explored with the partner.

Other Difficulties

Survivors include women who know that the sexual abuse is contributing to their present difficulties and those who have denied or repressed the abuse and its effects. The latter group may not have understood the influence of the past on the present. The helper's task here is to help make these links explicit and to enable a woman to begin to accept that past abusive experiences do continue to have an effect into adulthood.

The long-term effects of child sexual abuse have been described in Chapter 3. At the outset it is likely that a survivor will believe that all or none of her reactions and behaviour are due to the abuse. It is important, therefore, for the helper to state clearly the long-term effects of sexual abuse and to draw the woman's attention to them whenever possible. This is obviously much easier in a group setting, where other survivors will confirm that they too have suffered similar effects. In individual work, it can be useful to use material written by other survivors to show that she is experiencing problems similar to others. Considerable relief is usually felt by a survivor once she knows that her symptoms and suffering are normal responses to sexual abuse.

Much therapeutic work with a survivor will involve undoing many of the long-term effects of being abused. This will necessarily involve careful examination of these effects and encouragement for the woman to try and change them. Many changes come gradually as she begins to understand the relationship between past events and present feelings. The nature of this work varies from woman to woman but could involve work on anxiety, depression and its related negative thinking, alcohol abuse, sexual difficulties, and parenting problems (see Chapter 9).

Apart from the major psychological and relationship difficulties which result from being sexually abused as a child, there are many small elements which contribute to the problems of a survivor. It is important to draw a woman's attention to these because they may be easily changed. This gives her opportunities for taking control of her life, and can give her confidence for the future.

Example: Susan discovered that she did not like to sleep in a bed against a wall because she was abused in a bed which was in this position. Her own bed was against the wall; once she made the connection she decided to change the positioning of her bedroom furniture and slept properly for the first time in years. This encouraged her to recognize and change other behaviour. She decided that she did not need to sleep with the light on or to wear pyjamas rather than a nightie. She also discovered that she could safely have a bath when someone else was in the house.

Survivors frequently minimize and deny the effects of childhood sexual abuse. It is the helper's task to challenge this, reflecting the discrepancy between consequences of the abuse which a woman has already described and any ways in which she minimizes or denies its severity. A helper might say:

'You have already told me that being abused has left you with problems in your relationships, (especially sexually), has made you feel very bad about yourself and still gives you bad dreams and nightmares, and yet you are now telling me that it doesn't have much effect on your life any more. It sounds as if it still has quite a big effect'.

Helpers and survivors alike often assume that all of a survivor's problems originate in the sexual abuse. A distinction should be made between problems which are a result of being abused as a child and those which are a result of other life experiences.

Example: Jane was extremely frightened of men and had not recognized the links between her fears and her experience of being sexually abused. It was clear that these fears originated in the sexual abuse.

Example: Andrea believed that her anxiety about starting a new job was because she had been abused by her father when she was a child. It was obvious, however, that she was experiencing normal anxiety in this situation. The helper was able to use self-disclosure to help her to understand this.

Why Now?

A persistent concern for a survivor is understanding why she needs to seek help at a particular point in time. She is likely to see her action as a necessary step and also as a failure to cope. She may feel that she has coped with the effects of being abused for years, and cannot understand why she can no longer deal with them. Fears of 'going crazy' or of having a nervous breakdown are common. Exploration of the possible reasons for the timing of her request for help (see Table 7.1) is valuable and is likely to reduce some of these fears. It can also alert a survivor to potentially difficult situations she may have to face in the future; the anticipation of difficult situations helps a survivor to be realistic about coming to terms with her past. She learns that it is possible to become a survivor, and to take control of her life in a more effective way.

Becoming a Survivor

Becoming a survivor entails an acceptance of the past, a recognition of feelings associated with childhood sexual abuse and learning to take control of and make choices in life. It also involves gradually leaving any intensive sources of help and, for some, helping others who have suffered in a similar way.

Resolution of the effects of early abuse can be a daunting task, and it is not unusual for a woman and her helper to become overwhelmed from time to time with feelings of hopelessness and helplessness. However, for the majority of women, a considerable improvement in mental health and general well-being can be achieved with time and appropriate help. There are several factors which govern both the degree of improvement and the amount of time and help needed. These include:

— the personality and resources of the survivor, including her motivation to involve herself in therapeutic work;
— the frequency and severity of the abuse;
— the closeness of the relationship between the survivor and the abuser;
— her adult life experiences. Where these have been or continue to be problematic, resolution of her earlier experiences can be more difficult.

Given that many women who seek help are managing to cope with life in the community, it is important to confirm the strengths and resources which they manifestly possess. In spite of acute distress, they often show great courage and persistence in working on their difficulties. Confirming that she has survived her childhood experiences to get to this stage can be very reassuring. Detailed exploration of the methods she has used as an adult to cope with the sexual abuse also enables a woman to see that

Table 8.5: **Methods used by women to cope with the experience of sexual abuse**

Method of coping	Explanation
Denial of the abuse	— I imagined it — It didn't happen — I had a good childhood.
Denial of the frequency of the abuse	— It only happened once or twice — I forgot about it after each time, so each time became the first time.
Denial of the severity of the abuse	— He only touched me — He never had intercourse with me.
Protection of the abuser	— He was a nice man — He didn't know what he was doing — He wouldn't hurt a fly — He was a good father.
Rationalization	— I deserved it — It was my fault — There are people far worse off than me.
Repression/Blocking	— I don't remember the abuse — I don't remember things that occurred at a very young age.
Dissociation	— It didn't hurt me — It doesn't matter any more — I learned as a child not to feel anything, and I don't now.

she does have personal resources which have been useful to her. Table 8.5 gives an illustration of some of the methods which women use in this context.

Learning to live in the present without the spectre of the past haunting her may involve learning new skills. It could involve a woman in further education, occupational training or retraining. Many survivors write about their experiences before and during therapeutic work, and may want to publish these to help others in a similar position. Some want to become involved in media campaigns about sexual abuse, in training professionals to recognize and identify the long-term effects of abuse and particularly in supporting and counselling other survivors. All these activities are very important and valid activities because they can represent the first opportunity for a survivor to use her experiences in a positive way.

Chapter 9

Sexuality

As we have already seen in Chapter 3, the experience of childhood sexual abuse has major effects on and implications for the survivor's sexuality. Many of the effects are subtle and pervasive, and may not manifest themselves simply as problems with sexual relationships. Child sexual abuse can affect:

— her body image;
— her concept of herself as a sexual person;
— her view of herself as a woman;
— her attitudes and beliefs about sex;
— her knowledge about sexual and physical functioning;
— her automatic reactions to touch and sex;
— her ability to cope with intimacy and expressions of affection;
— her sexual behaviour;
— her confidence about her sexual orientation.

The survivor's sexuality is affected not only by the sexual abuse, but by her family's attitudes towards sexuality in its widest sense, by attitudes of her peer group and sexual partners in adolescence and adulthood, and by the prevailing attitudes in society. In addition, the effects of racial, religious and wider cultural influences may be important. These are influences that affect women in general, regardless of whether they have experienced sexual abuse.

The effects of the abuse on her sexuality vary from survivor to survivor and reflect the nature of the abuse, the messages given or implied by the abuser and the interpretation the survivor made of the abuse. In addition, her sexual experiences as an adult can often confirm or strengthen her beliefs about herself resulting from her childhood. For example, a sexually abusive relationship in adulthood might serve to enhance the survivor's view that there is something about her that attracts men who hurt her.

Changing attitudes and feelings about issues relating to her sexuality involves a process that goes alongside all the other work the survivor does in coming to terms with her childhood experiences. At some point, she may decide to do specific work on these issues. Critical concerns at that time may relate to her sexual functioning. Many survivors seek help because of sexual difficulties or the intrusion of abuse memories into a current sexual relationship.

The helper's task is to assist the survivor in assessing the effects of the sexual abuse on her sexuality, examining some of the above areas in detail. A useful starting point is the 'Sexual Effects Inventory' published in *The Sexual Healing Journey* by Wendy Maltz (1991). The origins of difficulties a survivor may experience in relation to her sexuality are set out in Table 9.1. As many of them relate to her childhood experiences and influences, it is often necessary to examine these in detail to begin to correct misinformation or to help the survivor change where she wishes to do so. The effects of the abuse itself are critical to this process and therefore some detailed disclosure work will be necessary to deal with concerns relating to sexuality.

Body Image

In a culture which is preoccupied with a body image for women which is youthful and slim, this can be a difficult area. Many survivors blame their bodies for having been attractive, being susceptible to stimulation, being small or large or for having been vulnerable. This is related to guilt feelings about the abuse. It is important for survivors to acknowledge that they have had their bodies 'stolen' from them in some way by the abuser. This may have led them to disguise or develop body size as a form of protection. Helping a survivor to acknowledge any protective strategies may be the first step in enabling her to let go of these strategies and to develop a body image with which she is comfortable. Examples of protective strategies include:

— being overweight;
— being over-thin;
— wearing clothes in which she feels protected or disguised;
— having her hair cut in styles which cover her face;
— developing eating disorders such as bulimia or anorexia.

The survivor can be encouraged to think about the body image she would like to have and to develop positive attitudes towards her body. With her helper she can:

Table 9.1: **Sexuality: Factors contributing to long-term effects**

Factor	Specific examples
The nature and context of the abuse	The actual nature of the abuse.
	The experience made her feel dirty.
	She could not wash afterwards.
	She became physically aroused.
	She believed the abuse would stop if she gained weight/ made herself unattractive.
	Any rewards, bribes or payment for the abuse.
	The age she was at the time of the abuse.
The abuser and his behaviour	What the abuser told her about herself physically.
	His justification for abusing her if stated (see Table 8.3).
	Whether he touched the survivor in non-sexual way for example as signs of affection or comfort.
	The way he behaved towards other children or women in the family in a physical — sexual and non-sexual — way.
	His behaviour, attitudes and beliefs about the human body and its functions.
	His attitudes and behaviour about nudity and personal hygiene.
	His behaviour, attitudes and beliefs about men and women, gender roles, and any contrasts between these stated beliefs inside and outside the home (particularly important where the survivor was abused within her own home).
	His beliefs about sexuality arising from religious, racial or cultural sources.
Mother and other significant women	Her behaviour as a woman in terms of body image, dress, sexual functioning, modesty, nudity.
	Her beliefs about and attitudes towards sex, bodily functions, male and female bodies, sex education, menstruation, puberty, contraception, childbirth.
	Her comfort at discussing the above issues with her children.
	Whether she was able to touch her child in a safe way, such as a sign of greeting, affection and comfort.
	Her behaviour, beliefs and attitudes about men and women, gender-roles and any other gender-related concerns.
	Her behaviour, beliefs and attitudes about sexuality arising from religious, racial or cultural sources.

Table 9.1: Continued

Factor	Specific examples
The survivor's beliefs and knowledge during childhood and adolescence	Whether she blamed herself, or 'something' about her body for the abuse.
	Her understanding of the abuse and whether she knew it to be sexual.
	The effects of the abuse on her.
	Her knowledge, beliefs, attitudes and feelings about sex, bodily functions, menstruation, puberty, contraception, childbirth, sexually transmitted diseases.
	What she learned from peers about sex, bodily functions, puberty, contraception, childbirth, sexually transmitted dieseases, relationships, homosexuality and heterosexuality.
	Her attitudes and beliefs about men and women, gender-roles and her future as a woman.
	Any learning about sexuality from religious, racial, cultural or media sources.
	Any sexual experience during adolescence.
The survivor's knowledge, beliefs and experiences as an adult	The nature of any sexual experiences as an adult.
	The effects of problems within close relationships with men and women.
	The intrusion or repression of the memories of the abuse in her adult life.
	The influence of her peer group on her understanding of sex, bodily functions, menstruation, menopause, childbirth, contraception, sexually transmitted diseases.
	The birth of any children and the surrounding medical care, education.
	The influence of a trusted partner on her sexuality, perception of herself, sexual functioning.
	Her beliefs about sexuality arising from religious, racial, cultural or media sources.
	The nature of the long-term effects of the abuse.

— learn about the positive effects of regular exercise;

— examine the effects of drugs and alcohol on her body;

— if necessary, find ways of taking care of herself physically;

— where appropriate, she can be encouraged to seek help with losing weight.

It has also been suggested (Bass and Davis, 1988) that a survivor can move from hating her body to liking, or even loving it by:

— thinking about one inch of her body which she feels good about, buying a present for it, such as some perfume or body oil, and gradually extending the area which she feels good about until she has reclaimed her whole body;

— counteracting the distorted messages she may have been given about her body by closely looking at herself in the mirror. By examining rather than criticizing she can become acquainted with her body, its strengths and any changes she would like to make.

— nurturing her body by taking soapy baths, long showers or soothing it with oils, powder or cream. Buying warm, comfortable clothes or material which is soft or smooth against the skin can also be used to nurture the body.

Survivors also frequently neglect their appearance. For many women this is associated with a wish to be seen as asexual or unfeminine. Other survivors dress to attract attention from men — attention which they do not always welcome. Challenging assumptions which she has about her appearance can be an important part of the work. Beliefs about her appearance may be the result of:

— direct comments from the abuser;

— suggestions or demands made by a partner to avoid or wear certain clothes;

— feeling ashamed about her appearance but unable to do anything about it.

It can help to explore:

— aspects of her appearance she is happy with and those which she would like to change;

— choosing to wear different styles and colours of clothes because she wants to rather than because of what someone thinks she ought to do;

— wearing make-up or jewellery that she wants to do;

— changing her hairstyle and wearing new or a different style of clothes that might increase self-confidence.

The most important point is that any work on self-image and appearance enables the survivor to change because she wants to rather than to conform to someone else's expectations of her.

View of Herself as a Woman

The survivor's view of herself as a woman may come from a number of sources as suggested in Table 9.1. It may also be confused by her concerns about her sexual orientation, her adult relationship with her mother, sisters, or female friends and by her attitudes about sex and the role of women in a sexual relationship.

She may need to reflect on how she perceives herself as a woman and how she perceives other women. This can be helped by having a female helper who can help her work through the issue, drawing on her own experience as a woman. If she is a member of a survivors' group she may find herself making friends with other women for the first time in her life. This can be important in valuing the support which women can give to one another and it can also encourage her to value her femininity.

Attitudes and Beliefs about Sex

One consequence of the sexual abuse is that survivors frequently view sex in a negative way. These negative attitudes are compounded by the way in which sex is portrayed and experienced. Examples of such attitudes are:

— sex is dangerous, painful, or causes hurt;
— sex is dirty;
— sex is frightening;
— sex is uncontrollable, or in the control of the survivor's partner;
— sex is secretive and shameful;
— sex is humiliating or degrading;
— sex is seen as a way of getting what the survivor wants;
— sex is a way of rewarding her partner;
— sex is a way of protecting oneself from worse harm in an abusive relationship;
— sex is no more than an obligation or duty;
— normal sex has no boundaries and all kinds of sexual act are acceptable;
— sex is unsafe;
— sex is irresponsible.

When a survivor shows some of these attitudes, her capacity for a satisfying sexual relationship is likely to be adversely affected. Communication with her partner about sexual matters may be restricted and uncomfortable. These attitudes and beliefs may also affect her ability to make changes within a sexual relationship. Some may lead her to withdraw from or avoid any situation that could be sexual.

Examples of more healthy attitudes towards sex might include some of the following:

— sex is an important part of an individual's identity;
— sex is a mutual sharing with someone else;
— sex is a natural drive;
— sex is an expression of love;
— sex is intimate and private;
— sex can be responsible and safe;
— sex has boundaries and limits;
— sex can be part of honest communication and it allows respect to be shown for both partners;
— sex requires open communication and choice;
— sex is empowering and healing.

Work on sexuality issues may start with an examination of the survivor's attitudes and where they originated (see Table 9.1). Challenging some of these attitudes is a gradual process and should begin with those that are clearly a consequence of the abuse. A survivor may find that challenging long-held attitudes is both painful and frightening, especially where they have protected her from having a healthy sexual relationship. Changing these attitudes is easier with the help of a supportive partner, but making a decision to examine these beliefs and their effects on her present behaviour is an important first step.

Table 9.2: **Basic rights in relation to sexual situations**

1	I have the right to information about my sexuality.
2	I have the right to choose my own sexuality.
3	I have the right to ask for what I want sexually.
4	I have the right to sexual pleasure.
5	I have the right to choose my sexual pleasure.
6	I have the right to change my mind.
7	I have the right to say no.

Developing positive attitudes about sex involves understanding and gradually testing out a number of rights within sexual situations. These are outlined in Table 9.2. Even without a partner, a survivor can look at the implications of these rights, and how they could have changed previous relationships. These rights also include the right not to have a sexual relationship if that is what she wants. For the survivor who has decided not to have a sexual relationship, there is often pressure from others to get involved sexually. This can put a heavy burden on her.

Other stages of changing attitudes involve deciding not to expose oneself to abusive sexual situations. The survivor might learn ways to avoid sexually abusive situations as an adult. This can have huge implications for the survivor who is already in an abusive adult relationship, if she concludes that this relationship is preventing her from recovering, and makes a choice to end it. If this is the case, she will need support from the helper, including the possibility of safety in a refuge or with family and/or friends.

Knowledge about Sexual and Physical Functioning

Assumptions are often made that a survivor of sexual abuse will be knowledgeable about sexual functioning because of her early sexual experiences. This is rarely the case. These early experiences are more likely to have prevented her from gaining accurate information at the appropriate time because of feelings of disgust, fear, shame and guilt. A survivor may describe sex education classes at school as being very difficult because:

— she fears that others will discover her secret;
— her strong negative feelings and fear may show and draw attention to her;
— she discovers, perhaps for the first time, what has been happening to her during the abuse, and discovers that it is behaviour that should not be perpetrated on a child;
— her levels of shame are increased with this knowledge;
— she cannot participate in any discussions with her peers, and so becomes more isolated and withdrawn;
— she is embarrassed.

As a result, she may have never had an opportunity to discuss sexual functioning. The helper may, therefore, need to supply good basic sex education information. In this context, the books listed in Appendix 3 are particularly useful. *Our Bodies, Ourselves* (Phillips and Rakusen, 1989) and *Women's Experience of Sex* are recommended. (Kitzinger, 1988) A survivor may find it extremely difficult to read such books, and the helper may need to go through the information with her in a clear and educative way.

For the survivor who experienced arousal during the abuse, it is important that she understands that her physical response was a normal response to being touched in certain ways. It was the abuser who created that situation, and it is not her fault that she reacted to him.

Automatic Responses to Touch and Sex

Automatic responses involve *thoughts*, *feelings* and *sensations* that echo the abuse. The survivor may repeat the responses she used as a way of coping with the sexual abuse. These reactions inhibit the development of a satisfying sexuality. Examples include dissociation, flashbacks and perceptual disturbances in sexual situations and in situations where the survivor is touched physically, such as in crowded places, as a sign of greeting, affection, or comfort. For a detailed discussion of these issues, readers are directed to Maltz (1991).

Automatic responses may also take the form of *physical reactions*, some of which may be the normal physical sensations experienced as a result of anxiety or a panic reaction (see section on Anxiety in Chapter 11). These reactions may be sweating, quickening of the heartbeat, over-breathing, nausea, and numbness. Some physical reactions may be those the survivor experienced as a child during the abuse including:

— unwanted sexual arousal;
— feeling very cold/hot;
— nausea;
— feeling faint.

Where these feelings were pleasurable, the survivor may seek out experiences which echo them. For example, she may seek sexual arousal with men who are exploitative or abusive without recognizing that she is continuing to be abused.

Further automatic responses involve *intrusive thoughts* that may lead directly back to the abuse and the abuser. An example is: 'He's going to come and get me', 'It's my Dad.' These thoughts may represent a frightened response of the survivor's inner child. They could also mirror the thoughts she had as a child which she used to explain the reasons for the abuse, such as 'He is doing this to me to punish me', or 'It's because I am unloveable.'

The final area of automatic responses concerns a survivor's *emotional responses* to situations involving touch, intimacy and sex. Her emotional reactions can affect whether she is prepared to tolerate the situation, and can involve fear, disgust, anger or distress. These may represent the feelings she had at the time of the abuse. For example, she may have started to cry after the abuser left her, and now as an adult, finds herself in tears after making love with her partner.

A survivor's automatic sexual responses may represent a learned response to the abuse or to the early association of abuse in its widest sense with sexual arousal. For example, a survivor might report that she is only able to feel sexual arousal if the sexual activity incorporates an element of violence. She may feel ashamed to admit to such feelings, but they are common, and often relate to the woman's first sexual experiences during the abuse. If a woman has experienced violation, humiliation and fear as a child at the same time as she experienced arousal, it can leave a legacy where the two elements are fused and confused. The consequence can be that the survivor associates pleasure with pain, and love with humiliation.

In addition, a survivor may report that she can only function sexually if she thinks or fantasizes about sex in an abusive context. The early experience of abuse is likely to have caused this, and for the survivor to overcome these thoughts, she will have to begin by understanding her reactions in the context of the sexual abuse.

The survivor may experience automatic responses in relation to touching her own children. She may fear that she will abuse her child, or be seen to be doing so. In this context, her appreciation of what is normal, safe and appropriate touch between a parent and child is critical. Most survivors are very clear about what is appropriate, and are able to touch their children safely.

Automatic responses rarely occur in isolation. They are more likely to connect with each other so that the survivor experiences a series of un-controllable responses that can be very inhibiting, and may precipitate a flashback. For example, a survivor might describe responding to her partner greeting her with a hug by feeling sick (a physical response), thinking that her partner just wants sex (intrusive thought), and feeling disgusted (emotional response). She may then turn away or feel extremely angry. Thus, a situation which could represent safe, non-sexual touch quickly becomes tainted by uncontrollable reactions that may belong to the original experience of being abused, or to some other sexually abusive experience.

The stages of dealing with these automatic responses involve:

— sometimes, the survivor can make sense of the trigger in terms of the abuse, but where she does not have the relevant memories, the triggers may be more difficult to understand. The triggers may indicate aspects of her childhood experiences that have been buried. They may be the first clues that she has experienced abuse in the past. Identification of the links with the abuse, the context in which the abuse occurred (time, place and family circumstances), and her childhood reactions, beliefs and assumptions may involve disclosure work, or may require detailed discussions leading to a better understanding of her childhood situation which provided the context for the abuse;

— the survivor should learn to understand that these responses are automatic, and that she is not to blame for experiencing them. It is only by understanding her responses that she may be able to work out ways of controlling them. In this context, the use of the concept of the 'inner child' can be useful, in that the helper might suggest that some of these reactions represent the responses of her inner child, and that as an adult, the survivor should not blame the 'child' for having them;

— the survivor should take control of the triggers and their accompanying automatic reactions. The key here is to be consciously aware of the triggers and their origins. When they occur in the context of a supportive relationship (with a partner, friend or family member), the survivor can enlist the support of that person to choose a new way of responding;

— she should try and stay as calm as possible. One way involves staying with the situation, and breathing more steadily;

— she should stay grounded in her present situation. She may have to talk herself through — confirming her name, age, and address of herself as an adult and where she is during the automatic reaction;

— she should choose a new response. For example, if she has had a strong reaction to her partner standing behind her and breathing deeply, she could ask him to move to a different position, or she could turn and face him. In more intimate situations, this could involve discussion with her partner about alternative responses, behaviour or other options, in order to help her take control of her reactions. This will require practice, and the choice of alternative responses may have to be broken down into several small steps before the chosen response is achieved.

Example: Sonia experienced a strong automatic reaction consisting of feelings of sickness, extremes of anger, and an urge to burst into tears whilst watching television with her boyfriend. She identified that the triggers for her reaction were aspects of the content of the TV programmes (if there was an attractive woman, particularly if she was lightly clad or in a sexual situation), and the fact that she and her boyfriend were alone together and relaxing. She related this to her experience of being abused by her uncle who used to look after her whilst her mother went to work. The abuse usually took place when she had been relaxed and absorbed in watching television. Her initial choice of response was to turn off the television, but she then decided to watch, with her boyfriend helping her to breathe calmly and grounding her in her adult environment. She was later able to do this for herself, and was able to stay in the situation whilst still experiencing some of the automatic response. It was several months before she could finally deal with her reactions.

— during the stage of choosing a new response, the survivor may need to learn about different forms of touch other than those she experienced during the abuse. It is important that throughout this learning process, the survivor is encouraged to be clear about her likes and dislikes regarding touch, and that she can learn the distinctions between safe and unsafe touch, and between sexual and non-sexual touch. In this respect, challenging her previously held beliefs, helping her to understand how her body reacts to touch, and enabling her to be more assertive about touch may have to accompany the work on examining and changing her automatic responses.

Automatic responses that occur in sexual situations can sometimes be dealt with by the survivor herself, but if she has a supportive partner, these situations may need to be explored and resolved with the help of her partner. Where her partner is unsupportive or abusive, resolving some of these reactions will be more difficult, as her adult situation may contain too many echoes of the abuse experienced in childhood. In either situation, a period of abstinence from sexual intercourse may be necessary as the survivor begins to deal with the complex issues surrounding her sexual responses. For women who do not have a partner, these automatic reactions can be dealt with to some extent, but may recur, if she does have a partner at a later stage.

Her Ability to Cope with Intimacy and Affection

We have already discussed a number of sexuality issues that can have widespread effects on the survivor's ability to cope with intimacy and affection. Beyond these, there are a number of additional concerns that can make it difficult for a survivor to have close relationships:

— problems of trust;
— confusion, perhaps because of the abuse, between affection, love and sex;

— problems in relation to women, because of unresolved issues with her mother, or because of concerns about her sexual orientation if she has a close relationship with a woman;

— difficulties in making a choice of partner and friends who will not exploit or abuse her;

— being able to recognize further abuse as abuse, and not discounting or minimizing it.

The survivor may have to work on some of these issues before she is able to deal with some of the more specific reactions outlined above. The helper can enable her to examine her confusion about relationships in general, many of which are experienced by people who have not been abused as a child.

Her Sexual Behaviour

The effects of sexual abuse on the survivor's sexual behaviour cannot be separated from other aspects of her sexuality. Within the context of a reasonably satisfying sexual relationship, the survivor can experience a number of difficulties, often related to her sexual beliefs and attitudes, and to her automatic responses. They may also relate to the nature and quality of her existing relationship with her partner, and his or her attitude towards the survivor's difficulties. However, there are a number of specific problems outlined in Chapter 3 that are often part of the survivor's reasons for seeking help.

Once sexual problems with a partner become established, it is often very difficult to resolve them without some help. It is recommended in this situation that survivors and their partners look for appropriate sources of help from people who have particular expertise in dealing with sexual problems.

Where a survivor is engaging in sexual behaviour that makes her vulnerable to further abuse, such as prostitution, the helper should encourage her to work on issues of self-esteem and self-worth together with an understanding of the abusive nature of her experiences. Obviously, the meaning and rewards of this behaviour for the survivor are highly relevant, but the helper can encourage her not to expose herself to further abuse. She may feel that her childhood experiences left her with no choice but to continue to be abused. The helper's task is to gradually help her to understand that she does not have to put herself in potentially dangerous or abusive situations any more.

This issue is more complex when the survivor is in a sexually and/or physically abusive adult relationship, and is not yet ready to leave it. In this situation, any children she has may be in danger of being abused, and the issue of her tolerance of abusive sexual behaviour may get swamped by concerns for her safety and those of her children. However, where there is no physical danger to herself or her children, the survivor may wish to gradually change her reactions in her relationship, and learn to be more assertive. She may, however, decide that she will not be able to make the changes she wants within her existing relationship, and decide therefore to leave it. In this case, she will need support from the helper, and where possible, from family and friends.

Her Confidence about her Sexual Orientation

A survivor may express a number of concerns about her sexual orientation. For the survivor who is gay, she has a double set of problems concerning her sexuality in that both the sexual abuse and her lesbianism may remain secret and a further source of confusion. Even if she is certain of her sexual orientation, she will be faced not only with society's homophobia but also with the attitudes of her family and friends. The survivor may ask some of the following questions:

— am I gay because I was abused by a man, and therefore do not like to have a close relationship with a man because it reminds me of the abuse?
— am I gay because I was abused by a woman, and she made me over-responsive sexually to women?
— am I gay because I like the company of women, although I do not wish to have a sexual relationship?

Heterosexual women do not usually have to ask the first two questions, and it is measure of the lack of acceptance of homosexuality in society that lesbian women have to test out the origins of their sexuality to such an extent. For some lesbian women, these issues are important, but acceptance of their sexuality and coming to terms with the implications of this in a society which is hostile to departures from the 'norm' of heterosexuality can be very difficult. The helper should be aware of the relevant issues for a woman and be available to help her with issues concerning her sexual orientation and any links it may have with her childhood experiences.

In this chapter, we have examined the pervasive nature of the effects of child sexual abuse on a survivor's sexuality. The helper's own comfort with discussing such issues may facilitate or impede the survivor's capacity to discuss such personal issues.

Chapter 10

Survivors' Groups

Some women feel more comfortable in a one-to-one therapeutic relationship, whilst others welcome the opportunity to share their experiences and get support from other survivors. Women may join a survivors' group and subsequently seek one-to-one support; others are already in an individual therapeutic relationship when they join a group.

Sgroi (1989) suggests that group members should plan to be seen individually by another helper outside a therapeutic group, at least once a month while the group is meeting. This, she suggests, will secure time for working through issues specific to the individual which have been triggered by the group experience. Another advantage of having the one-to-one support is that new feelings and emotional reactions experienced in one setting can be acknowledged or explored in another. The potential disadvantages include how much of her history is shared between helpers. This can heighten concerns about confidentiality. There is also the potential for group members giving contradictory messages. On balance, we would suggest that group members have access to on-going individual help outside the group whilst they are attending a self-help or therapeutic group.

This chapter examines issues which arise in the process of starting and maintaining a survivors' group. These issues include:

— models for survivors' group;
— open and closed groups;
— facilitating a survivors' group;
— starting a survivors' group;
— setting boundaries;
— joining a survivors' group;

— planning group meetings;
— structure of group meetings;
— responding to specific issues;
— ending a group.

Attending a survivors' group has a number of advantages for a survivor:

— she immediately sheds the isolation which she may have felt for years. Meeting other survivors helps her to see that she is not alone;
— she can see that she is not the abnormal person she perceived herself to be. Being in the company of other women who are working hard to recover enables her to validate her own strengths;
— group membership puts a survivor in touch with others with similar experiences. It also allows the woman to begin to develop her own support network;
— being part of a group enables the survivor to give and receive challenges in a supportive way, especially when they relate to the distortions of reality caused by the abuse. For example, a woman who feels guilty about an aspect of the abuse can find herself challenging another group member on a similar issue. In this way she can tell others what she needs to tell herself;
— being part of a survivors' group can also encourage a woman to develop skills which might help her to develop relationships in the future. These include identifying and communicating feelings, giving and receiving help and setting limits for herself and others in the group;
— there is often no substitute, no matter how good the quality of the relationship with her individual helper, for hearing herself and other survivors saying, 'It was not your fault.'

Many of the themes which arise in groups have been discussed in Chapter 8. It is, however, the experience of sharing them with other survivors that enables a woman to feel that

for the first time her . . . experience makes her one of a group rather than the deviant she usually perceives herself as being. She identifies with others the same guilt, anger, shame, fear and grief, needs and hopes. (Blake-White and Kline, 1985)

Models for Survivors' Groups

There are four types of group:

Self-help groups   These are formed by survivors themselves without the support of professionals or volunteers. These groups usually operate without a formal leader or they may rotate leadership between group members. Some self-help groups are structured, others are more flexible. The main problems for self-help groups are:

— there may be difficulty in maintaining continuity. They are usually open to anyone who chooses to come, and members often leave and rejoin;
— there may be difficulty in fostering trust between members because of their lack of continuity of membership;
— survivors may join the group before they are ready, and they can be retraumatized by the group experience;
— sometimes group members are too close to the issues and emotions which may arise in the group, and they may not be able to attend to the needs of a particular survivor.

The main advantages of self-help groups relate to their immediate availability to a survivor, and to survivors using their own strengths, resources and experiences to help each other.

Mutual support groups   These groups usually operate under the auspices of a voluntary organization such as Rape Crisis, Women's Aid or a community mental health resource. These groups can be self-help groups or have a more specific therapeutic set of aims. They may include facilitators, who may or may not have been sexually abused themselves.

Therapeutic groups   These are groups which are usually time-limited, more highly structured and facilitated by trained staff or volunteers. Potential members may be screened or assessed for membership, allowing the facilitator to assess the survivor's readiness for the group. The emphasis is on working together to understand, learn and move on from the experience of child sexual abuse.

Pressure/social action groups   The emphasis is on raising the public profile of the issue of sexual abuse; many survivors find these groups helpful in the recovery process. Organizing a group around a specific issue can be empowering and is also a way of informing the local community about a social issue of great importance. These groups can lobby for changes in the law, changes in investigative procedures, and they can campaign for more resources for survivors.

All four models offer the survivor a useful source of help and support. The presence of facilitators has some added advantages. They can:

— pay attention to the group process and also support individual group members;
— sustain the group through periods of low energy;
— have an enabling role within the group, ensuring that power is shared evenly.

Open and Closed Groups

A key feature of survivors' groups is whether they are run as open or closed groups. An open group has two major characteristics:

— members are free to join, leave and re-join at any time;
— the group is unlikely to be time-limited.

Open groups are more likely to be found in community-based settings and provide a continuing, long-term resource for survivors. Survivors themselves may have a strong preference for open access groups. They point to the importance of being able to join a group as soon as possible after making the decision to talk about the past with other survivors. Having to wait until there are sufficient members to start a new group can feel like a rejection at a time when acceptance is of great importance to them. Group facilitators, by contrast, may have stronger reservations about the admission of new members fearing disruption to the development of the group (Gordy, 1983; Sgroi, 1989).

A closed group has the following characteristics:

— membership of the group is fixed at the outset;
— the group is more likely to be time-limited;
— it is more likely to be found in a more formal setting, and will have at least one leader who is attached to that setting as a paid helper or volunteer.

Closed groups often have a limited number of meetings whose overall structure and general content may have been pre-determined by the facilitators or leaders (Gordy, 1983; Davenport and Sheldon, 1987; Tsai and Wagner, 1978).

The main advantages and disadvantages of open and closed groups for survivors are summarized in Table 10.1. Whilst groups may prefer to be either totally open or closed to new members after their first meeting, consideration of a third alternative may be helpful. A group may start as

Table 10.1: **Open and closed groups: Advantages and disadvantages**

Open Groups	
Advantages	Disadvantages
Access is available when women want it.	Trust may be more difficult to achieve.
New members can prevent group becoming stagnant.	New members may feel excluded from group culture.
Members may find it easier to leave the group when they want.	Newer members may not know group information which is important to aid their understanding of another member's problems.
Membership reduces the 'secretive' nature of a survivors' group and may contribute to breaking silence about sexual abuse.	More established members may not want to repeatedly share the same information with new members.
Repeated sharing of information lessens the power of the secret of sexual abuse.	There may be a greater risk of breaches in confidentiality.
Members at different stages can give each other encouragement and support.	Group may find it hard to resolve conflicts between group members with arrival of new members and uncertain attendance.
Not dependent on 'viable' number of members.	Attendance can be variable.
Membership allows women control over how they use the group in terms of attendance and input.	Group culture may never develop or be dominated by the beliefs, behaviour or emotions of one member.

Closed Groups	
Advantages	Disadvantages
Trust is more easily established.	Women may find it hard to leave, if group is not meeting their needs.
Members can get to know each other well over a period of time.	Women may be discouraged if they have to wait to join.
Group can move on together from one issue to the next.	A limited number of sessions may not be enough for some women to trust and feel safe.
It is easier to plan group activities together.	More formalized structure may result in members feeling less in control.
It is easier to establish and maintain group culture and rules.	

a closed group, enabling the development of trust and rapport between members, and remain closed for a limited number of sessions. At the end of the agreed number of sessions, the group starts again, admitting new members and allowing more established members to decide if they wish to continue in the group. Sgroi (1989) suggests that it is easier to convince people of the advantages of a time-limited group. She suggests that ten to fourteen weekly or fortnightly sessions is more reassuring than an open-ended group which can be unfamiliar and threatening. She also suggests that it is helpful to know in advance when a group is scheduled to stop, and to plan around that date. Open groups can be positively harmful if no trust develops, or if one member dominates. It is difficult to build trust and hard to do any planned work when membership of the group constantly changes. This can lead to new members feeling disillusioned and marginalized by more established members. New members can feel discouraged as well as encouraged by others who seem much further on or who have been group members for a long time. They may ask themselves, 'Is it going to take me so long to recover?' We would recommend closed survivors' groups as the safer forum for survivors.

Facilitating a Survivors' Group

The experience of facilitating a survivors' group can be exhausting, exhilarating, sad, exciting, angry, infuriating, and energizing. There are a number of important issues to consider for anyone planning to undertake the work. In the first place, it is our belief that, wherever possible, there should be two facilitators for groups because:

— the material expressed and exchanged is often stressful and painful, and is more easily coped with on a shared basis;
— it helps to reflect on the content and process of the group afterwards;
— if a woman is in distress, one facilitator can attend to the distress while the other pays attention to other group members;
— it is easier for two people to follow all the group interactions, particularly when some of the material is expressed non-verbally;
— mutual support and feedback is more readily available when there are two facilitators;
— cover for the group is maintained during holidays, sickness and in time of personal difficulties;
— ideas can be shared on how to plan future sessions.

Co-facilitating a Survivors' Group

The choice of co-facilitators should be made on the basis of the particular skills and experience of the facilitators in relation to the group's aims. However, sometimes an *ad hoc* or pressured decision is made to facilitate a group in response to the constraints of limited resources or the personal interests of facilitators themselves. Whatever the means by which facilitators embark on their work, they must do the following:

— they must have the capacity to work together. They may have already worked successfully together in the past. If not, they will need to check out their feelings about working together on this occasion. Discussing issues about child sexual abuse and planning the first session of the group can give an indication of their compatibility;

— they must trust each other and collaborate during the group sessions. Co-facilitators can provide a role-model during the meetings and they need to test their ability to do this;

— they must be clear about their roles and responsibilities during and between meetings. They will need to agree to share the facilitator role equally, or to work as a leader and assistant, with the former clearly taking overall responsibility. In the early stages of the group, it can be helpful to know who has responsibility for starting and ending the meeting, who takes special note of members' feelings, who introduces different themes or activities and so on. Some pairs split the group task and group process roles fairly explicitly; others prefer to wait and see how it develops naturally;

— they must be able to examine their working relationship. This is not always easy, but it is important and can be done together after a session or in supervision. Areas of conflict or collusion can often be more easily identified by a third party who can encourage frank dialogue and a sharing of difficulties.

Gender of Facilitators

There are strong arguments for ensuring that facilitators for female survivors' groups are women. These arguments include:

— women who have been sexually abused find it very difficult to trust male helpers, particularly during the early stages and during disclosure;

— they may see male facilitators as potential abusers;

— they may have learned to 'perform' for men and this could seriously affect the expression of honest feelings in the group;

— their early experiences have disempowered them, and the presence of a male facilitator could perpetuate feelings of powerlessness and loss of control;

— female facilitators can provide role models on some issues;

— facilitators who have not been abused can share their own experiences of being women. They can also share feelings of having felt vulnerable or powerless.

A male facilitator may present a number of difficulties for a group of survivors, not least of which is simply being in close proximity to a man (See Chapter 2). However, if some of these problems can be overcome, a male facilitator can provide a positive role-model of male behavior and may enable the woman to learn to trust a man again. The process of learning to trust and be in the company of a man can take a long time for some women.

Personal Qualities of Facilitators

The qualities needed to lead a survivors' group include consistency, honesty, calm, warmth and reliability, empathy and understanding. The ability to challenge constructively and deal with conflicts which arise between group members, to stick to the boundaries set and to be able to cope with distress in others are also important. Facilitators are often placed in a parenting role by the group. Many survivors have had impoverished early relationships with adult women, especially their mothers. Facilitators can provide the opportunity for group members to work through feelings relating to these early experiences — feelings of abandonment and not being cared for, and to have the experience of a warm relationship with adult women.

Overall, facilitators should be able to respond flexibly and with sensitivity to whatever the women bring to the group. This helps to ensure that the power invested in them does not perpetuate the powerlessness felt by the group members.

Attitudes and Feelings About Sexual Abuse

Group facilitators will not be helpful unless they have explored their own feelings about sexual abuse in some depth. This may involve a painful journey through their own childhood. It has been suggested (Gordy, 1983) that having a survivor to facilitate the group can accelerate feelings of mutual trust among group members. It is our view, however, that one of the facilitators should not have suffered sexual abuse. This enables the group to be provided with a yardstick of more 'normal' childhood experiences and enables the facilitators to acknowledge the pain of individual group members without triggering off their own pain. In groups where one of the facilitators is a survivor herself, she should be satisfied that she has resolved issues from her own past before starting with the group.

Support and Supervision For Facilitators

In addition to support which co-facilitators are able to give each other, it is helpful to enlist the help of another person for support and supervision. This person should be someone who has had experience of working with survivors. Regular meetings with a supervisor should:

— review the group content and process;
— give feedback on the work of each facilitator;
— pick up any potential problem areas for individual members at the next meeting;
— undertake some advance planning;
— explore any personal issues for the facilitators which have arisen during the session.

Facilitators should also decide how to inform the group about their arrangements for support and supervision. It is important to reassure them about the confidentiality of these meetings and to give an indication of their content and frequency.

Time Commitment for Survivors' Groups

Facilitators should be aware of the time they will have to commit to a survivors' group. Time-limited groups with an obvious terminating date are less demanding in terms of personal resources. Open-ended groups are, by definition, less easy to plan ahead. They can be very time-consuming for facilitators and are sometimes difficult to sustain through periods of low energy. Facilitators in open-ended groups should build into supervision a regular review of their time commitment to the group, noting any areas of difficulty and discussing possible solutions.

Starting a Survivors' Group

The impetus for starting a survivors' group can come from survivors themselves, with or without the support of organizations such as Rape Crisis or Women's Aid, from voluntary organizations or from professionals working in a hospital or community setting. If the group is started by survivors, it may be open to any woman who was sexually abused as a child. If, on the other hand, a group is started by professional workers, members may have to undergo some form of assessment or screening to determine their suitability for the group. The criteria for assessment might include:

— ability to work in a group setting;
— current support network;
— access to one-to-one help while attending the group;
— level of day-to-day pressures and how these are being managed.

An advantage of screening is that it gives some prior indication to facilitators of the stage which potential group members have reached in coming to terms with their childhood experiences. A further advantage of screening relates to a survivor's sense of feeling different from other people. Facilitators can attempt to have a group of mixed sexual orientation, ethnic background or age. Survivors often have strong feelings of being outsiders, as do women of colour and lesbian women. Survivors' groups should not do anything which serves to reinforce that sense of difference. The main disadvantage of screening is that women can feel excluded, and their sense of isolation is maintained, if they are assessed and fail to be included in a group.

The question of group size will need to be agreed by the facilitators beforehand, if the group is closed. A group of between six and eight members allows for absences and is not too large to inhibit participation by group members.

Resources and Finance

There are a number of issues relating to resources and finance to be considered:

1 the meeting place for the group should be easily accessible, sound-proof, safe, warm, comfortable and free from interruption. The premises of a sympathetic voluntary organization, such as family centre, rape crisis centre, women's centre might be suitable. It is not advisable to hold meetings in a member's home, since it can create problems if the member wants to miss a meeting, or if there are constant interruptions from visitors, telephone callers or her family. Access to the same meeting place for all meetings of the group is also important for continuity;

2 facilities for making tea and coffee should be available;

3 good quality childcare and/or care for dependents should be investigated whether meetings take place during the day or evening;

4   initial funding for booking a room, providing refreshments and care of dependents should be investigated. Once established, the group may want to embark on its own fundraising activities;

5   naming the group: Women who join a group may be worried about being identified as a survivor of child sexual abuse. Anonymity can be achieved by using a 'neutral' name when booking the room for meetings, for example, Tuesday Group, Self-Help Group, Women's Group. The group can decide its permanent name once it becomes established.

Starting a Community-based Group

In addition to finding a suitable meeting-place, the group will need to be advertised and the frequency of meetings agreed.

Advertising the group   Posters, leaflets, letters to potential referral sources and press statements are all useful and easy to compile. They should contain clear information about:

— the purpose of the group;
— proposed frequency of meetings;
— membership of the group;
— where/how to find out more details about the first meeting.

Details of the first meeting should be kept to a minimum in any publicity. Interested women will take the trouble to ring a contact telephone number, such as the local rape crisis centre, for further details. This can represent an important first step in encouraging survivors to acknowledge their past and take control of their lives.

Letters and posters can be circulated to community centres, health centres, libraries, community mental health resources, social work departments and psychiatric hospitals several weeks before the first meeting. Press statements can be sent to local radio stations and newspapers. If a survivor is involved at the planning stage, she should have the opportunity to say whether she wishes to be named as a contact person in publicity material, and if she is available for interview with the local media.

Example of Press Statement for first meeting

A new support group for women is to be formed in . . . .
. . . . within the next few weeks. The group aims to bring

together any women who have experienced sexual abuse by a trusted adult during their childhood.

The effects of such abuse can be long lasting, and it is hoped that the group will enable participant survivors to share their experiences and begin to come to terms with their past.

Further information about the group can be obtained by writing to or telephoning . . . .
. . . .

Example of Poster advertising initial meeting

Are you	a woman who has been sexually abused in childhood by a trusted adult?
Would you	like to meet other women with similar experience for mutual support?
A Group for Survivors of Child Sexual Abuse	will have its first meeting in a few weeks
If you would like to know more	Contact . . . .

Frequency of meetings The frequency of meetings should be agreed by the group, or be established before the group is started by the facilitators, but facilitators must also be clear about the limits of their commitment. It is helpful to hold meetings on the same day of the week, for example, alternate Thursdays, so that women who have missed meetings know when the group will meet again. Our experience indicates that fortnightly meetings allow enough time for members to reflect on issues raised in the group and, if a crisis arises, they have access to each other before the next meeting. When a woman joins a survivors' group she may find the time between meetings too long. This is understandable but, as time goes on, she may be better able to hold on to her feelings between meetings.

Figure 10.1 **Poster for Survivors' Group.**

Starting a Professionally-run Group

Although many of the issues are similar to those involved in starting a community-based group, there are some important additional factors to be considered:

Referrals   Referrals can be obtained by circulating colleagues with details of the group and asking them to pass on the information to potential group members. Posters can also be displayed in the organization, allowing potential members to self-select for referral or assessment to the group. Group facilitators may also wish to assess potential members for their suitability.

Three areas need to be addressed if potential group members are screened. These are:

— the stabilizing of severe long-term effects of the abuse, including alcohol and drug abuse. Unless potential members can demonstrate that they are reasonably stable, they will be unable to withstand the stress generated by group members in examining the meaning of their behavior;
— their ability to discuss their experiences of abuse. This does not imply that they will be expected to disclose all manner of details about the abuse, but could include the ability to understand its long-term effects;
— a willingness to participate in the group. The facilitator might explain the difference between a self-help and therapeutic group, and could outline the role of the facilitators, the format of the group meetings and other practical matters.

Location of meetings   Where possible, group meetings should be located in the community. This helps to allay fears of identification of stigma which might occur if the group met in a hospital setting.

Frequency and length of meetings   Published accounts of professionally led groups indicate that they are more likely to be closed and time-limited (Davenport and Sheldon, 1987; Gordy, 1983; Herman and Schatzow, 1984; Tsai and Wagner, 1978; Sgroi, 1989). The number of members averages between eight and twelve, and they usually meet weekly, over six to twelve weeks for an hour-and-a-half to two hours. Evaluation of the groups shows that members would have welcomed more sessions, and again there is some preference for an open-ended group.

Setting Boundaries

An important activity for a survivors' group is the establishment of boundaries for the group's operation. The setting of boundaries allows members some control over one aspect of their lives, and it can provide a positive framework for women whose childhood boundaries have been repeatedly violated. As one study puts it:

Repeated violation in childhood fragments ego boundaries and therefore consistent limits such as punctual timekeeping, and the same physical setting each week were of enormous importance. (Davenport and Sheldon, 1987)

The boundaries which are helpful to a group's functioning include the length of meetings, confidentiality, record-keeping and contact between meetings.

Length of meetings   It is important for the group to agree on a length of time for meetings, whilst acknowledging that it may be difficult to adhere to strict time limits. Two hours should be sufficient. If someone is in distress, or a woman is particularly needy during a session, it can be difficult for the facilitator to resist the pressure for more time. Asking each group member to take responsibility for ensuring that the group ends on time helps to alleviate this problem. Repeatedly extending the agreed time limit can:

— limit the effective work undertaken during the session;
— tire the group members and facilitators;
— impose additional stress on everyone present.

Confidentiality   Every new member should be reminded about the boundaries of confidentiality. The group will need to decide:

— with whom group meetings can be discussed;
— how confidentiality within the group is to be maintained.

There are two ways in which confidentiality can be a problem in groups. The first, particularly in a professionally-led group, concerns information the facilitators pass on to colleagues about the group. The second concerns what individual group members do with information about other members. Both of these issues should be discussed in the group as they may affect members' freedom to trust, take risks and share personal information.

Confidentiality may pose additional problems if:

— group members' families are known to each other outside the group. This may leave some women feeling particularly vulnerable;
— facilitators have made arrangements for support and supervision from someone outside the group. Members will need to be reassured that their confidentiality will be respected.

Record keeping   This also has important implications for confidentiality. The group will need to decide:

— should the group keep records of each meeting;
— what records will be kept (a historical record of the group, an account of issues covered, exercises undertaken);
— the form of records (individual diaries which women could decide whether or not to share, a group 'diary' which could be written by each member in rotation or by the facilitators);
— who will keep the records and where they will be kept;
— what will happen to records when the group finishes.

If facilitators are also planning to keep their own records for reflection and supervision purposes, the group should be informed.

Contact between meetings   Once trust is established between members, they might develop strong friendships and support networks. It is important that individuals have the choice of whether they can be contacted between meetings. They can then exchange addresses or telephone numbers, opting out if they want to. Facilitators also need to decide whether they are available to group members between meetings. Availability can pose problems, particularly when a woman discloses information to the facilitator which she would rather not share in the group. Contact between meetings also extends the boundaries of the availability of facilitators. They may find it difficult to sustain regular contact between meetings even if only one or two members contact them for additional support.

Group rules   The establishment of ground rules can be undertaken at the first meeting and reviewed regularly. Agreed ground rules could be made into a poster, to be displayed on the wall at each meeting, and amended as necessary. They might cover:

— membership of the group (a clear statement that the group is open to female survivors, arrangements for joining if the group is open or closed);
— financial arrangements (bank account, money for tea and coffee, etc.);
— confidentiality of the group (including record keeping);
— frequency and length of meetings;
— arrangements (if any) for follow-up if a woman misses one or more meetings.

Establishing group rules at the outset can be useful in promoting trust, group cohesion and participation.

Joining a Survivors' Group

Coming to a survivors' group for the first time can be a harrowing experience. A woman may get enormous relief from sharing her past with others, but it may also be the first time that she has publicly acknowledged her abuse. She may feel very apprehensive about meeting other survivors or worried that she will encounter someone known to herself or the abuser at a group meeting. It is important to acknowledge all of these issues with her at any pre-group meeting and, if appropriate, when she comes to a group for the first time.

Every woman who decides to join a survivors' group is bound to feel some anxiety. This is sometimes increased because she does not feel ready to join the group, but it has been suggested to her by well-meaning professionals or friends. Difficulties in asserting herself and saying 'No', may lead her to feel that she is obliged to attend the group. It is important to check, therefore, that she feels ready to join.

In *open groups*, at least one meeting with a prospective new member should be arranged before she joins the group. She should meet one of the facilitators and, if she wishes, a group member. At this meeting, information about the group can be given, and the woman herself has the chance to ask questions. Arrangements can then be made to accompany her to her first meeting; this gives her time to think over what she has heard before making a final decision about whether to attend. It also allows her to opt out if she wants, without losing face. If she decides to join the group, she knows that she will have the security of being accompanied to her first meeting by a familiar person.

When a woman attends the group for the first time it is essential that:

— she is welcomed and introduced to everyone;
— she knows that she has the choice to speak or listen;
— she knows that no pressure will be put on her to talk about her life experiences until she is ready to do so.

In *closed groups*, especially if members are assessed before joining, it is important to:

— explain the purpose of the group;
— outline the structure of meetings;
— explain the role of facilitators.

Just as group members might be assessed by facilitators, it is important that they too have the opportunity to get information and assess what the group proposes to offer to them. This can be done at a preliminary meeting with the facilitators.

The first meeting of a closed group obviously has to begin with introductions. The purpose of the group, the structure of and arrangements for the meetings should be shared before the main discussion of the meeting gets underway.

Introduction New members should always be introduced to an open group. This will not only break the ice but it can also confirm some of the ground rules of the group. At a first meeting one of the facilitators might say:

> Welcome to the survivors' group. My name is. . . . and I am one of the group facilitators. The other group facilitator is. . . . Neither one of us has been sexually abused by a trusted adult, and we hope that we are able to give support in the group to women who have.

It is also important to explain that women will not be 'put on the spot' in relation to disclosing details of their life experiences.

The women in the group can then be asked to introduce themselves using their first names. If a particular woman finds this too difficult, one of the facilitators could introduce her to the rest of the group. Similar introductions of new members to an open group must be made, with an emphasis placed on a woman's freedom to choose to talk or to remain silent.

Sometimes a woman who has come to the group for the first time may begin to talk at length when she is introduced. Just speaking may cause her such anxiety that she has difficulty limiting what she says. Facilitators should allow her to talk, but bring in other group members at the appropriate time, so that the new member does not monopolize the group's time.

The alternative methods of introduction might be considered:

1 Each member could be asked to introduce themselves by their first name.

They could also be asked:

— to identify the family member who abused them;
— who they first told or tried to tell about the abuse;
— what were the consequences of telling.

2   Members could be asked to pair with the person sitting next to them and to talk to each other about themselves for a few minutes. Each woman then introduces her 'partner' to the group, saying only what she has been given permission to share.

Planning Group Meetings

The planning of the content and structure of meetings is an important task for group facilitators. The nature of this task depends on whether the group is open, closed or time-limited. If the group is to be time-limited with a predetermined number of sessions, facilitators may plan the general outline of the content of group meetings in advance; examples of this are described by Davenport and Sheldon (1987), Deighton and McPeek (1985), Herman and Schatzow (1984) and Sgroi (1989). Typically, the first session involves introductions and the sharing of individual and group aims.

In groups that are not time-limited, a more flexible approach is necessary. Planning should be undertaken by the facilitators before each group meeting. The main areas to cover are:

— administrative tasks carried out from the previous meeting;
— planning the introduction to the meeting (including the introduction of new members and feedback of key issues/themes from the last session);
— arrangements for setting aside 'individual time' for any women who want to talk about a specific issue;
— group task as a means of exploring an agreed theme.

Structure of Group Meetings

Planning, starting, facilitating and ending a group meeting are tasks which require thought and co-ordination on the part of facilitators. A consistent structure can promote feelings of 'safety, containment and trust' (Davenport and Sheldon, 1987) although facilitators should be flexible enough to abandon an agreed structure if a woman is in crisis or a more immediate issue is presented.

Starting a group meeting   This is important in setting the atmosphere for the session. A few minutes to allow everyone to get seated can be followed by an introduction by one of the facilitators. This is a signal to everyone that the group is about to begin. In open groups, new members should be introduced at this point, and there are a number of introductory tasks and exercises that can be used at the start of a meeting. The facilitators should:

— remind the group of the previous meeting's discussion;
— check whether there are any aspects of the previous meeting's discussion that anyone wishes to raise;
— check briefly with each group member how she has been feeling since the previous meeting;
— remind the group of any decision that has been made about the content of the meeting (topic to be discussed).

In this way, the facilitators can quickly establish which group members may need individual time during the meeting; it also encourages some continuity between meetings. Beyond this, there are several useful introductory exercises that can help the group to begin:

1   Everyone, including the facilitators, could be asked to think about:

— three hopes;
— three fears;
— three expectations.

which they have for attending the group. These can then be shared in the group.
2   Everyone is asked to share something they feel good about having done since the last meeting. In order to set the tone, a facilitator might start by saying something brief. For example:

'I bought myself a new blouse today.'
'I went for a walk in the park last weekend.'
'I got here tonight!'

The sharing of achievements serves several important purposes:

— it allows women to take credit for things they have achieved;
— it reminds them that they can and should do nice things for themselves;
— it helps to reverse the process of self-criticism which may have been with them for years.

In spite of these more positive methods of starting a group, a woman may attend the group in such distress that she may blurt out her problems, hardly pausing for breath. Facilitators will need to exercise great tact in order to enable everyone to contribute.

They might say:

> We're trying to get round everyone just now, Jane. You sound very upset, and we'll come back to you in a little while, after everyone has had the chance to say something.

The group in process   After the introductory period, facilitators will have a good idea of what will be useful for the remainder of the session. They may have learned:

— that a woman is in crisis;
— that there are a few women who are so needy that they will use as much group time as is offered;
— whether there is any feedback or follow-up from previous meetings.

The next stage of the group should build on this information, or return to plans already made for the meeting. Broadly speaking, there are three types of group activities which can be used alone, or in combination, during a group meeting. These are:

— topics for discussion;
— exercises;
— individual time.

A topic has a number of advantages:

— it focuses the attention of group members on a common theme;
— it creates a sense of coming together for a shared purpose;
— it allows women to draw attention to an important aspect of their lives;
— it enables the facilitators to set limits by keeping group members on the topic;
— it enables every woman in the group to contribute.

A range of topics, by no means exclusive, is outlined in Table 10.2.

One of the most important tasks for the facilitator here is to ensure that everyone who wants to, gets the chance to speak in the group meeting. Facilitators can draw in other group members by saying,

Table 10.2: **Topics for discussion in a survivors' group**

Trust

Power and control

Dealing with feelings of anger towards abusers

Difficulties with mothering

Coping with emotions and memories

Problems with relationships

Dealing with feelings of guilt, anger, despair and revenge

Dealing with flashbacks and nightmares

Relationships with men

Relationships with partners

Feelings towards own children

Experiences with statutory services, such as hospitals, social work departments

Feelings towards mothers

Coping with anniversaries

> Jane, you sound very.... (describing the feeling) about your experience. I wonder if anyone else has had similar experiences or feelings.
>
> or
>
> Marion, you've talked about this issue in a previous meeting. Perhaps you could tell Jane how you dealt with it.

Group exercises may be an appropriate activity when there are more than four women in the group. They can be used to:

— build trust between group members;
— evoke difficult feelings, such as expressing anger in a 'safe' environment;
— re-create childhood experiences from which they were excluded;
— relax and enjoy each others' company.

There are some important guidelines for group exercises:

— they should be kept simple and straightforward;
— they should not make any member feel under pressure to participate;
— time should be set aside for feedback and support if needed.

Table 10.3: **Group activities and their purpose**

Activity	Purpose
Trust games	— building trust — acknowledging trust — taking risks
Touch activities	— building trust — giving support — accepting good feelings from others — learning safe touch
Childhood activities/games	— reclaiming lost childhood — having fun — discovering latent skills
Drawing	— expressing feelings — getting feedback from others — working together and building trust
Word plans	— acknowledging common feelings — saying difficult words or phrases
Use of poems (see Appendix 1)	— putting difficult feelings into words — sharing common feelings

Detailed examples of group activities and exercises are given in Chapter 11. Table 10.3 gives an indication of their purpose in a group. Individual time is the time during a meeting which individual women use to talk about pressing problems or issues from their past. It can form the main part of a meeting, or it can be time set aside for individual women to talk after a topic or activity. If the group breaks for coffee during a meeting, individual time could follow the break.

It is useful to remind women of the individual time available by saying:

'We can spend the next hour talking about individual concerns.'

This makes members aware that they are sharing a limited amount of time. It is also helpful to ask a woman if she would like feedback from the group or if she just wants to talk in the knowledge that others understand what she is saying. When she has finished speaking, a facilitator could say:

'I wonder is anyone else has ever felt like that?' 'Have you ever faced that problem? What did you do?'

Facilitators can give their ideas and reactions when other group members have spoken.

An important task for facilitators is to maintain their awareness of other group members while listening to a particular woman's experiences. Having two facilitators makes this task easier. One person can pay particular attention to the woman who is talking, while the other takes responsibility for noticing the reactions of the group members — if they are listening, emotionally shut off or showing signs of distress.

Sometimes a woman talks at length and it may be necessary for a facilitator to gently interrupt her in order to re-engage the attention of the group. A facilitator could say:

'You're talking about a lot of very painful things that have happened. I'm sure there are other women who are remembering similar experiences and feelings. Would you like to hear from them?'

or

'You seem very angry/sad/anxious. I'd like to check how everyone else is feeling and we'll come back to you.'

Once other group members have had the opportunity to share some of their feelings, the woman should be allowed to continue. This type of intervention is helpful on a number of counts:

— it breaks some of the tension which might have arisen in the group as a result of what the woman is saying;
— it draws the group together;
— it acknowledges common feelings between group members.

Breaks in the meeting should be agreed beforehand. Breaks can be used to:

— move from topic/exercise/individual time;
— have some refreshments;
— release some of the tension or lighten the atmosphere.

Ending the meeting   Ending the meeting properly is important, and ensures that the group does not drift to an uneven close. Using the same method of ending each meeting establishes an acceptable routine for group members. Facilitators should indicate when it is time for the meeting to draw to a close. They could say something like:

'We have fifteen minutes left. It's time to think about ending the meeting.'

It is important to try to end meetings on time, although this may not always be possible, and arrangements for the next meeting should be confirmed. These should include:

— checking that everyone knows the date of the meeting;
— making arrangements for lifts home and to the next group meeting;
— confirming what the group has agreed to do at its next meeting.

Finally, a check should be made to see how everyone is feeling and that they feel safe going home. If someone is feeling distressed she might welcome contact from other group members before the next meeting.

Evaluating the Group

Evaluation can be carried out by:

— asking women directly what they have gained from the group and what they would like to see changed;
— undertaking a follow-up of women after they have stopped attending the group.

If more formal evaluation is required, it may be necessary to ask the women to complete questionnaires and other evaluation material on a voluntary basis before they attend the group and after they leave. In this way, some measure of the changes, problems and benefits of the group can be made.

Responding to Specific Issues

Within survivors' groups there are a number of issues which may pose particular problems for members or facilitators. They are listed in Table 10.4.

Problems with Group Membership

Sometimes there are unforeseen difficulties which arise as a consequence of group membership. These include:

Table 10.4: **Issues which arise in survivors' groups**

Problems with group membership

Trust

Relationships with men

Lesbian women

Poverty and wealth

Issues for women in rural areas

Women with multiple problems

Silent women

Anger

Revenge

Not talking about the abuse

Minimizing individual experiences

Comparison of abuse experiences

Going over the same ground

Suicide attempts and self-abuse

Difficulties with touch

Previous acquaintances If a new member discovers that she knows another group member she may express shock, relief or surprise. For some women it is an awkward experience, especially if members of their respective families have ongoing contact. If this is the case, there may be questions about the confidentiality of material discussed in the group and trust between the two women may be difficult to establish. The facilitators have a responsibility to help them to confront the issue. This could be done in the context of a general discussion about trust. Alternatively a facilitator could say:

> 'Karen and Annette, we know that you were upset/dismayed/ frightened, etc, to meet each other in the group. How do you think that knowing each other might affect/has affected the way you are in the group?'

Siblings joining the group This can pose problems, especially if their experience of the abuse and its consequences has been different. Difficulties can arise if the group spends too great a proportion of its time on their relationship or experiences at the expense of other members. Again, it is important to address the issue openly. A facilitator might say:

'Katrina and Mary, you have spent a lot of time recently in the group discussing your relationship with each other. Perhaps there is no more help that the group can give you with this. What do you think. . . . What do other women think?'

On the other hand, the presence of sisters can enable the group to see that sexual abuse can continue for years, often without other family members being aware of it.

Trust

Trust is a central theme in a survivors' group, and it may take a long time to establish. The issue of trust is manifest in a number of different ways:

— women direct their contributions to the group and to each other through the facilitators;
— women find it difficult to show any form of physical affection to each other;
— there are difficulties participating in any trust games;
— women are unable to ask for support from other group members during or between meetings.

Openly drawing attention to these issues may improve the situation. Facilitators should therefore use every possible opportunity to confirm the achievements made by individual women and the group as a whole in trusting each other enough to share their experiences.

Relationships with Men

Within a survivors' group, women will have had a range of experiences in their relationships with men. These include:

— supportive or good relationships with male partners and/or colleagues;
— abusive heterosexual relationships;
— acquaintance/superficial relationships with men;

Women who have rejected relationships with men through fear are likely to find any discussion of sexuality or heterosexual relationships extremely threatening. They may express nausea or disgust and may even withdraw emotionally or physically from the group. This can be difficult for women who are in a heterosexual relationship, supportive or otherwise. A facilitator faced with this situation will rely on her co-worker to give her support if needed. She may also need to note any reaction in other group members which is in response to the topic under discussion rather than to the details of the group member's life.

Lesbian Women

Many of society's assumptions about the nature of female sexuality may be evident in a survivors' group. This is particularly so in relation to lesbian women. They may find it difficult to be open about their sexuality in a group. There can be additional fears and some resentment if other women:

— express homophobic sentiments;
— express a fear of being gay themselves.

Facilitators will need to check out with survivors who are lesbian how much information about their sexuality they wish other group members to know.

A group member may also be questioning her sexual orientation. The experience of being in an intensive, supportive group with other women, perhaps for the first time in her life, may blur the distinction between friendship, emotional attachment and sexual attraction. Facilitators should be alert to this possibility although it may not be appropriate to discuss it in the group.

Poverty and Wealth

A variation in income levels and relative standard of living can cause problems in the group in the following ways:

— some women might have difficulty finding money for group outings;
— there may be resentment of members who appear to have a higher income;
— there might be some disbelief that a women can have an adequate income and still have problems with her children or relationships.

A group 'kitty', into which members pay a small amount each week, can help resolve immediate problems with group outings. Otherwise it is important for facilitators to acknowledge the issue with the group as a whole. They might say:

> Although everyone in the group has a different standard of living, the common bond is your childhood experiences. Money can sometimes dull the pain of the past, and sometimes it also contributes to problems.

This could open up discussion on the issue.

Issues for Women in Rural Areas

There are a number of issues relating to group membership for women in rural areas. These include:

— identification as a survivor in a community where everyone knows each other can leave a woman feeling more vulnerable and isolated. She may not wish to identify herself in this way but may feel she has no choice;
— she may have problems of access to group meetings, especially if the woman is dependent on public transport;
— she may still live in the same community as the one she grew up in. The abuser and her family may be known to everyone. Her identification as a survivor has the potential for division, not only in her family of origin, but in the community as a whole;
— the preservation of confidentiality may also be more difficult than in larger urban communities.

These issues should be anticipated before the group starts, and ways of resolving them discussed alongside the needs of the survivors, the preservation of confidentiality and any particular feature of the community in which the group is to be based.

Women with Multiple Problems

Sometimes women who have had a lifetime of deprivation and abuse join the group. They seem to lurch from one crisis to the next, and the group as a whole can easily be overwhelmed by the apparently endless catalogue of disasters which a woman experiences. For some women this is undoubtedly their reality, but the issue for the group to face is whether the woman can realistically get support within it. It is important to help her to focus on one problem, but she may need one-to-one help before she can benefit from the support offered in the group context.

Silent Women

Sometimes women join a survivors' group and for many weeks say nothing at all. They might participate in group activities and come on group outings, but when the group starts to talk about sexual abuse in any detail, these women become silent. Their body language may also show signs of emotional distancing. The reasons for their silence include:

— they are too anxious or nervous to participate in the group;
— they cannot cope yet with the emotional content of the group;
— they do not feel that they have anything worthwhile to say;
— they do not trust the group enough to participate in it.

It is difficult to respond helpfully to a silent group member without her feeling under more pressure; sometimes another group member will address the issue, and a facilitator can follow this up. Asking her direct open questions can also gauge how she is feeling. A group review meeting, when members takes stock of their experiences, saying how far their expectations of the group have been met, what they like and what they would like to change about the group, can also enable a silent member to participate.

Anger

The expression of anger is often difficult for women who have experienced sexual abuse. Their anger may be associated with or masked by guilt and low-self-esteem. Women are sometimes frightened to express their anger for fear that it is not containable, or that it will make them go 'mad'. Doing word plans of feelings associated with anger (see Chapter 11), role-plays of situations in which women feel angry and games which allow the expression of anger can help to release some of these feelings in the safe environment of the group.

Revenge

Survivors often express strong feelings of revenge towards their abusers. They want their abusers to feel all the hurt, pain and humiliation which they have suffered themselves. They want to plan a violent or drawn-out death for their abusers, and may spend much time drawing up a hypothetical scenario for this event.

Sharing these violent thoughts helps women to get some of their deep feelings out into the open. Others can acknowledge that they have had similar thoughts and may even have tried to act on them. Reassurance that these feelings of revenge are common, given their childhood ordeal, can remove the sense of 'badness' which they produce. Facilitators should also be ready to point out that feelings of revenge, if held for too long, can sustain a women's anger and bitterness towards the abuser. It can keep her rooted in her past rather than allowing her to come to terms with it. Too much discussion of revenge can also be upsetting for other group members who may not have the confidence to seek a change of subject.

Example: In a survivors' group there were detailed discussions, over a number of meetings, of plans for the form of revenge towards abusers. This was carried out amidst much laughter and even glee. One woman, who left the group at this time, returned some months later to give her reasons for leaving. She said that she had found the prolonged revenge-planning upsetting because she started to have nightmares about her father and now felt that she would 'never be free of him'.

Not Talking about the Abuse

Survivors often avoid talking about the details of their abuse. The reasons for this avoidance include:

— it is still too painful for them to say exactly what happened;
— they have blocked out the details;
— they do not want to give the pain of their feelings to others who are disclosing similar experiences;
— they have never told anyone the details of what happened to them because they are frightened, disgusted or ashamed;
— they feel they cannot trust other group members with the details;

— they have convinced themselves that they have come to terms with their experiences, and they should forget about it all;
— they may still feel they are not believed.

In addition, referring in general terms to being 'bad-used' or 'abused' or talking about when 'it' happened, is all that some women can say about their experiences. The task for facilitators is to encourage individual women to unburden themselves of the details of their abuse, in their own time, under their own control and at their own pace. Facilitators should acknowledge the difficulty of the task and could say,

> We have been meeting now for 'x' meetings. We've all shared a lot with each other. Perhaps the time has come for us to talk about what actually happened when you were abused. Unless we all know what happened, we can't help you each to begin to deal with it.

It has been predicted that the silence following such a statement would not last for long (Tsai and Wagner, 1978). Group members could then be asked:

— at what age did the abuse begin?
— what was the nature of the abuse (in general or specific terms)?
— when, and how did it stop?

If group members can acknowledge the commonality of their experiences, and talk about them in this way, an atmosphere of safety and trust quickly develops around the common themes of secrecy, isolation, shame, and feelings of hurt, helplessness and fear. They can also build together on their strengths, by sharing, for example, the methods they used as children to survive the abuse.

Minimizing Individual Experiences

Sometimes women minimize their experience of being sexually abused because:

— they have not fully acknowledged to themselves its full impact on their lives;
— they compare themselves to other women in the group whom they perceive to have suffered greater pain, humiliation and betrayal of trust;

—they do not want to believe that their experiences really happened.

For these reasons they may not wish to burden other women with their 'lesser' problems. If this is the case, facilitators should point out that everyone's experience is equally valid because of its consequences for each woman. Minimizing the experiences may be an extension of the lack of self-worth that survivors often feel.

Comparison of Abuse Experiences

One of the most empowering experiences of belonging to a survivors' group is the way in which common issues can be explored and shared. Discovering that another survivor has experienced the same forms of abuse can be very reassuring.

On the negative side, however, there may be the possibility of group members feeling that their experiences are worse or less traumatic than other group members. If this happens, facilitators will have to work hard to ensure that all experiences are evaluated by the person who experienced them rather than by the rest of the group.

Going over the Same Ground

Survivors sometimes repeat a description of a particular incident of sexual abuse or a sequence of events over and over again. A signal that it is problematic comes when other group members appear to lose interest as the woman speaks. The issues should be addressed directly by the facilitator by saying:

Agnes, you have talked several times in the group about (name the incident). Perhaps other group members are finding it difficult to know what to say now.

The underlying reasons for this repetition may be that the woman has not told all the details of a particular incident, and is waiting for someone to ask the right question, or that she is frightened to move on for fear of uncovering new, more unpleasant memories. This issue is discussed in more detail in Chapter 7 when we examined the issue of pushing for memories.

Suicide attempts or Self-abuse

Survivors often talk about harming themselves or of wanting to 'forget about it all — for good'. They may have contemplated or attempted suicide in the past and return to the subject at times when they feel particularly vulnerable. For other women, the reminder of their past attempts stays with them in the form of scars from razor blade cuts. If they talk about self-mutilation, it may provoke an angry reaction from other women who might say, 'Haven't you suffered enough pain without putting yourself through this too?' or 'You can't give up now, you're letting him (the abuser) win.'

The urge to self-mutilate or to attempt suicide is a common one and all group members will be able to identify with it. Some group members can be afraid when they are confronted by a woman who is in a self-destructive phase. However, women can be encouraged to support any group member who experiences this sort of stress, and in doing so can learn to acknowledge their own strengths in times of crisis.

Example: Jane arrived at a group meeting one evening in an agitated state. She talked about wanting to die to stop the pain she felt, and half way through the meeting she rushed out of the room. One of the facilitators and another group member, Irene, eventually found her huddled in a corner of her flat. She had made several deep wounds with a blade to both her wrists. Irene immediately took control. She washed and bandaged Jane's wrists tightly and took her to the local hospital. Afterwards Irene was able to recognize that she reacted capably. Jane was able to accept and thank Irene for her concern and practical help.

Difficulties with Touch

Many survivors have difficulty with giving and receiving touch even for comfort or reassurance, because touching had such dangerous and unpleasant connotations in their childhood. Women talk about and show the effects of the problem by:

— having difficulties with expressing themselves in a physical way or responding physically to their children;
— having sexual problems with their partners;
— having difficulties in comforting another group member who is in distress;

— showing difficulty in participating in group exercises or games which involve touching.

The problem can only be dealt with by slowly building trust and acknowledging each woman's right to her 'defensible space'. Some of the exercises described in Chapter 11 might also help.

Leaving the Group

Leaving the group whether it be for all group members in a time-limited group, or for an individual woman in an open group, is a very important issue.

Time-limited Groups

In this situation, all group members leave together and know in advance that the group will be ending on a certain date. This allows both facilitators and members to prepare for the end of the group. For some women, the end of the group will represent a loss. It may also signal the beginning of a new phase of life which is much less troubled by the history of sexual abuse. Facilitators should therefore:

— prepare the women for the potential feelings of loss (including sadness, anger, emptiness, abandonment);
— look at ongoing support networks for the women;
— discuss arrangements for follow-up or further meetings;
— examine the positive achievements made in the group by each member.

One writer suggests making the final meeting a celebration of survival, with group members sharing their individual and collective accomplishments. She suggests that each member should bring food to share — as a symbol of nurturing and sustenance of group members by each other. This enables group members to leave on a high note and to enable the saying of good-byes to be a positive experience (Butler, 1978).

Open Groups

The main disadvantage in open groups is that people often leave without other group members being aware of their intentions. It is important for women to know that they can leave the group at any time. They should, however, be encouraged to let the group know their intentions, in person or in writing. A woman should also know that if she decides to leave or to limit her involvement in the group she can maintain a link with the group for support and encouragement. An open group enables members to drop in and report on their progress, or to seek support if they are in a crisis.

Support

Survivors' groups have a great deal to offer women who have been sexually abused. In our view a closed group has most to offer the women because it allows them to build trust in a safe atmosphere. It gives them time to feel more secure before disclosing details of the sexual abuse.

The words of group members themselves provide ample testimony of the usefulness of survivors' groups.

> I don't feel like a victim now, more like a survivor.
> I no longer feel wholly responsible for everyone and everything.
> I used to feel like the abuse was happening all over again, everytime something or someone triggered a reaction. Now I have a clearer sense of what is unsafe currently and what reminds me of past danger.

The single most valued experience in survivors' groups is the contact with other survivors. One woman wrote,

> Their presence proved .... to negate the message that it only happened to me and that it happened because I *was* me. (Herman and Schatzow, 1984).

The strength and courage of women who join survivors' groups is self-evident in their ability to share, to support others and to carry on with their lives with humour and goodwill. Acknowledging and reinforcing these qualities and other means of survival can take place in the group.

It is appropriate to end with another quotation, this time from a woman who saw the group in its historical perspective:

> When I look back at the group I see that it confronted me with a choice about whether to go on hating myself or to find a more constructive way to deal with the past.

In other words, survivors' groups can be the means to a new beginning for many women.

Chapter 11

Therapeutic Techniques

This chapter outlines methods that can be used with survivors to help them deal with particular issues and problems. The issues are summarized in Table 11. 1. The list is not exhaustive, but it offers a range of ideas that helpers might find useful in working with survivors. It will be necessary for them to adapt these techniques to suit individual women, and the helper may need to think about ways of doing this creatively.

Re-entering the World of the Child

One of the most important tasks for a survivor is to remember what it was like for her as a child. She will refer to her childhood from the perspective of an adult, and may have forgotten her physical size, her feelings of powerlessness and how it felt to be a child in her family. A number of therapeutic methods can be usefully employed to enable a survivor to get in touch with herself as a child. The methods described below can be modified to suit particular women.

Photographs

Studying photographs of herself at various ages throughout her childhood and adolescence can facilitate a more accurate perception of herself as a child. Group photographs of family occasions such as birthdays, anniversaries, holidays or excursions are particularly useful, as are photographs of other family members and the abuser. Photographs can used to:

— elicit memories of significant childhood events;
— compare and contrast photographs of the child and the abuser in

Table 11.1: **Themes and techniques in working with survivors**

Themes	Techniques
Re-entering the world of the child	Photographs Drawings/artwork Remembering key events Constructing a life history Describing places where the abuse took place Visiting places associated with childhood Description of significant adults Description of survivor as a child Use of childhood memorabilia.
Reclaiming childhood	Artwork Play Religious ceremonies Special occasions.
Dealing with guilt	Challenging beliefs and assumptions about responsibility. New strategies for dealing with responsibility.
Dealing with anxiety and fear	Awareness and recognition of feelings Situations and feelings that produce anxiety Dealing with physical signs of anxiety Dealing with avoidance Dealing with anxious thoughts Panic attacks.
Dealing with loss	Awareness of losses The experience of grief The tasks of grieving Coming to terms with loss.
Dealing with anger	Awareness and recognition of anger Describing angry feelings Awareness of situations and people that make her angry Expression of angry feelings Expressing anger towards the abuser and other family members Confrontation and challenge.
Dealing with flashbacks	Imagery techniques.
Building self-esteem	Negative self-image Building self-esteem.
Assertiveness	Defining assertiveness Identifying basic rights Assertiveness and aggression Role-play Ways of being assertive.
Challenging negative thoughts	Types of negative thoughts Methods for challenging negative thoughts.
Building trust in a group	Trust exercises Sentence completion exercises Confirming progress already made.
Role-play	Shared activities.

Table 11.1: Continued

Themes	Techniques
Writing	Letter writing Diaries and journals Personal writing Using other writers' work Using word-processors.
Brainstorming	
Word pictures	
Sentence completion exercises	
Dealing with other areas of difficulty	

order to reinforce the perception of the child as small and powerless in relation to an abusing adult;
— enable a survivor to gain a more complete picture of the important people in her childhood.

Sometimes the survivor has destroyed childhood photographs of herself
and other family members. She may find the memories which are elicited
by photographs too painful. If this is the case, the helper could ask if the
woman could obtain photographs from other family members.

Drawings/artwork

Artwork can be used in both individual and group settings. For further
ideas, *The Courage to Heal Workbook* (Davis, 1990) is useful. Artwork
can be used for:

— expressing feelings which may be difficult to share verbally;
— getting an immediate response on an issue without allowing too
much time to think about it;
— enabling a woman to express herself freely in a medium which is
fun to use.

Large sheets of drawing paper, lots of felt tipped pens, crayons or paints
are needed for artwork.

Initially a woman may feel inhibited about drawing, especially if she
has been told or feels that she is 'not good at art'. Acknowledging that
these feelings are widespread can reduce her anxiety, and she can then be

encouraged to enjoy the experience. Below, we give some examples of the ways in which artwork can be used.

'Me' at different stages   The helper asks the woman to draw a picture of herself and other significant family members at different stages of her childhood such as at the age of two, four, eight and twelve. The pictures may indicate:

— how the woman perceives herself in relation to other family members at different times;
— who were the significant adults in her life at various stages.

She could also be asked to draw pictures of:

— her relationship with other family members;
— where the sexual abuse took place;
— her current relationships with adults and/or children.

Artwork can also be used in the following ways:

— as part of the disclosure, especially if she has difficulty in verbalizing aspects of the abuse, a survivor might draw the place where the abuse took place. She can be encouraged to colour rooms as she remembers them and to locate significant individuals in them. This may enable to her to get a fuller picture of the location and to remember who else was present. It might also help her to make links between locations, colours, or fabrics which cause her distress and the abuse;
— as part of the disclosure, the survivor might draw, or ask her helper to draw, parts of the abuser's or her own body which hold significant memories for her. This might include positions she was forced to adopt during the abuse, the position of the abuser and anyone else who was present;
— survivors can be encouraged to draw a feeling which they have, especially when they are finding it difficult to express or are frightened by the intensity of it;
— matchstick people can be drawn to represent the survivor at various ages and stages. She might also draw other people in her life at the time or significant events.

Remembering Key Events

The survivor is asked to recall events from her childhood. These might include:

— moving house;
— school days (including teachers, friends, buildings, behaviour at school);
— birth of siblings;
— deaths of important people;
— pets;
— hobbies;
— leaving home;
— birthdays, Christmas and other celebrations.

The helper can discuss these in the context of the woman's memories. The discussion can build up an overall picture of her childhood including some of its less painful aspects.

Constructing a Life History

The helper asks the woman to write down the years since her birth and where she can, to note one or more significant events in each year. It can be useful to represent this on a large sheet or roll of paper.

Example

1952   Born at . . . hospital on . . .
1953
1954   Sister born
1955   Father got new job
1956   Moved house
1957   Started school
1958   Brother born
1959   Sexual abuse started
1960   Grandmother died

This exercise can:

— trigger memories about specific events and incidents;
— lead to the triggering of new memories through discussion;
— identify 'gaps' in a woman's early history and begin to work out reasons for the existence of these gaps (such as dissociating herself from the events because of the abuse, chaotic family background where the family were constantly on the move, etc.).

Describing Places where the Abuse Took Place

The helper asks the woman to describe or draw the places where the abuse took place. She can be asked:

— whether it was indoors, out of doors or some other place (such as car, shed);
— if it took place in a variety of locations or always in the same place;
— about any colours, smell, fabrics which she associates with the location;
— whether other adults or children were nearby when the abuse occurred;
— the time/s of the day when the abuse took place.

If the abuse took place in the family home, she can be asked to describe the house, inside and out. It is important to ask for descriptions of her bedroom (layout, furniture, bedding, ornaments and toys) and any room in which the sexual abuse took place.

If a woman finds it difficult to give a verbal description, drawings can be very useful. She can be asked to draw a plan of the house and details of its rooms. A picture of the exterior of the house might be drawn, together with a description of the street or neighbourhood in which it was situated. This exercise often triggers new memories.

Visiting Places Associated with Childhood

Taking or encouraging a woman to visit places which were important in her childhood is likely to induce memories of previously forgotten events. Once a woman begins to identify herself as a survivor by coming to terms with her past, she may feel ready and stronger to visit places where the abuse took place. She can be encouraged to visit:

— her school/s;
— the house she lived in;
— places where she played with other children;
— places where she felt safe as a child;
— the graves of dead family members;
— other important childhood places, such as houses of other family members.

Description of Significant Adults

The helper should ask the woman to identify significant adults in her life by compiling lists of 'people with whom I felt safe/trusted' and 'people with whom I did not feel safe as a child'. The lists can be examined together, with the helper asking questions such as:

'What made you trust/distrust these people?'
'How did they show you that they cared for you?'
'How much time did you spend with them?'
'Where did they live?'
'For how long were they significant in your life?'
'Did you ever try to tell them about the abuse?'
'If so, what were their reactions?'

By exploring these areas, a woman can begin to discover:

— that she may/may not have had significant adults in early life;
— the difficulties of talking about the sexual abuse with people whom she trusted as a child;
— that feeling frightened and upset because of the abuse affected her relationships with potentially safe and trustworthy adults.

Description of the Survivor as a Child

In addition to looking at photographs of herself as a child, it is helpful to get a description from a survivor of her physical size at various ages, her clothes, hobbies, toys, pets and so on. If it is too difficult or painful for her to remember herself as a child, she can be asked to describe children of relevant ages known to her. This enables her to gain a more realistic view of the size and situation of children in relation to adults around them. It may seem surprising that a survivor needs to be reminded of the relative size of children and adults, but many assume that in childhood they had the power and strength of an adult.

Use of Childhood Memorabilia

If a survivor has any toys, notebooks, school books or reports, or other childhood memorabilia, these might be used to facilitate general memories about childhood. Often, being given permission by the helper to bring these objects to her sessions can be enough to help the survivor recall general memories of her childhood as well as giving her additional clues about her reactions to the abuse.

Reclaiming Childhood

For many survivors there is an acute sense that they have lost important aspects of childhood. For example, play, sporting activities, friendship and schooling may all have been disrupted. This has implications not only for a woman herself, with feelings of loss, but it can also affect her role as a parent. She may have difficulties in playing with her own children, or she may be too over-protective of them. One way of enabling a woman to become less anxious is to help her to reclaim her childhood; this can involve doing art work, children's play, religious ceremonies, or re-creating special occasions.

Artwork

Artwork can be used to take women back to different stages in their childhood, and to express their feelings visually. The following exercises are useful:

1 The woman is given paper and crayons and told, 'Imagine that you are 18-months old, and you have just found paper and crayons under the kitchen table. Play and draw with the crayons and paper'. This exercise can be repeated for older age groups and the pictures are then compared.
2 The woman is given paper and crayons and told, 'You have just had your first day at school. Before you go home, your teacher asks you to draw a picture about your first day. Try to draw it now.' This exercise may evoke feelings and memories of an important day in every child's life. Women will be able to draw through a 'child's eye' rather than as an adult.
3 The woman can be supplied with drawing materials and encouraged to draw or paint whatever she wants. The freedom of expression gained from dabbling and dipping into paints can be both exhilarating and healing.

Play

Recreating a child's play can be fun, but can evoke strong feelings and memories of exclusion, prohibition or spoiling by parents. Some suggestions are given below:

— a doll's/teddy's tea party, complete with food, drink and games;
— pillow fights;
— playing with sand, play-doh or plasticine;
— bicycle rides;
— sports, for example, swimming, horse-riding, hill walking, football;
— collecting stones, shells, twigs or leaves on a walk;
— listening to a children's fairy or adventure story read aloud by the helper;
— building with Lego or other construction toys;
— experimenting in a group with musical instruments;
— singing nursery rhymes or local children's songs;
— playing children's board games.

Religious Ceremonies

Survivors who were abused and brought up in a home where religion was practised have an added confusion. This is likely to provide a source of considerable conflict for a woman because:

— she was aware that the abuser went to church and yet at home forced sexual activities on her;
— any religious activities or ceremonies she was involved in were spoiled, desecrated or made unclean by the sexual abuse;
— she may have felt it wrong to take part in special religious events when she felt dirty, unworthy or hypocritical;
— she may have been told that she must forgive people who wronged her.

As a result, key religious occasions may have left her feeling guilty and confused. It can be very important for a survivor to be given an opportunity to repeat these special religious occasions. The help and co-operation of key members of a relevant religious organization, congregation or church should be sought by the helper and the woman herself.

Many survivors return to the roots of their religion later in life, enabling them to gain comfort, hope and a sense of reparation. Forgiveness often remains a difficult problem. A useful book for use with survivors with a Christian background is *Child Sexual Abuse* by Hancock and Mains (1987).

Special Occasions

Birthdays, anniversaries or other family celebrations may have been absent or spoiled during a survivor's childhood. They can be re-created in adulthood, and can be marked by:

— a party, complete with cake, candles and party food;
— party games;
— small gifts to mark 'missed' birthdays and other occasions;
— dressing in clothes reserved for special occasions.

Dealing with Guilt

Guilt is often the predominant emotion that a survivor carries when she decides to seek help. The guilt may not just relate to the sexual abuse but also relates to other areas of her life. It is as if she has learned to blame herself for everything that happened to her as a child and has never stopped feeling guilty since. She therefore needs to learn to test her feelings of guilt in a realistic and rational way, instead of automatically believing herself to be guilty for everything that happens to herself and others.

Challenging Beliefs and Assumptions about Responsibility for the Sexual Abuse

It is important to examine issues of responsibility rather than blame. Blame is an emotive word that tends to allow the survivor's feelings of loyalty towards her family to interfere with her ability to realistically challenge her feelings of guilt.

The survivor can be helped to understand that:

— a child is never responsible for being sexually abused;
— a child is not responsible for experiencing physical arousal or orgasm during the abuse;
— a child is not responsible for being unable to stop the abuse;
— a child cannot be held responsible for remaining silent about the abuse (she may have been too frightened or did not know how to tell);

— a child is not responsible for failing to protect her siblings or other children from the abuser;

— a child needs attention and affection and is not to blame if she responds to whatever attention she is offered even if it is unhealthy unwanted sexual attention;

— even if the abuse continued through adolescence and adulthood, the survivor is still not responsible for it, as she is still in a powerless position in relation to the abuser. There is no magic day that she becomes an adult in relation to the abuser.

Specific Methods

1   There are a number of useful questions that can be asked to help a survivor to challenge her beliefs and thoughts about the guilt (see Table 11.2)

Table 11.2:   **Useful questions to challenge guilt feelings**

The occurrence of the sexual abuse

Whose idea was it to start the abuse?
How old were you when it started?
How tall were you?
How tall was the abuser?
Do you know a child of that age now? If so, would she or he be guilty/responsible?
What did you think the abuser was doing the first time?
When did you realise that what he was doing was wrong?
What told you that it was wrong?
What told you that it was sexual?

Stopping the sexual abuse

What could you have done to stop it?
What would have happened? (This should be asked about every response produced to first question).
Who could you have told?
How might they have reacted?
What prevented you from telling someone?
What did the abuser say about telling someone?

Inability to protect siblings

In what way could you have protected your sister(s) or brother(s)?
In what way could you have protected them (remembering you were a child too)?
Whose idea was it that they should be abused?
When did it happen to them?
Who should have been protecting them?

The context of the abuse

Where were you abused?
Was anyone else around?
Was it always in the same place?
What sort of things did the abuser do to keep the abuse secret?

2   Use of photographs of herself as a child to correct her misconceptions about the strength and size of herself as a child. These can be contrasted with photographs of the abuser.
3   Suggest that she looks at other children of an age close to the age she was when the abuse was occurring. This will enable her to get a more objective perspective on the size and powerlessness of a child.
4   She should be asked to examine the responsibilities of the abuser, her mother and other important adults in relation to her as a child. This should include protection, care, facilitating normal development, education.
5   A useful imagery technique is to ask the survivor to imagine her case of sexual abuse being brought before a court of law. She is asked to imagine a court with a judge, jury, prosecuting and defending lawyers, a witness stand, and the defendant's box. She should be asked to place the abuser in the defendant's box as he has been charged with the sexual abuse. Then she is to imagine herself as a child, and imagine herself in various places in the court-room first in the witness stand telling the court what the abuser did to her, then alongside the abuser to justify her feelings of guilt about the abuse.

Key points to stress are that:

— a child cannot be tried for a crime against herself;
— a child is not considered to be legally responsible for her actions;
— she is not charged with sexual offences against the child: the abuser is;
— no judge would allow her to be placed in the defendant's box.

This imagery technique enables her to recognize that feeling guilty is not the same as being guilty, and that it is always an adult's responsibility if he acts in a sexual way towards a child.

Learning New Strategies for Examining Issues of Responsibility

The main aim here is to examine situations in a realistic way. The following are useful:

1   Careful analysis of the sequence and the involvement of the survivor and other people.

2   A closer look at the responsibilities of all the individuals involved (including herself).
3   Awareness of her feelings, which may include a number of differing or conflicting emotions.
4   Effects of her emotional reactions on her actions and vice versa.
5   Acknowledgment of emotions that are justified and normal:

> — guilt when she has done something wrong, hurtful or thoughtless;
> — anger with others for their part in the situation;
> — anxiety/fear that other people may take some action against her;
> — disgust with someone's behaviour.

6   Any action that may need to be taken. For example:

> — she may need to confront someone with his/her behaviour;
> — she might want to apologize;
> — she might have to make a decision about the situation;
> — she may decide to do nothing.

Dealing with Anxiety and Fear

Most survivors have experienced significant problems with feelings of anxiety and fear. Some may have been prescribed tranquillizers to deal with these problems, and tranquilizer dependency can produce its own difficulties.

Anxiety develops into a problem in a variety of ways:

— it may have become a habit, and the woman reacts to many situations with anxiety;
— after experiencing unpleasant anxiety feelings, the woman may become sensitive to any slight physical sign of anxiety. This leads to fear of the symptoms themselves;
— if anxiety has been experienced once in a situation (e.g., in a crowded shop, or social situation), the woman is likely to feel anxious in similar situations;
— if anxiety has been experienced in a particular situation, the woman is likely to anticipate similar situations with anxiety.

Anxiety is, however, a normal emotion experienced by everyone at various times in their lives.

Figure 11.1: **Some common physical signs of anxiety**

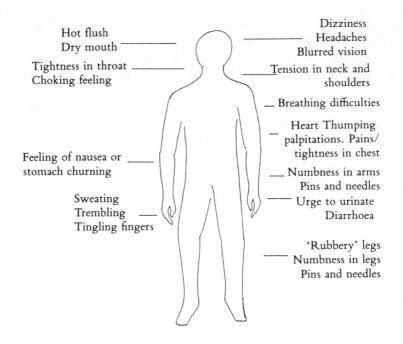

Awareness and recognition of anxiety   Anxiety affects an individual in three main ways:

1   Physical signs: Some of the more common physical signs of anxiety are shown in Figure 11.1.

Anxiety also manifests itself in the following ways:

— irritability, quick-temper or easily upset;
— sleeping difficulties;
— fatigue and exhaustion;
— loss of interest, motivation and confidence;
— unreal feelings;
— heightened sensitivity to noise;
— absent-mindedness, forgetfulness and inability to concentrate;
— indecision;
— restlessness;
— clumsiness.

The survivor needs to recognize and become aware of these signs of anxiety, as this is the first step in beginning to deal with them.

2 Effects on behaviour. If a survivor is anxious it is likely that she will be one of the following:

— over-active, rushing from task to task, rarely achieving anything satisfactorily;
— under-active and unable to motivate herself;
— showing signs of avoiding situations in which she fears becoming anxious;
— avoiding situations which she learnt to be frightened of as a child when she was abused.

3 Effects on an individual's thinking processes: Anxious thinking tends to be distorted or biased. The anxious person will interpret events and situations in such a way as to increase her anxiety. A full description of negative-thinking patterns of anxiety is to be found in the section on challenging negative thoughts.

Awareness of Situations and People that Produce Anxiety

As a child, the survivor may have developed anxiety in a number of situations and towards certain people as a result of the abuse. Common childhood-related situations are:

— being in the presence of men;
— being in places/houses/other situations that remind her of the environment in which the abuse took place;
— situations with authority figures (especially teachers, social workers or police);
— confined spaces which induce feelings of being trapped;
— sexual situations.

These should be distinguished from situations that might cause anyone to feel anxious such as job interviews, driving lessons, starting a new job, having a baby, going into hospital.

Dealing with Physical Signs of Anxiety

Bodily tension and physical signs of anxiety can be reduced through the use of relaxation techniques and deep breathing.

Table 11.3: **A programme for learning relaxation**

	Instructions	Length of relaxation period
Week 1	Arms	2–3 minutes
Week 2	Arms Legs	3–4 minutes
Week 3	Arms Legs Breathing	3–4 minutes
Week4	Arms Legs Breathing	4–5 minutes
Week 5	Repeat of Week 4 Lower part of body	5 minutes

Deep breathing Deep breathing exercises involve taking two or three slow deep breaths in the following way:

> Breath in very slowly
> Hold the breathe for 5–10 seconds
> Breath out very slowly
> Repeat twice more, then resume normal breathing

This can be particularly useful when actually in an anxiety-provoking situation.

Relaxation exercises There are a number of different relaxation exercises that can be taught. Relaxation techniques should be practised until the survivor feels comfortable with the exercises. The method known as autogenic relaxation is particularly useful for the following reasons:

> — it does not take long to do (5–6 minutes) and therefore can be easily and regularly practised;
> — it induces pleasant sensations of heaviness and warmth.

A version of this exercise is described below. It can be recorded by a helper onto a cassette, so that a survivor can replay it in a comfortable environment.

The exercise can be taught as a whole or in sections, gradually building up to doing the whole exercise. Suggestions for doing this are given in Table 11.3.

The woman should first be instructed to loosen tight clothing, remove contact lenses and shoes, and go to the toilet (relaxation is impossible with a full bladder). She should choose a comfortable but well-supporting chair. Although these exercises can be done lying on a bed, a chair is preferable because it means that the woman can adapt the exercises to situations outside her home (in a friend's house, on public transport, at work or in other situations where she can sit down).

She should be sitting in the following position:

— feet flat on the floor (or on a footrest if she is not very tall);
— back firmly against the back of the chair;
— lower arms resting on thighs;
— hands relaxed;
— fingers loosely resting on thighs;
— head down, chin resting on chest;
— eyes closed (optional). If left open, she should look straight ahead at a point on the floor.

Speaking in a slow, even and calm voice the helper says,

First of all, I want you to try and forget about any worrying thoughts, and just listen to my voice.

..... PAUSE .....

ARMS

Just think about your arms. I want you to allow them to become heavy, gradually feeling the weight of your arms pulling down from your shoulders. Allow them to become quite heavy.

..... PAUSE .....

Keep thinking about your arms. Allow them to become quite heavy. (Repeat as necessary).

..... PAUSE .....

At the same time, I want you to allow your arms to become warm. Imagine sitting beside a warm fire. Feel the warmth of that fire on your arms. Allow your arms to become quite heavy and warm.

..... PAUSE .....

Keep thinking about your arms. Feel them getting warmer and heavier.

Perhaps you are beginning to be aware that you are feeling a little less tense.

Keep allowing your arms to get warmer and heavier.

(This can be repeated several times).

. . . . . PAUSE . . . . .

LEGS

Now, keeping your arms warm and heavy, I want you to think about your legs. I want you to gradually allow your legs to get heavier and heavier. Feel the chair and floor supporting them. (Repeat as necessary).

. . . . . PAUSE . . . . .

Just as with your arms, I now want you to imagine that fire again, and allow your legs to become warm.

Feel the warmth of the fire on your legs.

Gradually you feel that your legs are getting heavier and warmer.

. . . . . PAUSE . . . . .

Keep thinking about your arms and legs. They are gradually getting heavier and warmer, and you are beginning to feel more comfortable and relaxed.

. . . . . PAUSE . . . . .

BREATHING

Now, keeping your arms and legs heavy and warm, I want you to think about your breathing.

I want you to allow your breathing to settle into a steady rhythm. Not too fast and not too slow. Not too deep and not too shallow. Let your breathing move along at a steady gentle rhythm.

Gradually you will notice that you are becoming more and more relaxed.

I want you to keep thinking of your breathing, and begin to enjoy the feeling of being more relaxed.

. . . . . PAUSE . . . . .

LOWER BODY

Now the last thing I want you to do is to think about the lower part of your body — imagine having a hot water bottle on that part of your body, and feel the warmth from the hot water bottle spread across your body.

Allow that part of your body to become quite warm and comfortable.

. . . . . PAUSE . . . . .

Keep thinking about the hot water bottle — feel the warmth.

. . . . . PAUSE . . . . .

Now I want you to keep thinking all these parts of your body in turn — your arms, legs, breathing and lower part of your body. Allow your arms and legs to become heavy and warm, your breathing steady and your body warm and comfortable. Notice that you are gradually becoming more and more relaxed.

Now I want you to stay like this for a few minutes until I speak again.

Relaxation period Up to five minutes silence from the helper.

Now I want you very slowly to open your eyes, put your head up, and gradually stretch yourself — your arms and legs. Just sit quietly for a few minutes. Don't get up and rush about. Just allow yourself the full benefit of being relaxed.

If the woman finds any part of the exercise very anxiety-provoking, she should be instructed to leave that section out. However, the breathing stage should **ALWAYS** be done.

These exercises can be modified for use in a variety of situations:

— in public situations, e.g. social situations or public transport, they can be done without the dropping of the head or closing of the eyes. They can be done for a very short time, or just by doing the easiest part of the exercises, (just the arms or the breathing);
— to help encourage sleep. In this case, the woman is told to lie comfortably in bed and do the exercises, but then to allow herself to drift into sleep rather than move on to the final 'waking-up' stage.

Dealing with Avoidance

Avoiding difficult or anxiety-provoking situations is common, but in the long run adds to a woman's problems. The most effective way of dealing with avoidance is for the woman to gradually confront the situations she avoids, so that she learns to cope with her anxious feelings. A helpful technique for coping with difficult situations includes the following:

1 The woman should list and rank situations which she finds difficult from most to least difficult.
2 She should choose a situation from the least difficult end of the list to work on.
3 A specific task should be set, for example, to visit a large shop for half an hour, or to tolerate being in the presence of a male colleague for ten minutes. Feelings of anxiety can be expected.
4 She should stay in the situation for the agreed amount of time, in spite of mounting anxiety. These feelings should be tolerated.
5 The task should be repeated several times until the woman learns she can cope with her anxiety.

If the avoidance of situations has reached an unmanageable level, the survivor may require to be referred to the local clinical psychology department for specific help with phobic problems. Examples are when she shows symptoms of:

— agoraphobic problems — she cannot tolerate being out of her home;
— specific phobias — dogs, birds or insects that prevent her from leading a normal life;

— phobias about medical procedures — injections, giving blood, or visits to the doctor dentist that prevent her from receiving appropriate treatment.

Dealing with Anxious Thoughts

Anxious thinking can become established as a habit, and a woman will find herself worrying continually about many things. The first step in dealing with this is to begin to recognize the anxious thoughts as they come to mind.

Some examples are:

— I won't be able to cope;
— everyone will think I'm stupid;
— if I go out, something is bound to go wrong;
— everything I do is a disaster;
— I'll never be any good at this;
— I shouldn't be worried about it.

The next step is to substitute more reasonable objective thoughts. For example:

Anxious thoughts	*Reasonable thoughts*
I shouldn't be worried about going to the hospital.	It is normal to be anxious about a situation like this.
I'll make a fool of myself at work if I feel like this.	I often feel like this at work but nothing bad happens. I am jumping to conclusions.

Learning to be more realistic in her thinking about situations takes practice and time. Anxiety is a normal feeling, but if it is too severe, it can be disruptive and prevent rational decision-making. It also affects self-confidence and self-esteem and often occurs in conjunction with symptoms of depression.

Panic Attacks

Panic attacks are different from high levels of anxiety, and consist of a combination of palpitations, shortness of breath, dizziness, nausea, shaking and sweating. A panic attack is a very physical and unpleasant experience. The body is responding as if it had had a very severe fright, but without any obvious cause. A panic attack often occurs during a period of stress, such as when a woman experiences difficulties at home or work, a bereavement or illness. For survivors, it can also occur in response to memories of the sexual abuse. For some survivors, panic attacks can be confused with flashbacks.

The first attack is an alarming experience and, as a result, most people misconstrue its nature and consequences. A women can perceive a panic attack as a very dangerous event, leading to serious physical harm, loss of control, mental breakdown or making a fool of herself in some way. The extreme fear reported in panic attacks is a result not only of the unpleasant physical sensations but also of the way the woman interprets the attack as extremely dangerous. As a result, she becomes extremely sensitive to and fearful of any physical signs reminiscent of the panic attack. This leads to a triggering of further fright responses, and a fear of panic attacks rapidly becomes established. Not surprisingly, this leads to the development of strategies to avoid or escape from any situation where she thinks that panic attacks might occur.

Dealing with panic attacks　The following information about panic attacks should be explained:

- — the body has a normal response to threat or danger. It can be useful if a woman has experienced a normal fright response to a real threat or danger (being followed at night or a near-miss situation in a car) to explore her physical responses on those occasions;
- — the panic attack is the body's fright response being triggered in the absence of any danger. This makes it difficult to understand;
- — it does not last for long;
- — it will not do any serious harm or have serious consequences.

This information is often sufficient to relieve a woman's anxiety about panic attacks. However, if her thinking about the panic attacks has led her to avoid situations, she may need to test out the possibility that nothing worse than the panic will occur. This can be achieved by risking going into these situations, allowing a panic attack to occur and discovering that:

- — the panic attack itself is the worst that will happen;
- — nothing more serious will happen;
- — the panic attack passes after some time.

During this stage she will need support to help her take the risk of going into the avoided situations. Gradually, as she becomes less afraid of the panic attacks, they will occur less often (McFadyen, 1989).

Dealing with Loss

Any woman who has been sexually abused as a child has suffered many losses. She may be unaware of her losses, or of her need to grieve for them. However, unexpressed or unresolved grief causes problems and leaves the woman emotionally chained to her past. As Bass and Davis (1988) explain to survivors:

> Buried grief poisons, limiting your capacity for joy, spontaneity, for life. An essential part of healing from traumatic experiences is to express and share your feelings . . . To release these painful feelings and to move forward in your life, it is necessary, paradoxically, to go back and to relive the experiences you had as a child — to grieve, this time with the support of a caring person and with the support of your adult self.

There are a number of stages in dealing with loss.

Awareness of Loss

The first stage is for the survivor to become aware of the losses that have resulted from the experience of being abused.

Losses in childhood These are numerous and include loss of innocence, the ability to enjoy and to play, normal peer relationships, safety and protection, of educational opportunities (because of difficulty in concentrating), of normal relationships within the family. The extent of the losses will vary from woman to woman, but each one should be explored in detail.

Losses in adulthood Again there are many losses including loss of normal sexuality, relationships, freedom, enjoyment, family relationships, friendships, the ability to sleep and to relax, peace of mind and trust.

Loss of normal relationships Where the abuser, mother or important person has died or where she is separated from them, a survivor may express the loss of her chance to have a normal relationship with that person or to confront them about issues from her childhood.

The Experience of Grief

Grief can be experienced in many ways, through emotional reactions, thoughts and behaviour patterns. It is often experienced physically. Table 11.4 outlines the normal reactions to loss.

The Tasks of Grieving

Worden (1983) outlines four tasks of mourning that are useful in determining the process of resolving grief. We have modified his ideas for survivors. The tasks are:

— to accept the reality of the loss;
— to experience the pain of grief;
— to adapt to life, bearing in mind the significance of the loss. For example, a survivor might have to adjust to the fact that she can never have a normal relationship with the abuser, and therefore learn to stop searching for the hoped-for opportunity to make this relationship perfect. In the case of loss of a person (through death, separation or divorce), the task is to adapt to the environment in which the person is missing;
— to withdraw the emotional energy bound up in the loss and to free it for use elsewhere. For example, when a survivor is very bitter about the loss of positive childhood experiences, much of her emotional energy is taken up with this bitterness. Once she has worked through the loss, that energy is gradually released for use in other areas of her life.

Coming to Terms with Loss

This process is similar whatever the loss — whether it be through traumatic experiences, sexual abuse, death, separation or normal life experiences such as loss of a job, moving house, or leaving home. A helper's task is to facilitate the grieving process by enabling:

The woman to become aware of the reality of her loss This involves detailed exploration of the causes and effects of the loss. This process

Table 11.4: **Normal reactions to loss**

Emotional reactions	Physical sensations
Numbness	Anxiety symptoms
Shock	Hollowness in stomach
Sadness	Tightness in chest/throat
Anger	Over-sensitivity to noise
Guilt/self-reproach	Sensations of unreality
Loneliness	Breathlessness
Apathy	Muscular weakness
Helplessness	Lack of energy
Relief	Loss of appetite
Yearning/pining	Loss of sleep
Emptiness	Dry mouth
Freedom	Weight gain/loss
Mental processes	*Behaviour*
Disbelief	Dreams/Nightmares
Denial	Avoiding reminders of loss
Confusion	Searching behaviour
Poor concentration	*Calling out
Loss of memory	Sighing
Preoccupation with thoughts of loss	Restlessness
*Sense of presence of lost person	Over-or under-activity
*Visual/auditory hallucinations of lost person	Crying
Repetitive thoughts about the events of the loss	*Carrying reminders of lost person Treasuring objects relating to loss
Absent-mindedness	*Refusing to disturb possessions of lost person
	*Behaviour like lost person in mannerisms or habits
	Social withdrawal

* Particularly common in situation where there is loss of a person
  through death, divorce or separation.

reduces the denial and minimization of loss. For example, a survivor might want to explore the loss of normal childhood experiences of play. Areas to discuss might include:

— What opportunities for play did she have?
— How were they spoiled?
— What effect has her lack of play opportunities had on her as an adult, such as playing with her children, knowing how to enjoy herself, allowing herself to have fun, missed learning opportunities, not feeling normal or worthwhile?

In the case of the loss of a person through death, the areas to discuss might include:

— How, when and where the death occurred (including any illness of the person).
— How did she find out about it?
— What was the period like before the person died?
— What were the days like between the death and the funeral?
— What were the funeral and any other family rituals like?
— What was her relationship with the dead person?

Help the woman identify and express her feelings   This usually occurs in conjunction with a growing awareness of the reality of the loss. Coming to terms with loss is a painful process, and this stage is often highly charged with mixed and confusing emotions. Common reactions include unaccountable periods of crying and sadness, anxiety, rage, anger and guilt. The woman may need to test out her guilty feelings to see if they are rational. She should be encouraged to release these emotions, even if it means spending many hours crying. Crying with a sympathetic friend, partner or helper can bring great relief, particularly if support and comfort are available. Survivors often feel that once they start crying, they will never stop, but through crying they release pent-up feelings that have been suppressed. And the crying does stop.

Provide time to grieve   This is important, as coming to terms with loss is a gradual process, and survivors find it very hard to justify to themselves that they are entitled to time for grieving over events and losses that occurred many years before.

Helping the woman to adapt to the loss   When the loss is of a person through death or separation, it is necessary to examine the various roles which that person played in the woman's life, both as an adult and a child. It is useful to ask her the following questions:

— What will you miss about that person?
— What will you not miss about that person?

Where the person has fulfilled roles in her adult life, she may have to learn new skills or make new arrangements to fill the gap. For example, the loss of a partner may leave her with decisions that she has never had to make before. In the case of losses relating to her childhood, she may have to learn skills and to re-experience childhood activities in order to compensate for the missing parts of her childhood.

Example: Rhoda had always had difficulties with literacy and numeracy. She discovered that her teacher had abused her when she was six, just after he had taught her to read and write. He had abused her in the classroom when the other children had gone home. As an adult she was able to make the links between her literacy difficulties and the abuse. She was encouraged by her helper to get in touch with an adult literacy project where she began to overcome her difficulties.

Normal grief behaviour and reactions should be noted   The woman needs to understand normal reactions during the grieving process. It is useful to help her understand that other survivors go through similar periods of grief. This can be achieved by encouraging her to read personal accounts by other survivors, or to join a survivors' group.

Help the woman to withdraw her emotional energy from the loss   This involves acceptance that she cannot change what happened to her, and that she may have to leave behind her many of her hopes and aspirations for better relationships within her family. As Gil (1983) suggests, she may have to say good-bye to the parents she never had.

This is gradual process and can only be achieved successfully once she has experienced the reality and the pain of loss. Usually, survivors find that they move gradually from an intense phase of reliving their childhood to a point where they begin to live for the present and the future. The process of grieving can be extremely emotional and the helper may find that she/he needs more support when taking a survivor through a particularly intense phase of grief.

Dealing with Anger

Awareness and Recognition of Anger

The task here is to help the survivor to recognize her angry feelings. Not only may she have little or no awareness of her reactions when she is angry, but she may also have no words to describe these feelings.

1 Anger is an emotion that can be detected through awareness of body language. Common signs are tension, particularly in the jaw and hands, clenched fists, gritted teeth, feelings of nausea, quickened heart-beat and shallow breathing.
2 It can be recognized through tone of voice and behaviour, such as shouting, door slamming, stamping feet, swearing.
3 It can be detected through thought patterns, such as thoughts of doing harm to someone, rudeness, or never wanting to be in a particular person's company again.

Describing Angry Feelings

1 The woman should be helped to find ways of describing angry feelings. 'Angry' may be too difficult a word to use. The following are alternatives that may be more acceptable: annoyed, irritated, cross, frustrated, wild, furious, put out, cheesed off, narked.
2 It is useful to help a woman describe her angry feelings through the use of phrases and sentences. Suggesting that she completes the sentence 'I was so angry that I . . .' can be helpful.

Example: I was so angry that I . . .

— felt like slamming the door in his face;
— wanted to hit her;
— could have exploded;
— went over the top;
— lost my temper.

Awareness of Situations and People that Make her Angry

This is an important step in dealing with angry feelings as it allows anticipation of and preparation for potentially difficult situations in the future.

It involves examination of situations and people in the past and present that have made a woman angry. This will inevitably include the sexual abuse, the abuser and other key adults in her childhood.

Validation of Angry Feelings

A survivor must be allowed to see that her angry feelings are valid emotions, and they are often entirely justified, especially when dealing with her childhood experiences. It is also important that she can distinguish between justifiable feelings of anger and those that are an over-reaction to a situation.

Expression of Angry Feelings

As we have already noted, anger is a very physical emotion. It is often best expressed in a physical way, but safely, so that this expression does not harm the woman, other people or possessions belonging to her or other people.

Suggestions for expressing anger safely include:

— finding an isolated place in which to scream loudly;
— screaming in a place where the sound is masked by other sounds, such as under a railway bridge when a train goes over, on a stormy beach;
— visiting a beach, river or other open space, for example, a field where stones can be thrown with force and abandon;
— visiting a beach where pictures can be drawn in the sand and then scrubbed out;
— punching a pillow/cushion;
— ripping up old newspapers or telephone directories.

Example: Members of a survivors' group went down to a beach. They were encouraged to draw pictures in the sand of their abusers, and then to scrub them out with force. It was suggested that they might get stones and boulders and throw them at a disused breakwater (imagining that the post of the breakwater represented the people with whom they were angry). They were encouraged to scream and shout with anger at the waves.

Remember that anger may have to be expressed many times before the survivor feels that it is manageable. Letting go of the anger can be both a relief and an extremely exhausting process, but in the end it is a necessary and justifiable part of the work with survivors. As one survivor said: 'He messed up my life. I have suffered enough because of what he did. Why shouldn't I be angry? I've every right to be.'

Expressing Anger Towards the Abuser and Other Family Members

There are two stages here: to identify the reasons for the anger and to explore ways to express it.

1　Identify specifically and in detail the reasons for her anger:

> In relation to the abuser:
> — he did sexual things to her;
> — he caused her problems (specify) in adulthood;
> — he did not take care of or protect her;
> — he had double standards, for example, don't go near strangers, don't do anything with boys (whilst he was also sexually abusing her).

> In relation to her mother:
> — she should have known what her daughter was trying to tell her;
> — she loved the abuser;
> — she protected the abuser rather than her;
> — she made her do too much in the house.

Similar examples could be generated for other family members. A woman may feel that she is not justified in being angry but at this stage, identifying all the possible reasons why she might feel anger is important.

2　Examining ways of expressing anger include:

> — methods outlined in the previous section;
> — writing letters to the abuser or other adults and not sending them. This leaves her free to write whatever she wants in the knowledge that it will not be seen. The woman does

not have to be reasonable, literate or polite in her letter. There will be no response or retaliation to what she writes. Letter-writing is particularly useful if the person has died, or if the survivor has lost contact with them;

— a letter could be sent to the person. This is a more difficult letter to write and the survivor may need help and support to write what she wants to say;

— role-play. This is a useful technique for expressing anger. It can be done in a one-to-one situation with the helper taking one role and the survivor taking the other, or in a group setting with two group members or a facilitator and the survivor, taking the roles.

The survivor may wish to role-play herself or another family member, and she should be encouraged to do both if possible. Again, the helper should assist her in her choice of words, responses, tone of voice. The role-play situation also allows her to examine the responses of the other person and her feelings about them.

Confrontation and Challenge

This requires considerable preparation and use of the techniques described earlier, so that the woman is clear about what she wants to say, can predict the responses of the other person and how she might react to those responses. Confrontation does not always go according to plan, and can leave the survivor more confused and upset than before. Only if she is determined to confront should she be encouraged to do so, as the responses from the abuser or others can compound her problems if the abuse is denied, its effects minimized, or the survivor is blamed for allowing the abuse to happen. It is important for a woman to think carefully about confrontation and the following work can be usefully undertaken in preparation for the event.

Initial Checking

1   Whose idea is it to embark on confrontation? (partner, sibling, therapist, friend, woman herself). The wish to confront must come from the woman herself.
2   Who does she want to confront? (abuser, members of family, friend, partner, children).

3 What is the purpose of the confrontation? The following are examples of the main aims:

— to tell about the abuse;
— finding out if he/she knew about the abuse.
— asking and getting answers to questions:

— why did he do it?
— why didn't he stop?
— is he sorry?
— did she know and if not, why not?
— did it happen to you as well?
— what did he get out of it?

— getting an explanation;
— getting an apology;
— getting angry;
— telling the person that she was not to blame;
— forgiving the person;
— telling the person what she thinks of him/her.

4 When is it to be done? (quickly, planned to coincide with family visit, sometime in the future).
5 How is the confrontation to be done? (face-to-face, by writing, on the telephone).
6 Who does she want to be present? (just herself and the person she is confronting, her partner/friend/helper/other support person.)

Preparation for the Confrontation

1 Collating the information from Initial checking stage.
2 What does she want to say?

— writing a letter: It should be done in draft form first. The helper might act as 'secretary' taking down what she says;
— face-to-face: The task here is to find the words the survivor wishes to say, and to practise saying them.

3 Predicting the reaction of the other person (denial, distress, accusation of lying, apology).

4 Working out how she will react to each of the above reactions:

> — what will she say if he/she denies it?
> — how will she feel if he/she denies it?
> — how will she handle these feelings?

5 Practising the various aspects of the confrontation in role-play so that any overwhelming or difficult feelings are dealt with before the real-life confrontation.
6 Is confrontation the best way to achieve her aims?
7 Does she still want to go ahead with the real-life confrontation?
8 Planning the time and place for confrontation.
9 Organizing support for herself before and after and during the confrontation.

Confrontation

Aftermath

This would include:

1 Immediate after-effects:

> — the woman's feelings and reactions;
> — the 'ripple' effect round the family (having to deal with the reactions of others);
> — the effect on her current relationships.

2 Feedback on the confrontation:

> Relevant questions are:
> — what did it achieve?
> — did it turn out as expected? If not, why not?
> — feelings it evoked at the time.

3 Longer term effects.

Repeating the Process of Preparation with Other People she Wishes to Confront

The survivor may find that by going through all of the stages above, she no longer wishes to undertake a face-to-face confrontation. Whatever her decision, preparation will enable her to plan, think ahead and assess possible outcomes with a supportive helper.

Dealing with Flashbacks

Imagery Techniques

These are particularly useful for helping a woman take control of flashbacks and perceptual disturbances. Survivors frequently experience images of the abuse, the abuser(s) and the situation in which incidents of the abuse took place. As these are images, it is possible to substitute alternative images which are less distressing.

Method

1   Clarify with the survivor the nature of these recurring images (for example, her abuser is about to abuse her).
2   Explain that these are *images* that frighten her, and because they are images, they can be replaced with less frightening images.
3   Examine alternative images that would allow her to remove the frightening or distressing elements of the images (for example, making the abuser leave the room before he attempts to abuse her). Table 11.5 outlines some alternative images.
4   Help the woman to find a safe place for the 'child' in her image (holding her mother's hand, putting her to bed in a 'safe' house.)

These imagery substitutes can be used within a session with a survivor, or can be recorded onto a cassette so that a woman can deal with the frightening images at home. If a cassette is to be used, the following sequence of events is helpful:

— ask the woman to think about the frightening images;
— substitute others that help her deal with the negative images;
— ask her to imagine going to a safe house/place where there are
  · adults who will take care of her;
— relaxation exercises can be recorded at the end of the tape with a suggestion that she rest or go to sleep for a while.

A cassette may have to be re-recorded regularly as the images and perceptual disturbances change with the recall of new memories.

Table 11.5: **Imagery techniques: images and substitutes**

Image	Possible substitute images
The child is alone.	Add a safe adult (the helper, her mother).
	Get her to go to another place/ room where there are safe people.
The child is injured.	Get a safe adult (the helper) to take her to a hospital or doctor's clinic where she will be looked after and her injuries dealt with. Then return her to a safe place where adults care for her.
The child is crying.	Get a safe adult to hold and comfort her.
The child is running away.	Imagine running to safe place (real or fictitious) where she will be cared for by adults who do not abuse her.
The abuser is present.	Make him leave the room.
The abuser is violent.	Introduce other adults to remove him.
The abuser sexually abuses her.	Introduce other adults to remove him.
Weapons (knife, broken glass) used during abuse.	Ask the woman or another adult to pick them up and throw them away.
Insects, especially if used during the abuse.	Introduce another adult (or the woman herself) into the scene to remove the insects or to kill them with insecticide.
Particularly frightening situations where she was abused.	Get the woman to take herself to a pleasant place/safe house.
	Go to imaginary safe place away from harm and danger.
	Have another adult (the helper) take her to a safe place.

Example: Helen was sexually abused by her father who used spiders and beetles to frighten her. He put them in her bed and clothes, and used them during the abuse. As an adult, she often had visual images of large numbers of spiders coming towards her and her father's voice gloating in the background. The rationale for changing these images was explained to her. She was asked to bring the frightening images to mind. She became agitated as she saw the insects coming towards her, and was then asked to imagine them all turning round and going back out of the door of the room. She was able to do this and her fear subsided but remained until her father's voice was dealt with. This was achieved by imagining him standing in the room, and two policemen coming in and taking him away. Helen then became calm and was able to use these simple substitute images as a way of dealing with the images at home. A cassette repeating these instructions was made to help her at home, and concluded with relaxation exercises. This procedure was repeated with other perceptual disturbances.

Building Self-esteem

This is associated with building self confidence. For many survivors, the right to determine their own lifestyle, priorities and values is something which they have never had the opportunity to do. A starting point might be to start thinking about what the survivor wants for herself, rather than what other people expect her to be. Change will be gradual and letting go of other people's expectations will leave a gap which may take time to fill. There are a number of areas on which the helper and survivor might work together.

Changing a Negative Self-image

The abused child grows up with many messages about herself that do not encourage the growth of a positive self-image. For example:

— she may have been told directly or indirectly that the abuse was her fault;
— she felt powerless and alone because of the abuse;
— she felt dirty and unloveable;
— she may have been told that she was no good at anything;
— she felt ashamed and guilty because of the sexual abuse.

As an adult, she may live a life which is based on these ideas about herself. A list of negative statements made by survivors is provided by Bass and Davis (1988). It emphasizes this lack of self-worth (see Table 11.6).

It is important that a survivor learns to discover the origin of her negative statements. Many are based on childhood experiences. By learning where these negative messages come from, she can discover that their origins do not lie within herself, but in how others made her feel.

Dealing with her feelings of guilt about her childhood is a vital stage in improving self-esteem. Once a survivor no longer feels guilty for the abuse, she begins to free herself from the negative image she has built of herself. She is then able to evaluate the negative thoughts she has about herself, as well as linking them to her past.

Example: Jane phoned her friend to invite her to supper when her friend refused abruptly, without giving a reason. Jane automatically assumed that her friend did not like her any more, that she had not invited her properly and that she didn't deserve to have friends anyway. When she re-assessed the situation she recognized that her friend would only have refused if she really couldn't come and that she might have refused more politely. Jane could also see that a refusal to supper did not mean the end of the friendship, even though she was hurt by it. The incident helped her to make links with her childhood by remembering her father's negative comments about her ability to keep friends.

Building self-esteem is also about learning that she does not have to continue giving herself negative messages. She needs to learn, therefore, to assess situations in a different way. She might begin by asking herself the following questions when she starts to think badly about herself:

— what started off this train of thought?
— what was I doing when it started?

for example — was I remembering something that happened recently?
— was I remembering something from my childhood?
— what happened just before I started thinking like this?

— did something frighten, upset or anger me?
— how would other people (for example, a friend) react in this situation?
— is there any reason for me to feel particularly vulnerable just now?

Table 11.6: **The origins of negative self-image (Adapted from Bass and Davis, 1988)**

Negative statement	Possible origins from childhood
I hate myself.	— I allowed myself to be abused. — I did not stop the abuse. — I got aroused during the abuse. — The abuser told me it was my fault.
I don't deserve it.	— Pleasant things have never happened to me. — I feel so bad about the abuse. — I don't deserve to have anything nice. — I don't deserve to be loved because I am guilty.
I can't do it.	— As a child I could never do anything right. — I was always in trouble. — My family and teachers told me I was no good (I couldn't concentrate on anything because of the abuse).
I have to be perfect.	— The abuser/my mother always found fault with everything I did. — Good was never good enough in my family.
Whatever I do, it'll never be enough.	— I'll never make up for all the lack of achievements in my childhood. — Even when I'd done everything he asked, there was always more abuse.
It's not worth trying.	— I tried stop him (abuser) but he wouldn't stop. — I'll never be normal after the abuse. — I feel like damaged goods because of the abuse.
What I want doesn't count.	— As a child, my wishes and needs were ignored. — I was just there to clean up round them. — I wanted him to stop but he didn't.
I have no right to feel good.	— He made me believe that the abuse was my fault.
I deserve to feel bad.	— He told me that he abused me because I was bad.

— is this a familiar feeling?

— does it remind me of something I learned as a child?

Building self-esteem

Discovering the positive A survivor often finds it extremely difficult to say anything good about herself. A helper can encourage her to construct a list of all the things she does well. To begin with, she may find it hard to write anything down because she undervalues good qualities, assuming that everyone has them.

For example:

1 Helpers can point out the qualities *they* have identified in the survivor, for example:

   — she manages her household finances;
   — she always attends her appointments on time;
   — she is a good listener;
   — she is good at making fruit cakes;
   — she can swim;
   — she is good at her job;
   — she knits her own jumpers.

2 A woman can be helped to construct a list of things she likes about herself. For example:

   — she is concerned about other people;
   — she has a good sense of humour;
   — she can make people feel at ease;
   — she likes helping at the Youth Club;
   — she likes her determination.

3 Help her construct a list of things that other people like about her. This will inevitably involve the helper (or friends and family if she is brave enough to ask) giving her feedback. The list may surprise the woman as she is probably not used to asking for or hearing anything positive about herself.

Positive feedback Most survivors find it difficult to hear anything positive about themselves, and tend to disqualify compliments and praise with, 'But it was only because of . . .'

— luck;
— someone else feeling sorry for me;
— someone trying to be nice/cheer me up;
— I just happened to be there.

Example: Working as a nurse, Anne was presented with an award naming her as the Best Nurse of the Year. She disqualified the achievement by saying that she only received the award because she was well known to the people who nominated her, and other, better nurses were not!

Constructing a list of things of which she is proud Here the survivor, on her own or with support from her helper, is encouraged to write down:

— any talents which she thinks she has, such as playing a musical instrument, communicating with children, doing crosswords;
— any things which she does better than other people;
— things about herself of which she is proud;
— difficulties which she is proud of having overcome;
— areas in which she has seen growth and change in the last year/ month/week;
— one thing on which she would like to receive compliments.

The survivor might find this difficult to do but by sharing the exercise with her helper she can get feedback from someone she is beginning to trust. She may have difficulty in accepting any positive feedback because she still has little confidence in herself as a worthwhile person. She may prefer to discount the compliments and feedback of others by using phrases such as:

— it was easy;
— anyone could do it;
— you are saying that just to be nice;
— you don't really know the real me;
— I did that but I couldn't manage other things.

It is important for the helper to give clear and accurate feedback, being very specific about her achievements, resources and strengths. The helper should make use of opportunities to give the woman positive feedback, no matter how small the change or achievement in her life. Positive feedback should:

— be very specific. For example it is better to say:

> 'You did well when you managed to go to your friend's house last Tuesday' rather than 'You are getting better at visiting your friend'. It is more difficult to disqualify specific and accurate feedback.

— contain a statement about the positive nature of the achievement. Examples are:

> — you did well when . . .
> — a few months ago you wouldn't have been able to do . . . and now you are able to . . .
> — it is good to see you doing . . .
> — you seemed pleased that you managed to . . .
> — statements which indicate the helper's approval, such as 'I am pleased that . . .', 'I am delighted that . . .' may be the first time she has received any genuine approval. The woman may, however, begin to do things just to gain the helper's approval rather than for her own sense of well-being.

— do not exaggerate the achievement by repeatedly drawing attention to it, 'I've told you so many times that . . .'

At times when she feels low about herself, it is useful for the survivor to find a task that she can do, rather than allowing herself to sink further into self-criticism. For example, she might do a routine task (clean a room, make a meal), read a book/magazine, listen to music she enjoys, phone a friend.

Buying herself something   This may seem a trivial task, but survivors have great difficulty in treating themselves to anything that is not strictly necessary. They prefer to buy things for other people. Encouraging a woman to buy herself something small because she wants to is an important first step in helping her see that she is a person of worth and has a right to treat herself. Examples of small things she might buy are: bath oil, earrings, a book, magazine, some favourite food, talc, bunch of flowers, colourful socks, a cassette.

Learning to be assertive   Improvements in self-esteem come with learning to be assertive. This is discussed in full in the following section and involves enabling a woman to learn that she has rights to her feelings and opinions and to make decisions and choices in her life. It will also help her to establish limits on the demands of others, and enable her to begin to say 'no' when she wants to.

Assertiveness

Many women feel that they lack control over different aspects of their lives, rarely feel confident, and they worry about criticism, comparison and security. For survivors these feelings can be magnified and they feel powerless in many areas of their lives. Some of the most frequently mentioned examples of lack of assertiveness include:

— not being able to speak to a stranger at the door;
— difficulties with authority figures, such as teachers, social workers, medical staff;
— difficulties with saying 'no' to friends, family, colleagues, partners and children;
— reluctance to challenge someone who is taking advantage of her goodwill, whether in a home or work situation;
— not being able to challenge a waiter, shop assistant or colleague on issues relating to poor service or standards of work;
— not feeling able to express sexual wishes or preferences;
— allowing others to make decisions on her behalf, even when they are not in her best interests.

There are a number of tasks which can be carried out with survivors, either in a group or one-to-one setting. These can help women to identify areas where they feel particularly unassertive, where they would like to change their behaviour and to reflect on changes made.

Ann Dickson's books *A Woman in Your Own Right* (1982) and *The Mirror Within: A New Look at Sexuality* (1985) are excellent handbooks to use when exploring the issue of assertiveness in everyday life and in personal relationships.

Defining Assertiveness

An important first step is to understand what assertiveness means. The survivor can be encouraged to list all the things she would include in her own definitions of assertiveness, aggressiveness and non-assertiveness. These might include some of the following:

— Assertiveness means:
> — being able to express your own needs, preferences and feelings in a way that does not threaten or put others down;
> — acting in a way that does not threaten or put others down;
> — having direct and open communication between people who take responsibility for themselves.

— Non-assertiveness means:
> — finding it difficult to stand up for yourself;
> — voluntarily giving up responsibility for your actions.

— Aggressiveness means:
> — being self-congratulatory at the expense of putting others down;
> — manipulating others by siding with one person and then another;
> — standing up for your own rights in such a way that others' rights are by-passed rather than respected.

A helper can point out that:

> — assertiveness is about the way in which someone uses 'personal power' — whether giving it away, using it to violate others or using it constructively and positively;
> — assertiveness and the ability to be assertive often depends on the situation a person is in. It can be easier to be assertive in some situations than in others.

Identifying Basic Rights

The idea that a woman has the right to a number of basic human rights can come as a surprise to survivors. Ann Dickson (1982) has produced a set of eleven basic rights which, she suggests, can be the basis for women to start changing their behaviour. She suggests that women should remind themselves of these basic rights if they begin to feel unsure of themselves. They are listed in Table 11.7.

Table 11.7: **The basic rights**

1   I have the right to state my own needs and set my own priorities as a person, independent of any roles that I may assume in my life.
2   I have the right to be treated with respect as an intelligent, capable and equal human being.
3   I have the right to express my feelings.
4   I have the right to express my opinions and values.
5   I have the right to say 'no' or 'yes' for myself.
6   I have the right to make mistakes.
7   I have the right to change my mind.
8   I have the right to say 'I don't understand' and to ask for more information.
9   I have the right to ask for what I want.
10   I have the right to decline responsibility for other people's problems.
11   I have the right to deal with others without being dependent on them for approval.

From Dickson (1982)

Assertiveness and Aggression

It is also important to distinguish between assertiveness and aggression. One way of enabling a survivor to see the difference is to create hypothetical situations and to work together to identify assertive and non-assertive responses. Situations can also be drawn from the survivor's own life.

Example:
1. You have been sold an item which has shrunk on its first wash. When you return it, the sales assistant suggests that it has shrunk because you have not followed the washing instructions.

   How would you respond assertively? — Point out that you followed the instructions carefully and suggest any other explanation.

   How would you respond aggressively? — Tell her that if she's not careful she might lose her job.

2. A relative telephones to say that she will call to see you at a time which is inconvenient.

   How could you respond in an assertive way? — Tell her the time she suggests is inconvenient and ask her to make another time to call.

   What would be an aggressive response? — 'You always ring when it's not convenient — don't you ever listen to what I say?'

3. Your manager at work has criticized an aspect of your work. You feel that her criticism is unjustified.

   What would be an assertive response? — 'I wonder if we

could look a bit more closely at the reasons for your criticism. I feel that they might be a little unjustified!'
What would be an aggressive response? — 'There's nothing wrong with me — it must be your problem.'

Role-play

Role-playing situations in which a woman feels that she would like to be more assertive can be a very helpful method. Role-play is described in some detail later in this chapter. Role-play which might be used to test out assertiveness includes:

— saying 'no' to repeated requests from family, friends or colleagues;
— telling someone that they have hurt her feelings;
— making an appointment with a school-teacher to discuss a child's progress or school report;
— telling a partner what your sexual needs are;
— returning shoddy goods to a shop;
— refusing to engage in conversation with doorstep sales personnel;
— refusing to baby-sit for a friend/relative because it is inconvenient.

Ways of Being Assertive

Once a woman begins to examine situations in which she would like to become more assertive, she will be able to examine issues such as:

— making clear and specific requests;
— saying 'no' directly and clearly;
— not automatically conceding her own needs and wants as less important than those of other people;
— recognizing feelings of anger, hurt and fear and being able to express them assertively;
— not allowing fear of criticism to dominate behaviour;
— finding ways of approaching difficult topics when communication is difficult or has broken down.

All of these issues can be discussed by looking at specific situations in a woman's life and working out how they could be improved. In addition, women can set themselves tasks in relation to the situations they have identified. An example of the way this can be done is given below.

Exercise

Working with her helper, a woman completes a sheet which asks her to identify situations which at the moment she feels she does not handle assertively (Figure 11.2). The woman picks one situation and discusses it in depth with her helper. They might choose to role-play the situation. This can lead to identifying ways in which the woman can become more assertive. It is important that the woman is also encouraged to try out these new approaches in real-life situations. She will need to review her progress and examine any set-backs she encounters. Set-backs can often provide useful information on a woman's difficulties with being assertive.

Figure 11.2: **Handling situations more assertively**

Think of a situation you don't handle assertively, which you would like to change, and fill in the sheet below.

Situation/ Action/Words of other person	My response	My feelings	What I wanted to say	How I would have chosen to handle the situation

Challenging Negative Thoughts

Survivors often have poor self-esteem, feel extremely guilty and show signs of anxiety and depression when they first come for help. These difficulties are characterized by a considerable number of negative thoughts about themselves, about their past and their present situation. In this section we consider some common negative thoughts and point out how survivors might learn to think more objectively and positively about themselves (Jehu, *et al*, 1986).

Types of Negative Thoughts

The following are common types of negative thinking:

'All or nothing' thinking   This is the tendency to see everything in very black or white terms, a complete failure or complete success. This is unrealistic, and is likely to lead to poor self-esteem, as one mistake will lead a woman to categorize herself as a total failure. Some examples are:

— I am a weak person because I can't forget about the abuse;
— I cannot do anything right (after making one mistake);
— I am a bad person because I forgot to telephone my mother.

Overgeneralization   This involves drawing a general rule from a single event. Some examples are:

— I had a bad day last week. I am never going to get over this;
— I will never be able to cope with anything because I can't handle the memories of my past;
— I was turned down for this job. I will never be able to get a job.

Mislabelling   The woman creates a totally negative view of herself because of a single weakness or mistake. For example:

— I am a useless person because I can't remember what happened to me during the abuse.

Mental filtering   This involves picking out a negative detail in any situation and dwelling on it to the exclusion of everything else. The whole situation becomes negative. Positive aspects are filtered out. For example:

— I was late for my appointment, and that made the rest of the day bad.

Disqualifying the positive   Another way of filtering out positive aspects is to discount them in some way. For example:

— I only got the job because they knew me;
— I had a good day on Tuesday but it won't last.

Jumping to conclusions   This involves drawing a negative conclusion that is not really justified by the facts of the situation. For example:

— I must have been to blame for the abuse because they took me away from home when I told about it;
— it was my fault that he abused me because he didn't force me;
— I must have enjoyed it because I didn't stop it;
— I got angry with my daughter today so I am a bad mother.

Catastrophizing This involves exaggerating the importance of mistakes or deficiencies and leads to poor self-esteem. For example:

— I will never be able to lead a normal life because the damage from the abuse is permanent;
— I made a mistake. I can never show my face there again.

Minimizing This is a tendency to play down good points or qualities. For example:

— I can sew, but so can most women;
— my kids have turned out all right — but it's nothing to do with me.

Emotional reasoning Feelings are taken to be evidence that something is true or real. For example:

— I feel guilty about the abuse, therefore I am guilty.

'Should' statements These involve beliefs that a woman should behave in ways that are unrealistic and overdemanding. For example:

— I should be able to forget about the abuse. It was in the past;
— I should be able to handle these flashbacks by myself;
— I should do everything for my children.

Personalization This involves assuming total responsibility for an event that was not her fault. For example:

— it was my fault that he abused me for so long because I didn't tell anyone;
— it was my fault that my sister was abused.

Methods for Challenging Negative Thoughts

1 The woman is asked to recall thoughts about herself, situations and events. This can be done by:

— asking her to keep to record of any thoughts that have made her distressed;

— role-playing a recent or past event so that she can identify any thoughts that provoked distress;

— describing a distressing event in detail so that the negative thoughts can be clarified.

2   She can be helped to identify negative thoughts and distorted beliefs.

3   The final stage is to explore more realistic and accurate thoughts and beliefs. This may be done through:

— the provision of accurate information in order to correct any misconceptions. For example, the helper might provide information about children's reactions to sexual abuse, the long-term effects into adulthood, incidence of sexual abuse as well as information about sexual and physical functioning;

— reviewing the evidence for her belief. This involves both her conclusion and any alternatives there might be. For example:

Her belief	*Alternative explanation*
I was to blame because I was removed from home.	I was removed for my protection.
I am guilty of the abuse.	The abuser, and not the child, did the abusing. I was only a child who did not know about sexual matters at that age.

— gaining a more objective perspective in her beliefs. This can be achieved by:

— asking the woman to assess how others would see the particular situation, for example if other people knew she had been sexually abused, who would they say was responsible?

— suggesting she reads the accounts of other survivors in order to check out how far their experiences as a child and adult relate to her own;

— encouraging her to join a group for survivors so that she can recognize that her problems are common amongst women who were abused as children;

— helping her to gain a wider perspective on current events. For example, her perspective might lead her to believe that just because she had a bad day she will never get over the abuse. Putting this into a wider context, she can be enabled to see that:

— she has had a lot of good days;
— everyone had bad days (including the helper!);
— by coming to talk about the abuse, she has taken the first steps in coming to terms with it;
— it is a difficult and painful process, and she may feel worse before she gets better.

— helping the woman to correct her tendency to assume responsibility for the abuse. This can involve examining:

— factors that were beyond her control (the abuser's wishes, intentions and behaviour) — she was a child;
— responsibilities of others who were involved, especially the abuser.

Building Trust in a Group

Chapters 8 and 10 emphasized the importance of trust for survivors. Here we describe some exercises which can be used to explore and confirm the issue of trust in a group setting. If trust exercises are used they should be planned carefully to ensure that participants feel safe. At no time should anyone feel pressured to participate there should always be the opportunity to opt out.

Trust Exercises

Trust in a circle Everyone stands in a close circle, and each group member takes it in turn go into the centre. The woman in the centre stands straight, legs stiff, feet together, eyes closed and body relaxed. She begins to rock herself backwards, forwards and from side to side. She allows others in group to gently catch her, and to pass her back and forth around the circle. If the woman really allows herself to trust other group members, she will be able to allow her body to go limp as she is passed from person to person. If she feels tense or cannot relax, she should try to be aware of what makes her feel like this. When everyone has had their turn in the centre of the circle, group members can discuss any feelings they had during the exercise.

Trust walk   This exercise is useful for highlighting feelings about trusting another person to care for you and experiencing dependency.

The group divides into pairs, one person is blindfolded and the other leads her on a walk around the room or outside. The 'leader' directs the blindfolded woman to a variety of objects, fabrics and textures, allowing her to explore each one for as long as she wishes. After about ten minutes the pairs swap roles. When everyone has completed her 'trust walk', the feelings they had doing the exercise can be discussed in then pairs and the in the whole group. Group facilitators should be aware that the experience of being blindfolded can be frightening for some women. If this is the case the woman should be reassured and given the opportunity to 'lead' the pair in the first instance.

A range of group trust exercises can be found in: *In Our Own Hands* by Ernst and Goodison (1981), *Gamester's Handbook* by Brandes and Phillips (1977), and *The Courage to Heal Workbook* (Davis, 1990).

Sentence completion exercise   The group facilitator writes the words to start a sentence on a large sheet of paper. Group members complete the sentence and the facilitator writes down each contribution. When the list is complete, it is discussed in the whole group. The exercise can be repeated with a range of sentences relating to trust: 'Trusting someone means . . .'; 'I find it difficult to trust people because . . .'; 'The things which help me to trust people are . . .'

Confirming Progress Already Made

In a group setting it is helpful to take stock of progress already made and to plan for the future. This is especially so in relation to the issue of trust. Some methods for doing this, together with exercises for 'taking stock' generally are given below.

1   Ask group members to write down three items in response to the sentence 'Things which have enabled me to trust women in this group are . . .'

2 Group members write a note to every other woman in the group starting

'Dear —

I value you as a member of this group because ...

from —'

The notes are distributed, read privately and, if anyone wishes, elaborated further or discussed.

3 Each woman is asked to write down what being in the group has meant to her. These thoughts are shared in the whole group with the facilitator writing them all down on a poster and helping group members to discuss them.

4 If group members identified their personal aims when they joined the group, these can be reassessed regularly.

Shared Activities

This is especially relevant to a group setting where members can plan and undertake a range of shared activities. These might include:

— an evening walk;
— a shared meal, with food prepared by group members;
— a meal in pub or restaurant;
— a visit to a swimming pool or other sports centre;
— a residential weekend in the country, planned in advance over a number of weeks;
— a visit to a funfair;
— an evening at the cinema, concert or theatre.

Role-play

Talking and thinking about behaviour is a prelude to changing it. Role-play is a useful method for trying out new ideas and ways of doing things. It can be used for:

— rehearsing what might be said and how to act in a particular situation;
— learning new ways of behaving in situations such as, being more assertive;
— expressing feelings towards someone, for example, anger with a family member;

— understanding why a woman behaves in a particular way in certain situations.

There are usually at least two roles to be played in role-play. The survivor plays herself, and a second person takes the complementary role of, shopkeeper, relative, partner or boss.

Many women initially express reluctance to try out role-play and they may feel embarrassed or self-conscious at the outset. Once the role-play has got under way, however, the pairs can get 'into role' very quickly. The person taking the complementary role can be a helpful source of insight and feedback on non-verbal behaviour such as tone of voice, posture and eye contact. These may be readily apparent to the woman herself.

Setting up a role-play　There are a number of helpful guidelines which include:

1　Do the role-play with someone you trust, preferably a friend.
2　Be specific about the subject of the role-play, rather than saying 'I want to try out being assertive', say 'I want to practise taking back a faulty jumper to a shop'.
3　Set the scene if this would be helpful — a shop assistant might stand behind a counter, a boss behind a desk.
4　Do not worry about having dramatic ability. The value of role-play lies in its ability to enable someone to practise a situation over and over again until she is reasonably happy with the way it has been handled.
5　Once a situation can be managed in role-play, there should be no need to try it out 'for real' immediately. This may take a long time.
6　The role-play does not need to last for long. Initially short role-plays are better until the individuals feel comfortable with the method.

The importance of role-play is that it allows someone to see how it feels to be in the situation. Any lessons learned through the exercise should only be put into practice when the person feels ready.

Example:　Hannah wanted to role-play a forthcoming meeting between herself and her daughter's teacher. She had received a complaint that her daughter had not been doing her homework. Hannah was very worried about the meeting. Her daughter had always assured her that her homework was done. The teacher frightened them both. Hannah role-played the meeting with a friend, acknowledging her daughter's problem, but pointing out possible reasons for it.

Writing

Many women resist writing down their thoughts and ideas simply because they dislike writing. They may think that writing is for other people or are worried about their spelling, grammar or handwriting. Also, women often find it difficult to find time to reflect and put their thoughts on paper. A woman should be encouraged to write, without worrying about spelling, grammar and punctuation. She should be offered the opportunity to share her writing with her helper if that is what she wants to do.

Writing down thoughts and feelings has a number of very important functions:

1 Writing makes things concrete. If a woman has conflicting or contradictory thoughts, writing them down will help to clarify them.
2 Writing can make a woman more aware of the thoughts. It is sometimes difficult for her to take note of things she tells herself; saying them out loud helps; writing them down can help even more.

Women should be encouraged to make some time to write. Writing can take the form of a diary or journal, a note of feelings at different stages, positive and negative emotions or reactions to specific situations, prose or poetry. Using a word processor can be helpful.

Bass and Davis (1988) and Davis (1990) suggest a variety of writing exercises which are summarized below:

— ask the woman to write down all the ways in which she thinks she is still affected by the abuse;
— ask her to write down the ways in which she coped with the abuse as a child;
— suggest she writes down how she feels she has come to terms with the abuse since coming for help. The list should include her achievements and successes as well as any difficulties she has encountered;
— suggest that she tries to talk to 'the child within' herself by writing a letter to her or engaging in a written dialogue with her, writing first as the adult and then as a child responding to the adult;

— ask her to make a list of all the things she did well today;
— ask her to write down what she did do this week to make things better for other people, such as:

> — preparing a meal;
> — controlling her temper with her partner;
> — listening to her neighbour's troubles;
> — kissing her daughter's knee better after a fall.

— ask her to write what she has done to begin to take control over her life, such as:

> — making a decision;
> — finding out about local evening classes;
> — finding out about driving lessons;
> — asking a welfare rights worker to check up on her benefits;
> — deciding to write a letter to her mother.

— ask her to write down what she has done to make herself feel better such as:

> — having a bubble bath;
> — going for a walk by herself;
> — going to bed early with a magazine;
> — buying herself something.

Women who have been abused often find it very hard to think of anything they have done well. Writing down accomplishments, however small, helps a woman confront the fact that she is not a total failure. If she is to begin to feel that she has some control over her life, she has to start giving herself credit for things well done, although this may not mean that a specific objective has been achieved.

In drawing up these sorts of lists, women should note whether they have added any negative qualifiers to their positive statements. Women often qualify a self-compliment with a criticism or they discount its importance, such as:

— 'I'm a good mother — but then anybody could do that.'
— 'I'm a fairly placid person — except when I get depressed I get really mean to my family.'

They should be encouraged to cross out any qualifying statements.

Letter Writing

Survivors can find it very helpful to write letters to significant people from their childhood but not necessarily send them. It allows them to express feelings which they might never have the courage to express verbally. Letters also have the advantage of no come-back if the woman chooses not to deliver them.

Letter writing is useful when:

— a woman feels that she will not have the confidence to confront someone (usually the abuser or her mother) about the sexual abuse;
— the abuser or other significant adult is dead or she is unable to make contact with them.

Writing a letter can be a very cathartic experience. Feelings and emotions are often easier and more clearly expressed in writing. Women can say what they want to in stages, without feeling the need to modify or camouflage any strong feelings. They need never post the letter, and may choose to destroy it or put it somewhere safe when they have completed it.

A survivor should be encouraged to:

— decide who she wants to write to, and why;
— equip herself with plenty of paper and pens;
— wait until she feels ready to put her thoughts on paper before starting;
— find somewhere she feels comfortable to write the letter. This might be at home, sitting in a crowded cafe or somewhere quiet such as an art gallery, library, church or park;
— write the letter in stages or in one sitting.

It may be helpful to start the letter with words such as,

'Dear —
I am writing to you because . . .'
                    or
'Dear —
This letter is important to me because . . .'

Women who have written letters, especially to an abuser, report that their thoughts flow freely and it is often hard to stop. Once complete, the letter can be shared with a helper, group members or whoever the woman chooses. Alternatively, she may wish to destroy it or put it somewhere secure. Letters can be written to:

— abusers;
— mothers;
— siblings;
— other family members;
— adults whom the woman tried to tell about the abuse;
— other significant adults such as, teachers, youth club leaders, family friends;
— themselves as children.

If the letter's recipient is still alive, the woman may want to personally deliver or post it. Alternatively she may suggest that the helper accepts it and destroys it at a later date. The helper should encourage the woman to accept responsibility for the letter and decide how to dispose of it herself.

Diaries and Journals

A diary or journal of her work with a helper or in a group might be kept. A woman can use it to write down:

— her expectations of a session or meeting;
— her thoughts on how it has gone;
— good and bad experiences during the session;
— new memories;
— connections with her past made during sessions;
— reflections on relationships past and present;
— points to follow up;
— her hopes for the future.

She may wish to keep her diary as her private record, or she can use it as a dialogue with her helper. Here she can ask for feedback from the helper on what she has written.

Keeping a diary is important for the following reasons:

— it is an important part of a woman's self-expression;
— it can be a significant means of acknowledging the process of change in her life;
— it can help to identify issues which are resolved and those which still recur in her life.

Personal Writing

Many survivors have turned to poetry and prose to express their feelings. They have produced emotional personal writing when it would have been difficult to express their feelings verbally; Appendices 1 and 2 give examples of material written by survivors. Women should be encouraged to write as much poetry or prose relating to their experiences as they can produce. It can be kept privately, shared with a helper or read aloud in a group and if the helper feels that a particular piece of writing may be useful for other survivors, permission must be sought to use it with other women. A survivor may be surprised that a piece of her writing could be used in this way, and it may be the first time she has felt that anything positive has come from her childhood experiences.

Using Other Writers' Work

Poetry and prose from survivors can be used to:

— reflect on and identify with feelings expressed by other survivors;
— encourage women to write down their own feelings;
— stimulate discussion on specific issues identified by other writers.

Helpers should try to have a selection of material to hand, so that women can be given appropriate material. The helper might suggest:

— giving material to a woman to take away and read. They could discuss it at a future session;
— reading it aloud together, checking out the impact of any particularly emotional passages;
— sharing reading of the material in a group and discussing its meaning for individual group members;
— giving women a selection of poetry, prose and autobiographical material which they can read at their leisure. Alternatively, a women could be directed to specific material at particular stages in her therapeutic work.

Brainstorming

The objective of brainstorming is to generate ideas on any subject or topic in a short space of time. It is also useful for producing material for further discussion. All that is needed for brainstorming is a large sheet of paper and a pen.

1 The helper explains the aim of the brainstorming session and asks for ideas on the topic which is written down on the paper or board, for example:

— ideas for a group to pursue;
— ways I could have stopped the abuser;
— people I could have told about the abuse.

2 There are some basic rules for the helper in a brainstorming session;

— write down every idea, without comment, and discard nothing;
— suspend judgment on each idea — they can be discussed individually later;
— aim for as many ideas as possible — quantity rather than quality;
— if ideas are slow to come, the helper might put down one or two of her or his own, but should wait before doing so.

3 When ideas have stopped flowing, the helper can:

— go through the list and group the contributions into smaller groups of related ideas;
— go through the list with a woman or group members pointing to each idea and checking if and how it should be followed up.

Example (taken from a group setting):

Ideas for the group to pursue
Feelings about mothers
Feelings about fathers
Feelings about own children
Feelings about sex
Reading some poems or stories
Playing games
Doing some drawings
Going for a swim together
A night out

Word Pictures

Word pictures can be used for:

— saying words which are difficult to say aloud;
— verbalizing feelings and thoughts relating to a particular topic;
— acknowledging common feelings and experiences in a group setting.

1 The helper puts a large sheet of paper on the floor or wall. In the centre of the sheet she/he writes the word or phrase which it has been agreed to explore.

Example:

2 She asks everyone present to say what they associate with the word or phrase. She writes down each contribution just as they are said.

Example:

3 Links between words and phrases can be drawn if they are apparent.

Example:

The picture is complete when everyone agrees that there is nothing more they wish to add.

4   Time is allowed for everyone to look at the picture and to ask for explanation or information if they need it. This leads to a general discussion of issues raised.

5   The helper checks how people are feeling and what they have learned from the exercise.

Topics for a word picture might include:

Sexual abuse is . . .
When I get angry I . . .
Reminders of the past
Feelings about abuser/father/mother/other trusted adults

The thing which frightens me most is . . .
Being a survivor means . . .
The effects of sexual abuse on my life are . . .
The ways I coped when I was young were . . .

Initially participants might feel too inhibited to contribute. Once the picture develops, however, the ice is broken and it becomes easier for people to participate. In a group setting, if one person dominates the construction of a word picture, the facilitator should ensure everyone who wants to contribute does so. This can be done at intervals during the exercise by asking women directly if they want to add anything.

Sometimes contributions do not directly address the issue, or they may be 'safe' thoughts or feelings. The facilitator can help by contributing her/his own ideas or material, changing the emphasis of the input. Finally, participants with poor literacy skills may be inhibited from joining in. The helper can help by repeating each word or phrase and summarizing the picture at regular intervals. This technique can also be used with a survivor in a one-to-one setting.

Sentence Completion Exercise

Most relevant in a group setting, sentence completion exercises are useful for:

— getting an immediate response on an issue;
— allowing women to respond individually to share their, individual responses and then to discuss their responses together;
— focusing thoughts on a specific topic.

1 The helper or group facilitator provides sheets of paper with the beginning of a sentence written on it. These are distributed to group members.

   I find it difficult to trust people because . . .

2 Women take five to ten minutes to complete the sentence, adding as many items as they can think of.

   I find it difficult to trust people because . . .

   — I don't expect them to trust me in return;
   — I'm afraid they will hurt me;
   — I don't usually get to know people well enough to be able to trust them;
   — It's better to keep your distance.

Once everyone has completed their individual lists, these can be shared by members of the group working in pairs, with the facilitator asking for one or two contributions from each group member in turn and noting these on a poster. The poster is complete when everyone has exhausted her personal list. Discussion may focus on:

— points of similarity or difference;
— clarification of specific points;
— situations in which women have experienced particular emotions or reactions;
— situations or conditions which help or hinder women in the area under discussion.

A sentence completion exercise can cover almost any topic. Some examples are given below:

The things which remind me of my past are . . .
For me, the effects of being sexually abused as a child are . . .
The feelings I have towards the abuser are . . .
The feelings I have towards my mother/sister/brothers etc are . . .
The things I like about myself are . . .
The things I dislike about myself are . . .
When I get angry I . . .
When I get angry I would like to be able to . . .
The things this group avoids talking about are . . .
The things I find easy to talk about in this group are . . .
The things I find hard to talk about are . . .

Dealing with Other Areas of Difficulty

There are a number of specific problems that are beyond the scope of this book. Survivors with these problems should be encouraged to seek help from appropriate agencies. They include:

Alcohol and drug abuse   These are serious problems that require the guidance of agencies dealing specifically with these problems. There are a number of agencies (Alcoholics Anonymous, Alcohol Advisory and Counselling Services, Drug Abuse Projects projects and professionals working within health and social services) with specific expertise in these areas. The woman's own doctor should be able to advise on referral procedures, and it is recommended that helpers have the relevant local information about appropriate sources of help.

Eating disorders (anorexia, bulimia, compulsive over-eating) These are serious problems that require professional help. Some health professionals are trained to deal with these difficulties and referral should be made through a woman's family doctor. Admission to a psychiatric hospital may be required if an eating disorder has reached a life-threatening stage.

Severe suicide attempts Referral to psychiatric services is appropriate here and may require admission to hospital. The woman's GP must be informed so that the referral can be made.

Severe depression Referral to psychiatric services is appropriate so that admission to hospital can be arranged if necessary. Again the woman's GP must be informed so that the appropriate referral can be made.

Significant obsessional problems Such difficulties such as compulsive hand-washing or contamination fears, can be dealt with by clinical psychologists and psychiatrists. Sometimes, admission to a psychiatric hospital may be necessary in order to work on the problems.

Tranquillizer dependency Withdrawal from tranquilizers is a difficult task, and should be done under medical supervision. The woman may require professional help to manage the withdrawal slowly and safely, to deal with the symptoms of withdrawal and any underlying problems that are revealed as the effects of the drugs wear off. Once a woman has de-cided to break her dependency, she should be informed of any support groups in her area.

Significant marital or relationship problems Help can be sought from appropriate agencies (marriage guidance agencies (Relate), social work departments, psychiatric and clinical psychology departments) which are willing to work with couples. Psychotherapy and other counselling services may also be available.

Problems with children Children in a family often have difficulties when one or both parents are having problems. Children's difficulties include truanting, school phobia, bed-wetting and soiling, sleep disturbance and eating problems. If a survivor's children are experiencing such difficulties, referral to child guidance, child psychiatry or child clinical psychology should be encouraged through the woman's GP. Parenting difficulties may also be dealt with in this way.

Chapter 12

Training for Working with Survivors

In Chapter 2 we drew attention to the personal and professional issues which need to be addressed by helpers working with survivors of child sexual abuse. Time set aside for specific training in this area of work is invaluable for exploring many of the issues described in earlier chapters of this book. Training needs will vary between one helper and the next. Some will have undergone professional training which may have included specific input for working with survivors; others will have had little preparation for the work.

In this chapter we draw attention to some general issues relating to training for working with survivors. These include:

— a framework for training;
— preparatory work;
— the training group;
— training methods.

Training should not be seen as the sole preserve of professional workers. It can range from a one-off session for helpers in a voluntary agency to a structured programme which is tailor-made for a range of helpers in a particular working environment. The most important features of effective training are its ability to:

— meet the specific needs of the participants;
— challenge assumptions and confirm the existing knowledge base;
— extend knowledge and skills.

We have not included training exercises or suggestions for specific topics. We would suggest that helpers adapt methods and ideas to the needs of specific training groups, spending time planning with the group if this is feasible.

Preparatory Work

A minority of helpers are attached to agencies whose main focus is in the area of sexual violence. For the remainder, they may find that a woman they have been working with for some time on another issue suddenly discloses a history of sexual abuse. It may help if the following aspects are covered before starting to work with survivors, although we acknowledge that often there is little time to prepare.

Counselling skills are a prerequisite for working with survivors. If this has not been part of any previous training, helpers should consider taking part in a basic training course. Counselling is an active process that enables the survivor to help herself. There are many models of counselling; one which we have found particularly useful and practical is Egan's three-stage model (1982). His three stages consist of:

— exploration of the individual's problems and feelings from her perspective;
— understanding and gaining new perspectives on her problems;
— action in dealing with them.

The model outlines the skills which are needed at each stage and emphasizes the importance of exploring a problem with a woman before moving towards finding a solution with which she is comfortable. It also involves building a therapeutic alliance between helper and survivor to facilitate the process.

Helpers should also examine their beliefs and feelings about child sexual abuse. This will certainly involve exploring attitudes and feelings about relationships between women and men and relationships within families. Sarah Nelson's book *Incest: Fact and Myth* (1987) is useful in this context. Helpers should also explore their own background for any history of child sexual abuse. If a helper discovers that she/he was abused as a child and has not resolved these issues, seeking help for her/himself before undertaking the work may be important. If they have not been sexually abused, helpers should be able to acknowledge any childhood and adult experiences which come closest to the betrayal, humiliation, sexual violence or violation experienced by a child who has been sexually abused. These experiences might include secrecy in the family, sexual assault or harassment in adulthood or situations in which the helper has felt powerless.

Helpers must be willing not only to believe women when they talk about their experiences of sexual abuse but also to accept that some women have experienced sadistic and cruel forms of abuse which challenge the boundaries of human understanding. It is useful to read personal accounts written by survivors in order to make themselves aware of the nature of sexual abuse and its effects on children and adult survivors. It is better to have emotional reactions of horror, disgust or sexual arousal to the contents of a book than to a survivor as she discloses details of her experiences.

Finally, helpers should be aware that although the majority of survivors were abused by male family members, women are increasingly disclosing sexual abuse by a mother, another female relative, or another child. Attitudes and feelings on these issues also need to be explored.

Facilitators for the Training

Facilitators for the training need to have:

— experience of working with survivors;
— checked out their ability to work together from a shared perspective;
— the ability to be flexible.

We would recommend that, when resources permit, one facilitator for each six to eight participants should be sought. This allows them to share the work and to give enough support for working in small and large groups.

A Framework for Training

In planning any training programme for working with survivors, it is useful for facilitators to establish a framework that will foster a safe and supportive atmosphere that will allow participants to explore the sensitive topic of sexual abuse. They can help to achieve this by spending time considering the following issues:

— the needs and experience of the training group in the context of the agency. Time spent on this can help to ensure that facilitators have examined the purpose of each exercise, the way in which the training as a whole fits together and the rationale for the sequence of exercises and activities;
— comfortable and quiet surroundings which are free from interruption. Rooms should be large enough to accommodate a range of training activities in large and small groups;

— regular breaks between activities so that there is time for reflection and relaxation;
— confidentiality. Three main areas need to be addressed:

> — sharing of personal information by participants during the training;
> — sharing information about any survivors with whom the participants are working;
> — how much of the issues discussed between members of small groups within a training session will be expected to be shared with the whole group;

— the availability of support during the training for anyone who gets upset or discloses painful experiences;
— a starting point for the training which allows the child's perspective to be understood and developed into an understanding of the reality of being a survivor;
— the timing of material and issues for discussion, so that participants do not leave the training feeling distressed or without having had time to wind down;
— flexibility of the trainers so that the programme can be altered if necessary;
— a training programme which maintains a balance between the distressing material relating to sexual abuse and other issues;
— a conclusion to the training which has time and space for examining 'issues for the helper'. This would include the effects of the work on the helper and how the helper might deal with these;
— a commitment to evaluating the training and using the evaluation to modify and improve future training courses.

The Training Group

Attention should be paid to membership of the group. The relative merits of the following should be addressed:

Stranger vs familiar group   A group of people who know each other may feel more at ease in this type of training. They may be more willing to challenge assumptions and values and can often give immediate support if someone discloses material of a personal nature.

Multidisciplinary vs single agency group   A multidisciplinary group has the advantage of bringing a range of perspectives to common issues. New working links can be made and professional stereotypes can be challenged. If specific professional jargon is used by any group members it can be challenged by facilitators in a way which does not alienate or patronize any of the individuals or professional groups involved. A single agency group, on the other hand, can have training which is tailor-made to a particular working environment and, if it works well, can be used to develop the team perspective on working with survivors. An added advantage can be the enhancement of team membership and development.

Single vs mixed gender group   Women often feel safer and less inhibited in an all-female group. Men should also be given this choice, where possible. Single gender groups can also be considered as an option for part of the training if the group is mixed;

Inexperienced vs experienced helpers   A range of experience in a training group can provide a good basis for discussion and ideas. It can also inhibit less experienced members.

Size of the group   The group should be small enough to enable everyone to contribute in a safe and supportive environment. We would recommend a group of twelve if there are two facilitators.

Content of Training Sessions

We would recommend that the following areas form the basis for a basic training programme for working with adult survivors of child sexual abuse:

— the meaning of sexual abuse;
— the long term effects of sexual abuse;
— perspective of the child and the adult survivor;
— disclosure;
— themes in therapeutic work;
— feelings towards abusers and other family members;
— personal issues raised by the work;
— helpers looking after themselves.

Training Methods

Participants on any training course will learn best if a range of training methods are used. Some of the methods which we have found useful are outlined below. We would also note the importance of:

— using methods which draw out the knowledge which is already held by members of the training group;

— starting each session with an orientation exercise. This can range from checking on how people are feeling, exploring any issues or feelings which have been carried from a previous session, or giving an introductory exercise which enables the participants to begin work;

— timing the methods to the overall structure of the training. Brainstorming can be useful as a 'starter' on a particular topic, but can lose impetus if used continuously throughout the training;

— creativity in adapting methods to suit the needs of the training group.

The following methods, some of which are described in more detail in Chapter 11, can be useful in the contexts described below:

Brainstorming　It is useful as a 'starter' for a particular topic. It can be used as a way of assessing knowledge in a group and it can also energize the group — especially after lunch!

Roleplay　The trainers should always be clear about their reasons for constructing roleplays. In order for roleplay to be useful it needs to be carried out in a safe environment. It can be helpful to say to participants that the purpose is to get in touch with the feelings of the roles which are being played rather than to give an outstanding acting performance. It is not advisable to ask course participants to 'perform' their roleplay in front of others. If everyone is doing the same roleplay, trust can be established and experiences shared.

Scenarios of particular situations　Here the trainer constructs short vignettes which are followed by specific questions which are discussed in a small group. This method is useful for getting a range of responses on a particular issue.

Responding to questions a survivor might ask　Working in small groups, one person takes the role of the survivor and the other group members act as a collective helper. For example, the 'survivor' asks questions which reflect the guilt she feels about the abuse and the helpers try to respond in a way which they feel might shift the responsibility for aspects of the abuse to the abuser. In addition to challenging guilt, this method is particularly useful for responding to questions a survivor might have about the abuser and other family members.

Understanding the reality of abuse It is important for training to enable helpers to get in touch with the survivor's childhood experiences. Care should be taken to ensure that the issue is explored in a supportive and sensitive way, as it may raise difficult or painful issues for helpers themselves.

Personal accounts from survivors Short extracts from books, poems and letters written by survivors are also an effective way of getting in touch with the child's or survivor's experience. They can be read aloud by the facilitators or group members. Facilitators should be alert to any strong reactions to the material from participants.

Whatever combination of methods are used in the training, they should all confirm existing strengths of group members in their work. Good practice in training for work with survivors is no different from good training for work in other areas. Creativity, adaptability, sensitivity and energy are needed in equal measure.

Chapter 13

Conclusions

Coming to terms with the experience of childhood sexual abuse can be a long process. Many women are now embarking on that process, and they show great determination and courage in their ability to recover from their childhood experiences. We hope that this book will encourage more survivors to seek help and that it will enable helpers in a variety of settings and organizations to feel more confident about working with survivors.

It is inevitable that, with new knowledge and ideas, helpers will remember women with whom they have worked in the past. They may wonder if the women were survivors, or if they could have helped them in a more positive way. Whilst these thoughts and feelings can be acknowledged, it is also important to look towards the future, to try to ensure that any woman who discloses a history of sexual abuse receives help and support which they find useful.

The process of helping a survivor is likely to challenge helpers in a variety of ways. Methods of working may need to be re-assessed and assumptions about the nature of the family and the status of childhood may need to be questioned. As a result of this re-evaluation and a clearer understanding of the issues raised in this book, helpers will hopefully be able to listen to survivors in ways which are better able to meet their needs. Many survivors will seek help having had a history of contact with psychiatric services. For some, they have been given psychiatric diagnoses on the basis of symptoms which have not been linked to their experience of childhood sexual abuse; such diagnoses are often unhelpful, misleading and they have served to isolate women even further.

With more survivors deciding to seek help and talking about their experiences, some women will consider taking legal action against their abusers many years after the abuse has stopped. If this happens, helpers may find themselves supporting women through a difficult legal process, with all its attendant publicity and distress.

Knowledge about child sexual abuse and its effects is still hampered by a lack of research in a number of key areas. Firstly, our knowledge about the frequency of child sexual abuse is limited by the lack of large-scale surveys of both men and women. This is particularly so in Britain. Not only is there a need for sensitive research questions and methods, but researchers need to acknowledge that child sexual abuse often remains repressed until an event in the present brings it to the surface. Secondly, more information is needed on abusers — who they are and the reasons they give for sexually abusing children. Thirdly, the views of survivors themselves need to be sought and taken into account in a more positive way. In particular, information about women's previous experiences of receiving help, how and by whom they would prefer to be helped in the future and which methods they have found most useful, need to be recorded and acted on.

Our final thoughts to anyone helping a survivor are:

— try to be creative, and do not disregard any therapeutic methods in the work just because they do not appear in textbooks;
— make sure that good support and supervision is arranged before starting the work, since the work can be both demanding and emotional;
— evaluate the work in the light of the woman's progress, new knowledge and experience;
— encourage women to write about their experiences as part of their recovery and as a means of helping other survivors;
— listen to and believe survivors. They have a great deal to teach their helpers and society at large about the experience of child sexual abuse;
— always bear in mind how difficult it is for a woman to disclose child sexual abuse. The helper should carefully consider their reactions and responses when a woman talks about her past.

Working alongside women who have experienced childhood sexual abuse is often a rewarding process, which offers hope for the future. Survivors are extremely courageous and resourceful women who have been weighed down by the burden of their past and as they start to recover, their burden gets lighter and they can begin to enjoy life — perhaps for the first time. The last words belong to a survivor:

At last I know I can be clean and whole again. There are times recently when I have been happy. Times when I have had the inner confidence to know I can be happy.

Appendix 1

Poems by Survivors

The poems included in this appendix were all written by survivors. They cover a wide range of issues and feelings, and are a powerful testimony of the experience and effects of being sexually abused. They can be used in working with survivors or in training helpers for the work.

This poem describes some of the many perceptual disturbances experienced by survivors. It is taken from Ellenson (1986).

> I still see the evil shadow in the darkness of the night from the
>   bed where warmth and safety should have been my given
>   right.
> I hear the voice which calls my name or cries out in distress.
> I'm terrified of being left alone in helplessness.
> For in the blackness — in the night when I am all alone is when
>   I hear the footsteps, bumps and breathing in my home.
> Even when I sleep I cannot find escape or peace.
> Nightmare earthquakes, floods and fires, vicious frightening beasts,
>   threaten me or family and chase me out of breath.
> And perhaps the worst of all of these are the dreams I dream of
>   death.
> Daylight drives the dreams away but not my haunting fear of
>   furtive shadows in the halls, of unseen eyes that leer,
> of sudden movements captured in the corners of my eyes,
> of the evil presence, the unseen touch that chills my soul to ice.
> I live in silence with all of these because I fear that maybe
> if I told you of these awful things, you would think I'm crazy.

The next two poems were written by a survivor who began to remember being abused when she was in her forties. This enabled her to make sense of her long-standing mental health problems.

I   is for the isolation we feel
N is for numbness and nothing feels real
C is for the cuddles of which there were none
E is for the emptiness and life's never begun
S is for the sleepless nights seeming endless in a row
T is for the tears that we were not allowed to show.

C is for the comfort, a feeling we never felt
A is for the anger at the hands we were dealt
U is for the understanding which never came our way
S is for the secret and the price we had to pay
E is for the emotions we felt no right to claim
S is for the scandal, the suffering and the shame.

P is for the protection which we never received
A is for the anguish that we may not be believed
I   is for the identity that we lost along the way
N is for the nobody who is writing this today.

Put them together. The message is clear.
It's what we've all run from year after year.
But talking can help and I'm finding that out;
Yes even those times when I may have a doubt
It's hard to remember the message is right
During dark days and during dark nights.
It has to be faced and worked through somehow
At least that's how I feel right now.

—

For once I know just how I feel
I'm standing on the ledge
A feeling I know very well
I'm back on the knife edge.

What am I, am I a freak
To be stared at in a fair
Or am I just a piece of meat
With everyone wanting a share.
I want to retract every word I said

For I just cannot see
How telling Tom, Dick and Harry will be
Of benefit to me.

What do they expect of me
What am I supposed to do
Walking into groups and say to all
'Have I got news for you'

What am I supposed to say
When they're playing fast and loose
'Hey everybody, what do you think
I'm a victim of child abuse'.

Why did I open this powder keg
I'm regretting the day I did
I just want it over and done with
But I can't find the lid.

The following poems are from Sisk and Hoffman (1987)

Caution: There's a Child Inside*

There is a child inside me, and though she's very small,
There was a time not long ago she seemed not there at all.
Then one day I was asked to tell a little of my past.
As I spoke and walls came down, a little comfort the child had
    found.
Hiding no longer would keep her content,
    though protecting her had been my intent.
Frantically now she tried to reach out
    to see what this feeling had all been about.
For while I was thinking I just couldn't cope.
Someone had given the child some hope.
Here began the struggle, you see,
    between this little child and me.
For she had to be quiet and remain inside,
    so her guilt and shame I could hide.
Now someone has told her she wasn't to blame;
    and there wasn't a reason for her to feel shame.
Even though she still felt guilt and shame,
    she clung to that hope just the same.

I continue to fight her for I feel I must,
    for I see her slowly beginning to trust.
And I don't want her to hurt for I remember too well,
Her painful experience, of which I tell.
But this one who continues to listen to me,
    reaches into the child and tells her she's free.

*My adult vs. the child**

Each night as the adult lays her in bed
    her childhood fears play in her head.

She tried hard to block out fear
    as the child's blue eyes begin to tear.

The child sits up as the adult wants to lay,
    the adult now explaining her fears away.

The child is still frightened yet tries to behave,
    in fear of the adult, as for now, she'll obey.

But as the adult begins to rest,
    the child's little mind flashes to the molest.

The child still trembling now silently screams,
    the adult still sleeping begins to dream.

The adult now sees, again the screams she can hear,
    Now she too trembles and awakens in fear.

And for awhile they both sit quivering in fright,
    as the child continues to experience each night.

But somehow between all the silent screams,
    the adult starts to realize it's only a dream.

Yet the child is still screaming for to her it is real,
    though the adult can numb-out, the child still can feel.

The adult now stifles the silent screams,
    in order to gain control of her dreams.

The child now looking for someone to hold her,
　　finds only that the adult ever ready to scold her.

*Not You But I**
You're the one who made me hurt,
　　Yet I'm the one who feels like dirt.
You're the one who is to blame,
　　Yet I'm the one who lives in shame.
You're the cause of my nightmares,
　　Yet I lay awake trembling, but what do you care?
And when I'd told what you had done,
　　I'm the one mom chose to shun.
You're the one who made me cry,
　　Then dared a tear to leave my eye.
How tough, how strong you must have been,
　　You had total control when I was ten.

*The Child in Me**
I didn't stop it because I didn't talk
　　or maybe it's the way I walk.
Whose fault was it? Yours or mine?
　　I dredge through my past to find a sign.
Each time I say it was his fault,
　　some inside voice speaks out.
One small forgotten issue
　　that seems to raise some doubt.
Who is that voice inside of me
　　that refuses to let my innocence be?
I thought it was those criticizing words,
　　that as a child I always heard.
But surprised I was to come to see
　　they're words of the little child in me.

*This Kind of Touch**
Tonight as I lay awake in bed
　　my hands propped beneath my head,
Afraid to close my eyes in sleep,
　　for fear that into my room he'll creep.
I see him standing at my door,
　　as he has so many nights before.

He doesn't think I know he's there;
    he doesn't know I see him stare.
And as he moves beside my bed,
    his ugly touch I start to dread.
For I feel frightened when I see his hand
    reaching out, touching me.
And I think that if I'd never been touched,
    it would have been better
Than this kind of touch.

* Excerpted from *Inside Scars: Incest Recovery as Told by a Survivor and her Therapist*, by Sheila L. Sisk and Charlotte Foster Hoffman. Copyright 1987. Pandora Press. Used with permission.

The following poem was written by Lynda E. D. Adams, a survivor. She wrote it in order to disclose some of her childhood experiences.

I was only '4'
How much younger could I have been. . . .
When you started to abuse my body?
'Come and sit on my knee' you say,
I love you because. . . .
You are my 'DADDY'
I love to sit on your knees.
You put your hands on my thighs
Then further up you would go. . . .
Until you reach between my legs,
You start to rub me. . . .
I feel funny in my tummy
You begin to frighten me
You didn't tell me what you were doing,
Only quietness. . . .
Then you push me away.

I was only '7'
Into the bathroom you came.
To dry me, I heard you say,
But what's this you're doing?
What is your finger doing there?
'Tell me if you hurt' I hear you say
Sure, I hurt!

But you don't hear me.
'Just a little longer' you once more say,
Then it's over. . . .
Until another time.

I was only '10'
'Want a lollipop' I heard you shout
Just a little child still,
Sure, I love lollipops!
I came to you with Innocence
Then I stood still with fear
Because you fooled me here.
'Sit down here, beside me'
You were already prepared
'Touch me . . . right here.'
I froze with fear.
Help me God. . . .
Don't leave me here
I feel you touch me. . . .
Between my legs.
Then you kiss me. . . . .
Dear God, why am I still here?

I was only '12'
Now you pin me to the floor,
With all your body weight
And for this, you couldn't wait.
I feel I wasn't your daughter then,
You treated me more like a lover
Or more like a Monster you were
For, you devoured my body,
While I was in despair,
For no lover would be so unfair?

I was only '13'
I had enough by then,
Too often have you raped me
Too often, I keep saying in my head
I had to undress in your view,
Like a hungry Monster, you watched me.
I tried to dress again,
You devoured my clothes,

Like you devoured my body,
But not this time
No, not this time,
But I had to fight,
So you left your dirty mark on me,
Because I won the fight!

I am much older now,
And I look back on my life
I was only a child then,
You were responsible for me,
You took advantage of a child,
And you knew what you were doing then.
I tell you how I feel,
You won't acknowledge it,
You only say 'it's all over now!'
For you!
But it still hurts inside me,
Because I won't let anyone near me.

The following three poems were written by Jane Wilkie, a survivor who was abused by her brother. The first is based on the poem 'How do I love thee?' by Elizabeth Barrett Browning, The other two are written for an abused child.

This poem is dedicated to my brother

How do I hate thee? let me count the ways,
I hate thee on a Monday and Wednesday,
and all other days in my year,
I hate thee in the morning and evening,
most of all I hate thee afternoons and nights,
I hate thee with my body and mind to the depths of my soul,
I hate thee with every breath, and every beat of my heart,
I hate thee with each step, each sneeze and cough,
I hate thee with every memory, remembered and forgotten,
with every wave of my hand and each hair on my head,
I hate thee for giving my life fear and disgust,
for robbing me of childhood and joy,
I hate thee for making me doubt, and for destroying my trust,
I hate thee for poisoning people against me,

I hate thee for your lack of conscience and your love of my pain,
I hate thee for your smell, your mind,
I hate thee for your foul body corrupting mine,
How do I hate thee?
I have counted some of the ways
I know I shall hate thee to the close of my days.

The Unknown Child

The unknown child sits with her unknown face,
just sits and stares, stiff, but with no grace.

She sits quiet and unmoving, intently listening,
no expression just tears in her eyes, glistening.

She looks alone, isolated and abandoned,
Strangely un-alive, what can I do, should she be questioned?

I turn away and feel her eyes burning into my mind,
they accuse me, 'you too, why are you so blind?'

There is deep regret that I turned away, distressed,
didn't help her play, I am as guilty as the rest.

It is easy to deny her, as though it is not our pain,
the tragedy is, it has happened before and will again.

The unknown child with her dead unknown face,
I now need her and search, too late, there is no trace.

Once I had a little girl

Once I had a little girl
now she is dead.
She lived inside my heart
locked away from all harm.

She was safe, but lonely
in the dark, afraid.
I didn't want her hurt
in ignorance I hurt her more.

She was alone and cold
slowly, so slowly I let her out,
to see and feel the world,
trying to protect her all the while.

Then I found her a safe place,
to laugh and cry and live,
to make friends to trust,
only it was not safe at all.

Once I had a little girl,
hope gone, she dies,
I failed her, now I am alone
in the dark, with only myself to blame.

The following three poems are taken from a series of poems based on traditional nursery rhymes. They were written by a survivor who used them as a way of contacting her inner child. She found the constraints of the nursery rhyme rhythms helpful in expressing her emotions and revealing the nature of the abuse she experienced.

(Little Boy Blue)

Little wee girl,
Come smile and sing.
The kids in the street dance in a ring.
Where is the child who lives o'er the street?
Alone on the doorstep, unable to weep.

(Polly Flinders)

Little Nettie Glover, snug beneath the covers,
Slept in her cosy little den.
Her father came and woke her, to fumble and to poke her,
And make her scared to ever sleep again.

(The Grand old Duke of York)

Oh, her mother and her dad,
They loved their Jenny Wren.

They gave to her the gift of life
And they took it back again.

Oh, and when she was good they refused her,
And when she was bad they misused her,
And when she was neither good nor bad
They demoralised and abused her.

Appendix 2   Hidden Memories

This is an extract from a longer piece written by a survivor who, after 47 years, has been recovering memories. When she began attending for help, she was experiencing intense emotional pain.

The Present

I have no visual memories of being sexually abused, I can't recall pictures in my mind of my father physically raping and violating me. But I know he murdered me when I was two years old, then abandoned me. I know the time of day he did it, where we were, how I felt before he started to do it, and how I felt after he finished violating me. So I know he murdered me because that's what it feels like, 47 years after he did it. Sometimes it feels as though he has just done it again.

After this first abuse I was separated from my mother for a few months as she was in hospital. Before I remembered the abuse I thought that my adult emotional insecurity was connected to this separation which occurred during a time of heavy wartime bombing, but I now know that although it must have been a difficult time, it was the sexual abuse I suffered that was the real cause of my trauma, because that's what it feels like, that's where the pain is. I had no memory of this trauma at all until I was able to bear what must have felt unbearable.

There are many reasons why I cannot recall images of the abuse itself, i.e., I was very young; it probably took place at night, in the dark, my face was turned away, covered up, smothered. I might have been lying on my stomach (adult males abusing children find that anal sex is easier than vaginal penetration). Some people remember the acts and repress their emotions. I recall the emotions very easily, but my conscious mind refuses to recall pictures of the acts. I forgot in order to live through it, I survived by repressing the memories at that time.

I have very strong feelings sometimes that I have been beaten on the right side of my body but I don't actually remember this happening, I've blocked it off — but it occurs in my nightmares, and that's as close as I get to remembering that kind of violence, because two-year-olds can't differentiate between physical and sexual acts, it's all violence felt by them. They probably would not see it coming, it's unexpected, and totally shocking and unexplainable to them. The severity, the duration of the abuse, the age at which it happened, the conditions surrounding the abuse, and the way it was handled have all been shown to influence my ability to remember. I think one of the most important reasons for my amnesia is fear, it is the strongest hidden memory I live with, it's always with me and impedes my recovery because I'm constantly two years old and fearful. As I begin to recover, the feeling slowly falls away and I literally brighten up.

In our visual culture we sometimes believe that picture memories are the only ones that count, but this clearly isn't true. You have only to think of popular culture images of sounds and smells, for instance, to realise that industries of music, perfumes, food, rely on our 'hidden memories'. A certain trigger is all we need to arouse images of intellectual or tactile expressions that are very difficult to resist.

I experienced great relief in releasing these hidden memories, and I was able to start recovering from the abuse when I began to start disclosing the emotions that I had experienced during those early years. I get very upset if anyone tries to suggest that it just didn't happen. I immediately know that it did.

Although I may have shut off the visual memory of the actual abuse I cannot prevent myself from recalling feelings, they overwhelm me and, as I recover from the almost overwhelming shock of discovering through therapy that I was sexually abused 47 years ago, other memories start to come through, memories of touch, taste, colour, sound, etc.

My Inner Child

Physical violence, rape, and sexual abuse feels like murder to two-year-olds, it would be quite difficult for them to differentiate what is happening to them. I know I was murdered, raped, when I was two years old, but I didn't discover this until a year ago when I started to visit a therapist. A series of losses had triggered my memory into altering me to a state of extreme terror that was connected to the two-year-old child within me, but I had no idea what the cause was.

My husband and I have always had a very good marriage so I knew it wasn't connected to our present life, but we had to spend the next two years adjusting to disturbed sleeping patterns as I had continuous nightmares that woke us up every night. I became so distressed during the day that I was treated for depression, but although it was depressing to live through I wasn't actually suffering from depression but post-traumatic stress disorder. Looking back it seems so obvious now, but I couldn't see what was causing the stress except I felt it was connected to a childhood loss of some kind, so I assumed it was probably the time when I had been separated from my mother when I was two.

My severe reaction to a bereavement finally made me ask a counsellor for help, and it was her recognition of my symptoms being associated with possible earlier traumas, perhaps even repressed memories from childhood, that enabled me to start therapy. By the time I started therapy I felt as if my emotions were boiling up with the lid about to come off, and my memories connected to the two-year-old within me started to emerge almost straight away. But I couldn't visually remember the origins of my emotional pain. What I remember are the emotions I felt then, I can't avoid them surfacing however hard I try to stop them. My therapist helped me to reach my inner child by sitting close to me and calling me my childhood name of Susie very softly, and I immediately felt so threatened she realized that we would have to find a different way round the process of disclosure. I wasn't frightened of her but of the hidden memory of someone close to me. I remembered being two years old and recalled the pain and trauma felt after the abuse but never the abuse itself.

These stored body memories cause me to react against all kinds of triggers that are set off without warning. I sometimes see, fleetingly, a look in a man's eye, an expression, that momentarily reminds me of someone else's face. It happens so quickly, like an electronic impulse, that I can't shut it off. The damage is done to the two-year-old within me, she sees it and tells me by the fearful reaction I get through her that I must be on my guard. Writing this makes me suddenly recall a man's expression that I saw a couple of years ago when I was out walking with my family. I immediately felt a two-year-old child again and started to feel terribly threatened. I had no idea then why I should react so strongly, but I do now. It's as though I'm seeing a face in the dark, with only the eyes visible, that's what scares me; it's not the man himself, I know that it's a kind of shadowy memory I get, but not vague, it's precise when it happens, and I can't stop my response to it, but I'm learning to control it and accept it by understanding its origin. I have to tell the child within me to differentiate between the expression and the reality. It has nothing to do with men I see today but has everything to do with my memories of my father a long time ago.

Hidden visual memories that occur also include being in unfamiliar surroundings; something triggers this off for me and I become devastated, a very frightened two-year-old again. As I begin to identify the cause I can cope a bit better with new places but I have to be aware of the problem very quickly otherwise I get overwhelmed by the knowledge that I'm in a strange place, away from home. Home, that is where I feel secure and protected, not home when I feel threatened.

There's a big area of hidden memories that includes fear of going upstairs to my bedroom, the doors I have to pass, oh the two-year-old inside me doesn't like going to bed at all. When I get into bed I have to brace myself for the sound of my husband coming out of the bathroom; he's usually humming to warn me he's coming as he knows I'll jump when he comes into the room; then it's the noise of the door handle that seems to threaten me, then he comes into bed and I have to cope with feelings of danger as I see his body and feel his physical presence. Only it's not my husband who frightens me, it's hidden physical memories that won't die down. After a bad dream I have to restrain myself, literally, from hitting my husband as he lies next to me, but it isn't him that I want to beat up, it's someone else that has angered my two-year-old.

It's also hidden memories of sight and sound, connected to strange surroundings, or my bedroom, that keep re-occurring. These include seeing the colour red, a red-striped shirt my husband has started to wear makes me feel really awful; it's not my dear husband or his shirt, it's the awful red stripes. If he wears a certain shade of blue it definitely has a calming effect on me, and I don't think this has much connection with colour therapy; it feels like a memory I have of my mother wearing blue, so it feels very safe to me.

Physical touching by my husband sets off more memories, it's not him or his touch, but the fearful anticipation that my body remembers; it has nothing to do with my relationship with my husband, it's to do with my childhood. He comes in and stands behind me as I sit writing, and the fear starts up again, I'm feeling vulnerable because I'm writing about the abuse. He puts his gentle hands on my shoulders, but they feel like the rough weight of my father's huge hands on my inner child, and instinctively I know that it's my back, he did it to my back, my father was behind me when he abused me. I never confuse the two men, but one man's touch sparks off a hidden memory of another's — that happened so many years ago. I can't create a situation where I might produce physical memories, that's putting the adult part of me in control, so they occur spontaneously, without warning.

Most of these memories are occurring since the disclosure of the sexual abuse, but every day I'm remembering things that have happened throughout my life that caused me emotional turmoil, and I now see where they originated from.

But I still can't remember the physical sexual abuse itself. I can't let myself remember that. So I get hidden memories that I can't control.

I've started to get memories of taste. And I have temporomandibular pain in my jaw (known as TMJ Syndrome), also a back problem and haemorrhoids, all possibly related to hidden memories. The stronger I become the more open I am to suggestion that physical memories stored in my body are caused by me being sexually abuse, raped and violated. I can be very adult one minute, not thinking about anything in the past, then the sudden feel of my hand when I use a tampon instantly makes me feel like I'm two years old again, and somebody is touching me in the wrong place and I don't like it. These feelings are like electronic impulses that I can't introduce or control myself, they just happen.

Feelings

The worst memory is of the feelings I had after the abuse. I feel as though I die again when I remember I was murdered. Murder is the only word that is strong enough to indicate how violently I was treated. I know I'm not dead, but sometimes the two-year-old inside me feels murdered, then worse than dead, much worse, abandoned, isolated and helpless. This feeling is the worst feeling in the world. My nightmares have been full of this pain, and now that I am getting better I tend not to remember the details so clearly of the night terrors, but the memory of the emotions remain, so I wake up feeling truly dreadful, worse than dead, dead means peace, so it's the abandonment. I have been abandoned forever, she is trying to recover from that. It felt terminal, sometimes it still does, but then the sound of people's voices lifts me, so that's another hidden memory. Death, abandonment, recovery.

But I still don't remember the actual physical abuse. I don't even want to remember it, not yet, maybe when I'm a bit further on in the recovery process. Although I sometimes think that it really wouldn't make much difference being able to actually see an image of the abuse, it wouldn't make me feel worse or better, I don't actually need to 'see it', as feeling it is as horrendous a pain as I am ever likely to experience. I used to want to be able to describe it, visually, to other people, to help me and them acknowledge what had been done to me, but it doesn't feel as though remembering the actual physical details now would make me recover more quickly. My therapist and I drew together every kind of physical abuse that a grown man could do to a child, I can't pick out one thing that feels worse than another, but I do feel that what we drew was really not enough to describe the pain I remembered.

But I know it happened because I can describe the feelings. These are so awful I have to deal with them, experience them again in therapy, otherwise I would never have started to recover. Talking about it is not enough, I have to feel it as well. We used symbolic descriptive drawing to replace my vocabulary. Two-year-olds in therapy don't have the appropriate words to describe their emotional pain, and drawings have an immediacy that words sometimes lack.

I have hidden memories of shame and guilt that I couldn't find the cause for until I started therapy, as well as feelings of being a 'bad' person, all these areas of worthlessness that couldn't be identified properly until I discovered that I had been abused. I always had trouble with personal boundaries, and it's given me a great feeling of self-esteem that I've never had before just to be able to identify that I am 'me'. I've never felt like a real 'me' before.

The list goes on and on. My previous attitude towards men, my behaviour in adolescence, my reactions to changes in my life, and always that awful feeling of abandonment and isolation that surfaces in times of stress without me being able to identify the cause. I feel it less often now, but it can re-occur if the least thing upsets me emotionally and I have to work very hard to get rid of it. It was the feeling of hopelessness and abandonment that finally made me realize I need to ask for help, I finally acknowledged to myself that something was wrong with my emotional health. And it's the feeling of abandonment that has made me feel I've had enough, I just want some peace.

The Process of Recovery

In the last month I've been able to lose over a stone in weight, because I now feel secure enough to give up some of my 'props', alcohol, over-eating, etc. My two-year-old never did like alcohol anyway, but I used to ignore this. I'm dieting sensibly, I don't know how long this will last, but it feels good to be able to be in control at the moment. I still get pain from piles and low back pain despite the new eating plan and my giving up caffeine altogether, but I'm learning to relax and meditate, which helps me cope with the pain. It also helps me to cope with the anguished feelings I get after bad dreams, I'm sleeping so much better these last weeks, whole nights free of internal trauma, BRILLIANT, but during the nights when I can remember the dreams, I just try to relax and visualize me being at peace, then I fall asleep again, and that seems to help a lot.

I'm reading everything I can find on self-help theories, and I'm finding that most books that I already have on child abuse have a section on relaxation anyway. They emphasize that our spiritual selves can be developed once we release our energies previously spent repressing so much pain. It seems to me that although I have read all this before, I was not able to use it myself. It feels increasingly, that there is a 'right' time for me to try different ways of relieving my stress, including writing, which occurs at a particular moment in my recovery, and I can't rush this process. However hard my intellect pushed me to move on, the adult part of me feels that I have little choice but to wait for this to happen, as I need to be quite strong to cope with the emotions coming back on my own, without my therapist at my side. Actually, I do have a choice and that involves listening to what the little me needs to do, so it's not so much a question of why I am sometimes appearing to be moving on slowly, but that my inner child needs to just pause and check that everything is alright, then it feels safe to move on again.

Once I realized that I could start writing, and maybe get upset, but recover and move on, on my own, I really started to come alive again. I don't need the tissue box today, or my Teddy (but I know exactly where he is. . . . .)

All the books I'm reading seem to be saying the same thing, whether they are talking about recovering from child abuse, back pain, general stress and disease: they recommend that you change your eating habits, lose weight, relax, meditate, visualize. It doesn't matter what your problem is, you have to start taking control over what you do to yourself in order to heal yourself. Well, I was aware of this, but I recognize that and experiencing security at long last, that I can actually relax enough to think about changing my old habits. It feels really good to be able to let go old patterns of behaviour and also to be in control if I get upset over something.

There are still things I can't do on my own, but I don't see them as being a problem in the future, I'm working on them, and I don't feel so frustrated about the time it takes for my 'complete' recovery as I used to be. If I go too fast the small me says 'hang on a minute, slow down', and that feels O.K., we seem to be working together well, we are working together very well.

Little children don't possess the vocabulary to describe their feelings, so they can't talk about them. I can't tell people what was done to me, my two-year-old doesn't have the words available to me like my adult does. And always there is this element of fear that stops me describing what happened to me. Every time my family walk in the room when I'm typing this 'disclosure' I feel it. It's fear, it's my strongest hidden memory. As I get in touch with my inner child I'm unable to use words with more than one syllable and my tone and posture begin to resemble that of a child rather than an adult. I've often driven home from therapy feeling like a two-year-old for several miles, I'm on a sort of auto-pilot with my child at the wheel. I have to concentrate very hard at keeping my distance from the car in front, I know that their red lights coming on means that I must brake too, and slowly I progress upwards to being 49 again. My adult knows I shouldn't start to drive until I'm in control, but my child is desperate to get home so off I go.

I'm not suffering anymore from childhood sexual abuse. It's all over now. I was violated, murdered, but I'm discovering. I never stopped driving myself home after therapy, despite being very distressed at times, so I must have been stronger than I realized. I never became an alcoholic, although I think I must have tried quite hard to become one. Discovering you have been abused is one thing, accepting this fact and its implications is something else. My recovery depends on my acceptance of the past. Oh, and I never lost my sense of humour. I was depressed but I never got depression.

After I was murdered at the age of two I buried my inner child for nearly 50 years, but she wasn't quite dead so she waited until I was strong enough to cope with her pain. I very nearly wasn't. But I had the constant support of my therapist and my family and friends who understood what was happening to me, and me and my inner child got through it in the end. And it was all achieved through identifying hidden memories, my stored feelings, not my visual recollection of these terrible events.

Appendix 3

Useful books

There are many books which can be used to help survivors recover from the effects of childhood sexual abuse. Some of these, together with a short description of their contents are outlined below.

* Specially recommended.

General Books for Working with Survivors of Child Sexual Abuse

BLUME, E.S. (1990) *Secret Survivors: Uncovering Incest and Its After effects In Women*, New York, New York: J. Wiley.

Gives a good overview, and has a useful checklist for assessing the long-term effects of sexual abuse.

BRAY, M. (1991) *Poppies on the Rubbish Heap: Sexual Abuse: The Child's Voice*, Edinburgh, Scotland: Canongate Press.

Good book by UK sexual abuse social worker on understanding the effects of abuse on the child.

COURTOIS, C.A. (1988) *Healing the Incest Wound: Adult Survivors in Therapy*, New York, New York Norton and Company.

A book for readers familiar with psychological concepts on the process of therapy with survivors.

DRAUCKER, C.B. (1992) *Counselling Survivors of Childhood Sexual Abuse*, London, England: Sage Publications.

A useful book with clear jargon-free text, good examples looking at the process of coming to terms with child sexual abuse.

* DINSMORE, C. (1991) *From Surviving to Thriving: Incest, Feminism and Recovery*, Albany, New York: State University of New York Press.

An excellent book acknowledging the strengths of survivors in overcoming the trauma of sexual abuse. Good sections on lesbian women, therapeutic issues and memory recall.

FINKELHOR, D. (1984) *Sexual Abuse: New Theory and Research*, New York, New York: Free Press.

Summarizes Finkelhor's research and looks at theoretical perspectives. Good overview.

GIL, E. (1988) *Treatment of Adult Survivors of Child Abuse*, Walnut Creek, California: Launch Press.

Looks at a wide range of issues including prevalence of sexual abuse, treatment of adult survivors and a number of specific problems (e.g. post-traumatic stress and multiple personality disorder, self-mutilation, etc.).

HERMAN, J.L. (1981) *Father-daughter Incest*, Cambridge, Massachusetts: Harvard University Press.

Examines sexual abuse, and some major myths, together with abusers' behaviour and the nature of families in which abuse occurs. A good overview.

JEHU, D., GAZAN, M. and KLASSAN, C. (1989) *Beyond Sexual Abuse*: *Therapy with Women Who were Childhood Victims*, London, England: John Wiley.

A book examining therapeutic methods with survivors within a cognitive therapy framework. Particularly useful on challenging the negative beliefs and thinking of survivors.

* NELSON, S. (1987) *Incest: Fact and Myth*, Edinburgh, Scotland: Stramullion.

Examines and refutes the commonly held myths about sexual abuse of children.

RUSSELL, D. (1986) *The Secret Trauma: Incest in the Lives of Girls and Women*, New York, New York: Basic Books.

This book discusses the research completed by Russell and her team.

SANDERSON, C. (1990) *Counselling Adult Survivors of Child Sexual Abuse*. London, England: Jessica Kingsley Publishers.

A general overview of the area with many helpful suggestions.

WALSH, D. and LIDDY, R. (1989) *Surviving Sexual Abuse*, Dublin, Ireland: Attic Press.

Gives good overall view of the subject and the problems involved.

Personal Accounts

ALLEN, C.V. (1980) *Daddy's Girl*, New York, New York: Berkeley Book.

A useful first-person account of the author's experience of being sexually abused by her father. The book gives a good insight into the child's way of coping with the abuse, and the effects of it on her subsequent development.

ANGELOU, M. (1983) *I know why the Caged Bird Sings*, New York, New York: Virago.

First in a series of autobiographical accounts about the effects of being sexually abused by her mother's boyfriend at an early age, and how she became mute for several years afterwards.

ATKINS, C. (1990) *Seeing Red*, London, England: Coronet Books.

The story of Coral Atkins' work in providing a stable home for disturbed children.

BRADY, K. (1979) *Father's Days: A True Story of Incest*, New York, New York: Dell.

A personal account of sexual abuse by her father.

CAMILLE, P. (1987, 1988) *Step on a Crack*, Chimney Rock, California, Freedom Lights Press.

An account of her foster sister's story of sexual and physical abuse.

* DANICA, E. (1988) *Don't: A Woman's Word*, Prince Edward Island, Gynergy Books.

Written by a survivor that goes beyond a mere description of her life. It describes her suffering and humiliation.

* EVERT, K. and BIJKERT, I. (1987) *When You're Ready*, Walnut Creek, California: Launch Press.

An account of the way Kathy Evert came to terms with sexual abuse by her mother. This book is especially helpful for a survivor who uses regression as a means of re-awakening her memories.

FRASER, S. (1987) *My Father's House*, London, England: Virago.

A personal account by a survivor who repressed the memories of being abused, and developed another 'self' to deal with the abuse.

GALEY, I. (1986) *I Couldn't Cry When Daddy Died*, Racine, Wisconsin: Mother Courage Press.

She describes her history of sexual abuse.

HILL, E. (1985) *The Family Secret*, New York, New York: Laurel Trade Paperback, Dell Publishing Co.

A moving account of a sexual abuse survivor's life.

MATTHEWS, C.A. (1986) *No Longer a Victim*, Canberra, Australia: Acorn Press.

Account of recovery from sexual abuse by her father. The book is particularly helpful for a woman who has no memories of her childhood abuse. It describes what happens when these memories start to emerge.

* MATTHEWS, C.A. (1990) *Breaking Through*, New South Wales, Australia: Albatross Books.

This book incorporates *No Longer a Victim*, but adds a section on the practical steps she took to be released from the pain of her childhood. It is also useful for survivors who want a Christian perspective on the healing process.

RANDALL, M. (1987) *This is About Incest*, Ithaca, New York: Firebrand Books.

A collection of images in poetry, photograph and prose about one woman's experience of being sexually abused by her grandfather. Very useful.

* SISK, S.L. and HOFFMAN, C.F. (1987) *Inside Scars*, Gainesville, Florida: Pandora Press.

The account of a woman's recovery from sexual abuse by her stepfather. Gives a good insight into the process of therapy, both from the survivor's point of view and that of her helper. Highly recommended.

SPRING, J. (1987) *Cry Hard and Swim*, London, England: Virago.

A personal account of a Scottish woman's journey in coming to terms with sexual abuse by her father. It describes how she sought and found help, together with the difficulties she encountered in the process. A readable and moving account.

* UTAIN, M. and OLIVER, B. (1989) *Scream Louder*, Deerfield Beach Florida, Health Communications Inc.

Describes the survivor's healing process with detailed comments from the therapist. It looks at issues beyond the sexual abuse — particularly co-dependency and the effects of living in a dysfunctional family.

WISECHILD, L.M. (1988) *The Obsidian Mirror*, Seattle, Washington: Seal Press.

The author describes the pain and healing from the experience of child sexual abuse. She was abused by several different adults.

* WYNNE, C.E. (1987) *That Looks Like a Nice House*, Walnut Creek, California: Launch Press.

A story with pictures of a woman's recovery from sexual abuse.

Collections of Short Accounts

We would add a general cautionary note to these books especially for survivors. Reading a series of personal accounts can lead to unhelpful comparisons between the survivors' experiences, and to generally feeling overwhelmed.

ARMSTRONG, L. (1978) *Kiss Daddy Goodnight*, New York, New York: Pocket Books.

A series of personal accounts of sexual abuse.

BASS, E. and THORNTON, L. (Eds) (1983) *I Never Told Anyone: Writings by Women Survivors of Child Sexual Abuse*, New York, New York: Harper and Row.

Series of personal accounts of child sexual abuse.

McNARON, T. and MORGAN, Y. (Eds) (1982) *Voices in the Night: Women Speaking About Incest*, Minneapolis, Minnesota: Cleis Press.

Women, including lesbian women, talk about their childhood experiences.

PORTWOOD, P., GORCEY, M. and SANDERS, P. (1987) *Rebirth of Power*, Racine, Wisconsin: Mother Courage Press.

A variety of short accounts written by survivors of child sexual abuse.

WARD, E. (1984) *Father-daughter Rape*, London England: Women's Press.

A series of personal accounts is contained in the earlier sections of this book.

* WOOD, E. and HATTON, L. (1988) *Triumph Over Darkness*, Hillsboro, Oregon, Beyond Words Publishing.

This is an organized collection of personal accounts looking at the healing process.

Novels

GAITSKILL, M. (1991) *Two Girls, Fat and Thin*, London, England: Chatto and Windus

A moving account of two women who both experienced abuse and suffered different long-term effects.

HART, T. (1979) *Don't Tell Your Mother*, London, England: Quartet Books.

This book examines the effects of a man's sexual abuse of his daughter on the father, the mother and their daughter and the subsequent effects of legal action on the family.

MOGGACH, D. (1983) *Porky*, Harmondsworth, England: Penguin Books.

This is a story of a father's sexual abuse of his daughter, and the effects on her development into adulthood. This can be quite upsetting to read.

* MORRIS, M. (1982) *If I Should Die Before I Wake*, London, England: Black Swan Books.

A very powerful book describing the life of a girl who was sexually abused by her father. Is likely to provoke strong emotional reactions.

MURPHY, P.A. (1987) *Searching for Spring*, Tallahassee, Florida: Naird Press Inc.

About a lesbian woman who remembers she was sexually abused as a child.

TASANE, S. and DREYFUSS, C. (1989) *Bird of Prey*, London, England: Clubman Books.

A novel about sexual abuse written for both men and women.

WALKER, A. (1983) *The Color Purple*, Women's Press, London, England.

A moving story of a woman's early and adult years of abuse and her pathway to recovery, told in the form of letters.

Books Written for Survivors of Sexual Abuse

ALLENDER, D.B. (1991) *The Wounded Heart*, Farnham, England: Crusade for World Revival.

This book is written within a Christian framework, and offers helpful advice on forgiveness.

* BAIN, O. and SANDERS, M. (1990) *Out in the Open*, London, England Virago Press.

A book for teenage survivors, written in a very clear style.

* BASS, E. and DAVIS, L. (1988) *The Courage to Heal*, New York, New York: Harper and Row.

An excellent book packed with information and ideas for use in the recovery process from the experience of sexual abuse. Written for sexual abuse survivors.

CROSSAN TOWER, C. (1989) *Secret Scars*, Harmondsworth, England: Penguin Books.

A book for survivors on the healing process and examines different types of therapy.

* DAVIS, L. (1990) *The Courage to Heal Workbook*, New York, New York: Harper and Row.

A workbook to accompany *The Courage to Heal*.
Highly recommended.

ENGEL, B. (1989) *The Right to Innocence: Healing the Trauma of Child-hood Sexual Abuse*, New York, New York: Ivy Books.

A positive self-help book stressing the need for confronting the past and the strengths and resources of survivors.

* FINNEY, L.D. (1990) *Reach for the Rainbow*, Park City, Malibu, California Changes Publishing.

This book attempts to answer many of the questions survivors have about aspects of their childhood. It covers a wide range of issues, and is very useful.

GALLAGHER, V (1991) *Becoming Whole Again: Help for Women Survivors of Childhood Sexual Abuse*, Bradenton, Florida: HSI and TAB Books.

Looks at the long-term effects, and working with survivors in groups.

GANNON, P. (1989) *Soul Survivors: A New Beginning for Adults Abused as Children*, New York, New York: Prentice-Hall Press.

This is a useful book examining the effects of different types of abuse, and presenting ways of overcoming the long-term effects of abuse.

* GIL, E. (1983) *Outgrowing the Pain*, Walnut Creek, California: Launch Press.

A good little book explaining aspects of the healing process. Cartoon illustrations and a simple clear text make for easy reading.

HANCOCK, M. and MAINS, K.B. (1987) *Child Sexual Abuse: A hope for healing*, Crowborough, England: Highland Books.'

This book examines recovery from child sexual abuse from a Christian point of view, and examines the religious and spiritual difficulties experiences by survivors.

HANSEN, T. (1991) *Seven for a Secret*, London, England: S.P.C.K.

Useful book, examining healing from sexual abuse from the Christian perspective and has many useful ideas.

* KUNZMAN, K.A. (1990) *The Healing Way: Adult Recovery from Childhood Sexual Abuse*, Minneapolis, Minnesota Hazelden Foundation.

A very useful book examining the reality of abuse, and the connections between addictions and sexual abuse. The healing process is outlined.

* MALTZ, W. and HOLMAN, B. (1987) *Incest and Sexuality*, Lexington, Massachusetts: Lexington Books.

An extremely useful book for survivors, their helpers and partners. It examines issues relating to sexuality and suggests ways of working through sexual problems.

* MALTZ, W. (1991) *The Sexual Healing Journey: A Guide for Survivors of Sexual Abuse*, New York, New York: Harper Collins.

An excellent book for helping survivors deal with the sexual problems resulting from sexual abuse.

McLURE, M.B. (1990) *Reclaiming the Heart: A Handbook of Help and Hope for Survivors of Incest*, New York, New York: Warner Books.

A book looking at recovery from the effects of being sexually abused. Has some detailed case studies.

* PARKS, P. (1990) *Rescuing the Inner Child: Therapy for Adults Sexually Abused as Children*. London, England: Souvenir Press.

An excellent book with many ideas about working with the inner child.

PARRISH, D.A. (1990) *Abused: A Guide to Recovery for Adult Survivors of Emotional/Physical Child Abuse*, Barrytown, New York: Station Hill Press.

Looks at the consequences of child abuse. The book gives some therapeutic methods for survivors which should only be considered with appropriate support.

POSTON, C. and LISON, K. (1989) *Reclaiming our Lives*, Boston, Massachusetts: Little, Brown and Co.

A book validating the feelings, resources and problems of the survivor, and offering a fourteen step approach to healing.

SANFORD, L.T. (1990) *Strong at the Broken Places*: *Overcoming the Trauma of Child Abuse*, New York, New York: Random House.

Identifies common problems of survivors and the importance of their strengths and resources in the healing process.

TURNER, J. (1989) *Home is Where the Hurt Is*, Wellingborough, England: Thorsons Publishers.

A book written partly by survivors who were able to write of their experiences and the effects. It looks at many difficult issues and follows the progress of the survivors.

WILLIAMS, M.J. (1991) *Healing Hidden Memories*, Deerfield Beach, Florida: Health Communications Inc.

This is a useful book for helping survivors to look for potential memories in her reactions to aspects of her daily life.

WILSON, E.D. (1986) *A Silence to be Broken*, Leicester, England: Inter-Varsity Press.

A book for survivors written from a Christian perspective.

WOITITZ, J.G. (1989) *Healing Your Sexual Self*, Deerfield Beach, Florida. Health Communications Inc.

A book for survivors dealing with sexuality and sexual problems.

* WOMEN'S RESEARCH CENTRE (1989) *Recollecting our Lives*: *Women's Experience of Childhood Sexual Abuse*, Vancouver, British Colombia Canada Press Gang Publishers.

Particularly useful in identifying survival skills, childhood family issues and the number of ways abusers 'disguise' their abusive behaviour (for example, games, affection).

Books for Working with Survivors with Multiple Personalities

* GIL, E. (1990) *United We Stand: A Book for Individuals with Multiple Personalities*, Walnut Creek, California: Launch Press.

A useful little book for survivors at the early stages of understanding the development and use of multiple personalities.

KEYES, D. (1981) *The Minds of Billy Milligan*, New York, New York: Random House.

The story of a man with multiple personalities.

MAYER, R. (1988) *Through Divided Minds*: *Probing the Mysteries of Multiple Personalities*, New York, New York: Avon Books.

An account of the author's work with survivors with multiple personalities, and his recognition that traditional psychological models of therapy do not provide the answers.

ROSS, C.A. (1989) *Multiple Personality Disorder*: *Diagnosis, Clinical Features and Treatment*, New York, New York: John Wiley and Sons.

Looks at the development of multiple personality disorder (MPD) in the context of a response to early and sustained trauma. Written in the American psychiatric tradition with a tendency to be prescriptive. Its description of some of the features of MPD is useful.

SCHREIBER, F.R. (1975) *Sybil*, Harmondsworth, England: Penguin.

The story of a survivor with multiple personalities.

* The Troops for TRUDDI CHASE (1987) *When Rabbit Howls*, London, England: Pan Books.

   A book about a woman who developed multiple personalities to survive her experience of sadistic and sexual abuse by her stepfather. Has a very useful introduction to working with survivors with multiple personalities.

Books for Partners/Families

BYERLY, C.M. (1985) *The Mother's Book*, Dubuque, Iowa: Kendall/Hunt Publishing.

   Written particularly for mothers of children who have been abused.

* DAVIS, L. (1991) *Allies in Healing*, New York, New York: Harper Collins.

   This is an excellent book attempting to answer the many questions asked by partners, friends and families of survivors.

* GRABER, K. (1991) *Ghosts in the Bedroom*, Deerfield Beach, Florida: Health Communications Inc.

   A useful book dealing with issues for partners of survivors.

General Self-Help Books

BRADSHAW, J. (1988) *Bradshaw On: Healing the Shame that Binds You*, Deerfield Beach, Florida, Health Communications Inc.

   Useful for identifying types of shame and ways of overcoming 'toxic' shame.

* BRADSHAW, J. (1990) *Homecoming: Reclaiming and Championing your inner child*. London, England: Judy Piatkus.

   A very helpful book looking at the effects of a difficult childhood, with many suggestions for working through the inner child.

Burns, D.D. (1980) *Feeling Good*, New York, New York: Signet Book.

A useful book for dealing with problems of self-esteem. Looks at how to change the negative-thinking patterns that are experienced by individuals with low self-esteem.

Davies, J. (1990) *Protect Yourself: A Woman's Handbook*, London, England: Judy Piatkus.

A useful book with practical suggestions for women who are concerned about their physical safety.

* Delvin, D. (1974) *The Book of Love*, London, England: New English Library.

Concise and readable book about sexual problems and ways of dealing with them.

* Dickson, A. (1982) *A Woman in Your Own Right*, London, England: Quartet Books.

An excellent book on the issue of assertiveness in women.

Dickson, A. (1985) *The Mirror Within*, London, England: Quartet Books.

A very readable book about women's sexuality. Lots of useful ideas for changing attitudes and behaviour.

Forward, S. (1989) *Toxic Parents: Overcoming their Hurtful Legacy and Reclaiming your Life*, New York, New York: Bantam Books.

An interesting book examining the effects of toxic parenting on the way adults interract with others.

* Kitzinger, S. (1985) *Woman's Experience of Sex*, Harmondsworth, England: Pelican.

An excellent, readable book which places sex in the context of life experiences, and includes material on a wide range of issue. Clear illustrations and photographs.

* LERNER, H.G. (1986) *The Dance of Anger*, New York, New York: Harper and Row.

Very useful book about anger looking at the effects of anger within relationships, and how to change situations with the constructive use of anger.

LERNER, H.G. (1989) *The Dance of Intimacy*, New York, New York: Harper and Row

Looks at issues of intimacy and the relation of adult problems to childhood family experiences. It stresses the need for confrontation of family members which may be unhelpful or impossible for survivors.

LEVER, J., BRUSH, M. and HAYNES, B. (1980) *P.M.T. The Unrecognised Illness*, London, England: New English Library.

Useful, clearly written book about pre-mentrual tension.

MUELENBELT, A. (1981) *For Ourselves: Our Bodies and Sexuality*, London, England: Sheba.

Examines aspects of women's sexuality, with chapters on sexual orientation, sexual violence and sources of help available for problems related to a woman's sexuality.

NORWOOD, R. (1986) *Women who Love too Much*, London, England: Arrow books.

An interesting book on relationship addictions. Written in co-dependency framework. Has a lot to offer survivors and their relationship problems.

* PHILLIPS, A., and RAKUSEN, J. (1988) *Our Bodies, Ourselves*. Harmondsworth, England: Penguin Books.

An invaluable sourcebook on women's health issues, originally, published by the Boston Women's Collective in Boston, Massachusetts in 1971.

REITZ, R. (1985) *Menopause: A Positive Approach*, London, England: Unwin Paperbacks.

Examines issues relating to the menopause, and how to deal with difficulties.

ROBERTSON, I. and HEATHER, N. (1986) *Let's Drink to your Health*, Leicester, England: British Psychological Society.

A readable and useful book on assessing and dealing with problems with alcohol.

WHITFIELD, C.L. (1987) *Healing the Child Within*. Deerfield Beach, Florida: Health Communications Inc.

This is written from the perspective of the effects of alcoholism and dependency on a child's life. It has some useful ideas about the 'child within', although overemphasizes the need for reliving the memories.

Books for Parents to use in Talking to their Children

CORCORAN, C. (1987) *Take Care! Preventing Child Sexual Abuse*, Dublin, Ireland: Poolbeg Press.

Straightforward, direct book examining the myths of sexual abuse and strategies for teaching children to be safe. Written from the principle that 'an informed child is a safe child'.

ELLIOTT, M. (1988) *Keeping Safe*, London, England: New English Library.

A practical guide for parents and other adults talking with children about a whole range of problems from sexual abuse to teenage drug-taking and AIDS.

FAGERSTROM, G. and HANSSON, G. (1979) *Our New Baby*, London, England: McDonald Educational.

Useful book describing puberty, conception, pregnancy and childbirth through the story of the new baby's arrival in a family.

HINDMAN, J. (1985) *A Touching Book*, Ontario, Oregon: Alexandria Associates.

Looks at safe and unsafe touching and what to do about it.

RAYNER, C. (1979) *The Body Book*, London, England: Piccolo Books.

A useful book describing the working of the human body for primary school children.

Books for Groups

ERNST, S. and GOODISON, L. (1981) *In Our Hands*: *A Woman's Book of Self-help Therapy*, London, England: Women's Press.

Full of ideas that can be adapted for use in a survivors' group.

KRZOWSKI, S. and LAND, P. (Eds) (1988). *In Our Experience*, London, England: Women's Press.

A useful sourcebook for groups and workshops run by women for women.

NICARTHY, G., MERRIAM, K. and COFFMAN, S. (1984) *Talking It Out*: *A Guide to Groups for Abused Women*, Seattle, Washington: Seal Press.

Although written for women who have been physically, sexually and emotionally abused by their partners, it has lots of useful ideas and advice for running groups.

Useful Training Books

BRAUN, D. (1988) *Responding to Child Abuse*, London, England: Bedford
Square Press.

A valuable book for use in basic training for working with children
and adults who have been sexually abused.

Bookshop where many of the American books can be obtained:
Compendium, 234 Camden High Street, London 071–485–8944

Bibliography

ALLEN, C.V. (1980) *Daddy's Girl*, New York, New York: Berkeley Book.
ALLENDER, D.B. (1991) *The Wounded Heart*, Farnham, England: CWR.
ANGELOU, M. (1984) *I Know Why the Caged Bird Sings*. London, England: Virago.
ARMSTRONG, L. (1978) *Kiss Daddy Goodnight*, New York, New York: Pocket Books.
ARMSWORTH, M. (1989) 'Therapy of incest survivors: abuse or support?', *Child Abuse and Neglect*, **13**(4), pp. 549–62.
ARMSWORTH, M. (1990) 'A qualitative analysis of adult incest survivors' responses to sexual involvement with their therapists', *Child Abuse and Neglect*, **14**(4), pp. 541–54.
ASH, A. (1984) *Father-daughter Sexual Abuse: The Abuse of Paternal Authority*, Bangor, Wales: Department of Social Theory and Institutions. University of North Wales.
ATKINS, C. (1990) *Seeing Red*. London, England: Coronet Books.
BAGLEY, C. and RAMSAY, R. (1986) 'Sexual abuse in childhood; psychosocial outcomes and implications for social work practice', *Journal of Social Work and Human Sexuality*, 4, pp. 33–47.
BAIN, O. and SAUNDERS, M. (1990) *Out in the Open*. London, England: Virago.
BAKER, A.W. and DUNCAN, S.P. (1985) 'Child sexual abuse: a study of prevalence in Great Britain', *Child Abuse and Neglect*, **9**, pp. 457–67.
BASS, E. and DAVIS, L. (1988) *The Courage to Heal*, New York, New York: Harper and Row.
BASS, E. and THORNTON, L. (Eds) (1983) *I Never Told Anyone: Writings by Women Survivors of Child Sexual Abuse*, New York, New York: Harper and Row.
BECK, A.T. (1976) *Cognitive Therapy and the Emotional Disorders*, New York, New York: International Universities Press.

BECKER, J.V., SKINNER, L.J., ABEL, G.G. and TREACEY, E.C. (1982) 'Incidence and types of sexual dysfunction in rape and incest victims', *Journal of Sex and Marital Therapy*, **8**, pp. 65–74.

BERLINER, L. and CONTE, J. (1990) 'The process of victimisation: the victim's perspective', *Child Abuse and Neglect*, **14**(1), pp. 29–40.

BLAKE-WHITE, J. and KLINE, C.M. (1985) 'Treating the dissociative process in adult victims of childhood incest', *Social Casework*, **66**, pp. 394–402.

BLUME, E.S. (1990) *Secret Survivors: Uncovering Incest and its Aftereffects in Women*, New York, New York: Wiley.

BRADY, K. (1979) *Father's Days: A True Story of Incest*. New York, New York: Dell.

BRADSHAW, J. (1988) *Bradshaw On: Healing the Shame that Binds You*, Deerfield Beach, Florida: Health Communications, Inc.

BRADSHAW, J. (1990) *Homecoming: Reclaiming and Championing Your Inner Child*, London, England: Judy Piatkus.

BRANDES, D. and PHILLIPS, H. (1977) *Gamesters Handbook*, London, England: Hutchinson.

BRAUN, D. (1988) *Responding to Child Abuse*, London, England: Bedford Square Press.

BRAY, M. (1991) *Poppies on the Rubbish Heap: Sexual Abuse: The Child's Voice*, Edinburgh, Scotland: Canongate.

BRIERE, J. and RUNTZ, M. (1986) 'Suicidal thoughts and behaviors in former sexual abuse victims', *Canadian Journal of Behavioral Science*, **18**, pp. 314–423.

BRIERE, J. and ZAIDI, L.Y. (1989) 'Sexual abuse histories and sequelae in female psychiatric emergency room patients, *Americal Journal of Psychiatry*, **146**, pp. 1602–6.

BROWNE, A. and FINKELHOR, D. (1986) 'Initial and long-term effects: a review of the research', in FINKELHOR, D. (Ed.), *A Sourcebook of Child Sexual Abuse*, pp. 143–79, Beverly Hills, California: Sage.

BUTLER, S. (1978) *Conspiracy of Silence: The Trauma of Incest*, San Francisco, California: Volcano Press.

BYERLY, C.M. (1985) *The Mother's Book*, Dubuque, Iowa: Kendall Publishing Co.

BURNS, D.D. (1980) *Feeling Good*, New York, New York: Signet Books.

CAMILLE, P. (1988) *Step on a Crack*, Chimney Rock, California: Freedom Lights Press.

CAVALLIN, H. (1966) 'Incestuous fathers: a clinical report', *American Journal of Psychiatry*, **122**, pp. 1132–38.

CONTE, J.R. and SMITH, T. (1989) 'What sexual offenders tell us about prevention strategies', *Child Abuse and Neglect*, **13**(3), pp. 293–301.

CORCORAN, C. (1987) *Take Care! Preventing Child Sexual Abuse*, Dublin, Ireland: Poolbeg Press.

COURTOIS, C.A. (1979) 'The incest experience and its aftermath', *Victimology*, **4**, pp. 337–47.

COURTOIS, C.A. (1988) *Healing the Incest Wound: Adult Survivors in Therapy*, New York, New York: Norton and Company.

COURTOIS, C.A. and WATTS, D.L. (1982) 'Counselling adult women who experienced incest in childhood or adolescence', *Personnel and Guidance Journal*, **6**, pp. 275–79.

CROSSAN TOWER, C. (1989) *Secret Scars*, Harmondsworth, England: Penguin Books.

DANICA, E. (1988) *Don't. A Woman's Word*, Charlottetown, Prince Edward Island: Gynergy Books.

DAVENPORT, S. and SHELDON, H. (1987) 'From victim to survivor', *Changes*, **5**, pp. 379–82.

DAVIES, J. (1990) *Protect Yourself: A Woman's Handbook*. London, England: Judy Piatkus.

DAVIS, L. (1990) *The Courage to Heal Workbook*, New York, New York: Harper and Row.

DAVIS, L. (1991) *Allies in Healing*, New York, New York: Harper Collins.

DEIGHTON, J. and MCPEEK, P. (1985) 'Group treatment: adult victims of childhood sexual abuse', *Social Casework*, **66**, pp. 405–410.

DELVIN, D. (1974) *The Book of Love*, London, England: New English Library.

DEMPSTER, H. (1989) The Reactions and Responses of Women to the Sexual Abuse of their Children: A Feminist View and Analysis, *Unpublished M.Sc. thesis*, Stirling, Scotland: University of Stirling.

DE YOUNG, M. (1982) 'Self-injurious behaviour in incest victims: a research note', *Child Welfare*, **61**, pp. 577–84.

DICKSON, A. (1982) *A Woman in Your Own Right*, London, England: Quartet Books.

DICKSON, A. (1985) *The Mirror Within*, London, England: Quartet Books.

DINSMORE, C. (1991) *From Surviving to Thriving: Incest, Feminism and Recovery*, Albany, New York: State University of New York.

DRIVER, E. and DROISEN, A. (1989) *Child Sexual Abuse: Feminist Perspectives*, London, England: Macmillan.

EGAN, G. (1982) *The Skilled Helper*, (2nd edition) Monterey, California: Brooks/Cole.

ELLENSON, G.S. (1985) 'Detecting a history of incest: a predictive syndrome', *Social Casework*, **66**, pp. 525–32.

ELLENSON, G.S. (1986) 'Disturbances of perception in adult female incest survivors', *Social Casework*, **67**, pp. 149–59.

ELLIOT, M. (1988) *Keeping Safe: A Practical Guide to Talking with Children*, London, England: New English Library.

ENGEL, B. (1989) *The Right to Innocence: Healing the Trauma of Childhood Sexual Abuse*, New York, New York: Ivy Books.

ERNST, S. and GOODISON, L. (1981) *In Our Own Hands: A Woman's Book of Self-Help Therapy*, London, England: Women's Press.

EVERT, K. and BIJKERK, I. (1987) *When you're Ready*, Walnut Creek, California: Launch Press.

FAGERSTROM, G. and HANSSON, G. (1979) *Our New Baby*, London, England: MacDonald Educational.

FALLER, K. (1987) 'Women who sexually abuse children', *Violence and Victims*, **2**, pp. 263–76.

FARIA, G. and BELOHLAVEK, N. (1984) 'Treating female adult survivors of childhood incest', *Social Casework*, **65**, pp. 465–71.

FIELDS, M.D. (1988) *Legal and Social Work Responses to Sexual Abuse of Children*, Paper presented at the Conference of Social and Legal responses to Child Sexual Abuse, Stirling, Scotland: University of Stirling, Institute for the Study of Violence.

FINKELHOR, D. (1979) *Sexually Victimized Children*, New York, New York: Free Press.

FINKELHOR, D. (1984) *Child Sexual Abuse: New Theory and Research*, New York, New York: Free Press.

FINKELHOR, D. (1986) *A Source book on Child Sexual Abuse*, London, England: Sage.

FINKELHOR, D. and BROWNE, A. (1986) 'Initial and long-term effects: A conceptual framework', in FINKELHOR, D. (Ed.), *A Sourcebook on Child Sexual Abuse*, London, England: Sage.

FINKELHOR, K. and RUSSELL, D. (1984) 'Women as perpetrators', in FINKELHOR, D., *Child Sexual Abuse: New Theory and Research*, New York, New York: Free Press, pp. 171–85.

FINNEY, L.D. (1990) *Reach for the Rainbow*, Park City, Malibu, California, Changes Publishing.

FLUGEL, J. (1926) *The Psychoanalytic Study of the Family*, London, England: Woolf.

FORWARD, S. (1989) *Toxic Parents: Overcoming their Hurtful Legacy and Reclaiming your Life*, New York, New York: Bantam Books.

FORWARD, S. and BUCK, C. (1981) *Betrayal of Innocence: Incest and its Devastation*, Harmondsworth, England: Penguin.

FRASER, S. (1987) *My Father's House*, London, England: Virago.

FROMUTH, M.E. (1986) 'The relationship of child sexual abuse with later psychological and sexual adjustment in a sample of college women', *Child Abuse and Neglect*, **10**, pp. 5–15.

GAITSKILL, M. (1991) *Two Girls, Fat and Thin*, London, England: Chatto and Windus.

GALEY, I. (1986) *I Couldn't Cry When Daddy Died*, Racine, Wisconsin: Mother Courage Press.

GALLAGHER, V. (1991) *Becoming Whole Again: Help for Women Survivors of Childhood Sexual Abuse*, Bradenton, Florida: HSI and TAB Books.

GANNON, P. (1989) *Soul Survivors: A New Beginning for Adults Abused as Children*, New York, New York: Prentice Hall.

GELINAS, D. (1983) 'The persisting negative effects of incest', Psychiatry, **46**, pp. 312–32.

GIL, E. (1983) *Outgrowing the Pain*. Walnut Creek, California: Launch Press.

GIL, E. (1988) *Treatment of Adult Survivors of Child Abuse*, Walnut Creek, California: Launch Press.

GIL, E. (1990) *United We Stand: A Book for Individuals with Multiple Personalities*, Walnut Creek, California: Launch Press.

GOODWIN, J., SIMMS, M. and BERGMAN, R. (1979) 'Hysterical seizures: a sequel to incest', *American Journal of Orthopsychiatry*, **49**, pp. 698–703.

GORDY, P.L. (1983) 'Group work that supports adult victims of childhood incest', *Social Casework*, **64**, pp. 300–7.

GRABER, K. (1991) *Ghosts in the Bedroom*, Deerfield Beach, Florida: Health Communications Inc.

GROSS, M. (1980) 'Incest and hysterical seizures', *Medical Hypnoanalysis*, **3**, pp. 146–52.

GROSS, R.J., DOERR, H., CALDIROLA, D., GUZINSKI, G.M. and RIPLEY, H.S. (1980) 'Borderline syndrome and incest in chronic pelvic pain patients', *International Journal of Psychiatry in Medicine*, **10**, pp. 79–99.

GUTTMACHER, M.S. (1951) *Sex Offences: The Problem, Causes and Prevention*, New York, New York: W.W. Norton.

HANCOCK, M. and MAINS, K.B. (1987) *Child Sexual Abuse: A Hope for Healing*, Crowborough, England: Highland Books.

HANSEN, T. (1991) *Seven for a Secret*, London, England: Society for the Promotion of Christian Knowledge S.P.C.K.

HART, T. (1979) *Don't Tell your Mother*, London, England: Quartert Books.

HAYS, K.F. (1985) 'Electra in mourning: grief work and the adult incest survivor', *Psychotherapy Patient*, **2**, pp. 45–58.

HERMAN, J.L. (1981) *Father — Daughter Incest*, Cambridge, Massachusetts: Harvard University Press.

HERMAN, J. and HIRSCHMAN, L. (1977) 'Father-daughter incest', *Signs: Journal of Women in Culture and Society*, **2**, pp. 735–56.

HERMAN, J., RUSSELL, D. and TROCKI, K. (1986) 'Long-term effects of incestuous abuse in childhood', *American Journal of Psychiatry*, **143**, pp. 1293–96.

HERMAN, J. and SCHATZOW, E. (1984) 'Time-limited group therapy for women with a history of incest', *International Journal of Group Psychotherapy*, **34**, pp. 605–16.

HERMAN, J. and SCHATZOW, E. (1987) 'Recovery and verification of memories of childhood sexual trauma', *Psychoanalytic Psychology*, **4**, pp. 1–14.

HILL, E. (1985) *The Family Secret*, New York, New York: Dell.

HINDMAN, J. (1985) *A Touching Book*, Ontario, Oregon, Alexandria Associates.

JACKSON, S. (1978) *On the Social Construction of Female Sexuality*, London, England: Women's Research and Resources Centre.

JAMES, J. and MEYERDING, J. (1977) 'Early sexual experience and prostitution', *Americal Journal of Psychiatry*, **134**, pp. 1381–85.

JEHU, D. and GAZAN, M. (1983) 'Psychosocial adjustment of women who were sexually victimized in childhood or adolescence', *Canadian Journal of Community Mental Health*, **2**, pp. 71–82.

JEHU, D., GAZAN, M. and KLASSEN, C. (1985) 'Common therapeutic targets among women who were sexually abused in childhood', in VALENTICH, M. and GRIPTON, J. (Eds) *Feminist Perspectives on Social Work and Human Sexuality*, pp. 25–45, New York, New York: Haworth.

JEHU, D., KLASSEN, C. and GAZAN, M. (1986) 'Cognitive restructuring of distorted beliefs associated with childhood sexual abuse', *Journal of Social Work and Human Sexuality*, **4**, pp. 49–69.

JEHU, D., GAZAN, M. and KLASSEN, C. (1989) *Beyond Sexual Abuse: Therapy with Women Who were Childhood Victims,* London, England: Wiley.

JOSEPHSON, G.S. and FONG-BEYETTE, M.L. (1987) 'Factors assisting female clients' disclosure of incest during counseling', *Journal of Counseling and Development*, **65**, pp. 475–78.

KEMPE, C.H. (1980) 'Sexual abuse: Another hidden pediatric problem', in COOK, J.V. and BOWLES, R.T. (Eds) *Child Abuse: Commission and Omission*, Toronto, Canada: Butterworth.

KEMPE, R.S. and KEMPE, C.H. (1984) *The Common Secret: Sexual Abuse of Children and Adolescents*, New York, New York: Freeman.

KENDALL-TACKELL, K.A. (1991) 'Characteristics of abuse that influence when adults molested as children seek help', *Journal of Interpersonal Violence*, **6**, pp. 486–93.

KENWARD, H. (1987) Workshop on Child Sexual Abuse held in Aberdeen, Scotland: October 1987, Personal Communication.

KEYES, D. (1981) *The Minds of Billy Milligan*, New York, New York: Random House.

KINDER, J.M., MATHEWS, R. and SPELTZ, K. (1991) 'Female Sexual Offenders: A Typology', in PATTON, M.Q., *Family Sexual Abuse*, London, England: Wiley.

KITZINGER, S. (1985) *Woman's Experience of Sex*, Harmondsworth, England: Pelican.

KRZOWSKI, S. and LAND, P. (Eds) (1988) *In Our Experience*, London, England: Women's Press.

KUNZMAN, K.A. (1990) *The Healing Way: Adult Recovery from Childhood Sexual Abuse*, Minneapolis, Minnesota: Hazelden Foundation.

LERNER, H.G. (1986) *The Dance of Anger*, New York, New York: Harper and Row.

LERNER, H.G. (1989) *The Dance of Intimacy*, New York, New York: Harper and Row.

LEVER, J., BRUSH, M. and HAYNES, B. (1980) *P.M.T. The Unrecognised Illness*, London, England: New English Library.

LISTER, E.D. (1982) 'Forced silence: A neglected dimension of trauma', *Americal Journal of Psychiatry*, **139**, pp. 872–76.

LOULAN, J. (1987) *Lesbian Passion: Loving Ourselves and Each Other*, San Francisco, California: Spinsters/Aunt Lute Book Company.

LUKIANOWICZ, N. (1972) 'Incest, I Paternal incest, II Other types of incest', *British Journal of Psychiatry*, **120**, pp. 301–13.

McCARTY, L. (1986) Mother-child incest: Characteristics of the offender, *Child Welfare*, **65**, pp. 447–58.

McCORMACK, A., JANUS, M.D. and BURGESS, A.W. (1986) 'Runaway youths and sexual victimization: Gender differences in an adolescent runaway population', *Child Abuse and Neglect*, **10**, pp. 387–95.

McFADYEN, M. (1989) 'The cognitive invalidation approach to panic', in BAKER, R. (Ed.) *Panic Disorder: Theory, Research and Therapy*, Chichester, England: John Wiley.

McGUIRE, L.S. and WAGNER, N.N. (1978) 'Sexual dysfunction in women who were molested as children: One response pattern and suggestions for treatment', *Journal of Sex of Marital Therapy*, **4**, pp. 11–15.

MACLEOD, M. and SARAGA, E. (1987) 'Abuse of trust', *Journal of Social Work Practice*, November 1987, pp. 71–9.

MACLEOD, M. and SARAGA, E. (1988) 'Challenging the orthodoxy: Towards a feminist theory and practice', *Feminist Review*, **28**, pp. 16–56.

McLURE, M.B. (1990) *Reclaiming the Heart: A Handbook of Help and Hope for Survivors of Incest*, New York, New York: Warner Books.

McNARON, T. and MORGAN, Y. (1982) *Voices in the Night: Women Speaking about Incest*, Minneapolis, Minnesota: Cleis Press.

MAISCH, H. (1973) *Incest*, London, England: Andre Deutsch.

MALTZ, W. (1991) *The Sexual Healing Journey: A Guide for Survivors of Sexual Abuse*, New York, New York: Harper Collins.

MALTZ, W. and HOLMAN, B. (1987) *Incest and Sexuality: A Guide to Understanding and Healing*, Lexington, Massachusetts: Lexington Books.

MARVASTI, J. (1986) Incestuous Mothers, *American Journal of Forensic Psychiatry*, **7**(4), pp. 63–9.

MASSON, J.M. (1985) *The Assault on Truth: Freud's Suppression of the Seduction Theory*, Harmondsworth, England: Penguin.

MATHEWS, R., MATTHEWS, J. and SPELTZ, K. (1989) *Female Sexual Offenders: An Exploratory Study*, New York, New York: Safer Society Press.

MATTHEWS, C.A. (1986) *No Longer a Victim*, Canberra, Australia: Acorn Press.

MATTHEWS, C.A. (1990) *Breaking Through*, New South Wales, Australia: Albatross Books.

MATTHEWS, J.K., MATHEWS, R. and SPELTZ, K. (1991) 'Female Sexual Offenders: A Typology' in PATTON, M.Q. (1991) (Ed.) *Family Sexual Abuse, Frontline Research and Evaluation*, London, England: Sage, pp. 199–219.

MAYER, R. (1988) *Through Divided Minds: Probing the Mysteries of Multiple Personalities*, New York, New York: Avon Books.

MEISELMAN, K. (1978) *Incest — A Psychological Study of Causes and Effects with Treatment Recommendations*, San Francisco, California: Jossey-Bass.

MILLER, A. (1984) *Thou Shalt Not be Aware: Society's Betrayal of the Child*, London, England: Pluto.

MILLER, A. (1990) *The Untouched Key: Tracing Childhood Trauma in Creativity and Destructiveness*, London, England: Virago.

MILLER, A. (1991) *Breaking Down the Wall of Silence: To Join the Waiting Child*, London, England: Virago.

MOGGACH, D. (1983) *Porky*, Harmondsworth, England: Penguin.

MORRIS, M. (1982) *If I Should Die before I Wake*, London, England: Black Swan.

MUELENBELT, A. (1981) *For Ourselves: Our Bodies and Sexuality*, London, England: Sheba.

MURPHY, P.A. (1987) *Searching for Spring*, Tallahassee, Florida: Navid Press Inc.

NAKASHIMA, I. and ZAKUS, G. (1977) 'Incest review and clinical experience', *Pediatrics*, **60**, pp. 696–701.

NATIONAL CHILDREN'S HOME (1992) *The Report of the Committee of Enquiry into Children and Young People who Sexually Abuse Other Children*, London, England: National Children's Home.

NELSON, S. (1982) *Incest — Fact and Myth*, (1st edition) Edinburgh, Scotland: Stramullion.

NELSON, S. (1987) *Incest — Fact and Myth*, (2nd edition) Edinburgh, Scotland: Stramullion.

NICARTHY, G., MERRIAM, K. and COFFMAN, S. (1984) *Talking It Out: A Guide to Groups for Abused Women*, Seattle, Washington: Seal Press.

NORWOOD, R. (1986) *Women Who Love Too Much*, London, England: Arrow Books.

O'BRIEN, M.J. (1991) 'Taking sibling abuse seriously', in PATTON, M.J. (Ed.) *Family Sexual Abuse*, London, England: Sage.

O'HARE, J. and TAYLOR, K. (1983) 'The reality of incest', *Women and Therapy*, **2**, pp. 215–29.

OPPENHEIMER, R., HOWELLS, K.L., PALMER, R.L. and CHALONER, D.A. (1985) 'Adverse sexual experience in childhood and clinical eating disorders: a preliminary description', *Journal of Psychosomatic Research*, **19**, pp. 357–61.

PARKS, P. (1990) *Rescuing the Inner Child: Therapy for Adults Sexually Abused as Children*, London, England: Souvenir Press.

PARRISH, D.A. (1990) *Abused: A Guide to Recovery for Adult Survivors of Emotional/Physical Child Abuse*, Barry Town, New York: Station Hill Press.

PATTON, M.Q. (Ed.) (1991) *Family Sexual Abuse: Frontline Research and Evaluation*, London, England: Sage.

PETERS, S.D. (1984) *The Relationship Between Childhood Sexual Victimization and Adult Depression among Afro-American and White Women*, Unpublished doctoral dissertation, Los Angeles, California: University of California.

PHILLIPS, A. and RAKUSEN, J. (1988) *Our Bodies Ourselves*, Harmondsworth, England: Penguin.

PORTWOOD, P. GORCEY, M. and SAUNDERS, P. (1987) *Rebirth of Power*, Racine, Wisconsin: Mother Courage Press.

POSTON, C. and LISON, K. (1989) *Reclaiming our Lives*, Boston, Massachusetts: Little, Brown and Co.

RANDALL, M. (1987) *This is about Incest*, Ithaca, New York: Firebrand Books.

RAYNER, C. (1979) *The Body Book*, London, England: Piccolo Books.

REITZ, R. (1985) *Menopause: A Positive Approach*, London, England: Unwin Paperbacks.

RESEARCH TEAM (1990) *Child Sexual Abuse in Northern Ireland. A Research Study of Incidence*, The Research Team from the Department of Child Psychology, Royal Belfast Hospital for Sick Children and

Department of Public Health Queen's University of Belfast. Belfast, Northern Ireland, Greystone Books.

ROBERTSON, I. and HEATHER, N. (1986) *Let's Drink to Your Health*, Leicester, England: British Psychological Society.

ROCKLIN, R. and LAVETT, D.K. (1987) 'Those who broke the cycle: Therapy with non-abusive adults who were physically abused as children', *Psychotherapy*, **24**, pp.769–78.

ROSS, C.A. (1989) *Multiple Personality Disorder: Diagnosis, Clinical Features and Treatment*, New York, New York: John Wiley and Sons.

RUSH, F. (1980) *The Best Kept Secret: Sexual Abuse of Children*, Englewood Cliffs, New Jersey: Prentice-Hall.

RUSSELL, D.E.H. (1986) *The Secret Trauma: Incest in the Lives of Girls and Women*, New York, New York: Basic Books.

SANFORD, L.T. (1990) *Strong at the Broken Places: Overcoming the Trauma of Child Abuse*, New York, New York: Random House.

SCHREIBER, F.R. (1975) *Sybil*, Harmondsworth, England: Penguin.

SCOTT, A. (1988) 'Feminism and the seductiveness of the real event', *Feminist Review*, **28**, pp. 88–102.

SGROI, S. (1982) *Handbook of Clinical Intervention in Child Sexual Abuse*, Cambridge, England: Lexington Books.

SGROI, S. (1989) 'Healing together: peer group therapy for adult survivors of child sexual abuse', in: Vulnerable Population, **2**, Cambridge, England: Lexington Books.

SGROI, S.M., BLICK, L.C. and PORTER, F.S. (1982) 'A conceptual framework for child sexual abuse', in SGROI, S. (Ed.), *Handbook of Clinicial Intervention in Child Sexual Abuse*, pp. 11–17.

SHELDON, H. (1987) 'Living with a secret', *Changes*, **5**, pp. 340–43.

SISK, S.L. and HOFFMAN, C.F. (1987) *Inside Scars: Incest Recovery as Told by a Survivor and Her Therapist*, Gainesville, Florida: Pandora Press.

SLOAN, G. and LEICHNER, P. (1986) 'Is there a relationship between sexual abuse or incest and eating disorders?', *Canadian Journal of Psychiatry*, **31**, pp. 656–70.

SPRING, J. (1987) *Cry Hard and Swim*, London, England: Virago.

TASANE, S. and DREYFUSS, C. (1989) *Birds of Prey*, London, England: Clubman Books.

THE TROOPS FOR TRUDDI CHASE (1987) *When Rabbit Howls*, London, England: Pan Books.

TSAI, M. and WAGNER, N.N. (1978) 'Therapy groups for women sexually molested as children', *Archives of Sexual Behaviour*, **7**, pp. 417–27.

TSAI, M. and WAGNER, N.N. (1979) 'Women who were sexually molested as children', *Medical Aspects of Human Sexuality*, **13**, pp. 55–6.

TURNER, J. (1989) *Home is Where the Hurt is*, Wellingborough, England: Thorsons Publishers.

UTAIN, M. and OLIVER, B. (1989) *Scream Louder*, Deerfield Beach, Florida, Health Communications Inc.

WALKER, A. (1982) *The Color Purple*, New York, New York: Pocket Books.

WALSH, D. and LIDDY, R. (1989) *Surviving Sexual Abuse*, Dublin, Ireland: Attic Press.

WARD, E. (1984) *Father-Daughter Rape*, London, England: The Women's Press.

WEST, D.J. (Ed.) (1985) *Sexual Victimization*, Aldershot, England: Gower.

WHITFIELD, C.L. (1987) *Healing the Child Within*, Deerfield Beach, Florida, Health Communications Inc.

WILLIAMS, J.J. (1991) *Healing Hidden Memories*, Deerfield Beach, Florida, Health Communications.

WILSON, E.D. (1986) *A Silence to be Broken*, Leicester, England: Inter-Varsity Press.

WINESTINE, M.C. (1985) 'Compulsive shop lifting as a derivative of childhood seduction', *Psychoanalytic Quarterly*, **54**, pp. 70–2.

WISECHILD, L.M. (1988) *The Obsidian Mirror*, Seattle, Washington: Seal Press.

WOITITZ, J.G. (1989) *Healing your Sexual Self*, Deerfield Beach, Florida, Health Communications Inc.

WOMEN'S RESEARCH CENTRE (1989) *Recollecting Our Lives: Women's Experience of Childhood Sexual Abuse*, Vancouver, British Colombia, Press Gang Publishers.

WOOD, E. and HATTON, L. (1988) *Triumph Over Darkness*, Hillsboro, Oregon Beyond Words Publishing.

WORDEN, J.W. (1983) *Grief Counselling and Grief Therapy*, London, England: Tavistock Publications.

WYNNE, C.E. (1987) *That Looks Like a Nice House*, Walnut Creek, California: Launch Press.

Index